SENSATION COMICS FEATURING
WONDER ★ WOMAN
VOLUME 2

Michael Jelenic
Adam P. Knave
Alex de Campi
Amy Chu

D1295369

WRITERS

Matthew Dow Smith
Drew Johnson
Ray Snyder
Neil Googe
Bernard Chang
Noelle Stevenson
Ryan Benjamin
Mike Maihack
Chris Sprouse
Karl Story
Christian Duce
Aaron Lopresti
ARTISTS

Lizzy John
Rex Lokus
Len O'Grady
Carrie Strachan
Wendy Broome
Jordie Bellaire
Hi-Fi
COLORISTS

Saida Temofonte
Deron Bennett
Todd Klein
LETTERERS

Jae Lee with June Chung
COLLECTION COVER ARTISTS

WONDER WOMAN created by
William Moulton Marston

KRISTY QUINN Editor – Original Series
JESSICA CHEN Assistant Editor – Original Series
JEB WOODARD Group Editor – Collected Editions
LIZ ERICKSON Editor – Collected Edition
SARABETH KETT Publication Design

BOB HARRAS Senior VP – Editor-in-Chief, DC Comics

DIANE NELSON President
DAN DIDIO and JIM LEE Co-Publishers
GEOFF JOHNS Chief Creative Officer
AMIT DESAI Senior VP – Marketing & Global Franchise Management
NAIRI GARDINER Senior VP – Finance
SAM ADES VP – Digital Marketing
BOBBIE CHASE VP – Talent Development
MARK CHIARELLO Senior VP – Art, Design & Collected Editions
JOHN CUNNINGHAM VP – Content Strategy
ANNE DEPIES VP – Strategy Planning & Reporting
DON FALLETTI VP – Manufacturing Operations
LAWRENCE GANEM VP – Editorial Administration & Talent Relations
ALISON GILL Senior VP – Manufacturing & Operations
HANK KANALZ Senior VP – Editorial Strategy & Administration
JAY KOGAN VP – Legal Affairs
DEREK MADDALENA Senior VP – Sales & Business Development
DAN MIRON VP – Sales Planning & Trade Development
NICK NAPOLITANO VP – Manufacturing Administration
CAROL ROEDER VP – Marketing
EDDIE SCANNELL VP – Mass Account & Digital Sales
SUSAN SHEPPARD VP – Business Affairs
COURTNEY SIMMONS Senior VP – Publicity & Communications
JIM (SKI) SOKOLOWSKI VP – Comic Book Specialty & Newsstand Sales

SENSATION COMICS FEATURING WONDER WOMAN VOLUME 2

DC Comics, 4000 Warner Blvd., Burbank, CA 91522
A Warner Bros. Entertainment Company.
Printed by RR Donnelley, Salem, VA, USA. 9/11/15. First Printing.
ISBN: 978-1-4012-5862-7

Library of Congress Cataloging-in-Publication Data

Tynion, James, IV, author.
  Sensation Comics featuring Wonder Woman. Volume 2 / James
Tynion, writer ; Noelle Stevenson and Ryan Benjamin, artists.
     pages cm
  ISBN 978-1-4012-5862-7 (paperback)
 1. Graphic novels. I. Benjamin, Ryan, illustrator. II. Stevenson, Noelle,
illustrator. III. Title.
  PN6728.W6T96 2015
  741.5'973—dc23
                                  2015014162

GENERATIONS

MICHAEL JELENIC
WRITER

DREW JOHNSON
PENCILLER

RAY SNYDER
INKER

LIZZY JOHN
COLORIST

SAIDA TEMOFONTE
LETTERER

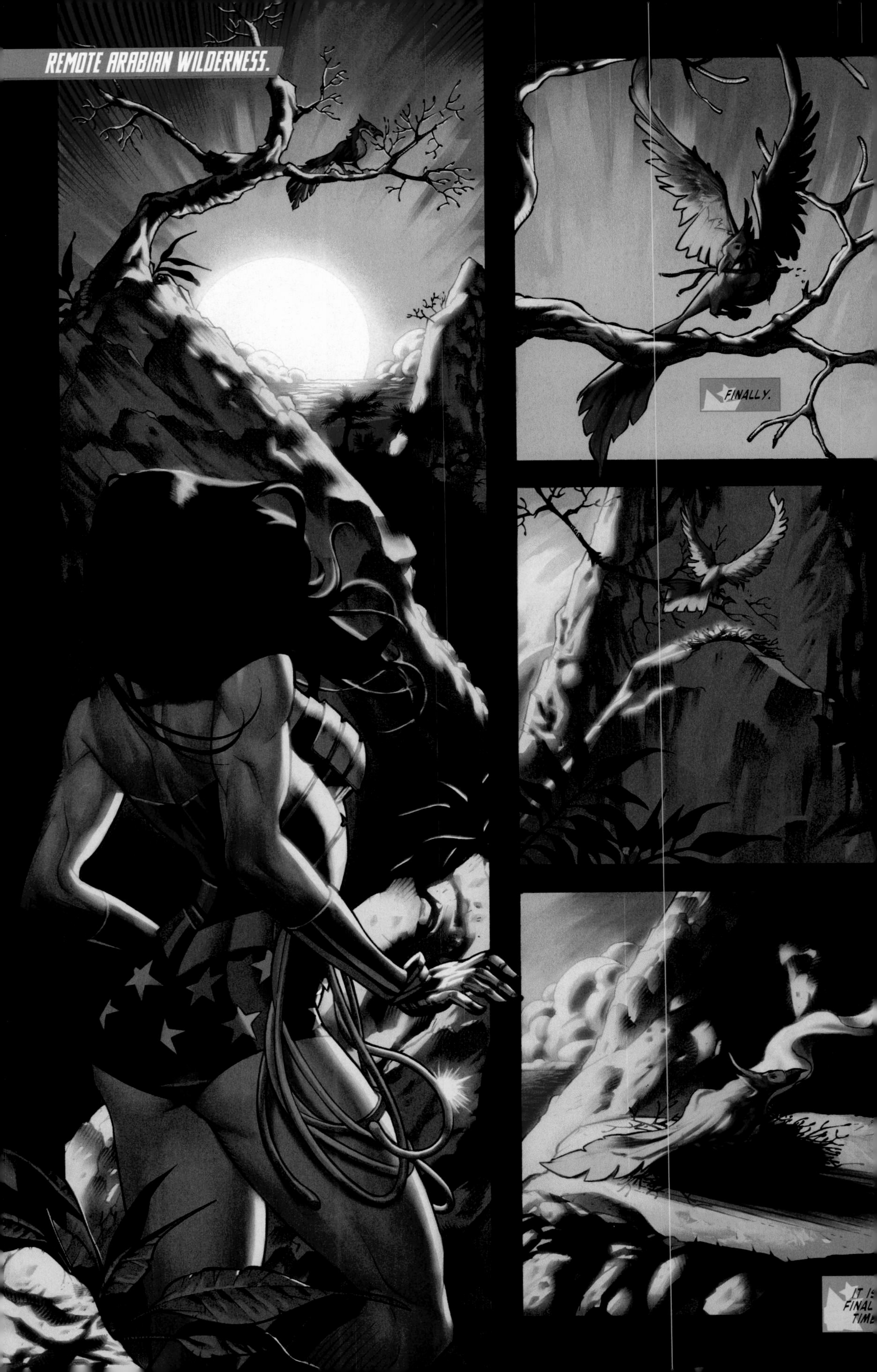
REMOTE ARABIAN WILDERNESS.
FINALLY.
IT I
FINAL
TIM

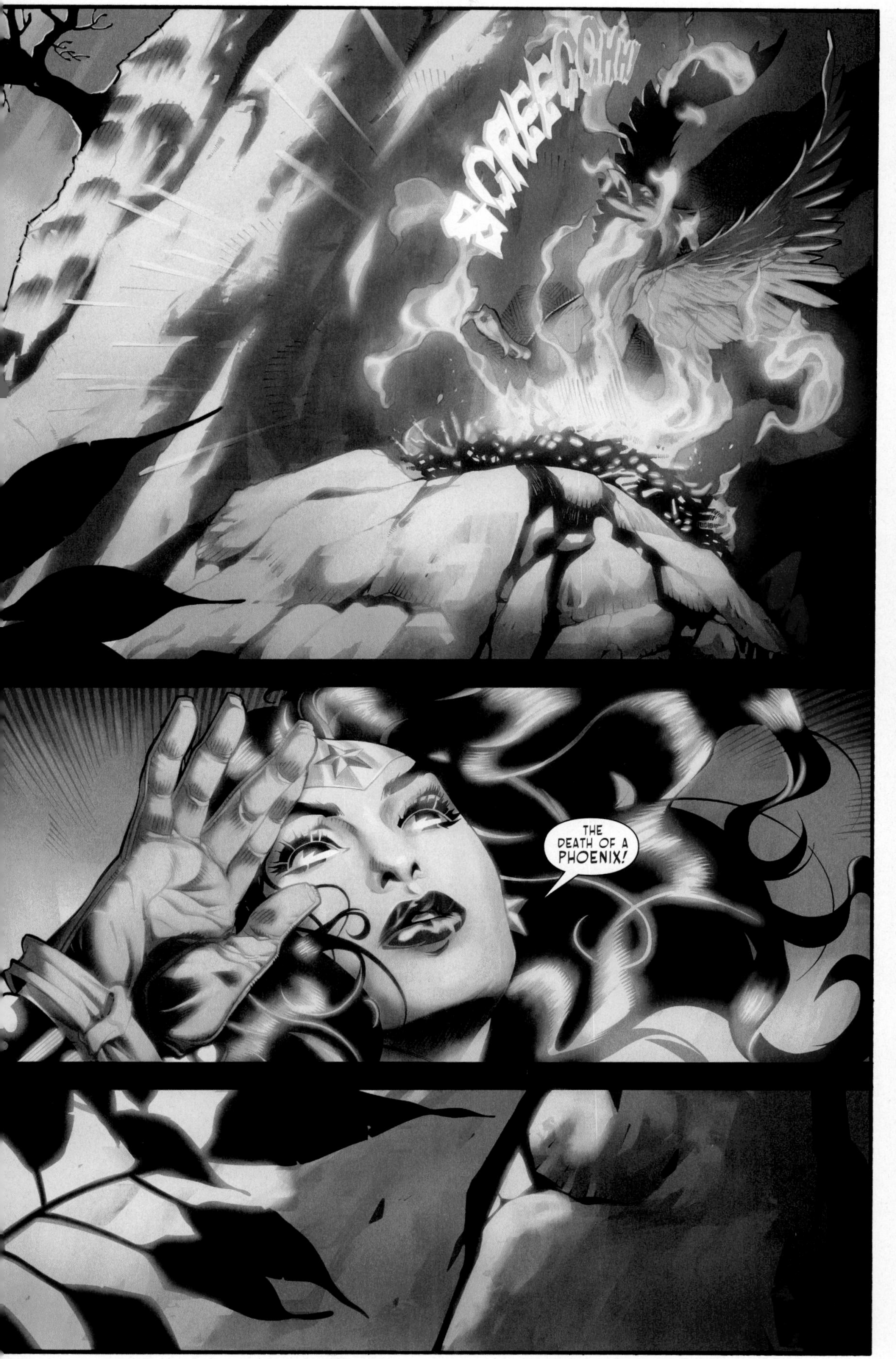
SCREECHH!
THE DEATH OF A PHOENIX!

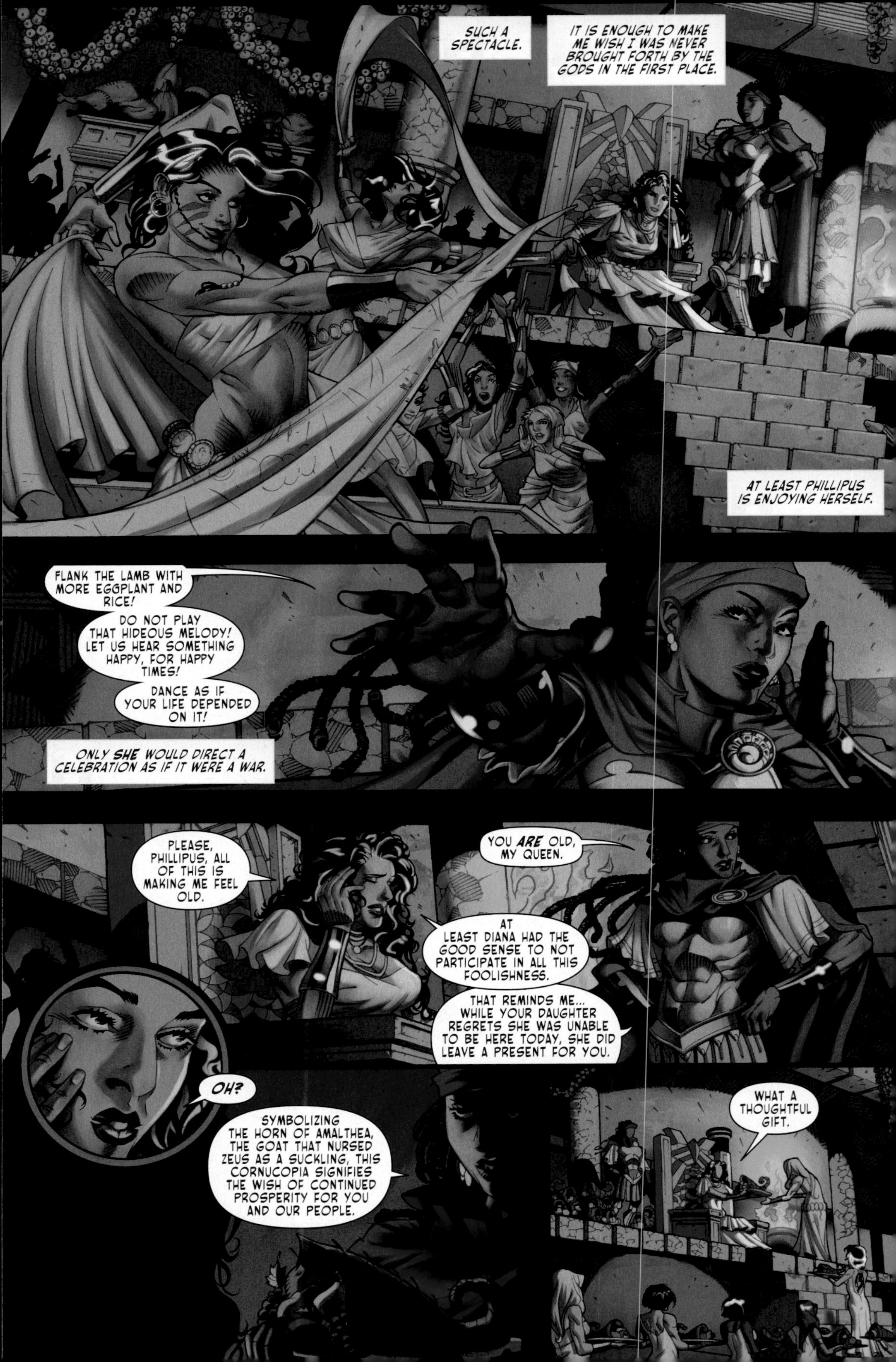
SUCH A SPECTACLE.
IT IS ENOUGH TO MAKE ME WISH I WAS NEVER BROUGHT FORTH BY THE GODS IN THE FIRST PLACE.
AT LEAST PHILLIPUS IS ENJOYING HERSELF.
FLANK THE LAMB WITH MORE EGGPLANT AND RICE!
DO NOT PLAY THAT HIDEOUS MELODY! LET US HEAR SOMETHING HAPPY, FOR HAPPY TIMES!
DANCE AS IF YOUR LIFE DEPENDED ON IT!
ONLY SHE WOULD DIRECT A CELEBRATION AS IF IT WERE A WAR.
PLEASE, PHILLIPUS, ALL OF THIS IS MAKING ME FEEL OLD.
YOU ARE OLD, MY QUEEN.
AT LEAST DIANA HAD THE GOOD SENSE TO NOT PARTICIPATE IN ALL THIS FOOLISHNESS.
THAT REMINDS ME... WHILE YOUR DAUGHTER REGRETS SHE WAS UNABLE TO BE HERE TODAY, SHE DID LEAVE A PRESENT FOR YOU.
OH?
SYMBOLIZING THE HORN OF AMALTHEA, THE GOAT THAT NURSED ZEUS AS A SUCKLING, THIS CORNUCOPIA SIGNIFIES THE WISH OF CONTINUED PROSPERITY FOR YOU AND OUR PEOPLE.
WHAT A THOUGHTFUL GIFT.

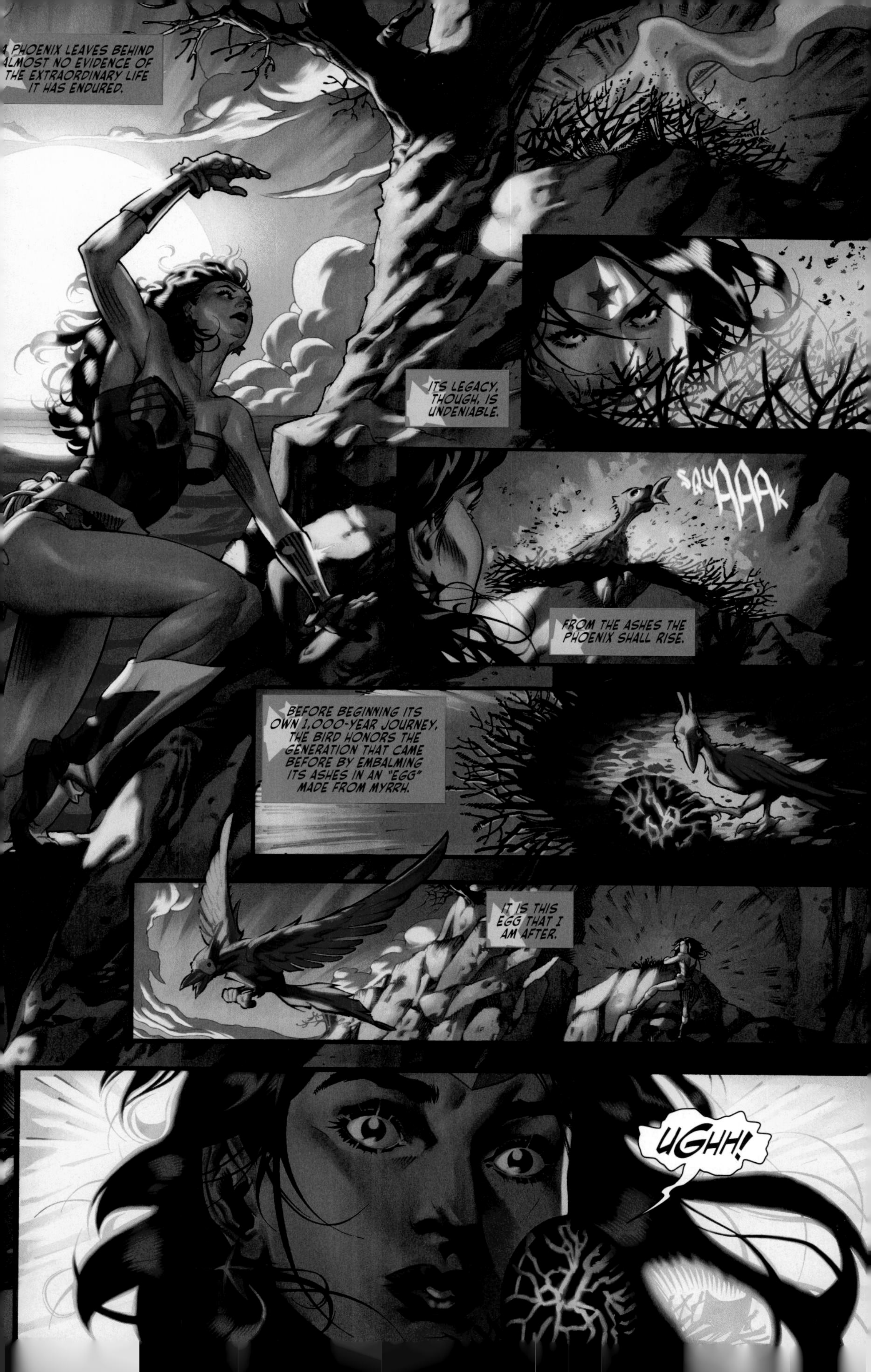
A PHOENIX LEAVES BEHIND ALMOST NO EVIDENCE OF THE EXTRAORDINARY LIFE IT HAS ENDURED.
ITS LEGACY, THOUGH, IS UNDENIABLE.
SQUAAAK
FROM THE ASHES THE PHOENIX SHALL RISE.
BEFORE BEGINNING ITS OWN 1,000-YEAR JOURNEY, THE BIRD HONORS THE GENERATION THAT CAME BEFORE BY EMBALMING ITS ASHES IN AN "EGG" MADE FROM MYRRH.
IT IS THIS EGG THAT I AM AFTER.
UGHH!

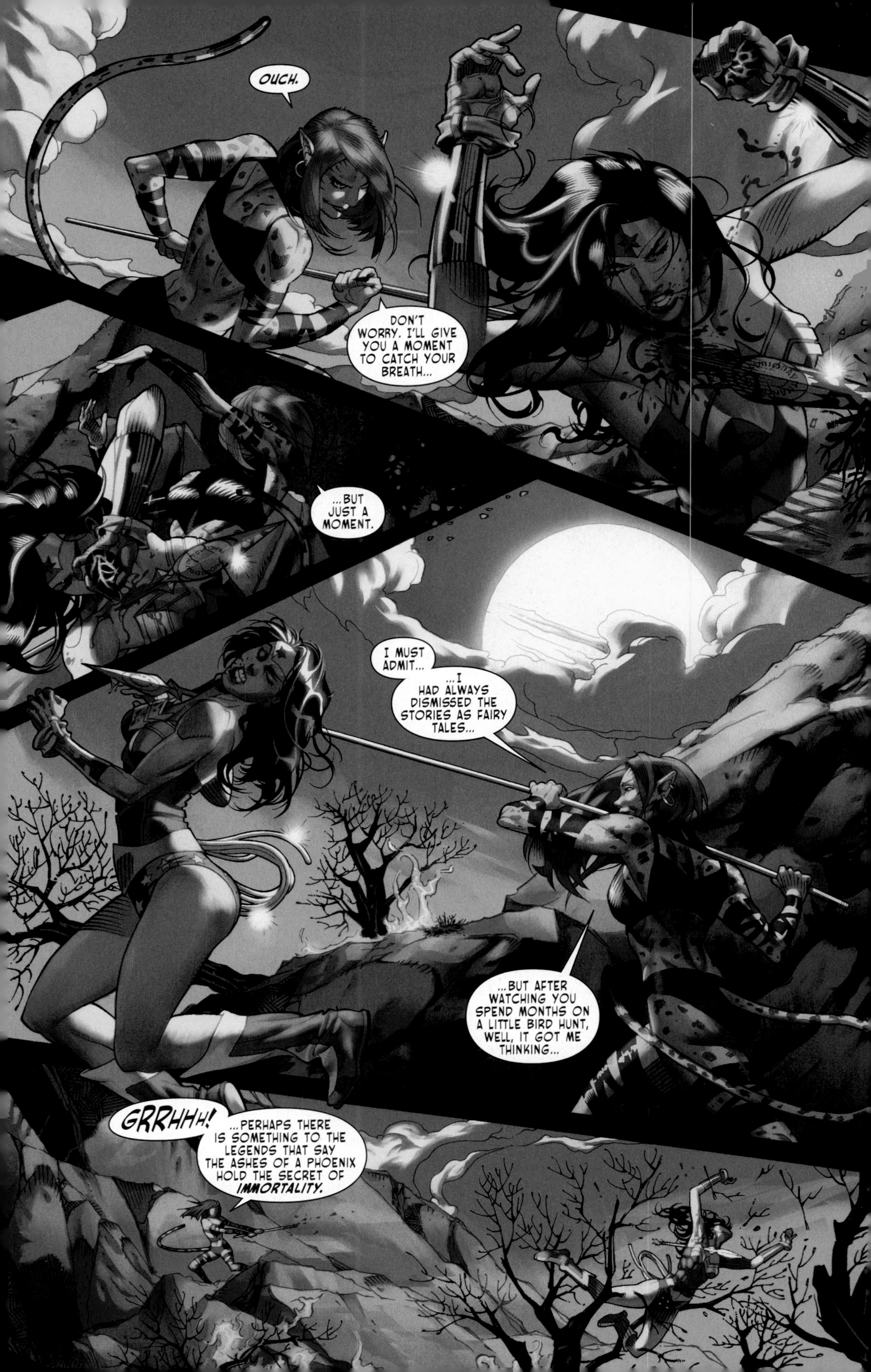
OUCH.
DON'T WORRY. I'LL GIVE YOU A MOMENT TO CATCH YOUR BREATH...
...BUT JUST A MOMENT.
I MUST ADMIT...
...I HAD ALWAYS DISMISSED THE STORIES AS FAIRY TALES...
...BUT AFTER WATCHING YOU SPEND MONTHS ON A LITTLE BIRD HUNT, WELL, IT GOT ME THINKING...
GRRHHH!
...PERHAPS THERE IS SOMETHING TO THE LEGENDS THAT SAY THE ASHES OF A PHOENIX HOLD THE SECRET OF IMMORTALITY.

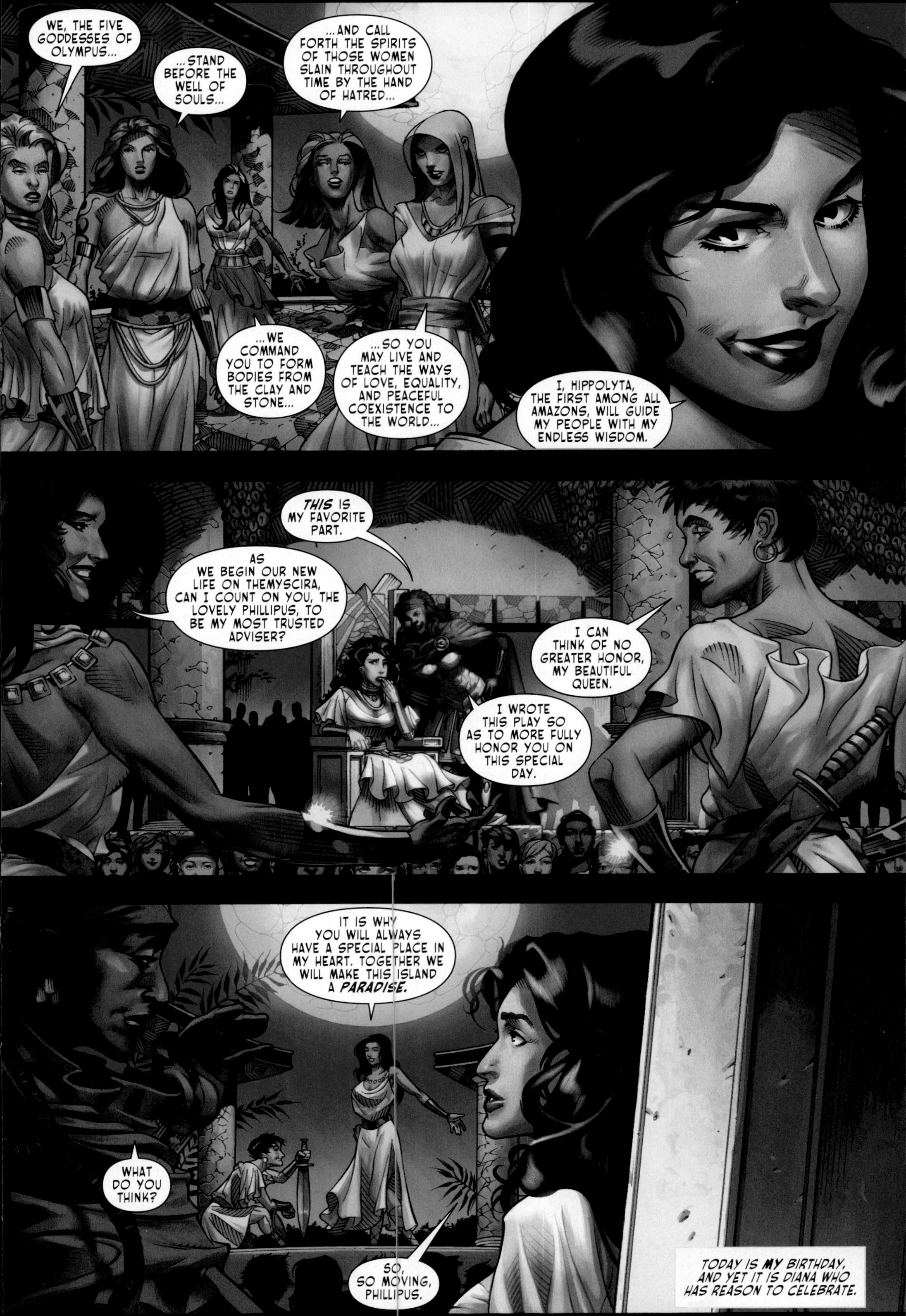
WE, THE FIVE GODDESSES OF OLYMPUS...
...STAND BEFORE THE WELL OF SOULS...
...AND CALL FORTH THE SPIRITS OF THOSE WOMEN SLAIN THROUGHOUT TIME BY THE HAND OF HATRED...
...WE COMMAND YOU TO FORM BODIES FROM THE CLAY AND STONE...
...SO YOU MAY LIVE AND TEACH THE WAYS OF LOVE, EQUALITY, AND PEACEFUL COEXISTENCE TO THE WORLD...
I, HIPPOLYTA, THE FIRST AMONG ALL AMAZONS, WILL GUIDE MY PEOPLE WITH MY ENDLESS WISDOM.
AS WE BEGIN OUR NEW LIFE ON THEMYSCIRA, CAN I COUNT ON YOU, THE LOVELY PHILLIPUS, TO BE MY MOST TRUSTED ADVISER?
THIS IS MY FAVORITE PART.
I CAN THINK OF NO GREATER HONOR, MY BEAUTIFUL QUEEN.
I WROTE THIS PLAY SO AS TO MORE FULLY HONOR YOU ON THIS SPECIAL DAY.
IT IS WHY YOU WILL ALWAYS HAVE A SPECIAL PLACE IN MY HEART. TOGETHER WE WILL MAKE THIS ISLAND A PARADISE.
WHAT DO YOU THINK?
SO, SO MOVING, PHILLIPUS.
TODAY IS MY BIRTHDAY, AND YET IT IS DIANA WHO HAS REASON TO CELEBRATE.

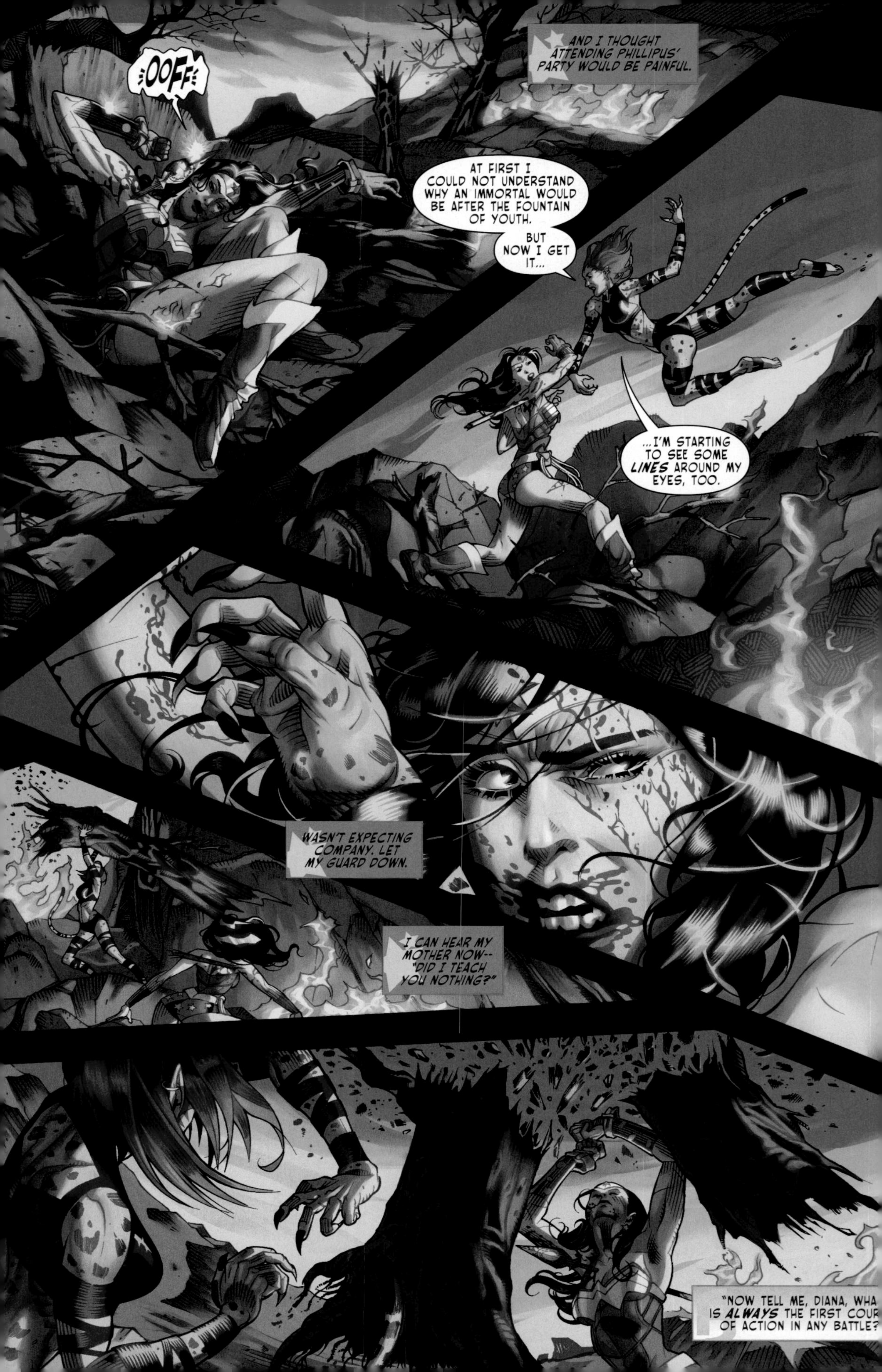
OOFF
AND I THOUGHT ATTENDING PHILLIPUS' PARTY WOULD BE PAINFUL.
AT FIRST I COULD NOT UNDERSTAND WHY AN IMMORTAL WOULD BE AFTER THE FOUNTAIN OF YOUTH.
BUT NOW I GET IT...
...I'M STARTING TO SEE SOME LINES AROUND MY EYES, TOO.
WASN'T EXPECTING COMPANY. LET MY GUARD DOWN.
I CAN HEAR MY MOTHER NOW-- "DID I TEACH YOU NOTHING?"
"NOW TELL ME, DIANA, WHA IS ALWAYS THE FIRST COUR OF ACTION IN ANY BATTLE?

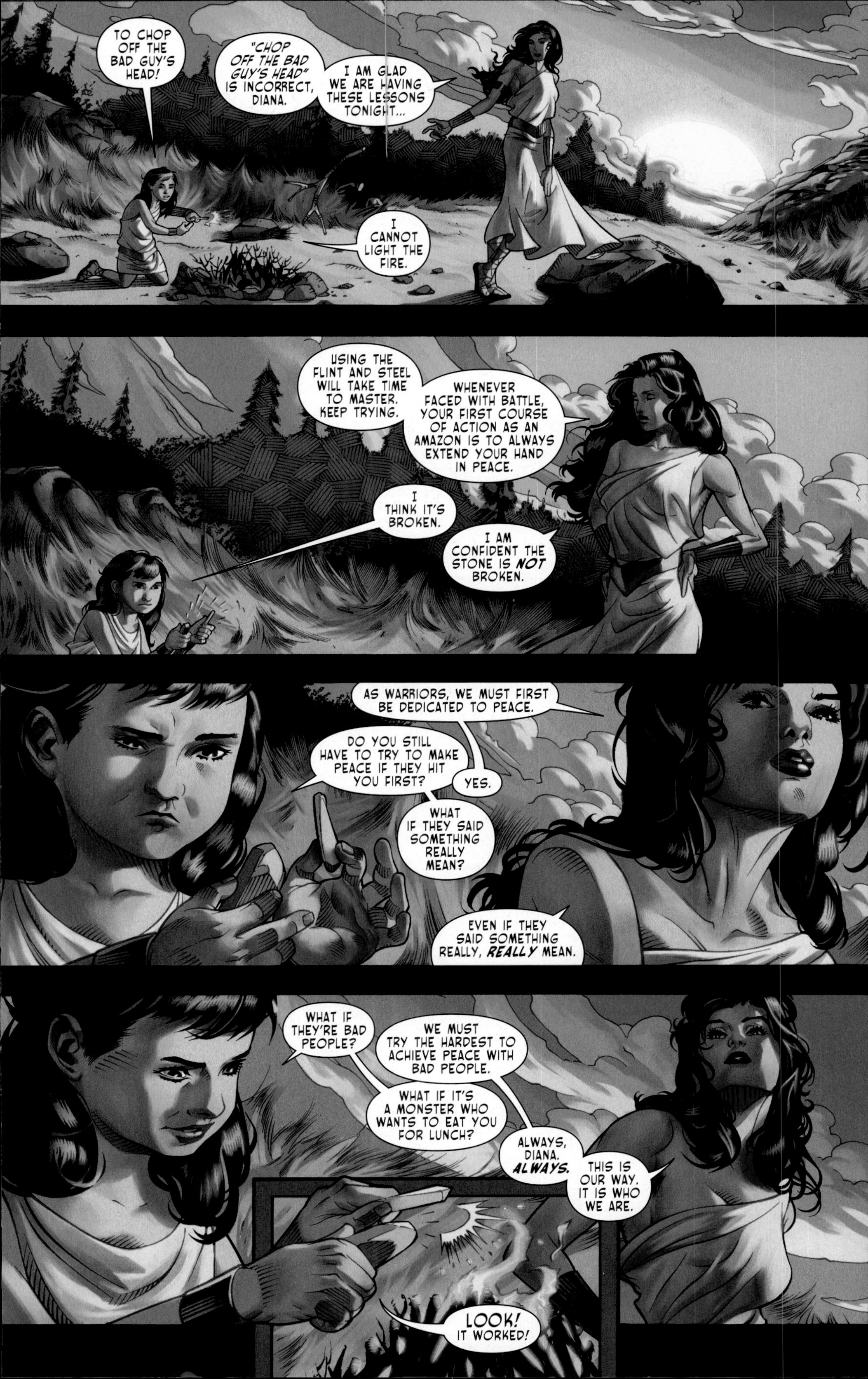
TO CHOP OFF THE BAD GUY'S HEAD!
"CHOP OFF THE BAD GUY'S HEAD" IS INCORRECT, DIANA.
I AM GLAD WE ARE HAVING THESE LESSONS TONIGHT...
I CANNOT LIGHT THE FIRE.
USING THE FLINT AND STEEL WILL TAKE TIME TO MASTER. KEEP TRYING.
WHENEVER FACED WITH BATTLE, YOUR FIRST COURSE OF ACTION AS AN AMAZON IS TO ALWAYS EXTEND YOUR HAND IN PEACE.
I THINK IT'S BROKEN.
I AM CONFIDENT THE STONE IS NOT BROKEN.
AS WARRIORS, WE MUST FIRST BE DEDICATED TO PEACE.
DO YOU STILL HAVE TO TRY TO MAKE PEACE IF THEY HIT YOU FIRST?
YES.
WHAT IF THEY SAID SOMETHING REALLY MEAN?
EVEN IF THEY SAID SOMETHING REALLY, REALLY MEAN.
WHAT IF THEY'RE BAD PEOPLE?
WE MUST TRY THE HARDEST TO ACHIEVE PEACE WITH BAD PEOPLE.
WHAT IF IT'S A MONSTER WHO WANTS TO EAT YOU FOR LUNCH?
ALWAYS, DIANA. ALWAYS.
THIS IS OUR WAY. IT IS WHO WE ARE.
LOOK! IT WORKED!

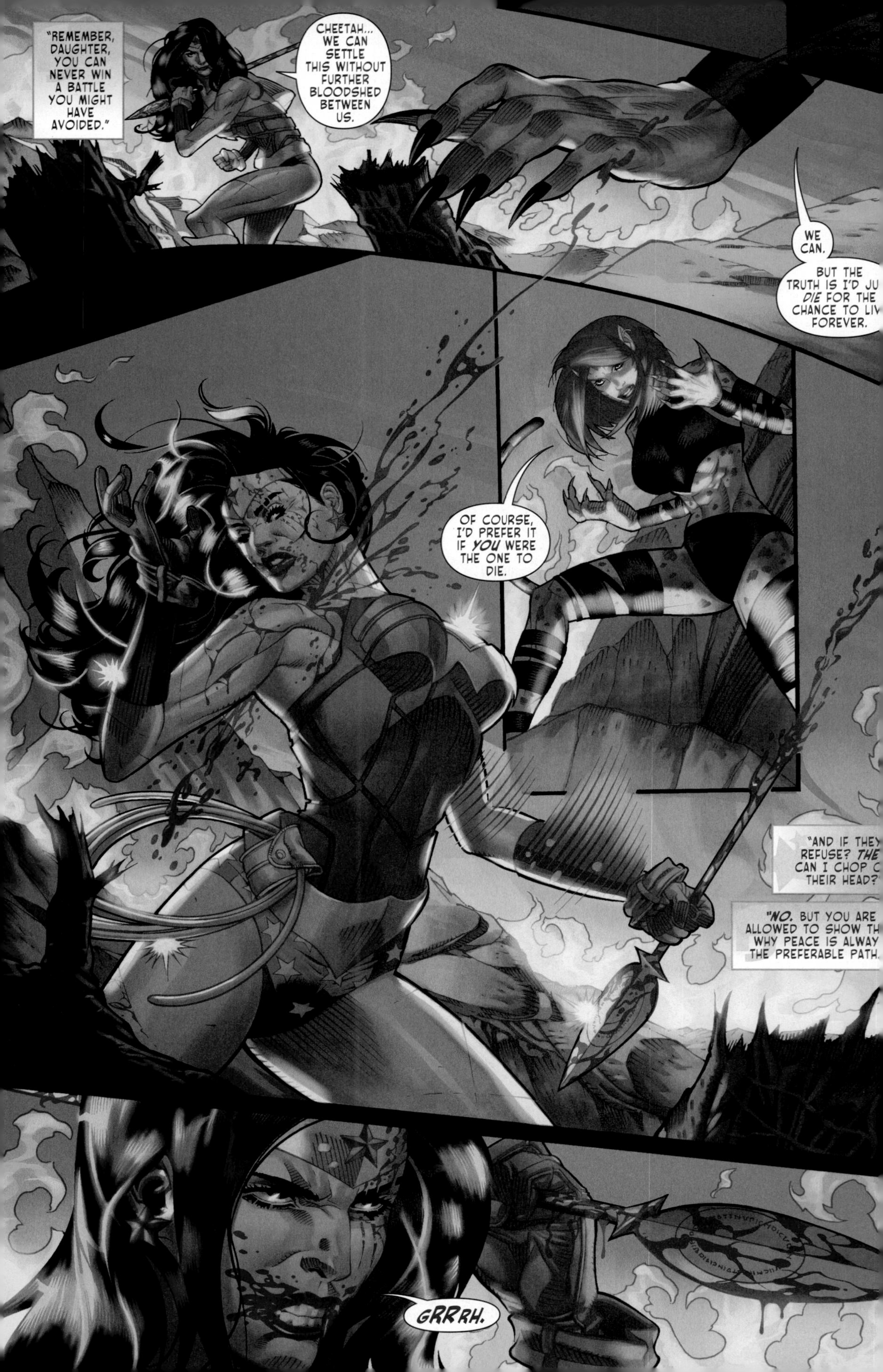
"REMEMBER, DAUGHTER, YOU CAN NEVER WIN A BATTLE YOU MIGHT HAVE AVOIDED."
CHEETAH... WE CAN SETTLE THIS WITHOUT FURTHER BLOODSHED BETWEEN US.
WE CAN.
BUT THE TRUTH IS I'D JU DIE FOR THE CHANCE TO LIV FOREVER.
OF COURSE, I'D PREFER IT IF YOU WERE THE ONE TO DIE.
"AND IF THEY REFUSE? THE CAN I CHOP C THEIR HEAD?
"NO. BUT YOU ARE ALLOWED TO SHOW TH WHY PEACE IS ALWAY THE PREFERABLE PATH.
GRRRH.

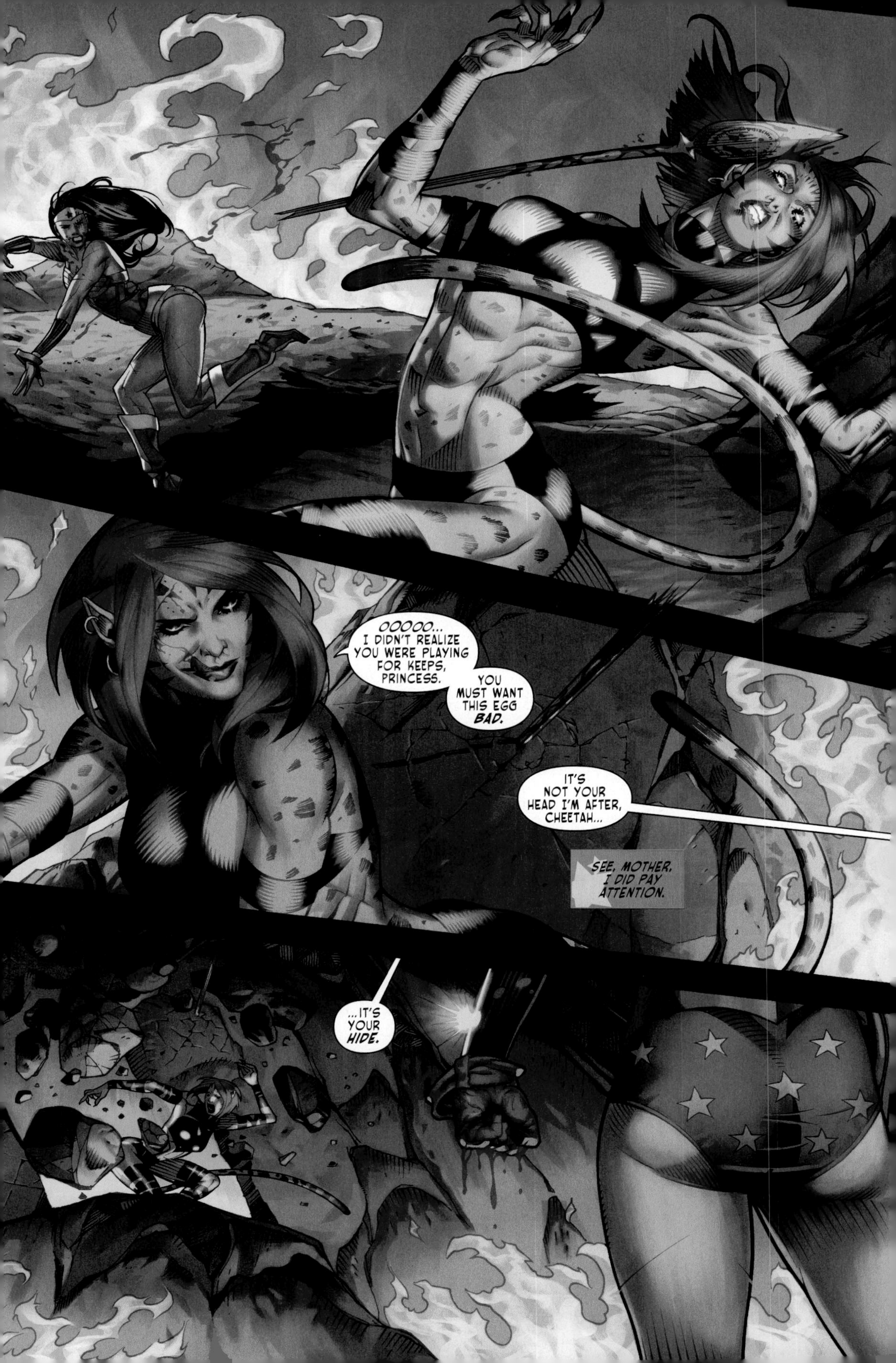
OOOOO... I DIDN'T REALIZE YOU WERE PLAYING FOR KEEPS, PRINCESS.
YOU MUST WANT THIS EGG BAD.
IT'S NOT YOUR HEAD I'M AFTER, CHEETAH...
SEE, MOTHER, I DID PAY ATTENTION.
...IT'S YOUR HIDE.

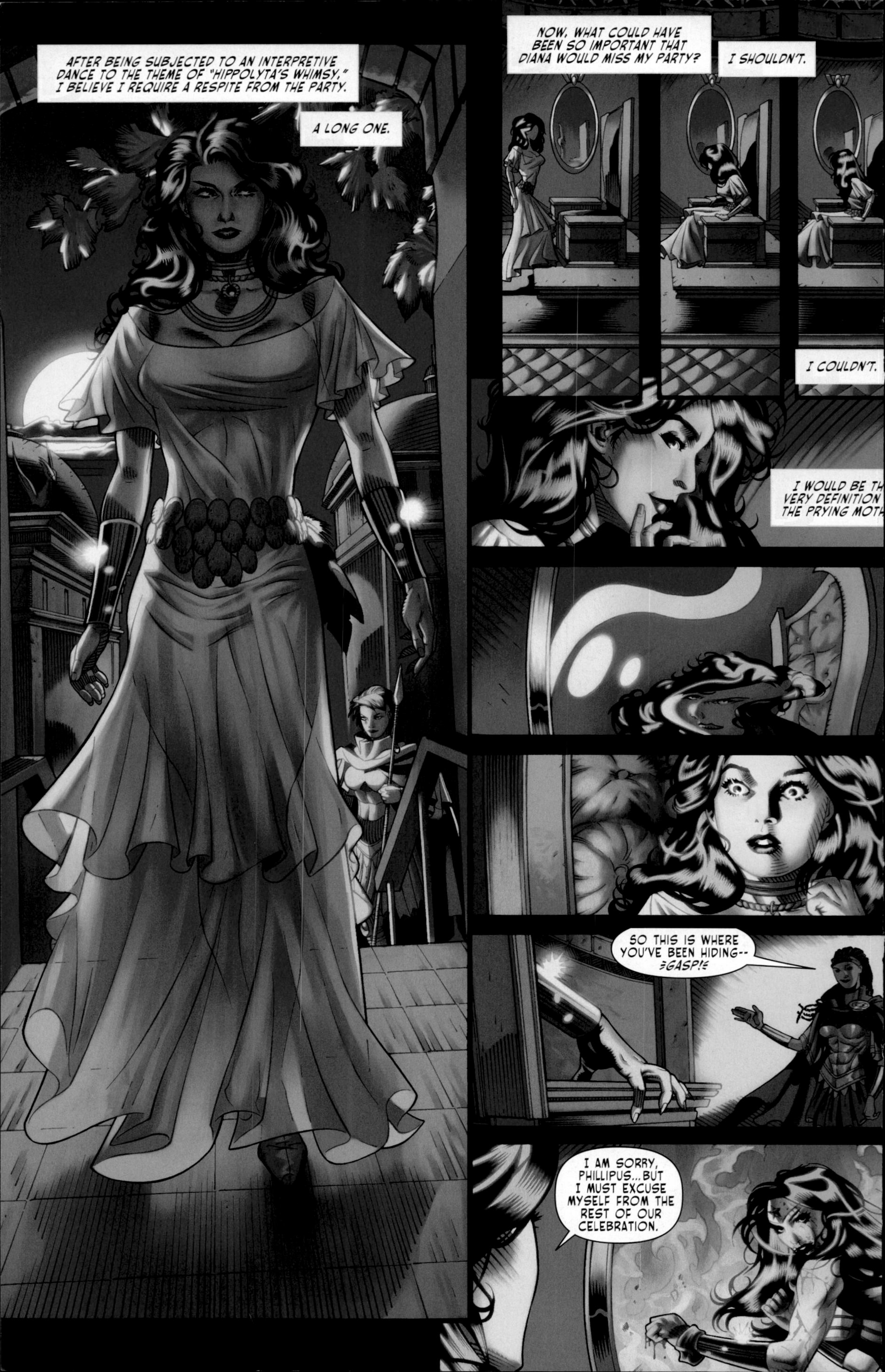
AFTER BEING SUBJECTED TO AN INTERPRETIVE DANCE TO THE THEME OF "HIPPOLYTA'S WHIMSY," I BELIEVE I REQUIRE A RESPITE FROM THE PARTY.
A LONG ONE.
NOW, WHAT COULD HAVE BEEN SO IMPORTANT THAT DIANA WOULD MISS MY PARTY?
I SHOULDN'T.
I COULDN'T.
I WOULD BE TH
VERY DEFINITION
THE PRYING MOTH
SO THIS IS WHERE YOU'VE BEEN HIDING-- ≶GASP!≷
I AM SORRY, PHILLIPUS... BUT I MUST EXCUSE MYSELF FROM THE REST OF OUR CELEBRATION.

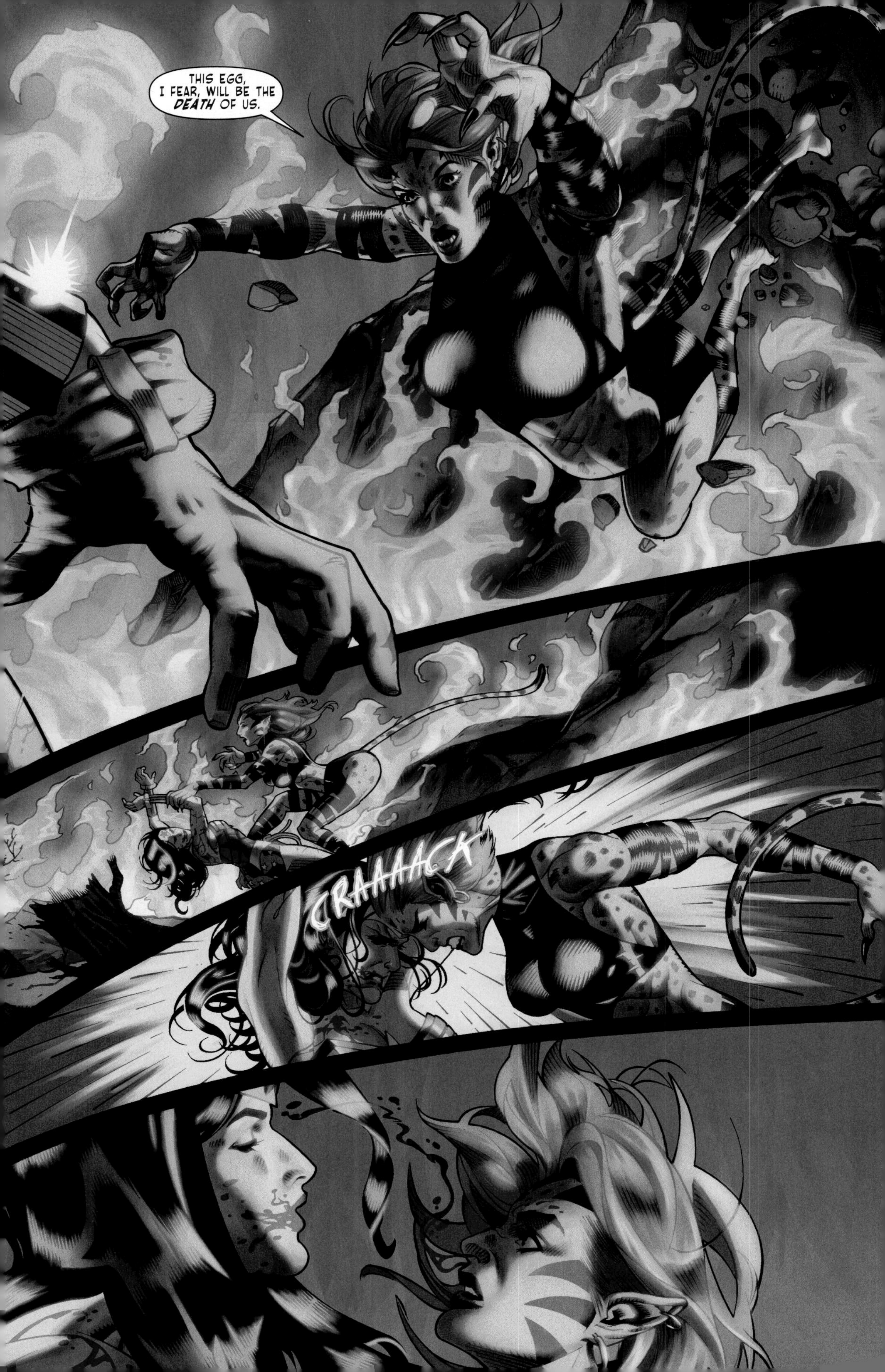
THIS EGG, I FEAR, WILL BE THE *DEATH* OF US.
CRAAAACK

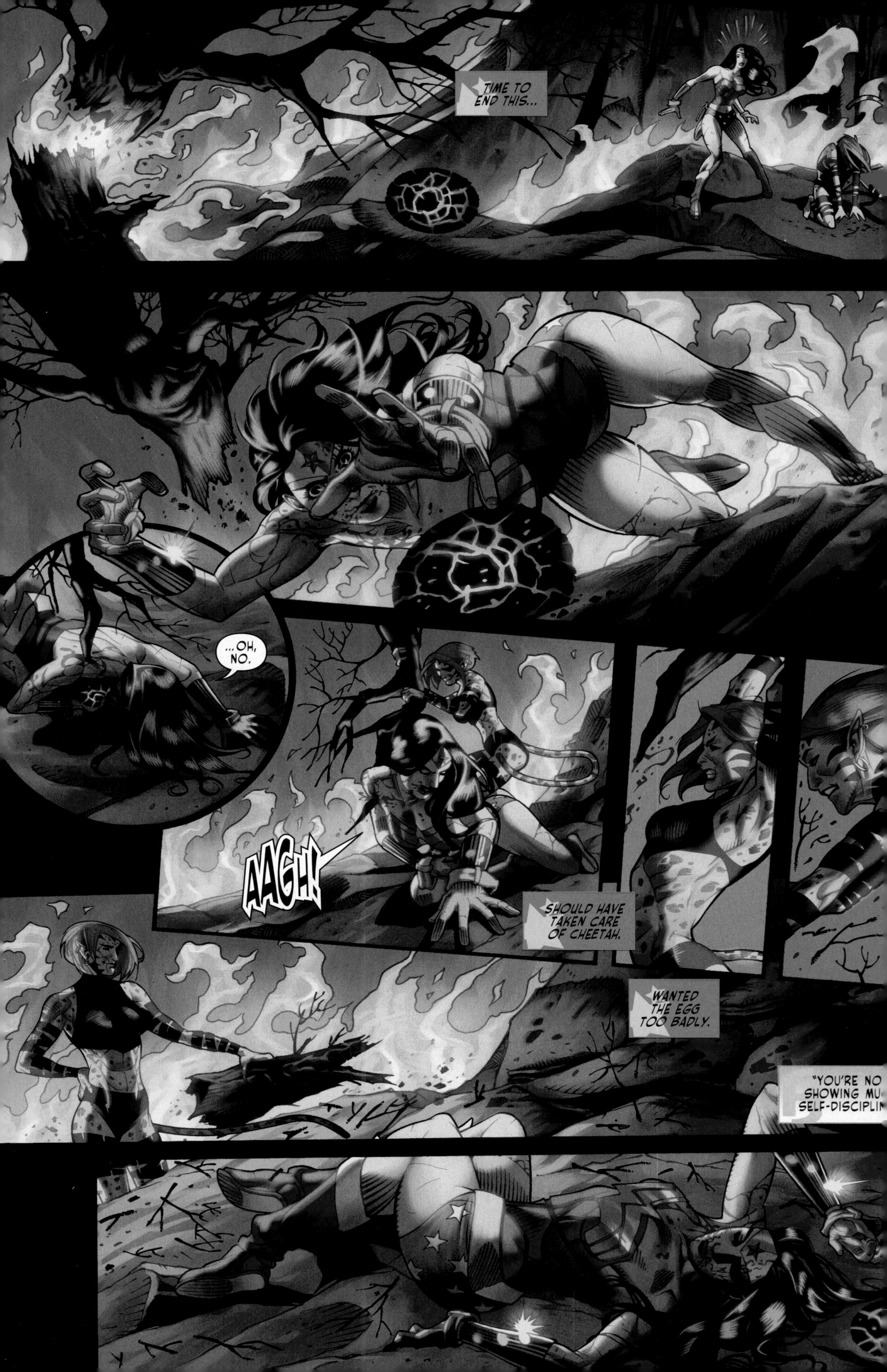
TIME TO END THIS...
...OH, NO.
AAGH!
SHOULD HAVE TAKEN CARE OF CHEETAH.
WANTED THE EGG TOO BADLY.

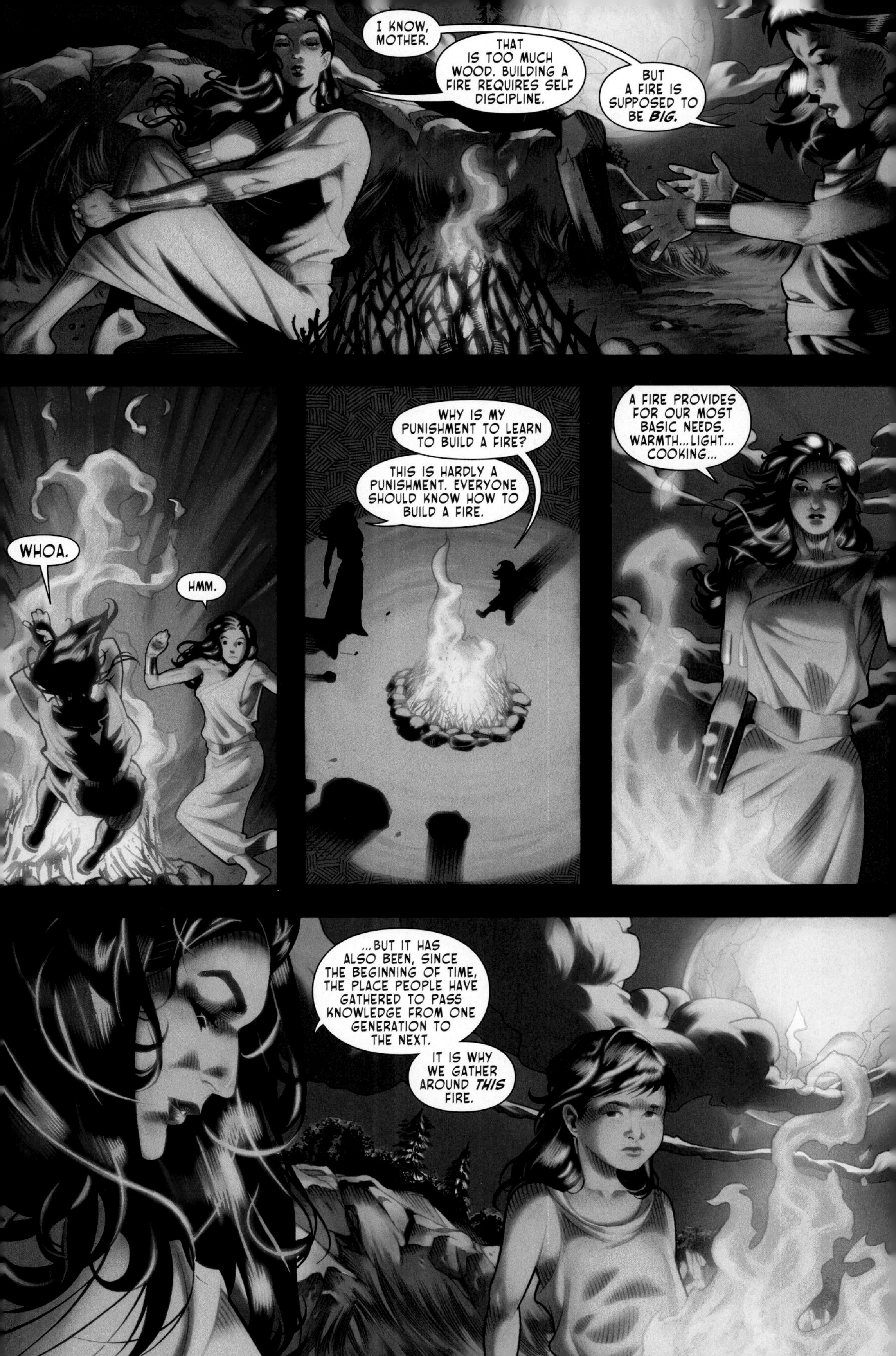
I KNOW, MOTHER.
THAT IS TOO MUCH WOOD. BUILDING A FIRE REQUIRES SELF DISCIPLINE.
BUT A FIRE IS SUPPOSED TO BE *BIG.*
WHOA.
HMM.
WHY IS MY PUNISHMENT TO LEARN TO BUILD A FIRE?
THIS IS HARDLY A PUNISHMENT. EVERYONE SHOULD KNOW HOW TO BUILD A FIRE.
A FIRE PROVIDES FOR OUR MOST BASIC NEEDS. WARMTH...LIGHT... COOKING...
...BUT IT HAS ALSO BEEN, SINCE THE BEGINNING OF TIME, THE PLACE PEOPLE HAVE GATHERED TO PASS KNOWLEDGE FROM ONE GENERATION TO THE NEXT.
IT IS WHY WE GATHER AROUND *THIS* FIRE.

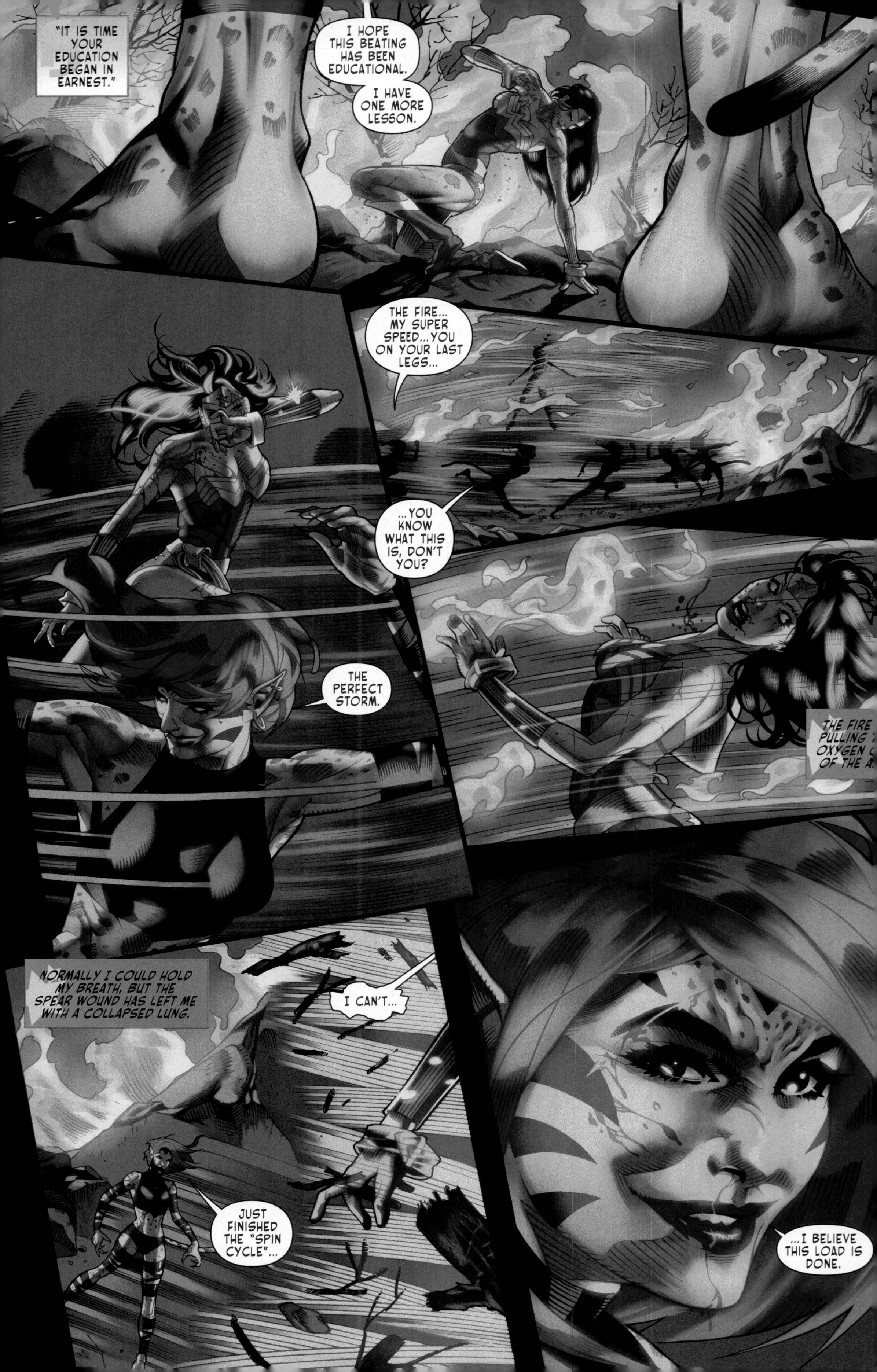

"IT IS TIME YOUR EDUCATION BEGAN IN EARNEST."
I HOPE THIS BEATING HAS BEEN EDUCATIONAL.
I HAVE ONE MORE LESSON.
THE FIRE... MY SUPER SPEED...YOU ON YOUR LAST LEGS...
...YOU KNOW WHAT THIS IS, DON'T YOU?
THE PERFECT STORM.
THE FIRE PULLING OXYGEN OF THE A
NORMALLY I COULD HOLD MY BREATH, BUT THE SPEAR WOUND HAS LEFT ME WITH A COLLAPSED LUNG.
I CAN'T...
JUST FINISHED THE "SPIN CYCLE"...
...I BELIEVE THIS LOAD IS DONE.

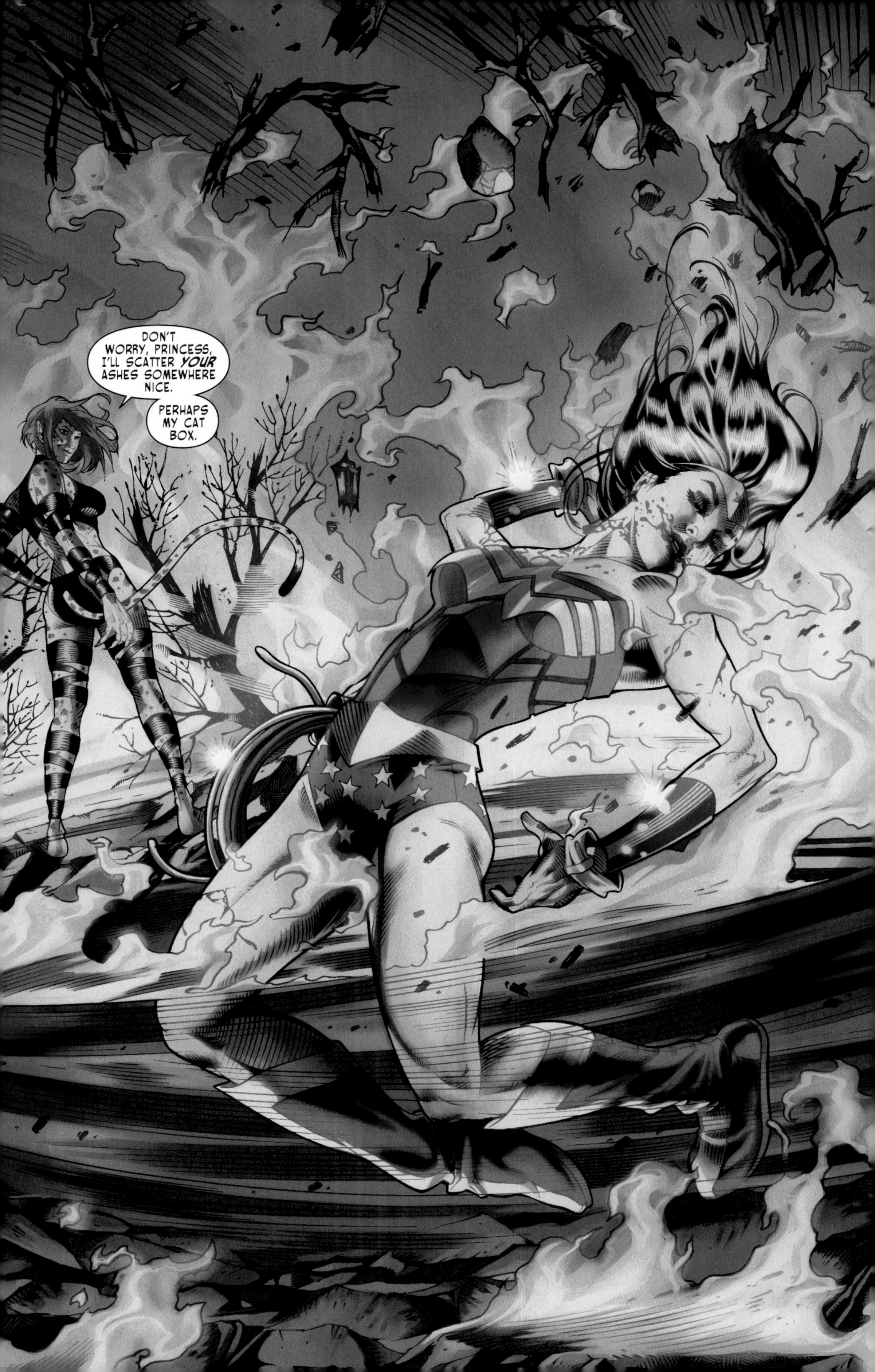
DON'T WORRY, PRINCESS, I'LL SCATTER YOUR ASHES SOMEWHERE NICE.
PERHAPS MY CAT BOX.

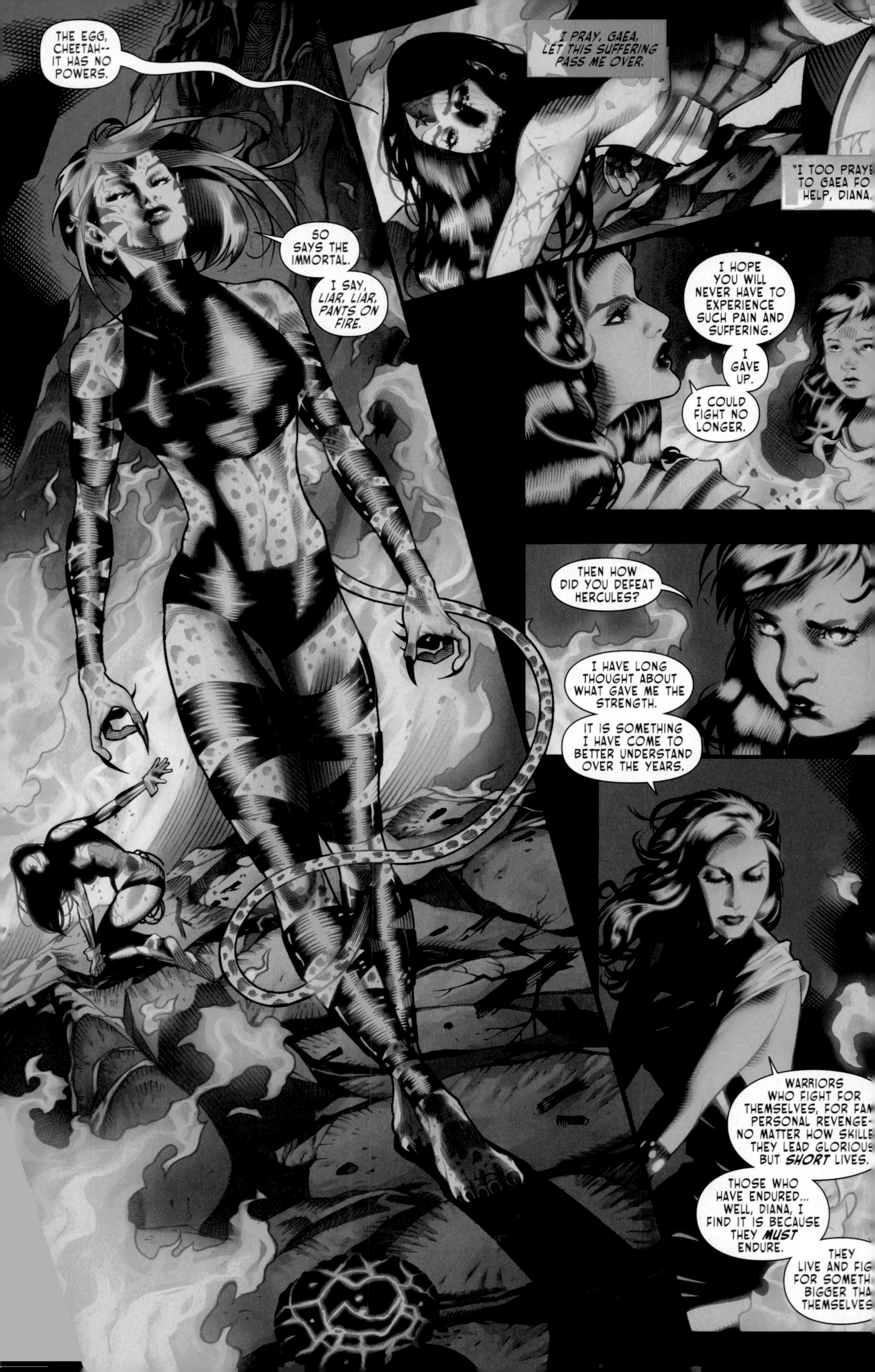
THE EGG, CHEETAH-- IT HAS NO POWERS.
I PRAY, GAEA. LET THIS SUFFERING PASS ME OVER.
"I TOO PRAYE TO GAEA FO HELP, DIANA.
SO SAYS THE IMMORTAL.
I SAY, *LIAR, LIAR, PANTS ON FIRE.*
I HOPE YOU WILL NEVER HAVE TO EXPERIENCE SUCH PAIN AND SUFFERING.
I GAVE UP.
I COULD FIGHT NO LONGER.
THEN HOW DID YOU DEFEAT HERCULES?
I HAVE LONG THOUGHT ABOUT WHAT GAVE ME THE STRENGTH.
IT IS SOMETHING I HAVE COME TO BETTER UNDERSTAND OVER THE YEARS.
WARRIORS WHO FIGHT FOR THEMSELVES, FOR FAM PERSONAL REVENGE- NO MATTER HOW SKILLE THEY LEAD GLORIOUS BUT *SHORT* LIVES.
THOSE WHO HAVE ENDURED... WELL, DIANA, I FIND IT IS BECAUSE THEY *MUST* ENDURE.
THEY LIVE AND FIG FOR SOMETH BIGGER THA THEMSELVES

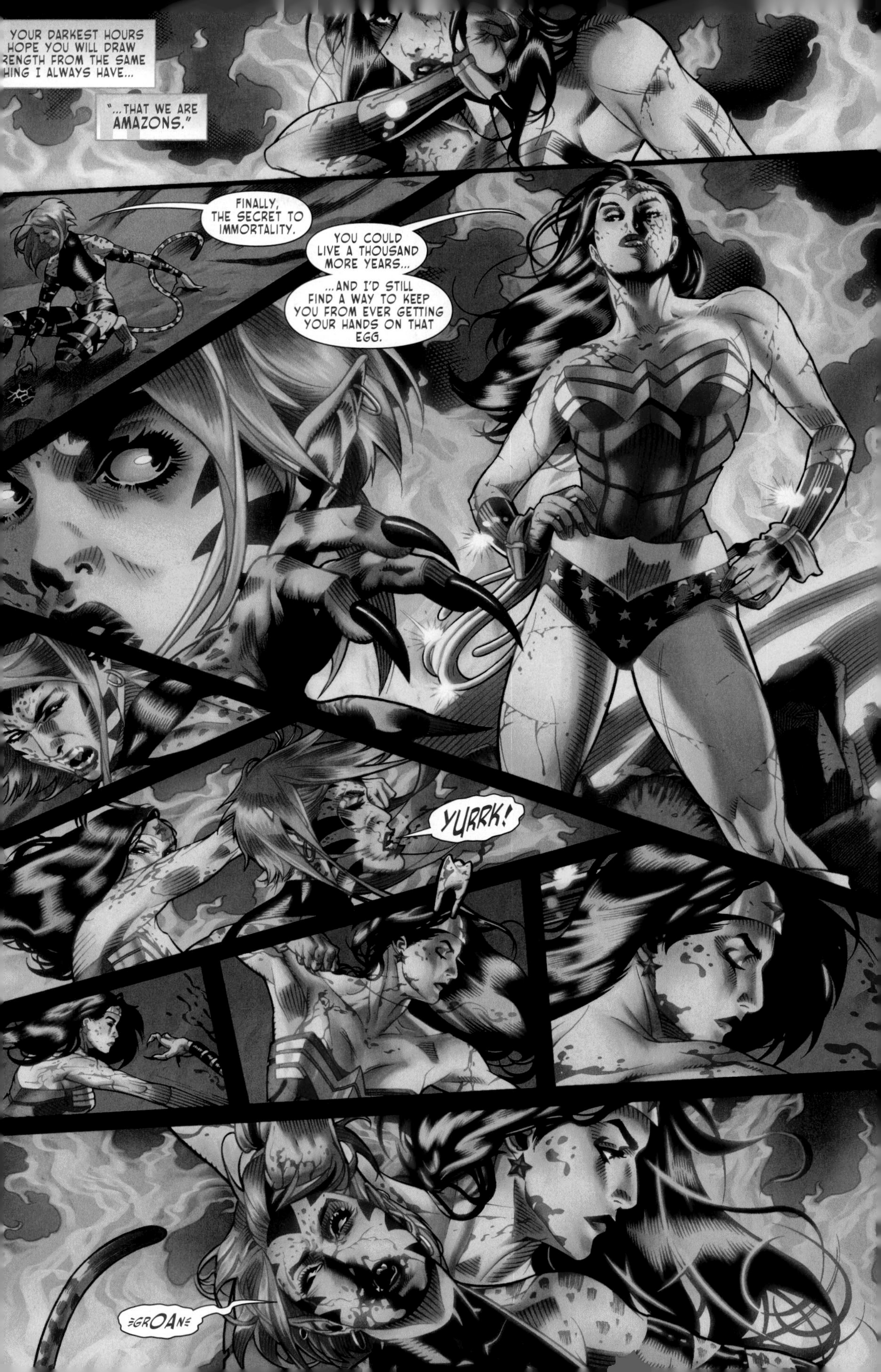
YOUR DARKEST HOURS HOPE YOU WILL DRAW RENGTH FROM THE SAME HING I ALWAYS HAVE...
"...THAT WE ARE AMAZONS."
FINALLY, THE SECRET TO IMMORTALITY.
YOU COULD LIVE A THOUSAND MORE YEARS...
...AND I'D STILL FIND A WAY TO KEEP YOU FROM EVER GETTING YOUR HANDS ON THAT EGG.
YURRK!
GROAN

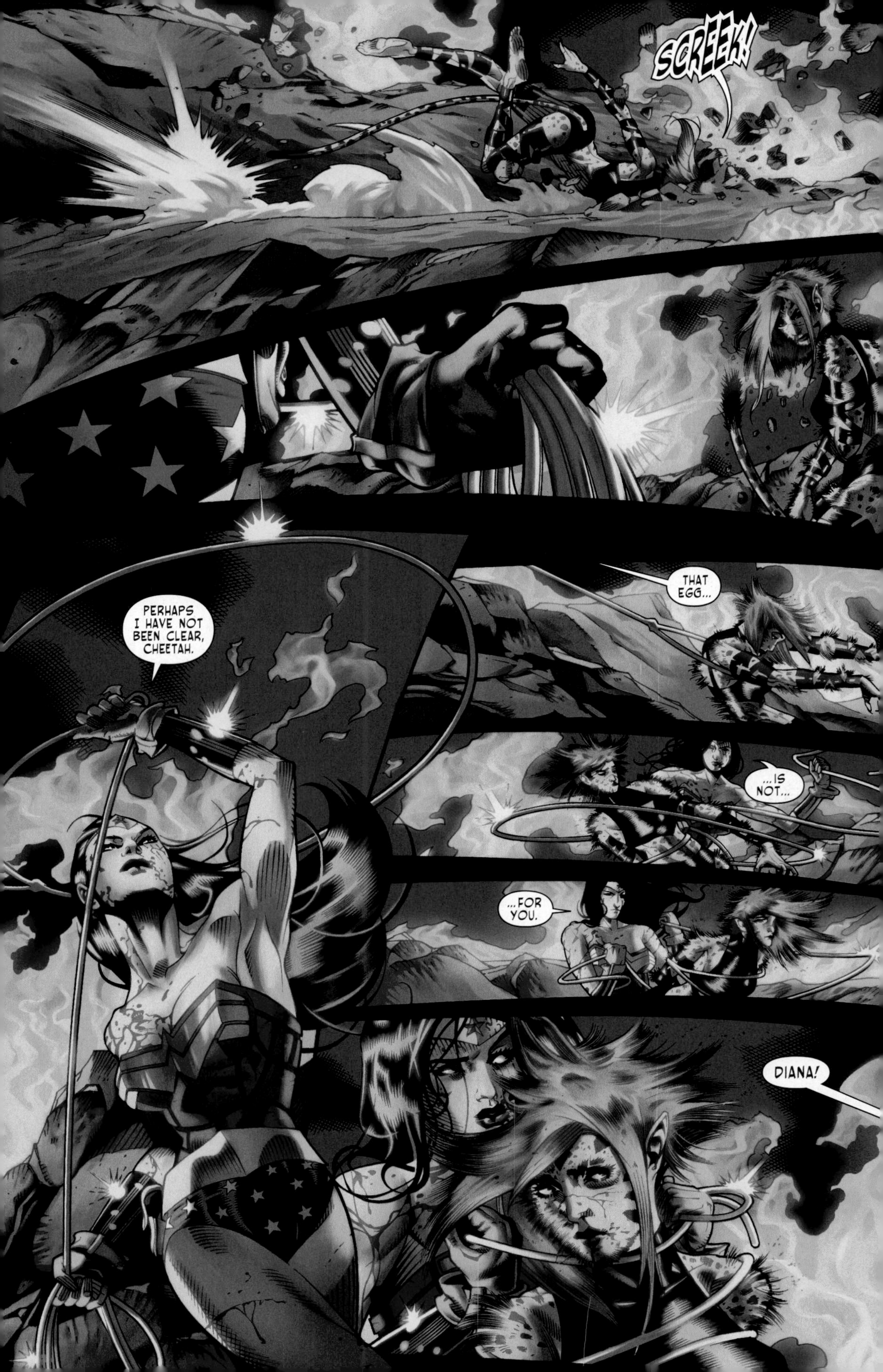
SCREEK!
PERHAPS I HAVE NOT BEEN CLEAR, CHEETAH.
THAT EGG...
...IS NOT...
...FOR YOU.
DIANA!

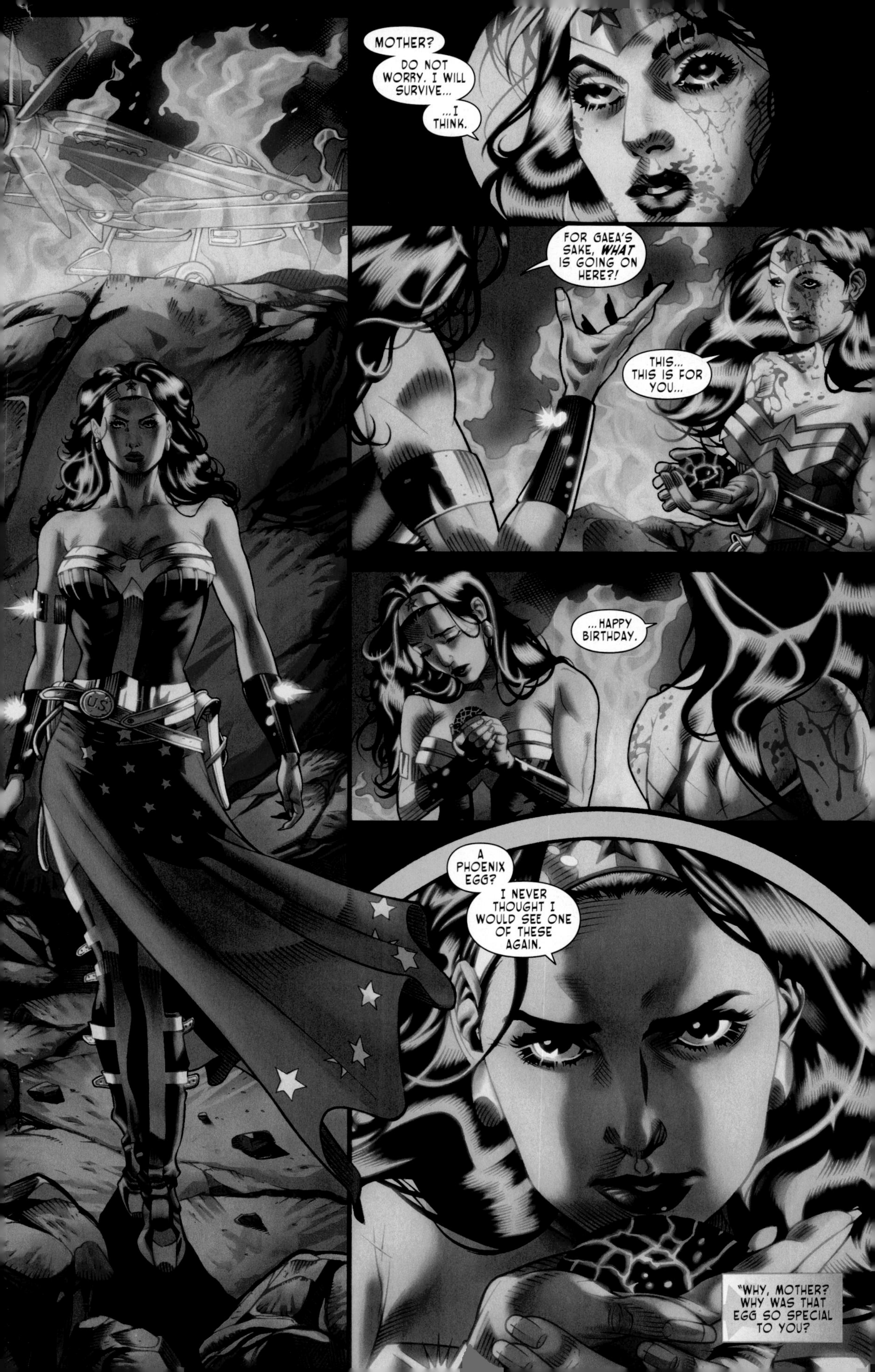
MOTHER?
DO NOT WORRY. I WILL SURVIVE...
...I THINK.
FOR GAEA'S SAKE, **WHAT** IS GOING ON HERE?!
THIS... THIS IS FOR YOU...
...HAPPY BIRTHDAY.
A PHOENIX EGG?
I NEVER THOUGHT I WOULD SEE ONE OF THESE AGAIN.
"WHY, MOTHER? WHY WAS THAT EGG SO SPECIAL TO YOU?

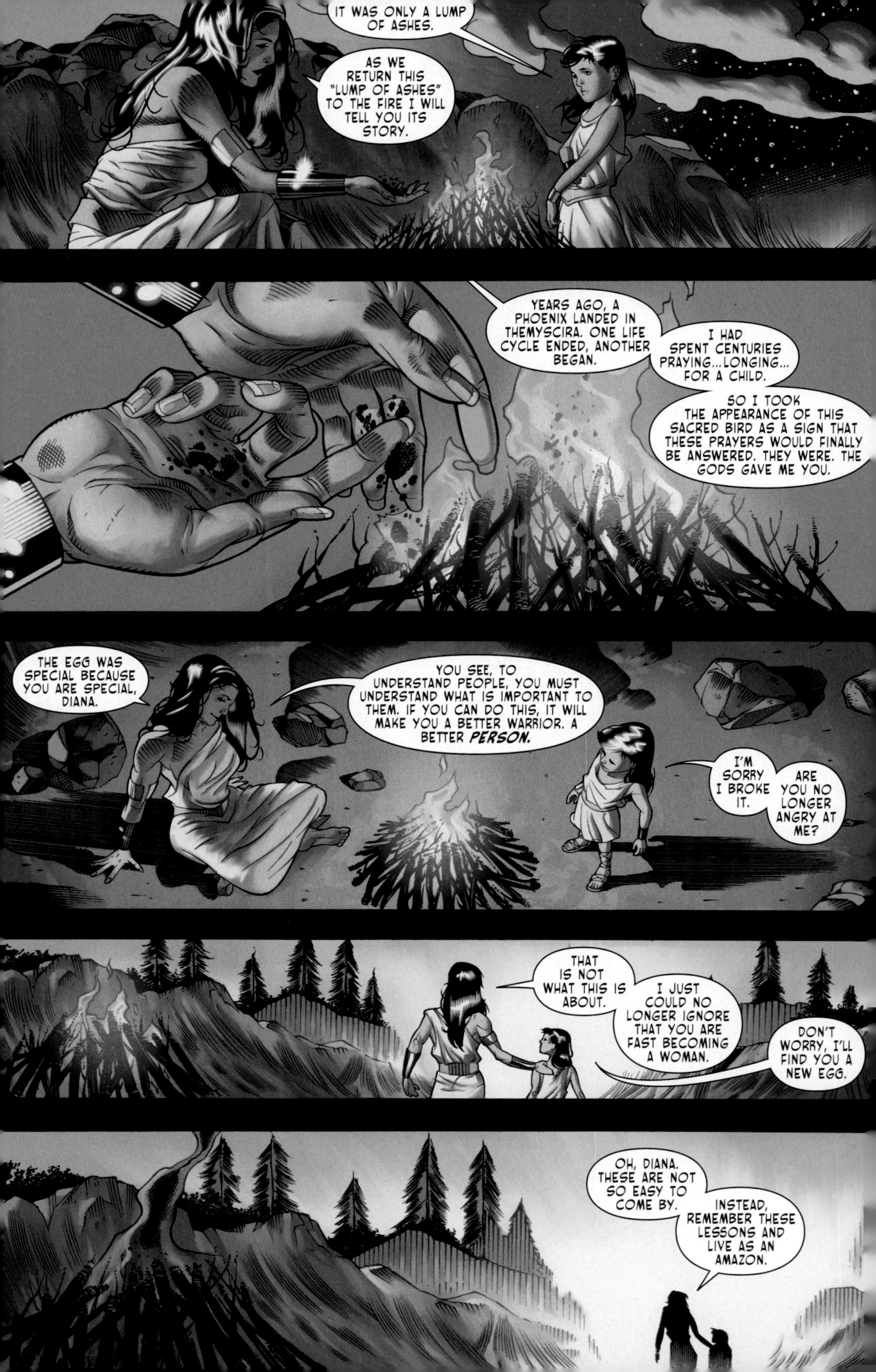
IT WAS ONLY A LUMP OF ASHES.
AS WE RETURN THIS "LUMP OF ASHES" TO THE FIRE I WILL TELL YOU ITS STORY.
YEARS AGO, A PHOENIX LANDED IN THEMYSCIRA. ONE LIFE CYCLE ENDED, ANOTHER BEGAN.
I HAD SPENT CENTURIES PRAYING...LONGING... FOR A CHILD.
SO I TOOK THE APPEARANCE OF THIS SACRED BIRD AS A SIGN THAT THESE PRAYERS WOULD FINALLY BE ANSWERED. THEY WERE. THE GODS GAVE ME YOU.
THE EGG WAS SPECIAL BECAUSE YOU ARE SPECIAL, DIANA.
YOU SEE, TO UNDERSTAND PEOPLE, YOU MUST UNDERSTAND WHAT IS IMPORTANT TO THEM. IF YOU CAN DO THIS, IT WILL MAKE YOU A BETTER WARRIOR. A BETTER PERSON.
I'M SORRY I BROKE IT.
ARE YOU NO LONGER ANGRY AT ME?
THAT IS NOT WHAT THIS IS ABOUT.
I JUST COULD NO LONGER IGNORE THAT YOU ARE FAST BECOMING A WOMAN.
DON'T WORRY, I'LL FIND YOU A NEW EGG.
OH, DIANA. THESE ARE NOT SO EASY TO COME BY.
INSTEAD, REMEMBER THESE LESSONS AND LIVE AS AN AMAZON.

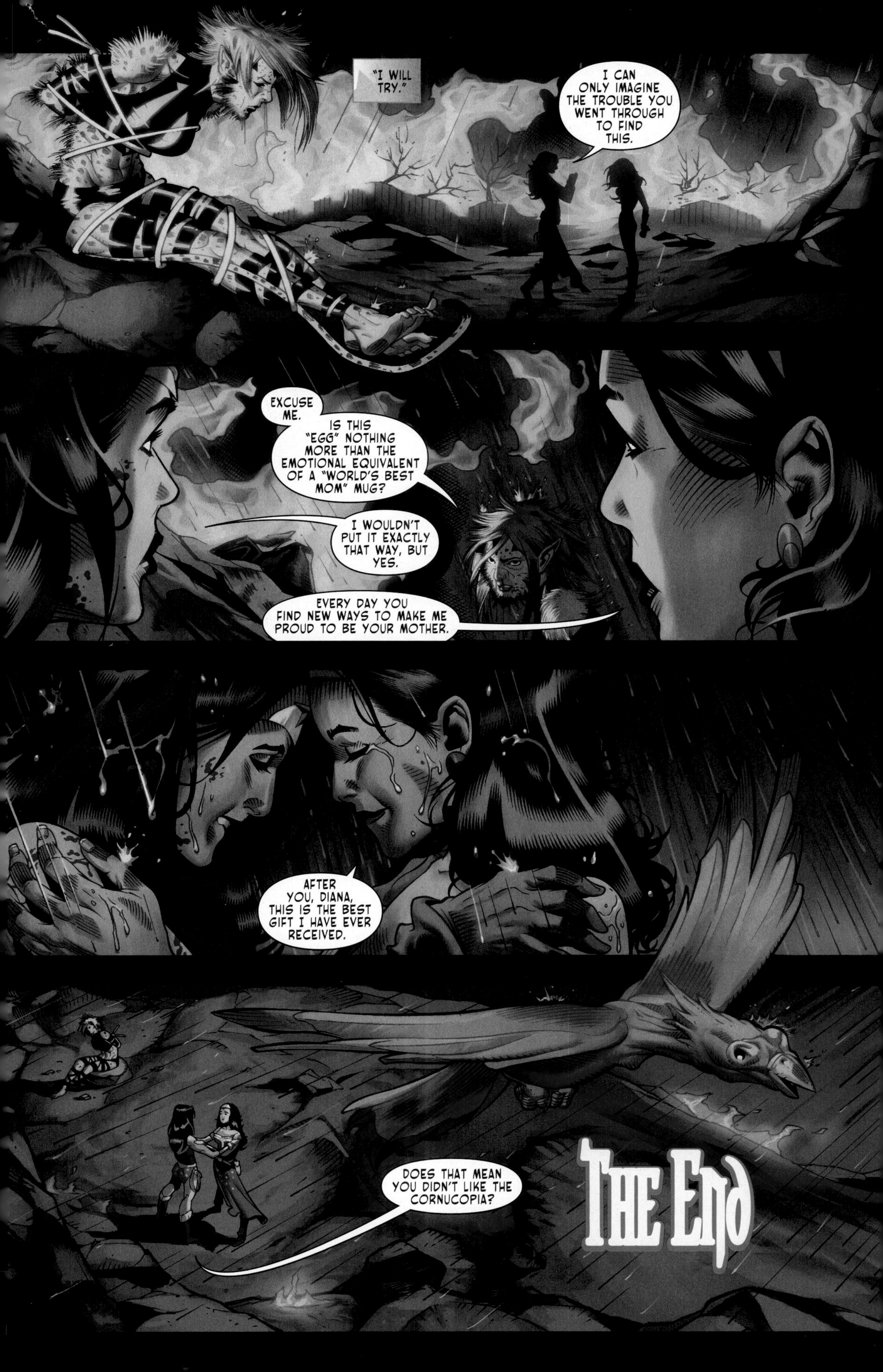
"I WILL TRY."
I CAN ONLY IMAGINE THE TROUBLE YOU WENT THROUGH TO FIND THIS.
EXCUSE ME.
IS THIS "EGG" NOTHING MORE THAN THE EMOTIONAL EQUIVALENT OF A "WORLD'S BEST MOM" MUG?
I WOULDN'T PUT IT EXACTLY THAT WAY, BUT YES.
EVERY DAY YOU FIND NEW WAYS TO MAKE ME PROUD TO BE YOUR MOTHER.
AFTER YOU, DIANA, THIS IS THE BEST GIFT I HAVE EVER RECEIVED.
DOES THAT MEAN YOU DIDN'T LIKE THE CORNUCOPIA?
THE END

NOT INCLUDED

ADAM P. KNAVE
WRITER

MATTHEW DOW SMITH
ARTIST

REX LOKUS
COLORIST

DERON BENNETT
LETTERER

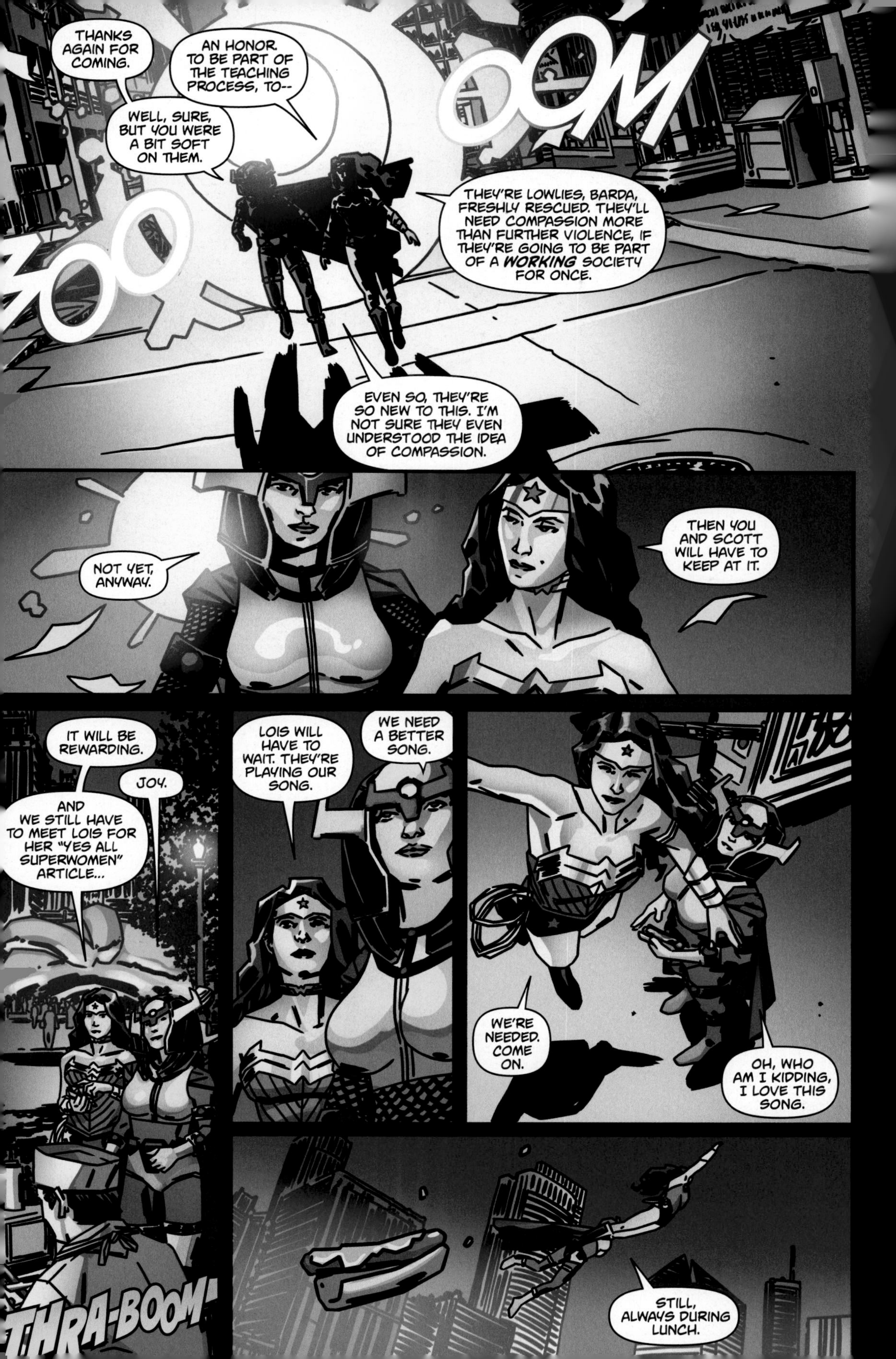
BOOOOOM
THANKS AGAIN FOR COMING.
AN HONOR. TO BE PART OF THE TEACHING PROCESS, TO--
WELL, SURE, BUT YOU WERE A BIT SOFT ON THEM.
THEY'RE LOWLIES, BARDA, FRESHLY RESCUED. THEY'LL NEED COMPASSION MORE THAN FURTHER VIOLENCE, IF THEY'RE GOING TO BE PART OF A WORKING SOCIETY FOR ONCE.
EVEN SO, THEY'RE SO NEW TO THIS. I'M NOT SURE THEY EVEN UNDERSTOOD THE IDEA OF COMPASSION.
NOT YET, ANYWAY.
THEN YOU AND SCOTT WILL HAVE TO KEEP AT IT.
IT WILL BE REWARDING.
JOY.
AND WE STILL HAVE TO MEET LOIS FOR HER "YES ALL SUPERWOMEN" ARTICLE...
THRA-BOOM
LOIS WILL HAVE TO WAIT. THEY'RE PLAYING OUR SONG.
WE NEED A BETTER SONG.
WE'RE NEEDED. COME ON.
OH, WHO AM I KIDDING, I LOVE THIS SONG.
STILL, ALWAYS DURING LUNCH.

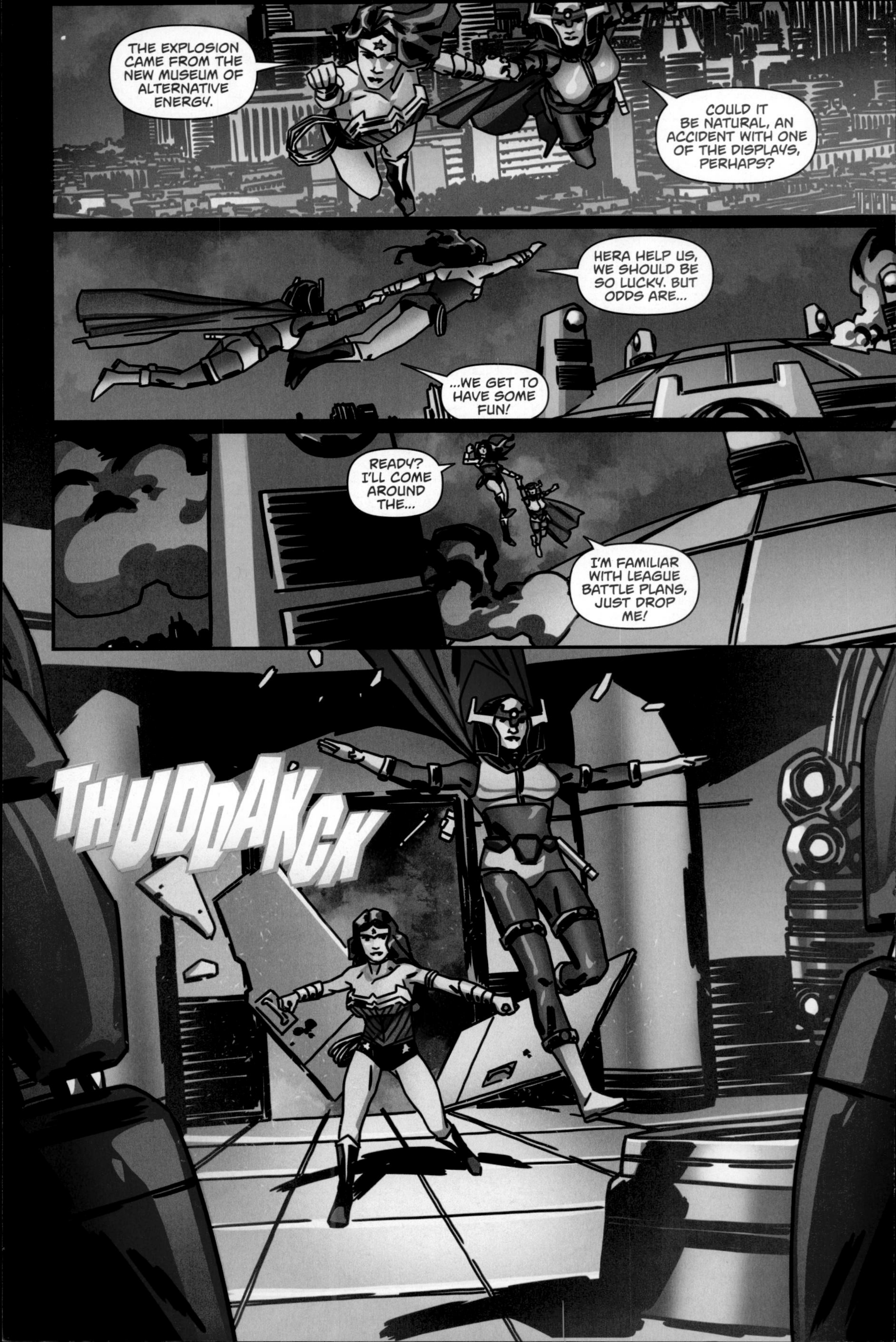
THE EXPLOSION CAME FROM THE NEW MUSEUM OF ALTERNATIVE ENERGY.
COULD IT BE NATURAL, AN ACCIDENT WITH ONE OF THE DISPLAYS, PERHAPS?
HERA HELP US, WE SHOULD BE SO LUCKY. BUT ODDS ARE...
...WE GET TO HAVE SOME FUN!
READY? I'LL COME AROUND THE...
I'M FAMILIAR WITH LEAGUE BATTLE PLANS, JUST DROP ME!
THUDDAKCK

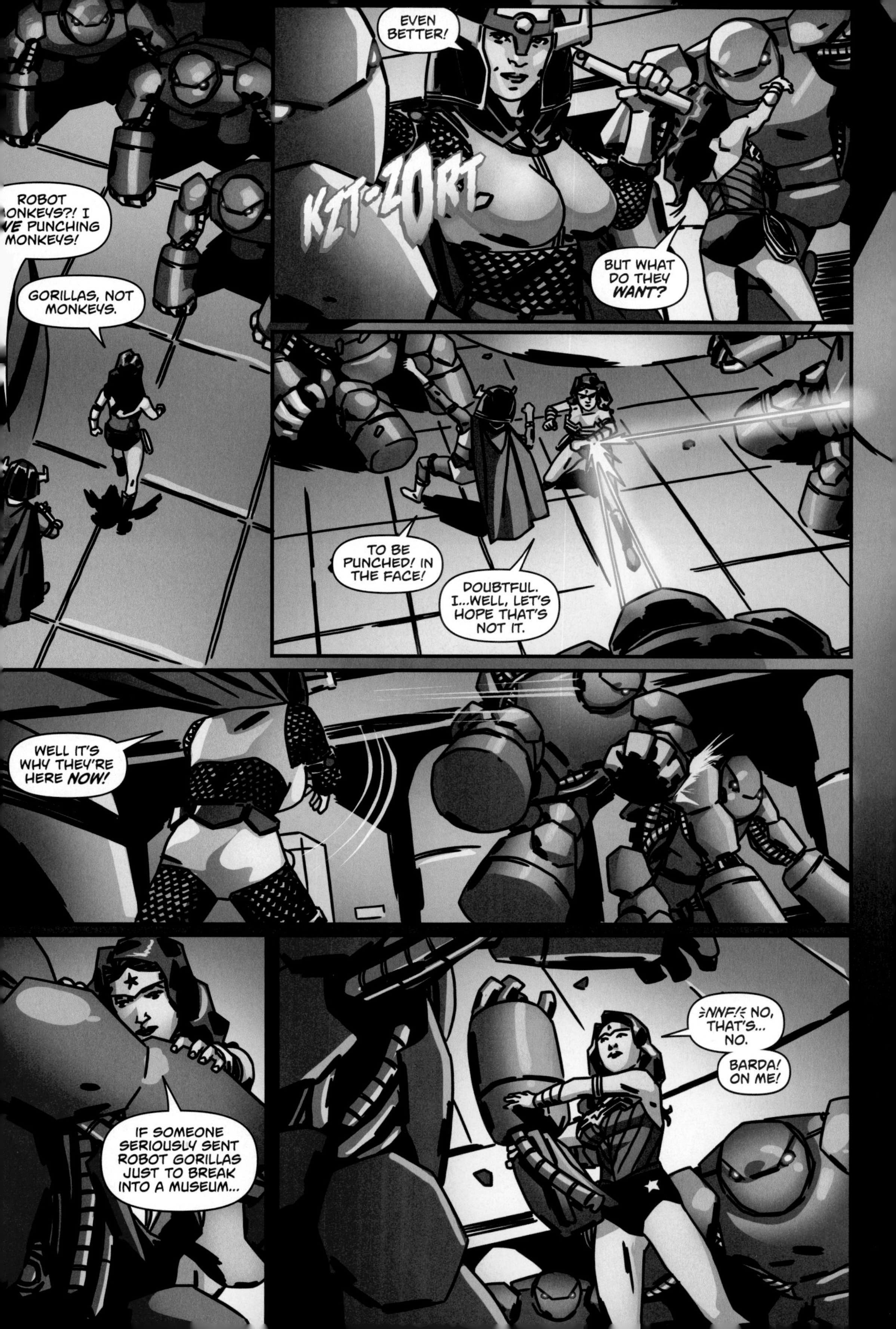
ROBOT
ONKEYS?! I
VE PUNCHING
MONKEYS!
GORILLAS, NOT MONKEYS.
EVEN BETTER!
KZT-ZORT
BUT WHAT DO THEY *WANT?*
TO BE PUNCHED! IN THE FACE!
DOUBTFUL. I...WELL, LET'S HOPE THAT'S NOT IT.
WELL IT'S WHY THEY'RE HERE *NOW!*
IF SOMEONE SERIOUSLY SENT ROBOT GORILLAS JUST TO BREAK INTO A MUSEUM...
NNF! NO, THAT'S... NO.
BARDA! ON ME!

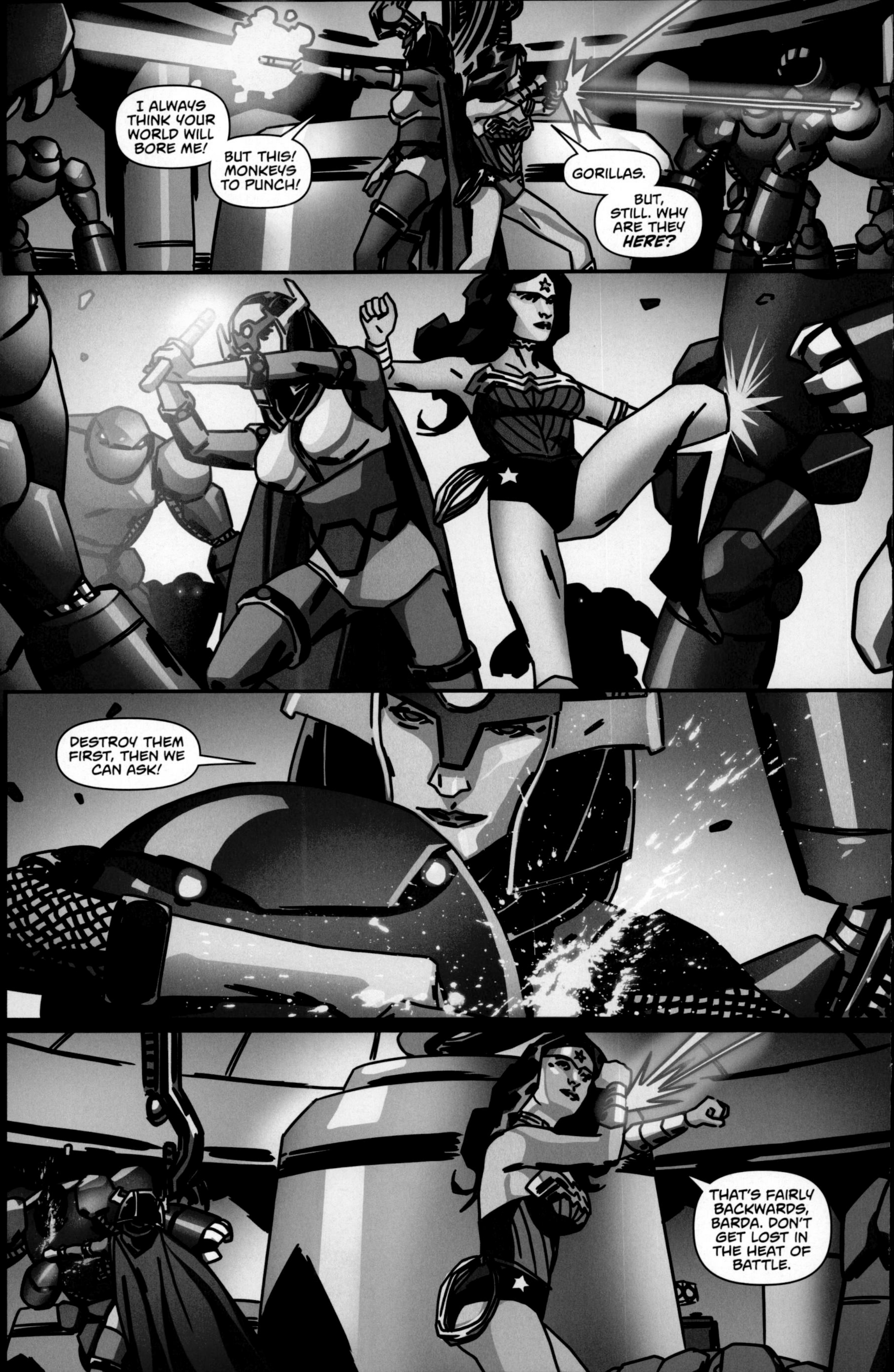
I ALWAYS THINK YOUR WORLD WILL BORE ME!
BUT THIS! MONKEYS TO PUNCH!
GORILLAS.
BUT, STILL. WHY ARE THEY *HERE?*
DESTROY THEM FIRST, THEN WE CAN ASK!
THAT'S FAIRLY BACKWARDS, BARDA. DON'T GET LOST IN THE HEAT OF BATTLE.

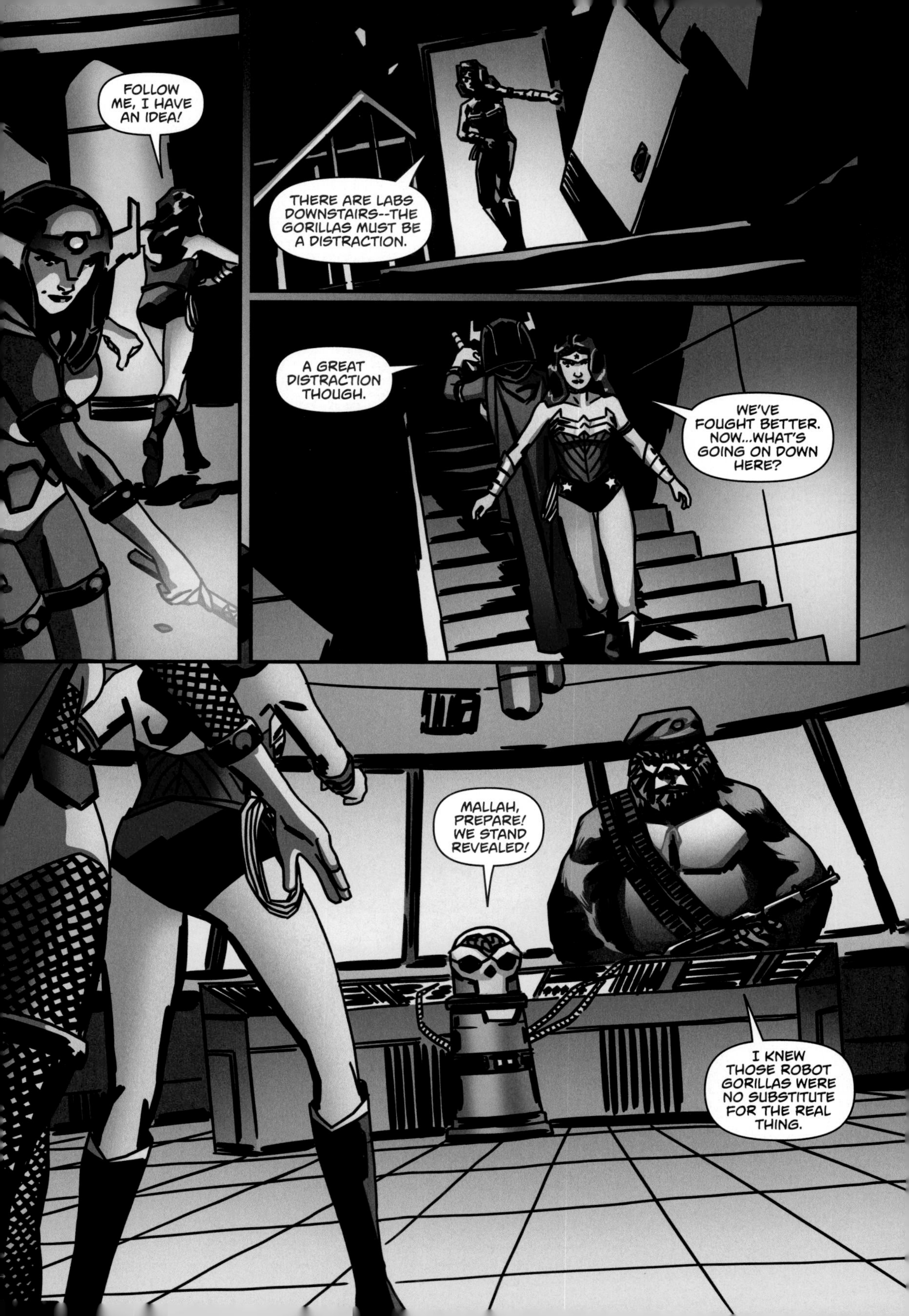
FOLLOW ME, I HAVE AN IDEA!
THERE ARE LABS DOWNSTAIRS--THE GORILLAS MUST BE A DISTRACTION.
A GREAT DISTRACTION THOUGH.
WE'VE FOUGHT BETTER. NOW...WHAT'S GOING ON DOWN HERE?
MALLAH, PREPARE! WE STAND REVEALED!
I KNEW THOSE ROBOT GORILLAS WERE NO SUBSTITUTE FOR THE REAL THING.

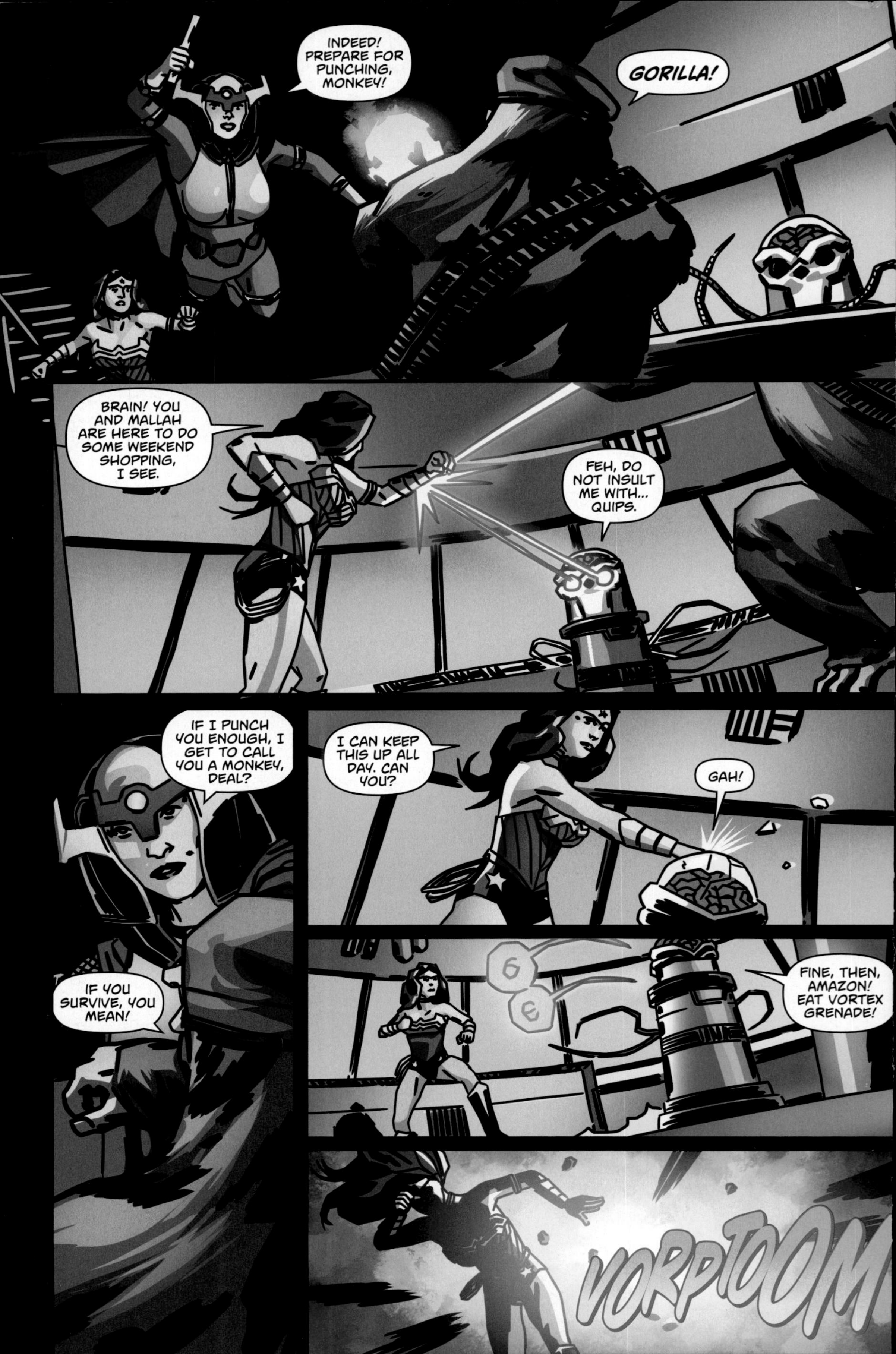
INDEED! PREPARE FOR PUNCHING, MONKEY!
GORILLA!
BRAIN! YOU AND MALLAH ARE HERE TO DO SOME WEEKEND SHOPPING, I SEE.
FEH, DO NOT INSULT ME WITH... QUIPS.
IF I PUNCH YOU ENOUGH, I GET TO CALL YOU A MONKEY, DEAL?
IF YOU SURVIVE, YOU MEAN!
I CAN KEEP THIS UP ALL DAY. CAN YOU?
GAH!
FINE, THEN, AMAZON! EAT VORTEX GRENADE!
VORPTOOM

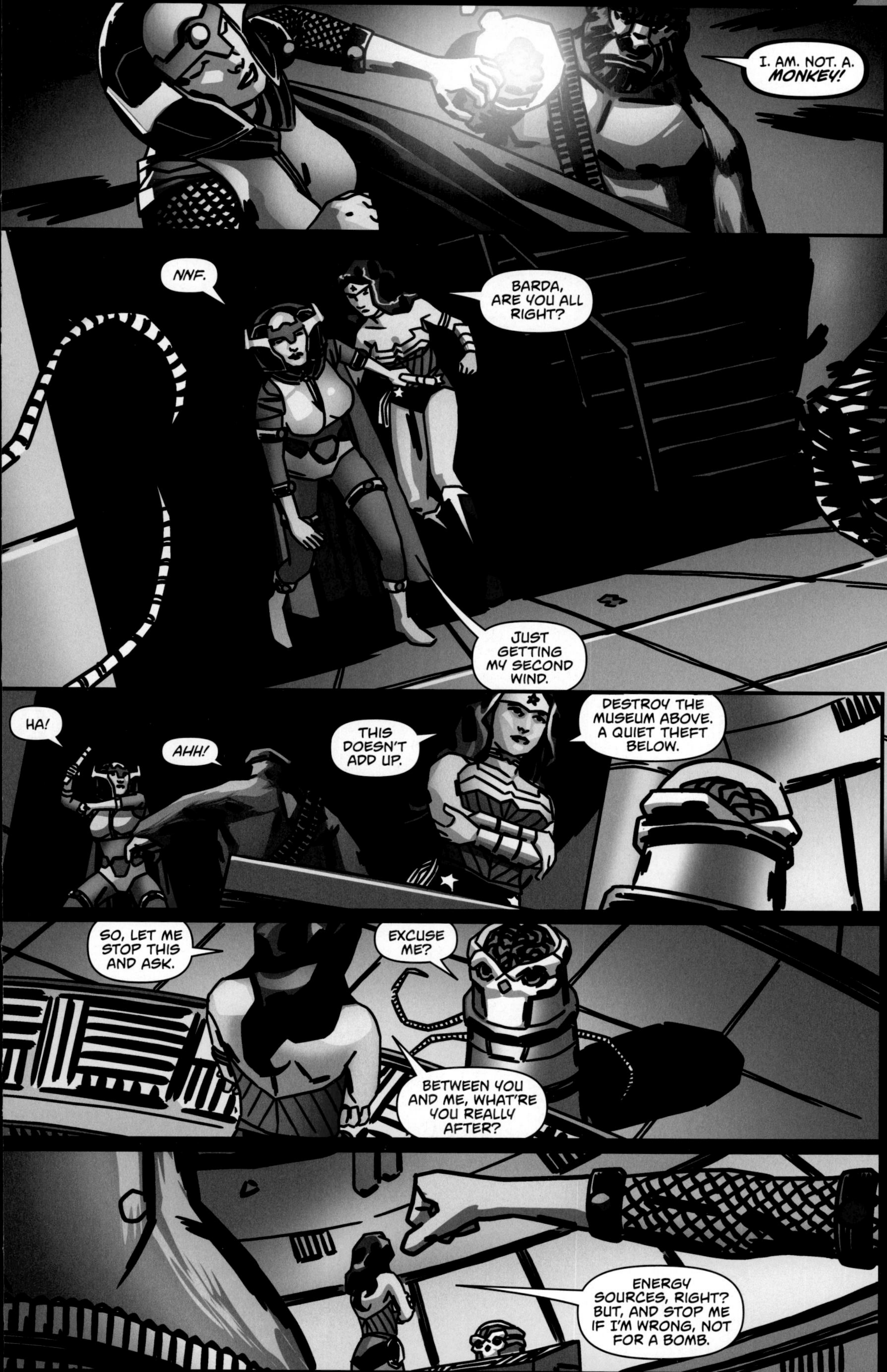
I. AM. NOT. A. *MONKEY!*
NNF.
BARDA, ARE YOU ALL RIGHT?
JUST GETTING MY SECOND WIND.
HA!
AHH!
THIS DOESN'T ADD UP.
DESTROY THE MUSEUM ABOVE. A QUIET THEFT BELOW.
SO, LET ME STOP THIS AND ASK.
EXCUSE ME?
BETWEEN YOU AND ME, WHAT'RE YOU REALLY AFTER?
ENERGY SOURCES, RIGHT? BUT, AND STOP ME IF I'M WRONG, NOT FOR A BOMB.

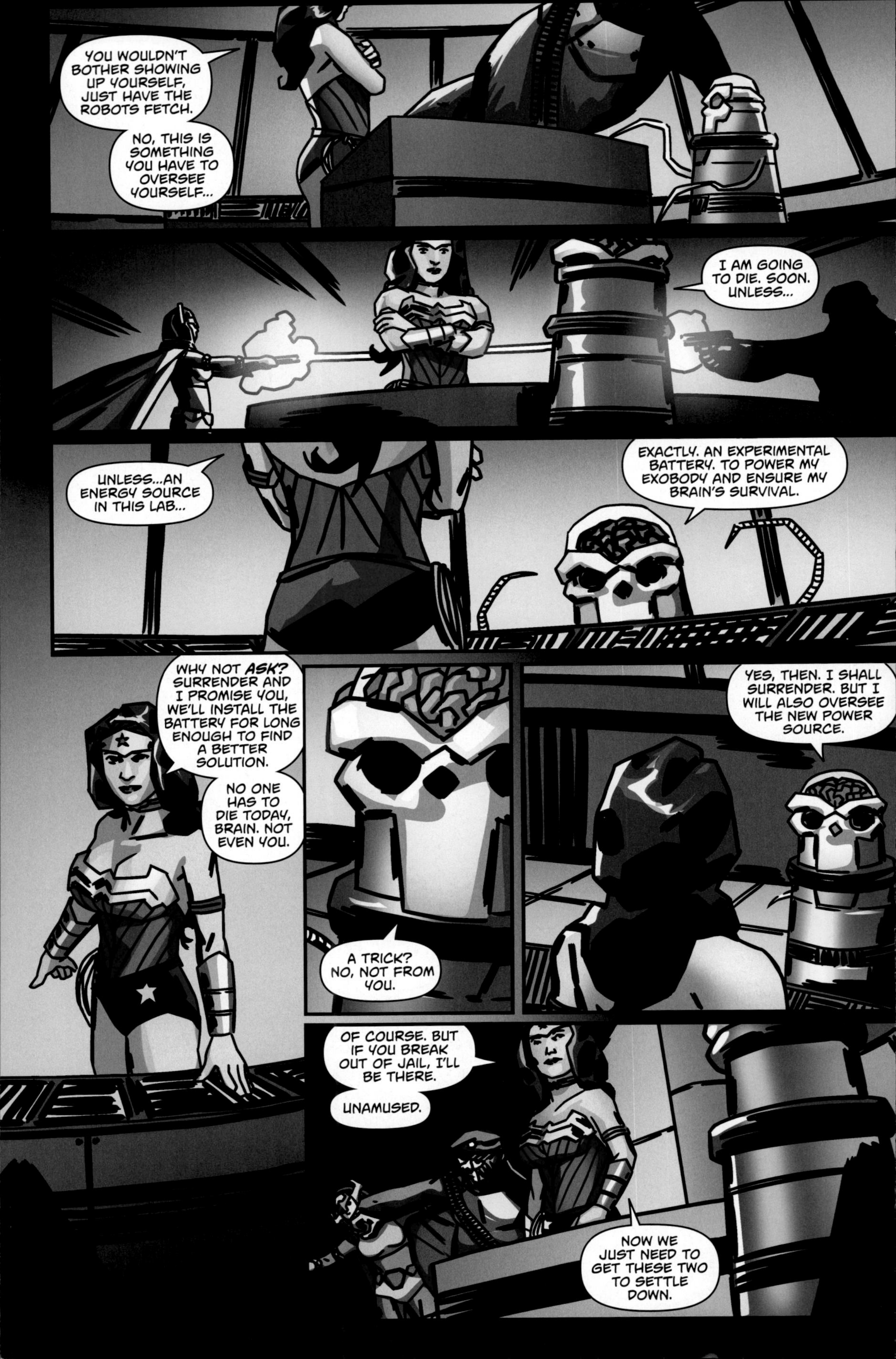
YOU WOULDN'T BOTHER SHOWING UP YOURSELF, JUST HAVE THE ROBOTS FETCH.
NO, THIS IS SOMETHING YOU HAVE TO OVERSEE YOURSELF...
I AM GOING TO DIE. SOON. UNLESS...
UNLESS...AN ENERGY SOURCE IN THIS LAB...
EXACTLY. AN EXPERIMENTAL BATTERY. TO POWER MY EXOBODY AND ENSURE MY BRAIN'S SURVIVAL.
WHY NOT ASK? SURRENDER AND I PROMISE YOU, WE'LL INSTALL THE BATTERY FOR LONG ENOUGH TO FIND A BETTER SOLUTION.
NO ONE HAS TO DIE TODAY, BRAIN. NOT EVEN YOU.
A TRICK? NO, NOT FROM YOU.
YES, THEN. I SHALL SURRENDER. BUT I WILL ALSO OVERSEE THE NEW POWER SOURCE.
OF COURSE. BUT IF YOU BREAK OUT OF JAIL, I'LL BE THERE.
UNAMUSED.
NOW WE JUST NEED TO GET THESE TWO TO SETTLE DOWN.

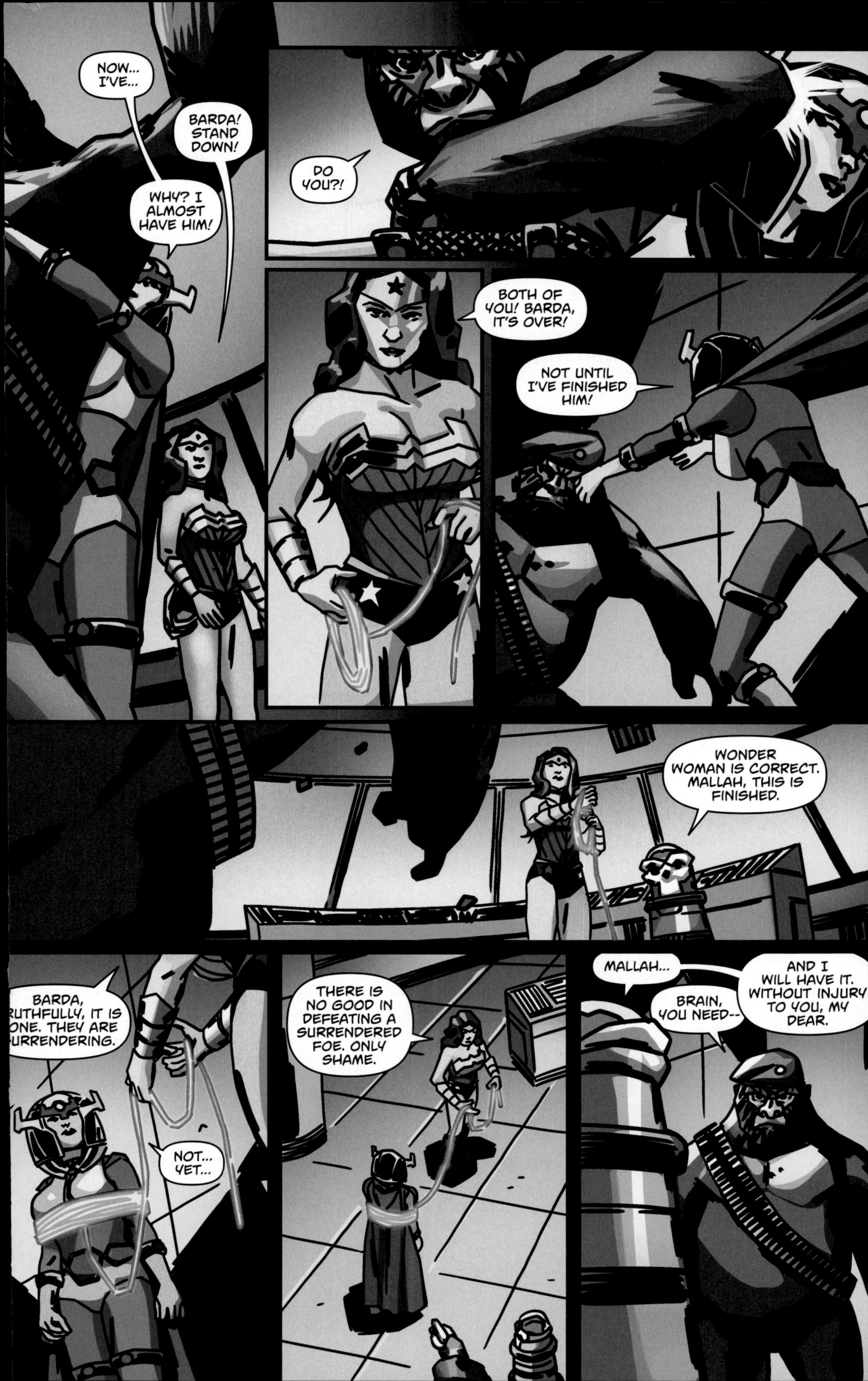
NOW... I'VE...
BARDA! STAND DOWN!
WHY? I ALMOST HAVE HIM!
DO YOU?!
BOTH OF YOU! BARDA, IT'S OVER!
NOT UNTIL I'VE FINISHED HIM!
WONDER WOMAN IS CORRECT. MALLAH, THIS IS FINISHED.
BARDA, TRUTHFULLY, IT IS DONE. THEY ARE SURRENDERING.
NOT... YET...
THERE IS NO GOOD IN DEFEATING A SURRENDERED FOE. ONLY SHAME.
MALLAH...
BRAIN, YOU NEED--
AND I WILL HAVE IT. WITHOUT INJURY TO YOU, MY DEAR.

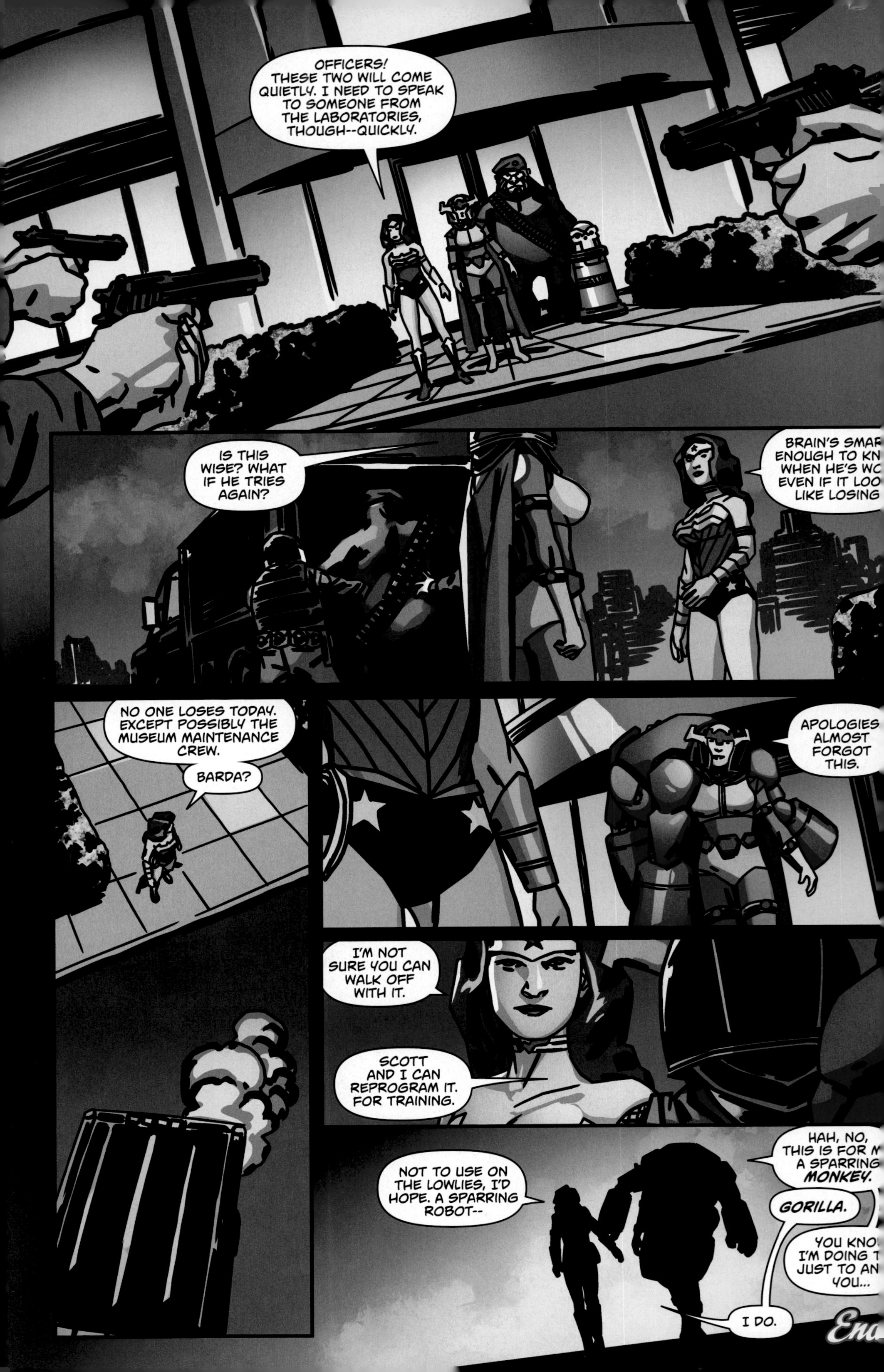

OFFICERS! THESE TWO WILL COME QUIETLY. I NEED TO SPEAK TO SOMEONE FROM THE LABORATORIES, THOUGH--QUICKLY.
IS THIS WISE? WHAT IF HE TRIES AGAIN?
NO ONE LOSES TODAY. EXCEPT POSSIBLY THE MUSEUM MAINTENANCE CREW.
BARDA?
I'M NOT SURE YOU CAN WALK OFF WITH IT.
SCOTT AND I CAN REPROGRAM IT. FOR TRAINING.
NOT TO USE ON THE LOWLIES, I'D HOPE. A SPARRING ROBOT--
GORILLA.
I DO.

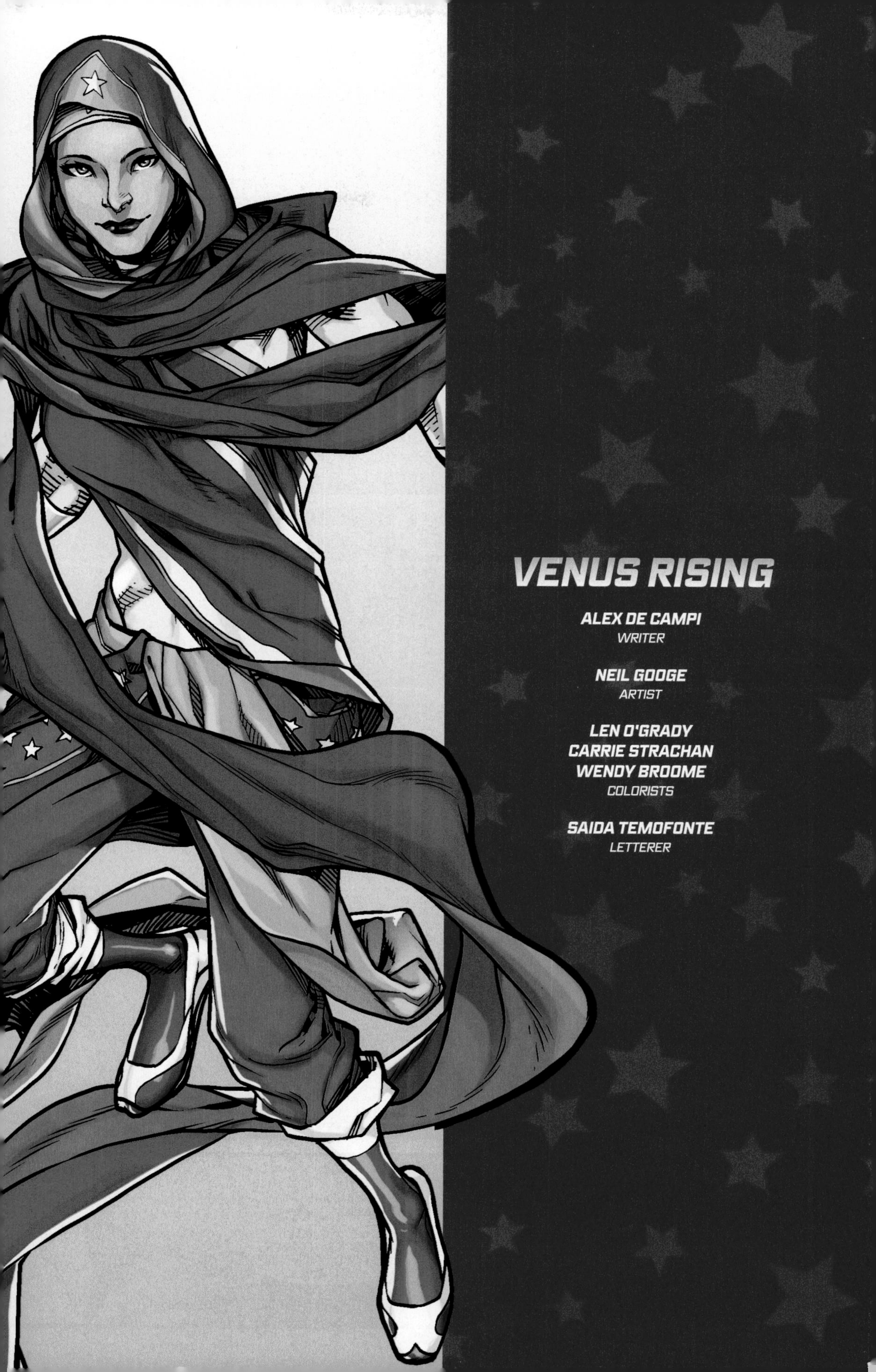

VENUS RISING

ALEX DE CAMPI
WRITER

NEIL GOOGE
ARTIST

LEN O'GRADY
CARRIE STRACHAN
WENDY BROOME
COLORISTS

SAIDA TEMOFONTE
LETTERER

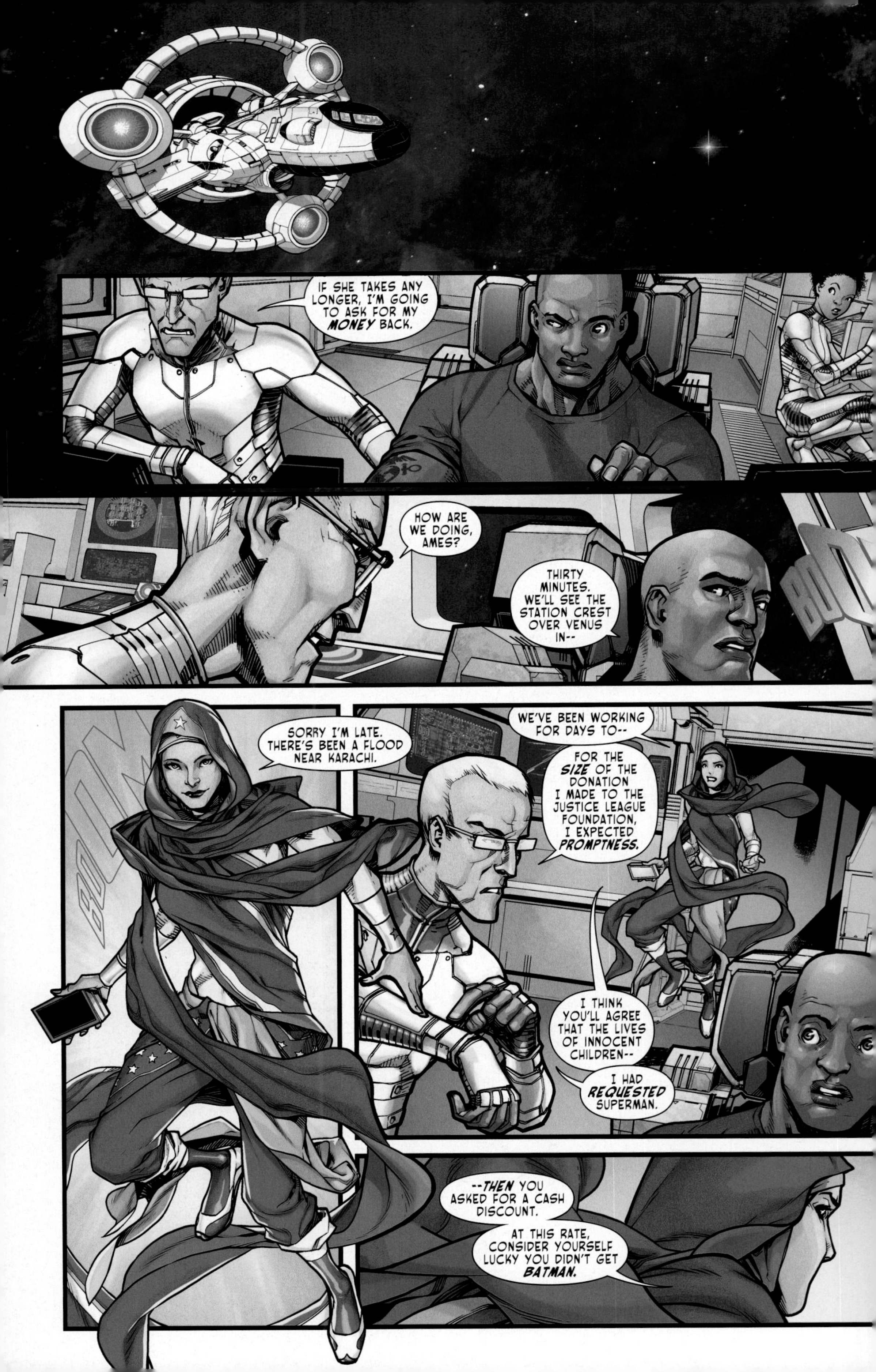
IF SHE TAKES ANY LONGER, I'M GOING TO ASK FOR MY MONEY BACK.
HOW ARE WE DOING, AMES?
THIRTY MINUTES. WE'LL SEE THE STATION CREST OVER VENUS IN--
SORRY I'M LATE. THERE'S BEEN A FLOOD NEAR KARACHI.
WE'VE BEEN WORKING FOR DAYS TO--
FOR THE SIZE OF THE DONATION I MADE TO THE JUSTICE LEAGUE FOUNDATION, I EXPECTED PROMPTNESS.
I THINK YOU'LL AGREE THAT THE LIVES OF INNOCENT CHILDREN--
I HAD REQUESTED SUPERMAN.
--THEN YOU ASKED FOR A CASH DISCOUNT.
AT THIS RATE, CONSIDER YOURSELF LUCKY YOU DIDN'T GET BATMAN.

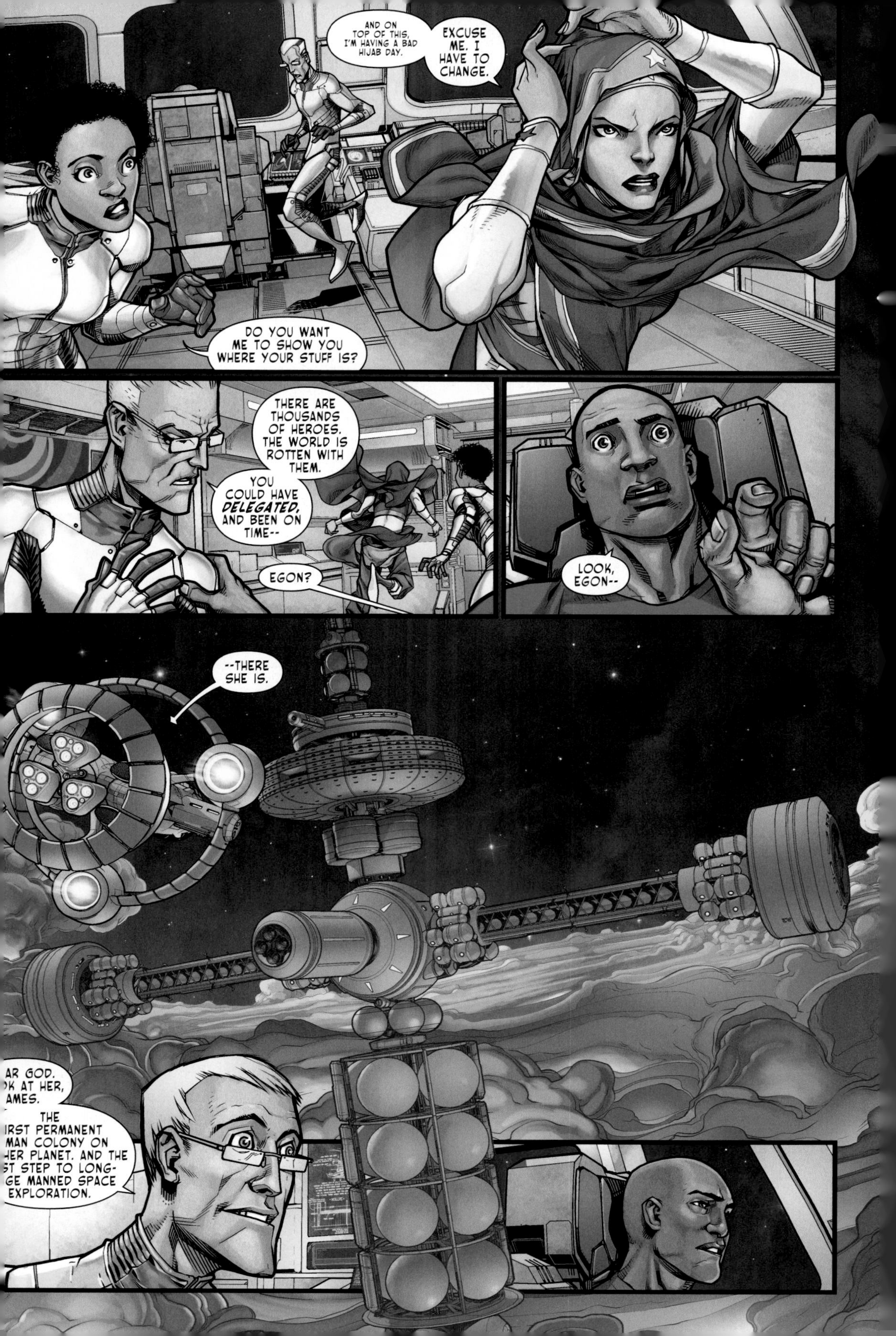
AND ON TOP OF THIS, I'M HAVING A BAD HIJAB DAY.
EXCUSE ME. I HAVE TO CHANGE.
DO YOU WANT ME TO SHOW YOU WHERE YOUR STUFF IS?
THERE ARE THOUSANDS OF HEROES. THE WORLD IS ROTTEN WITH THEM.
YOU COULD HAVE *DELEGATED*, AND BEEN ON TIME--
EGON?
LOOK, EGON--
--THERE SHE IS.
AR GOD. OK AT HER, AMES.
THE IRST PERMANENT MAN COLONY ON HER PLANET. AND THE ST STEP TO LONG-GE MANNED SPACE EXPLORATION.

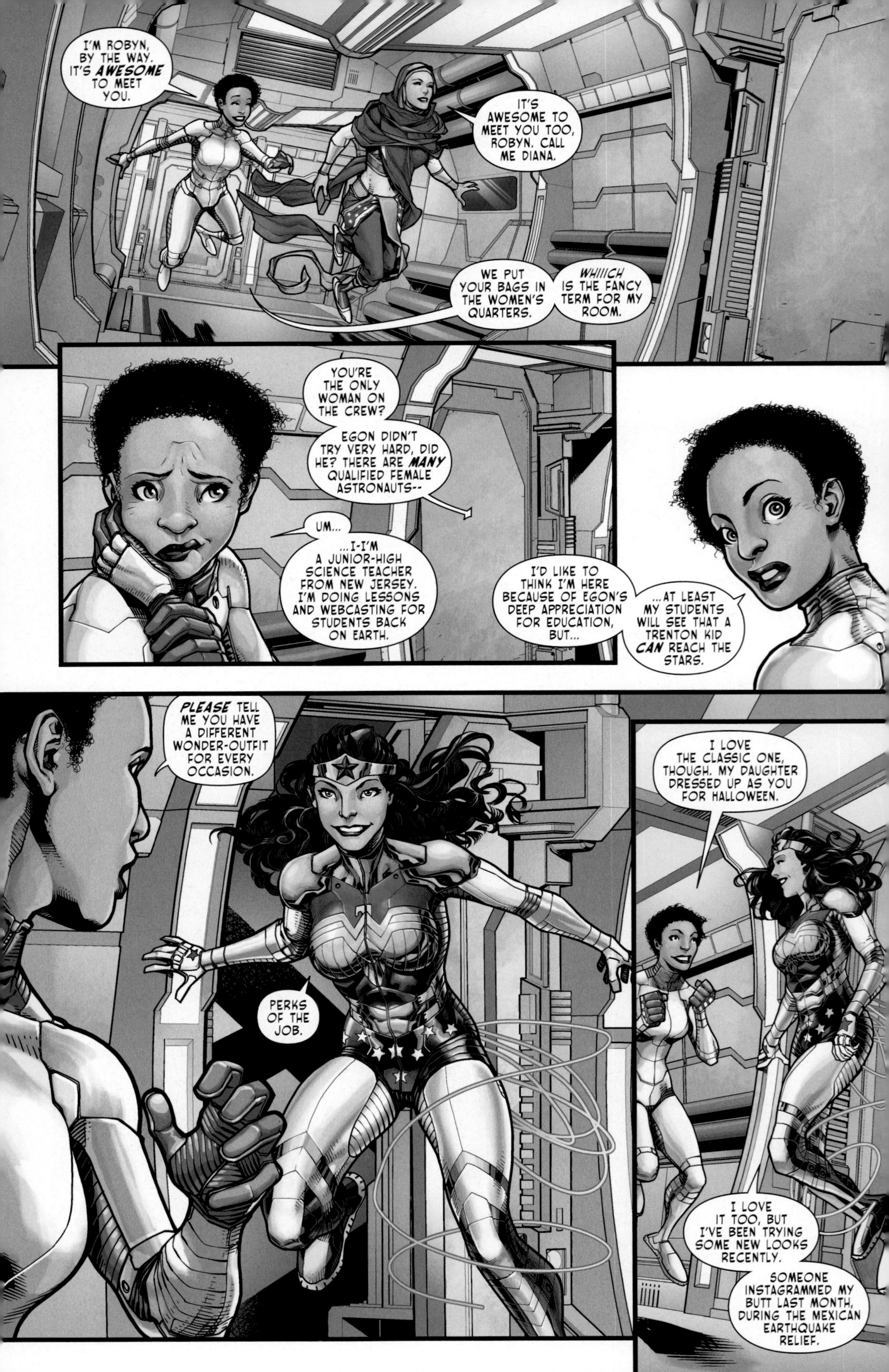
I'M ROBYN, BY THE WAY. IT'S AWESOME TO MEET YOU.
IT'S AWESOME TO MEET YOU TOO, ROBYN. CALL ME DIANA.
WE PUT YOUR BAGS IN THE WOMEN'S QUARTERS.
WHIIICH IS THE FANCY TERM FOR MY ROOM.
YOU'RE THE ONLY WOMAN ON THE CREW?
EGON DIDN'T TRY VERY HARD, DID HE? THERE ARE MANY QUALIFIED FEMALE ASTRONAUTS--
UM...
...I-I'M A JUNIOR-HIGH SCIENCE TEACHER FROM NEW JERSEY. I'M DOING LESSONS AND WEBCASTING FOR STUDENTS BACK ON EARTH.
I'D LIKE TO THINK I'M HERE BECAUSE OF EGON'S DEEP APPRECIATION FOR EDUCATION, BUT...
...AT LEAST MY STUDENTS WILL SEE THAT A TRENTON KID CAN REACH THE STARS.
PLEASE TELL ME YOU HAVE A DIFFERENT WONDER-OUTFIT FOR EVERY OCCASION.
PERKS OF THE JOB.
I LOVE THE CLASSIC ONE, THOUGH. MY DAUGHTER DRESSED UP AS YOU FOR HALLOWEEN.
I LOVE IT TOO, BUT I'VE BEEN TRYING SOME NEW LOOKS RECENTLY.
SOMEONE INSTAGRAMMED MY BUTT LAST MONTH, DURING THE MEXICAN EARTHQUAKE RELIEF.

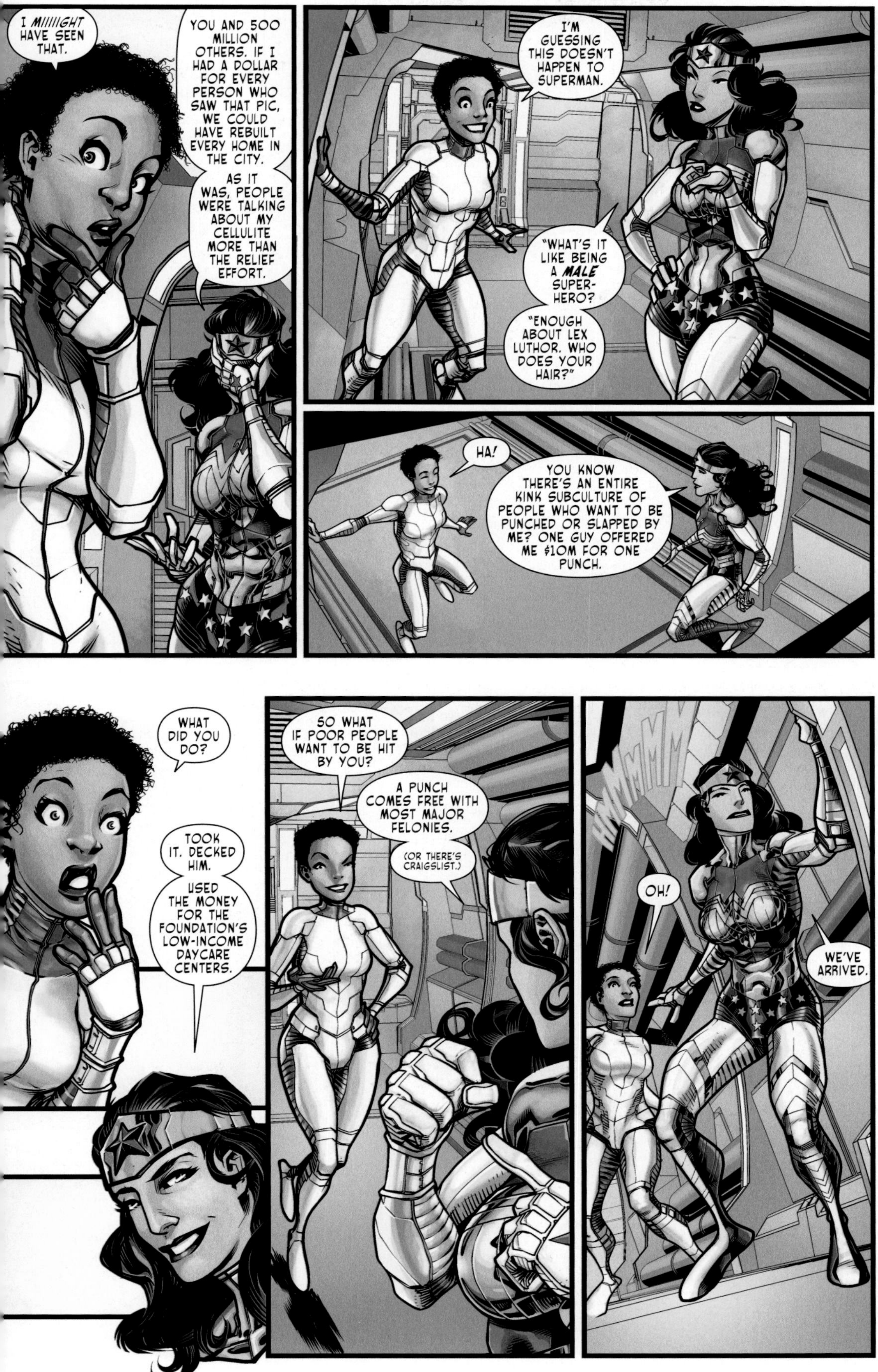
I MIIIIGHT HAVE SEEN THAT.
YOU AND 500 MILLION OTHERS. IF I HAD A DOLLAR FOR EVERY PERSON WHO SAW THAT PIC, WE COULD HAVE REBUILT EVERY HOME IN THE CITY.
AS IT WAS, PEOPLE WERE TALKING ABOUT MY CELLULITE MORE THAN THE RELIEF EFFORT.
I'M GUESSING THIS DOESN'T HAPPEN TO SUPERMAN.
"WHAT'S IT LIKE BEING A MALE SUPER-HERO?
"ENOUGH ABOUT LEX LUTHOR. WHO DOES YOUR HAIR?"
HA!
YOU KNOW THERE'S AN ENTIRE KINK SUBCULTURE OF PEOPLE WHO WANT TO BE PUNCHED OR SLAPPED BY ME? ONE GUY OFFERED ME $10M FOR ONE PUNCH.
WHAT DID YOU DO?
TOOK IT. DECKED HIM.
USED THE MONEY FOR THE FOUNDATION'S LOW-INCOME DAYCARE CENTERS.
SO WHAT IF POOR PEOPLE WANT TO BE HIT BY YOU?
A PUNCH COMES FREE WITH MOST MAJOR FELONIES.
(OR THERE'S CRAIGSLIST.)
HMMMMMM
OH!
WE'VE ARRIVED.

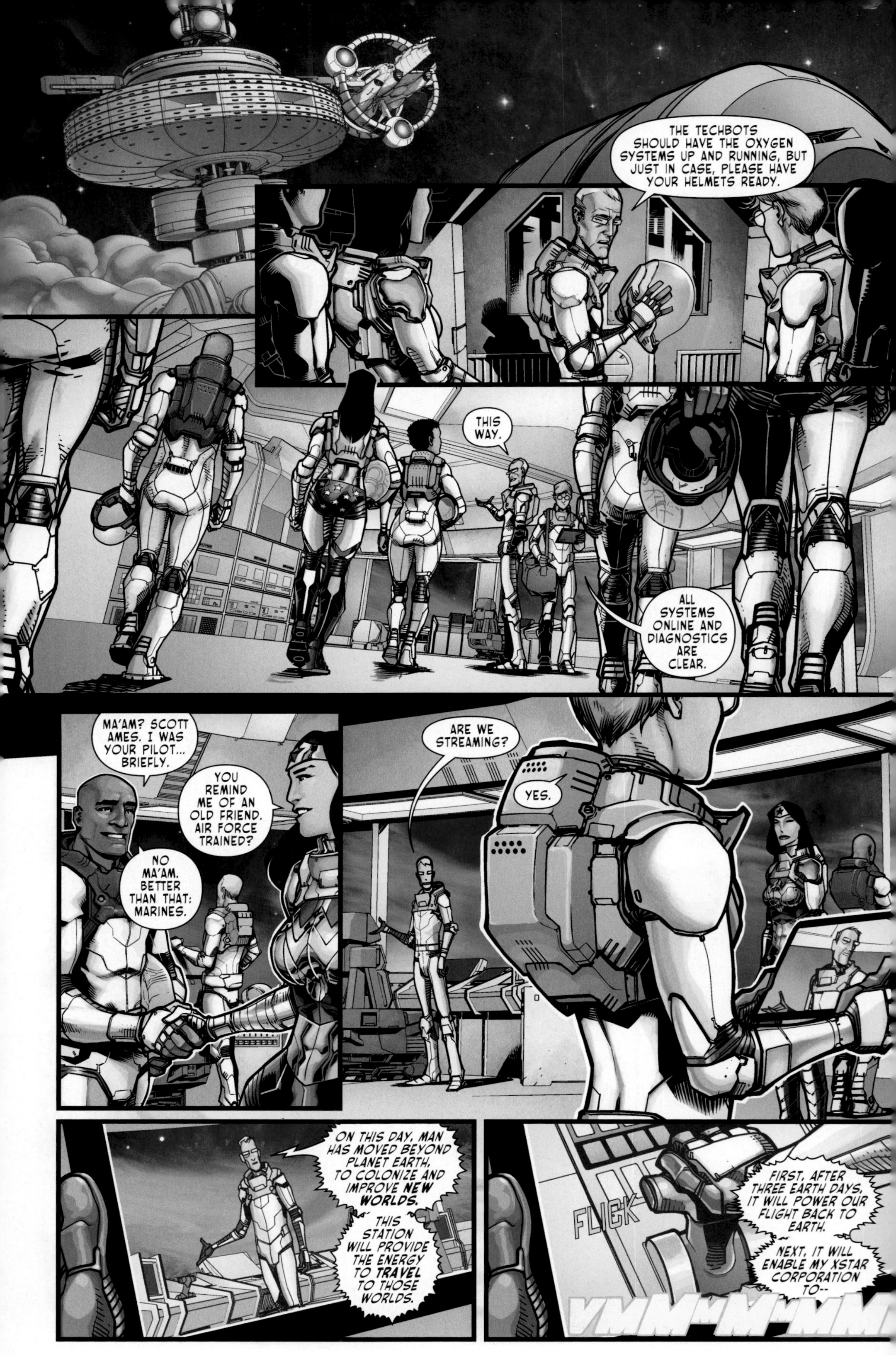
THE TECHBOTS SHOULD HAVE THE OXYGEN SYSTEMS UP AND RUNNING, BUT JUST IN CASE, PLEASE HAVE YOUR HELMETS READY.
THIS WAY.
ALL SYSTEMS ONLINE AND DIAGNOSTICS ARE CLEAR.
MA'AM? SCOTT AMES. I WAS YOUR PILOT... BRIEFLY.
YOU REMIND ME OF AN OLD FRIEND. AIR FORCE TRAINED?
NO MA'AM. BETTER THAN THAT: MARINES.
ARE WE STREAMING?
YES.
ON THIS DAY, MAN HAS MOVED BEYOND PLANET EARTH, TO COLONIZE AND IMPROVE NEW WORLDS.
THIS STATION WILL PROVIDE THE ENERGY TO TRAVEL TO THOSE WORLDS.
FLICK
FIRST, AFTER THREE EARTH DAYS, IT WILL POWER OUR FLIGHT BACK TO EARTH.
NEXT, IT WILL ENABLE MY XSTAR CORPORATION TO--
VMMMMMMMM

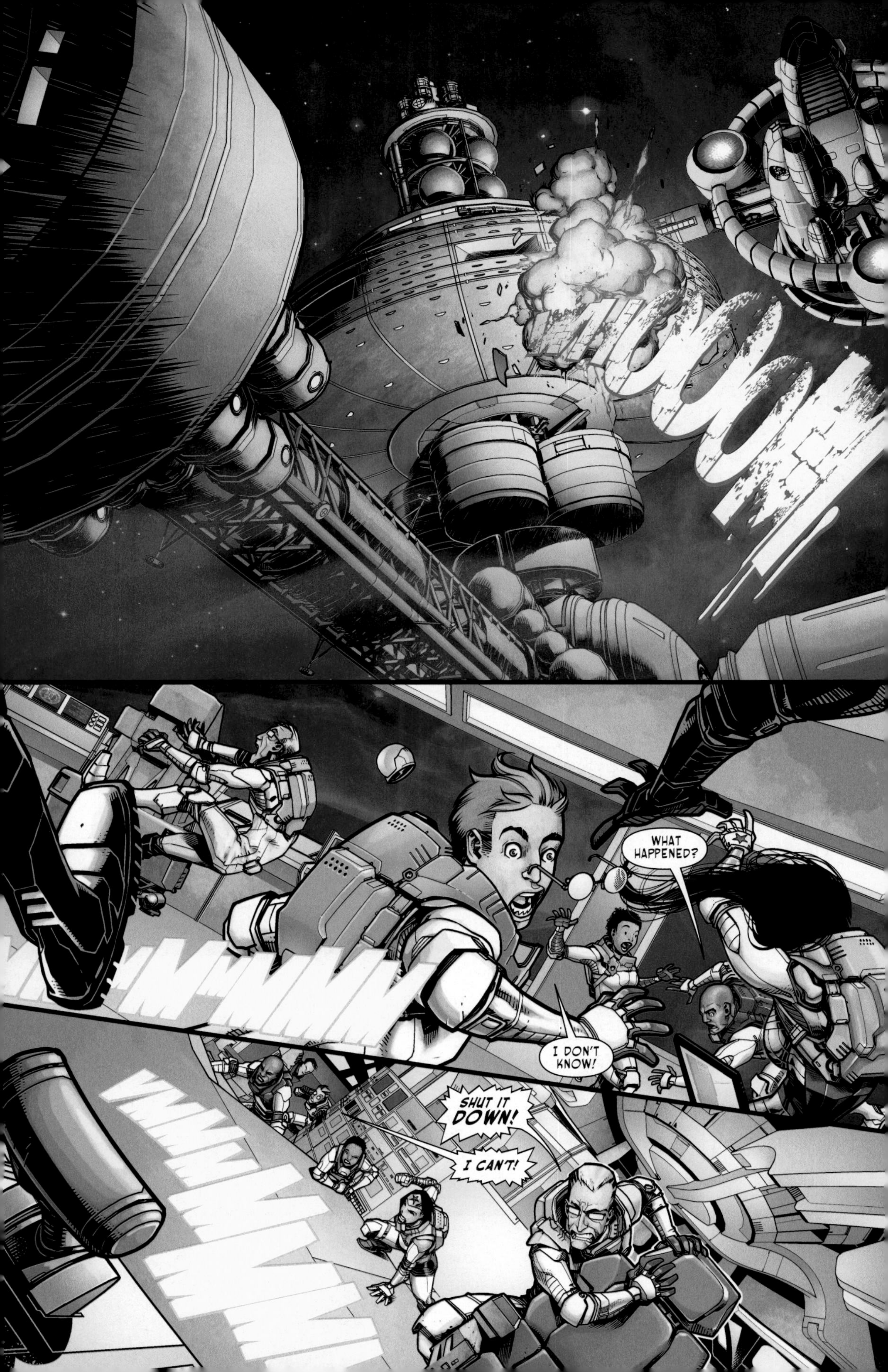
WHAT HAPPENED?
I DON'T KNOW!
SHUT IT DOWN!
I CAN'T!

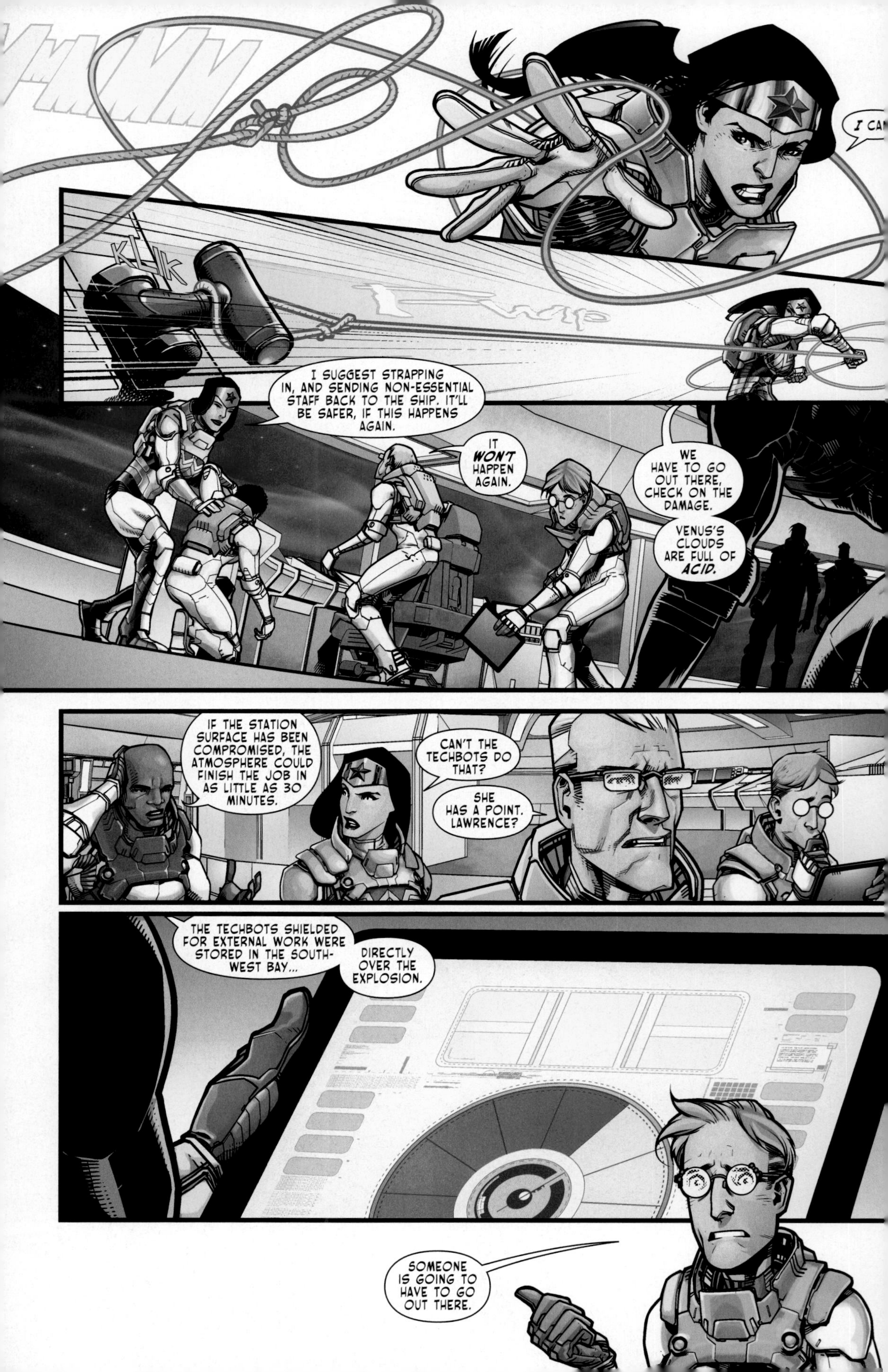
I SUGGEST STRAPPING IN, AND SENDING NON-ESSENTIAL STAFF BACK TO THE SHIP. IT'LL BE SAFER, IF THIS HAPPENS AGAIN.
IT WON'T HAPPEN AGAIN.
WE HAVE TO GO OUT THERE, CHECK ON THE DAMAGE.
VENUS'S CLOUDS ARE FULL OF ACID.
IF THE STATION SURFACE HAS BEEN COMPROMISED, THE ATMOSPHERE COULD FINISH THE JOB IN AS LITTLE AS 30 MINUTES.
CAN'T THE TECHBOTS DO THAT?
SHE HAS A POINT. LAWRENCE?
THE TECHBOTS SHIELDED FOR EXTERNAL WORK WERE STORED IN THE SOUTH-WEST BAY...
DIRECTLY OVER THE EXPLOSION.
SOMEONE IS GOING TO HAVE TO GO OUT THERE.

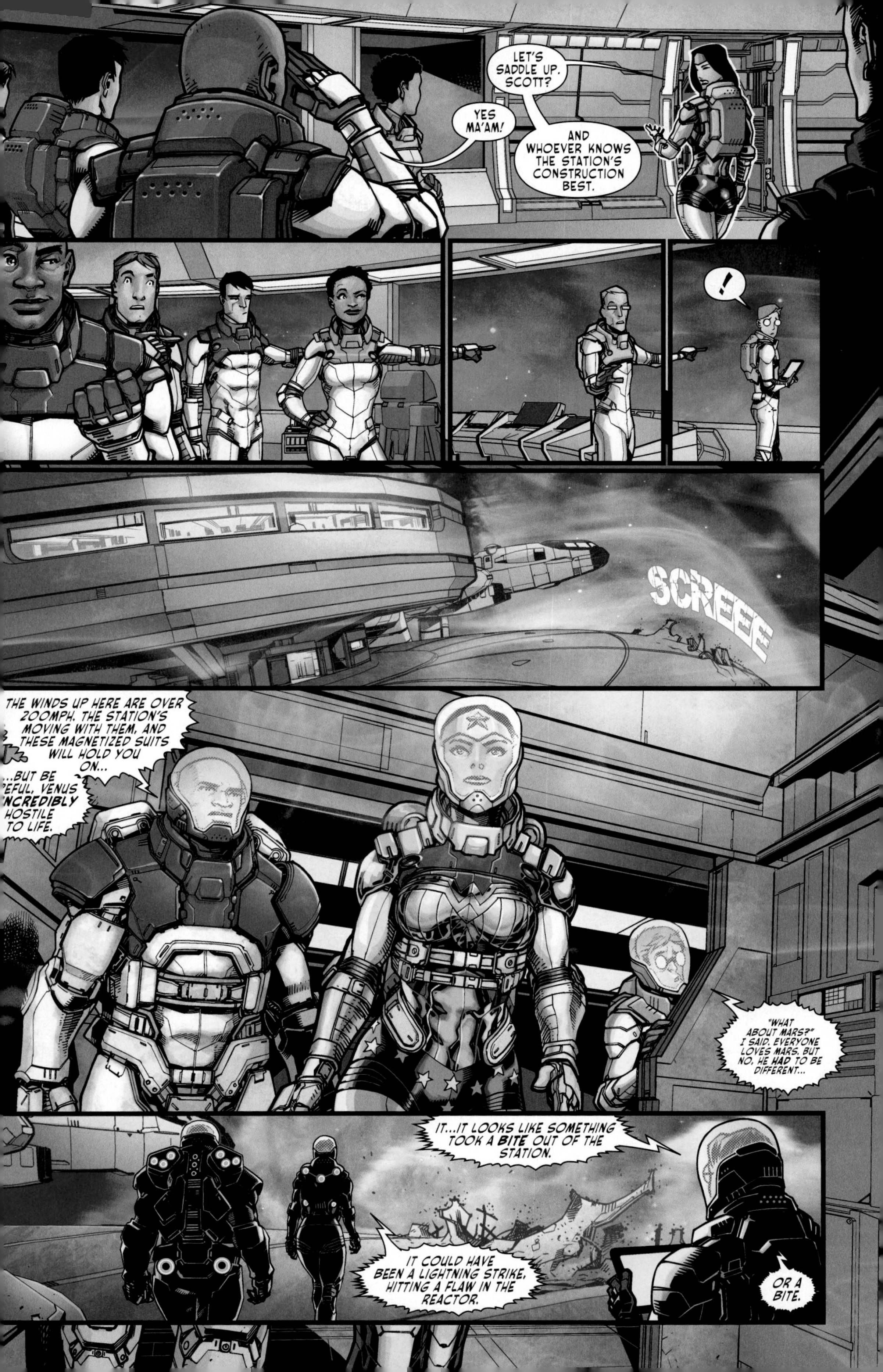
LET'S SADDLE UP. SCOTT?
YES MA'AM!
AND WHOEVER KNOWS THE STATION'S CONSTRUCTION BEST.
!
SCREEEE
THE WINDS UP HERE ARE OVER 200MPH. THE STATION'S MOVING WITH THEM, AND THESE MAGNETIZED SUITS WILL HOLD YOU ON...
...BUT BE EFUL. VENUS NCREDIBLY HOSTILE TO LIFE.
"WHAT ABOUT MARS?" I SAID. EVERYONE LOVES MARS. BUT NO, HE HAD TO BE DIFFERENT...
IT...IT LOOKS LIKE SOMETHING TOOK A BITE OUT OF THE STATION.
IT COULD HAVE BEEN A LIGHTNING STRIKE, HITTING A FLAW IN THE REACTOR.
OR A BITE.

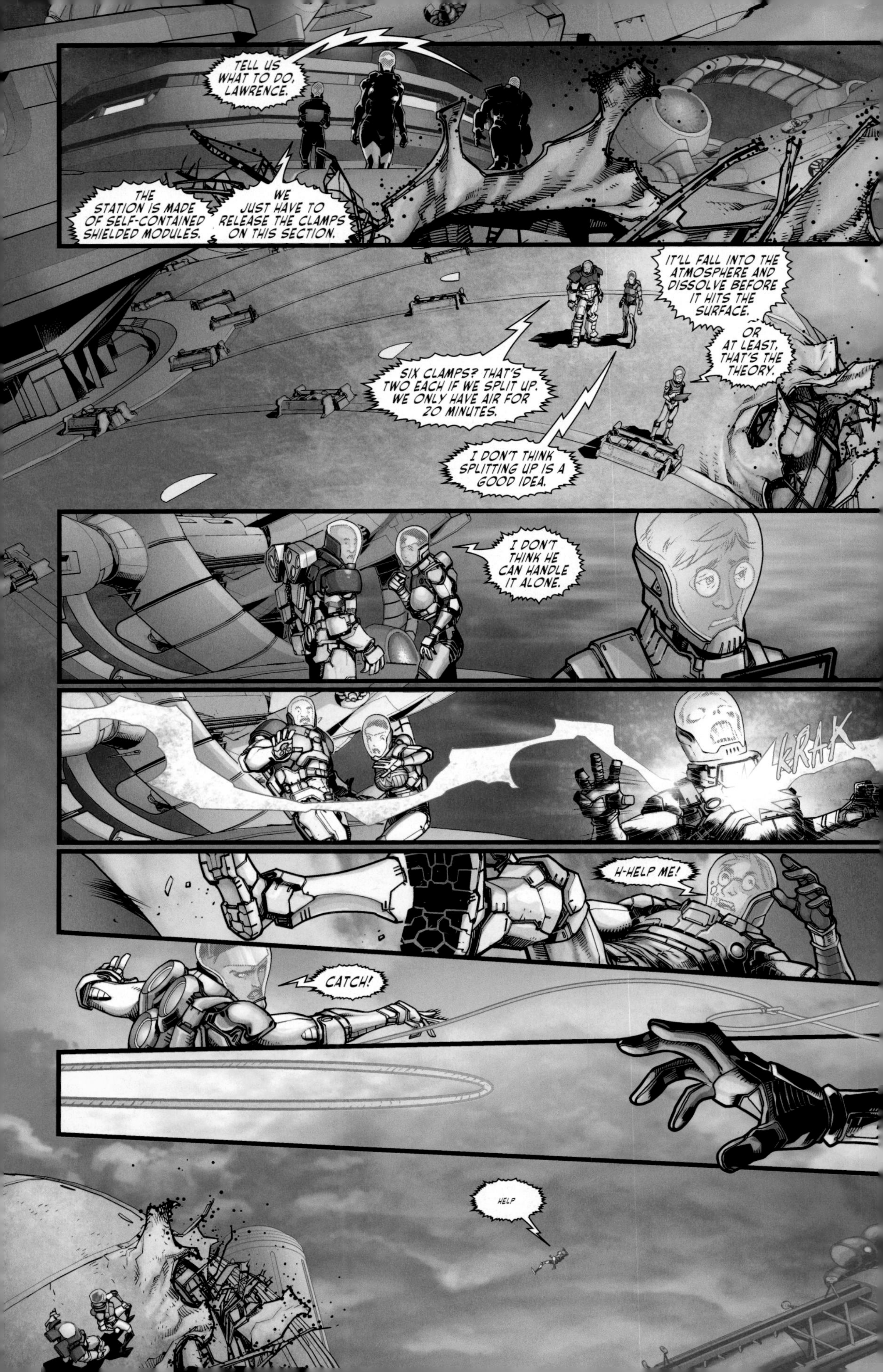
TELL US WHAT TO DO, LAWRENCE.
THE STATION IS MADE OF SELF-CONTAINED SHIELDED MODULES.
WE JUST HAVE TO RELEASE THE CLAMPS ON THIS SECTION.
IT'LL FALL INTO THE ATMOSPHERE AND DISSOLVE BEFORE IT HITS THE SURFACE.
OR AT LEAST, THAT'S THE THEORY.
SIX CLAMPS? THAT'S TWO EACH IF WE SPLIT UP. WE ONLY HAVE AIR FOR 20 MINUTES.
I DON'T THINK SPLITTING UP IS A GOOD IDEA.
I DON'T THINK HE CAN HANDLE IT ALONE.
KRAK
H-HELP ME!
CATCH!
HELP

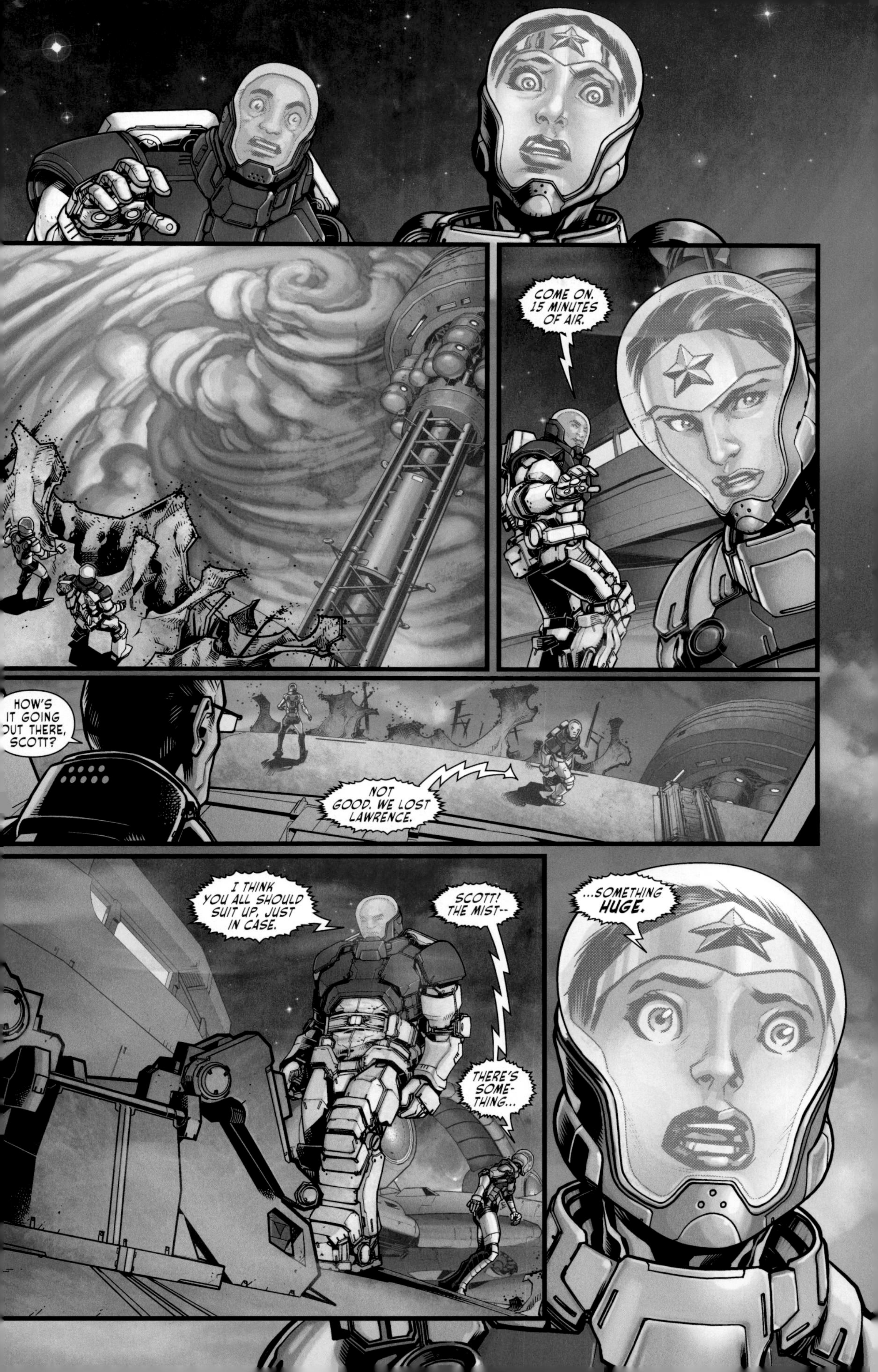
COME ON. 15 MINUTES OF AIR.
HOW'S IT GOING OUT THERE, SCOTT?
NOT GOOD. WE LOST LAWRENCE.
I THINK YOU ALL SHOULD SUIT UP, JUST IN CASE.
SCOTT! THE MIST--
THERE'S SOME-THING...
...SOMETHING HUGE.

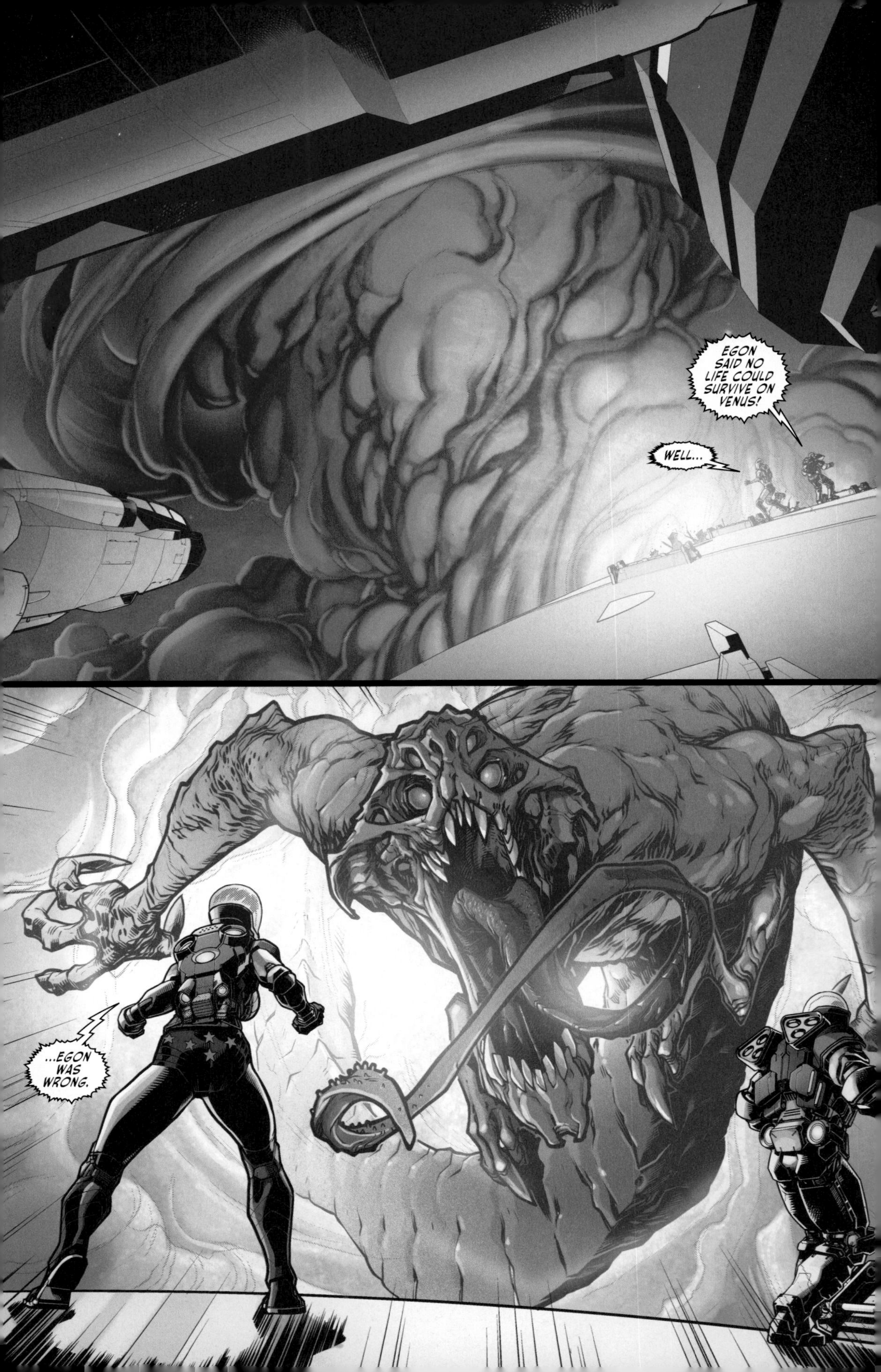
EGON SAID NO LIFE COULD SURVIVE ON VENUS!
WELL...
...EGON WAS WRONG.

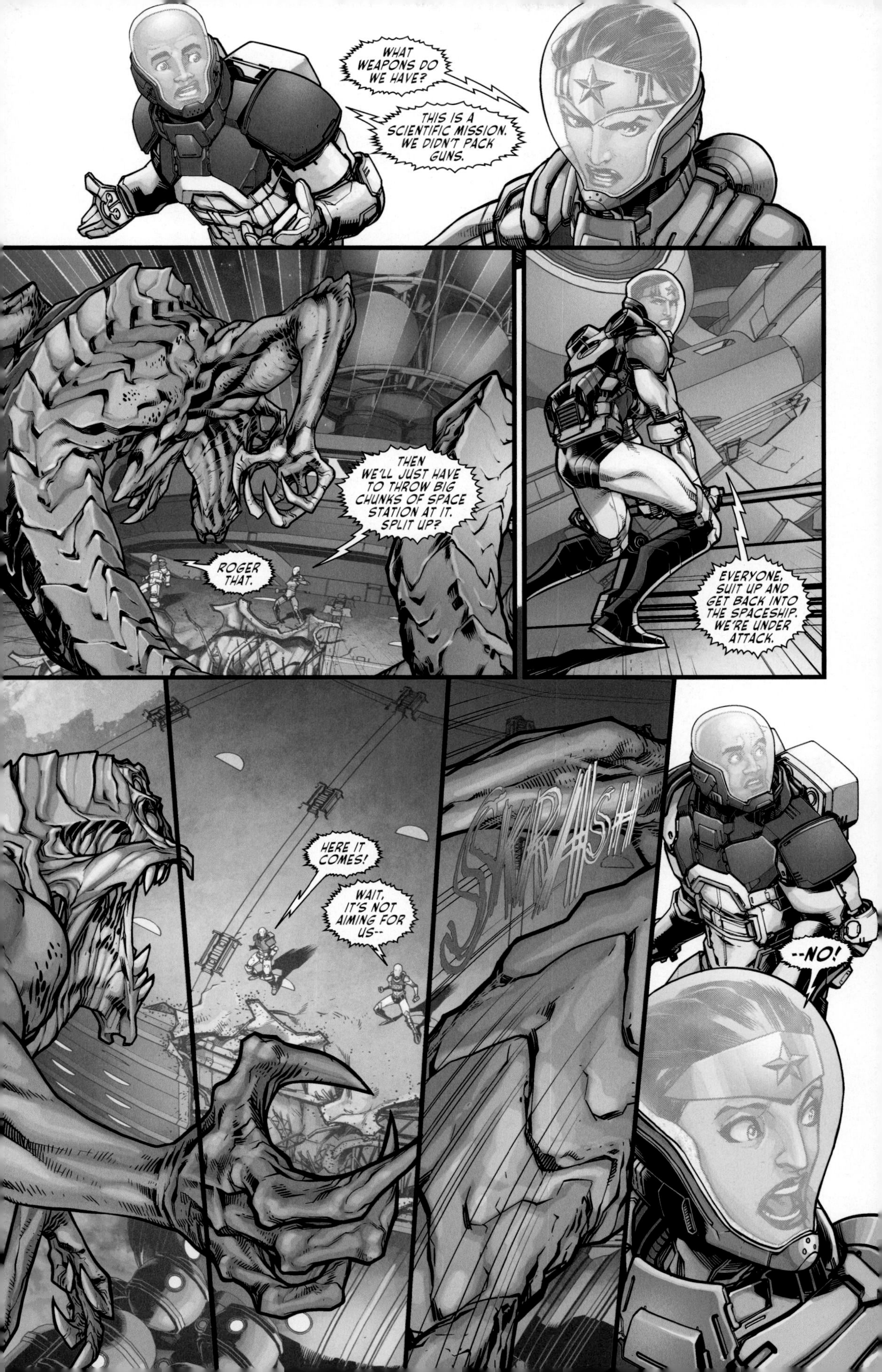
WHAT WEAPONS DO WE HAVE?
THIS IS A SCIENTIFIC MISSION. WE DIDN'T PACK GUNS.
THEN WE'LL JUST HAVE TO THROW BIG CHUNKS OF SPACE STATION AT IT. SPLIT UP?
ROGER THAT.
EVERYONE, SUIT UP AND GET BACK INTO THE SPACESHIP. WE'RE UNDER ATTACK.
HERE IT COMES!
WAIT, IT'S NOT AIMING FOR US--
SKRASH
--NO!

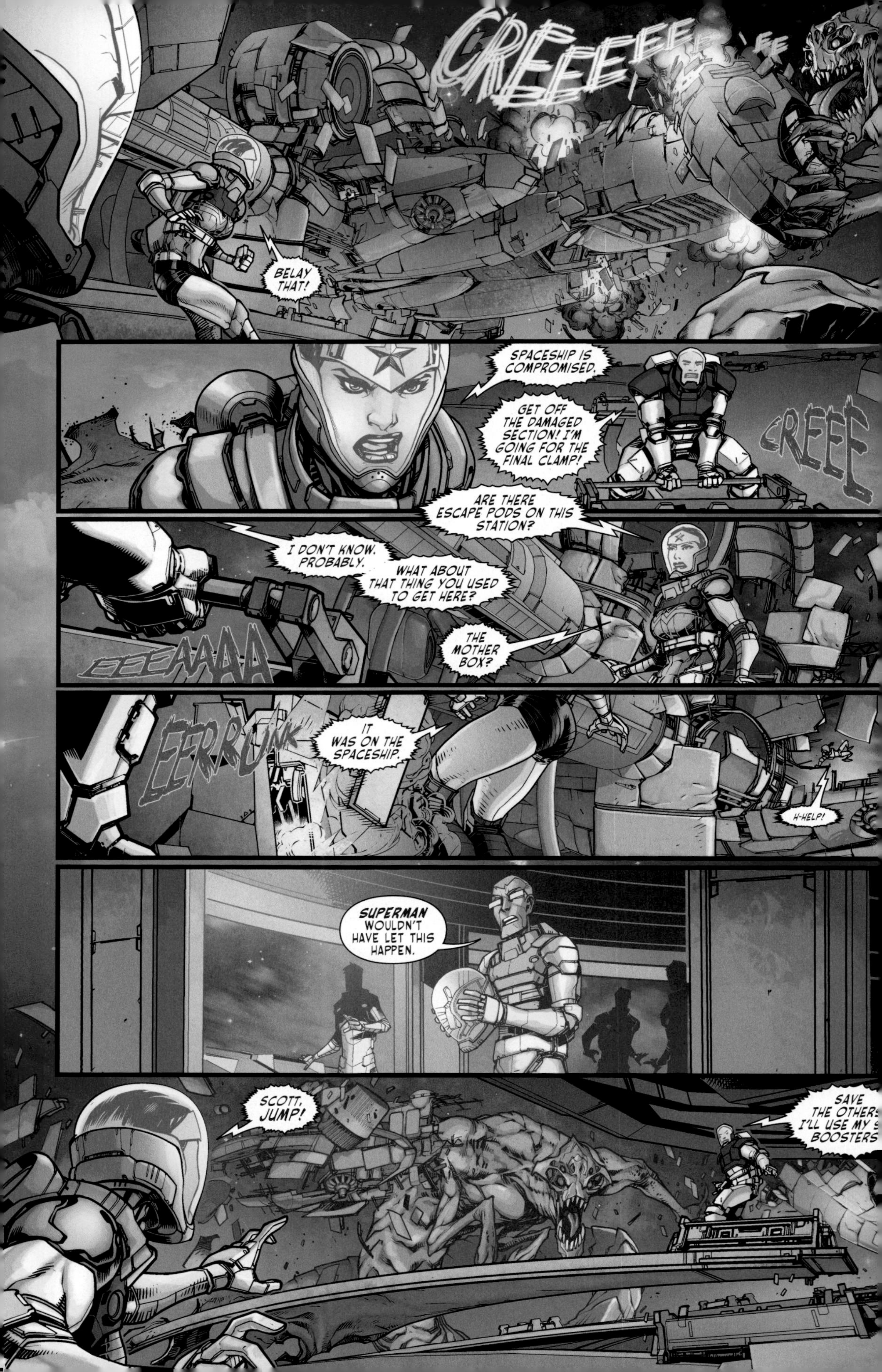
CREEEEEEEE
BELAY THAT!
SPACESHIP IS COMPROMISED.
GET OFF THE DAMAGED SECTION! I'M GOING FOR THE FINAL CLAMP!
CREEE
ARE THERE ESCAPE PODS ON THIS STATION?
I DON'T KNOW. PROBABLY.
WHAT ABOUT THAT THING YOU USED TO GET HERE?
THE MOTHER BOX?
EEEAAAA
EERRUNK
IT WAS ON THE SPACESHIP.
H-HELP!
SUPERMAN WOULDN'T HAVE LET THIS HAPPEN.
SCOTT, JUMP!
SAVE THE OTHERS! I'LL USE MY BOOSTERS!

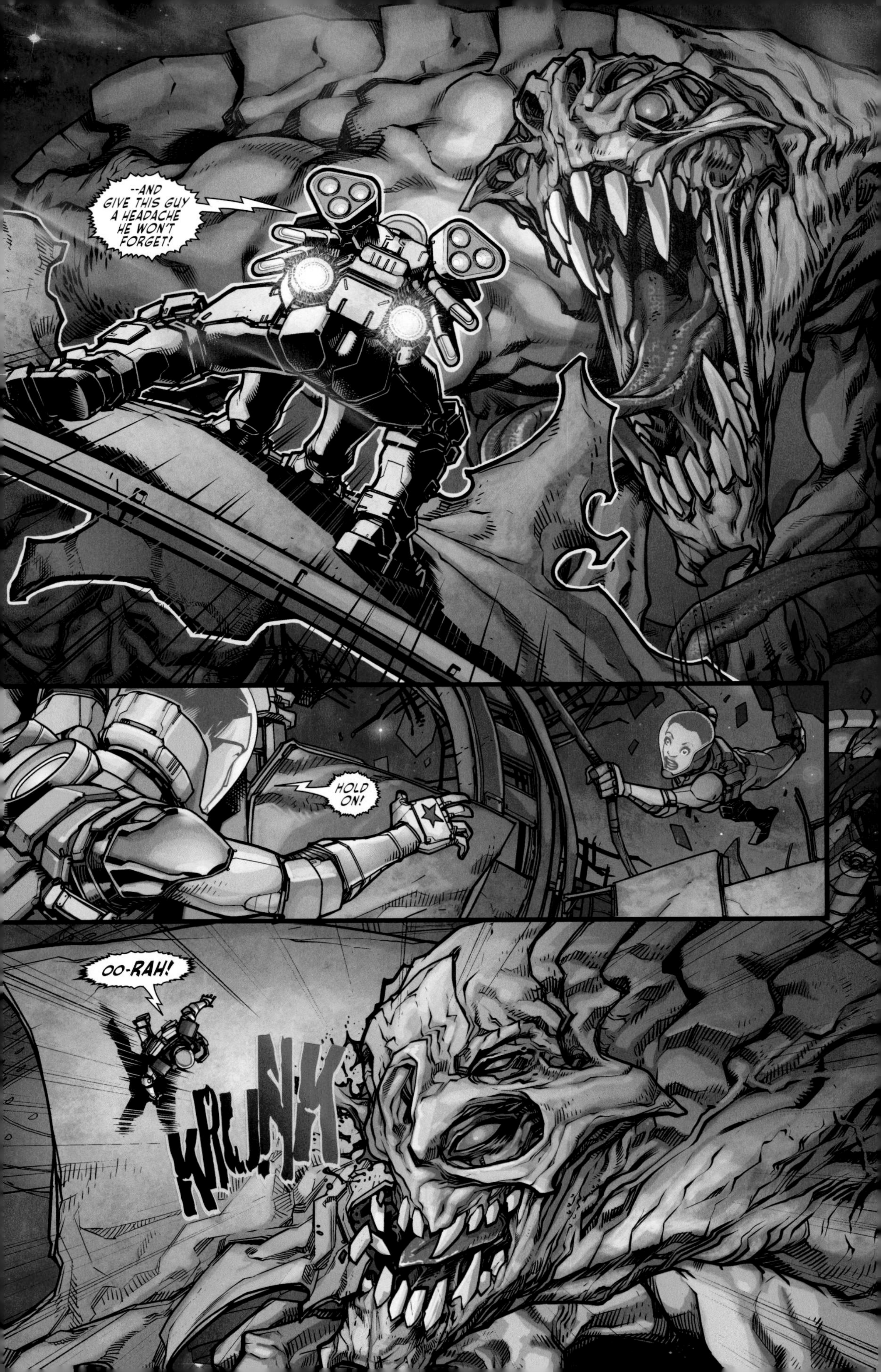
--AND GIVE THIS GUY A HEADACHE HE WON'T FORGET!
HOLD ON!
OO-RAH!
KRUNK

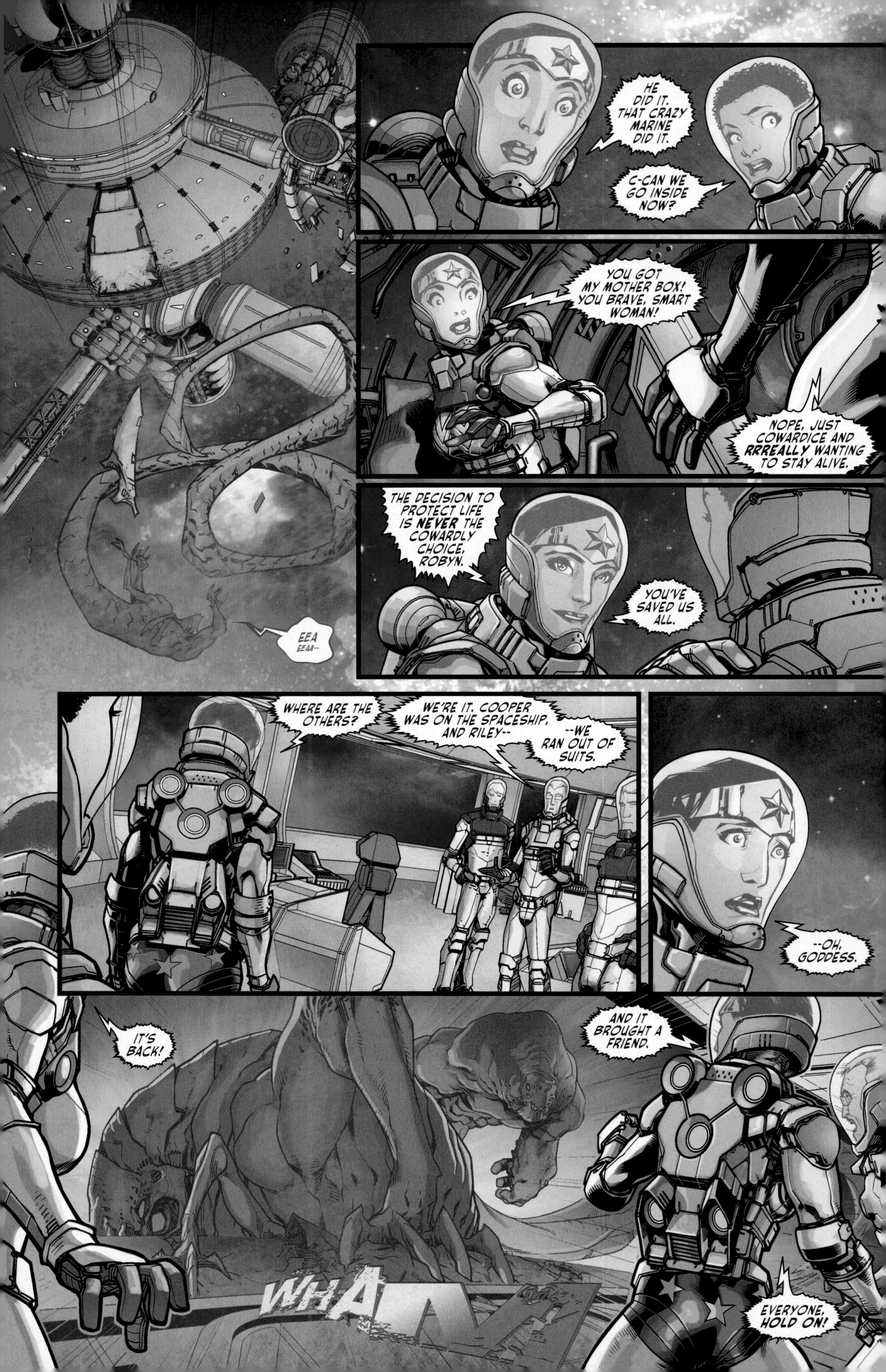

EEA EEAA--
HE DID IT. THAT CRAZY MARINE DID IT.
C-CAN WE GO INSIDE NOW?
YOU GOT MY MOTHER BOX! YOU BRAVE, SMART WOMAN!
NOPE, JUST COWARDICE AND RRREALLY WANTING TO STAY ALIVE.
THE DECISION TO PROTECT LIFE IS NEVER THE COWARDLY CHOICE, ROBYN.
YOU'VE SAVED US ALL.
WHERE ARE THE OTHERS?
WE'RE IT. COOPER WAS ON THE SPACESHIP, AND RILEY--
--WE RAN OUT OF SUITS.
--OH, GODDESS.
IT'S BACK!
AND IT BROUGHT A FRIEND.
WHAM
EVERYONE, HOLD ON!

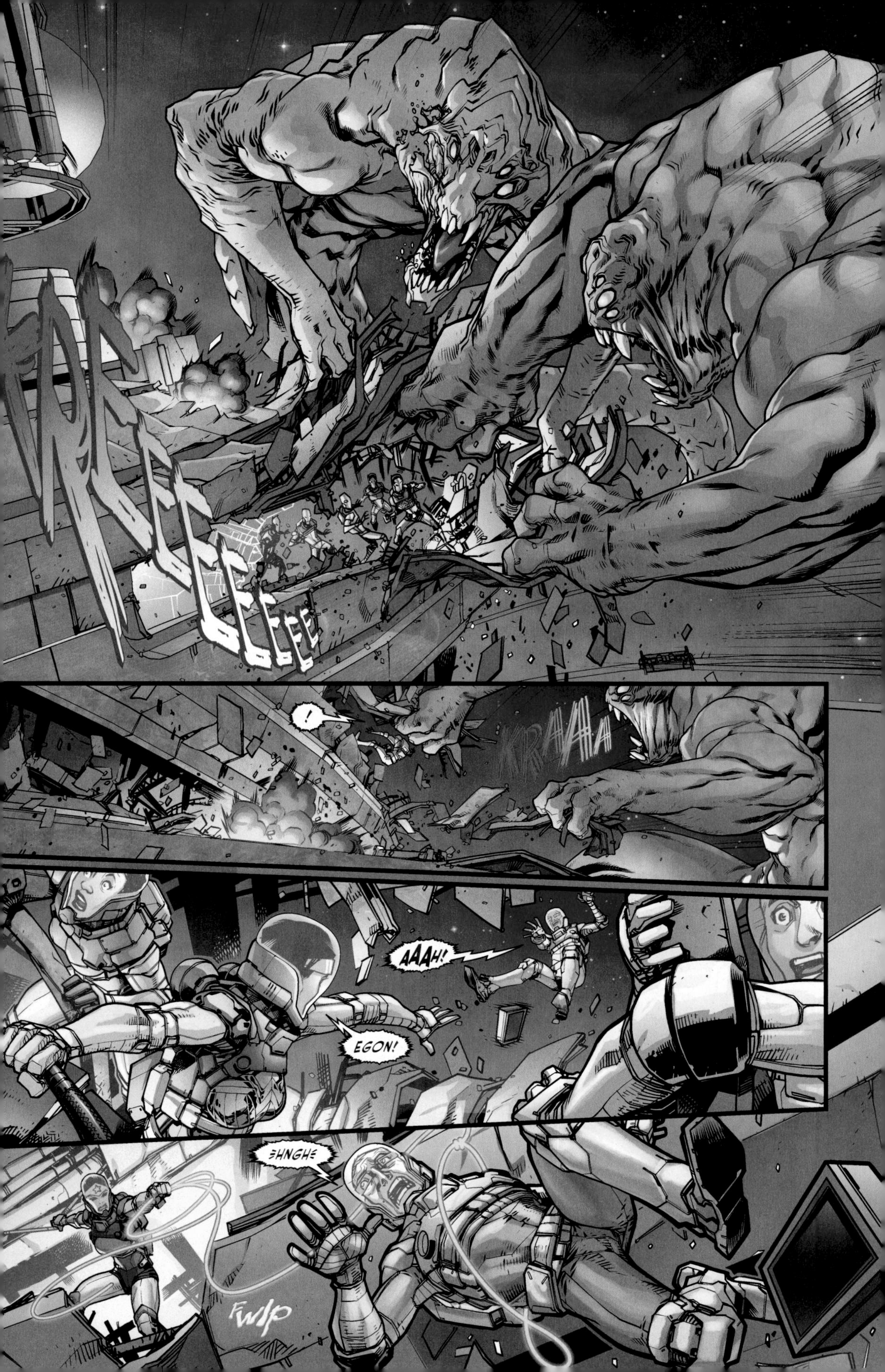
!
KRAAAA
AAAH!
EGON!
HNGH
FWIP

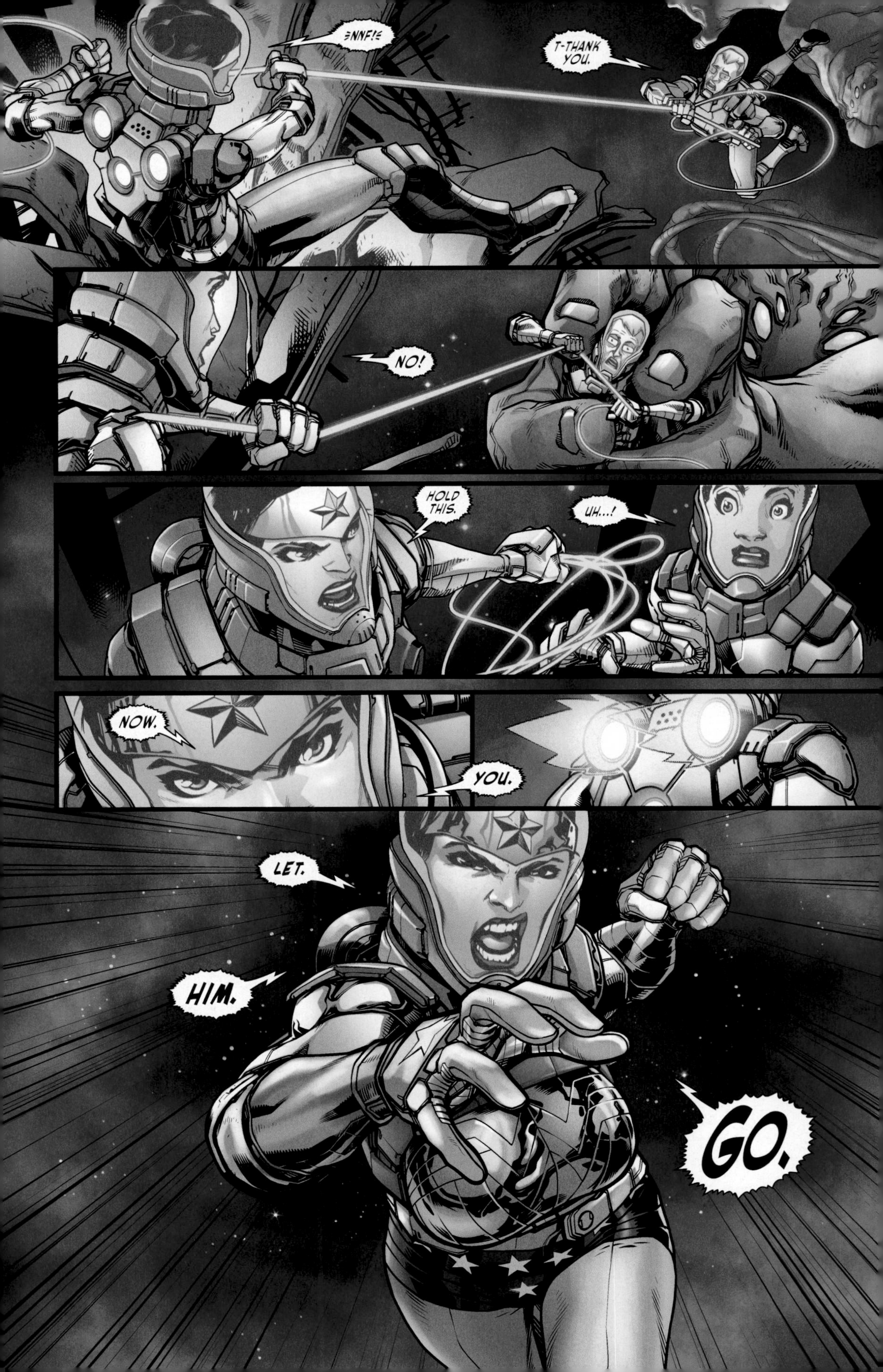

ƎNNF!Ǝ
T-THANK YOU.
NO!
HOLD THIS.
UH...!
NOW.
YOU.
LET.
HIM.
GO.

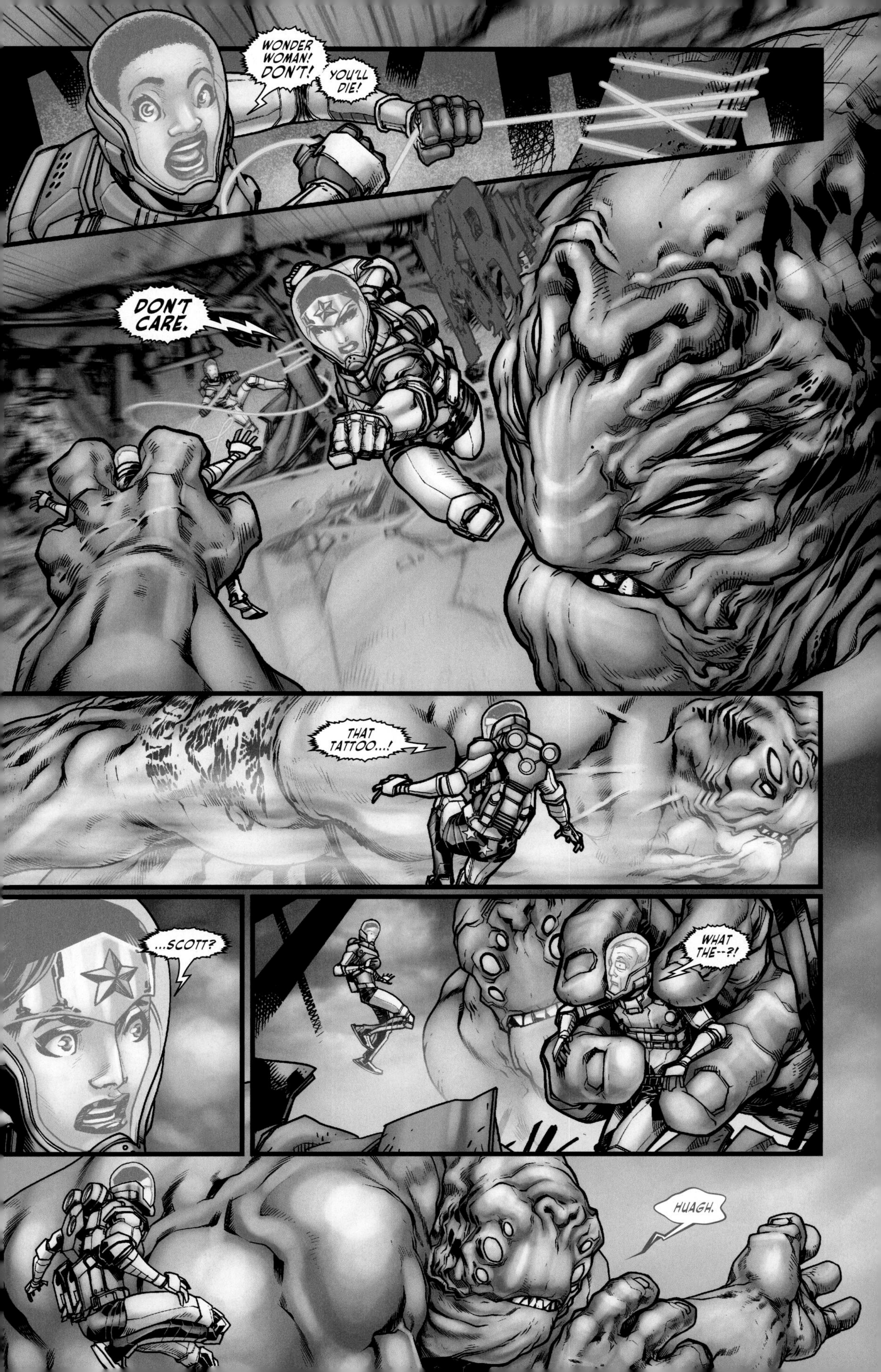
WONDER WOMAN! DON'T!
YOU'LL DIE!
KRAK
DON'T CARE.
THAT TATTOO...!
...SCOTT?
WHAT THE--?!
HUAGH.

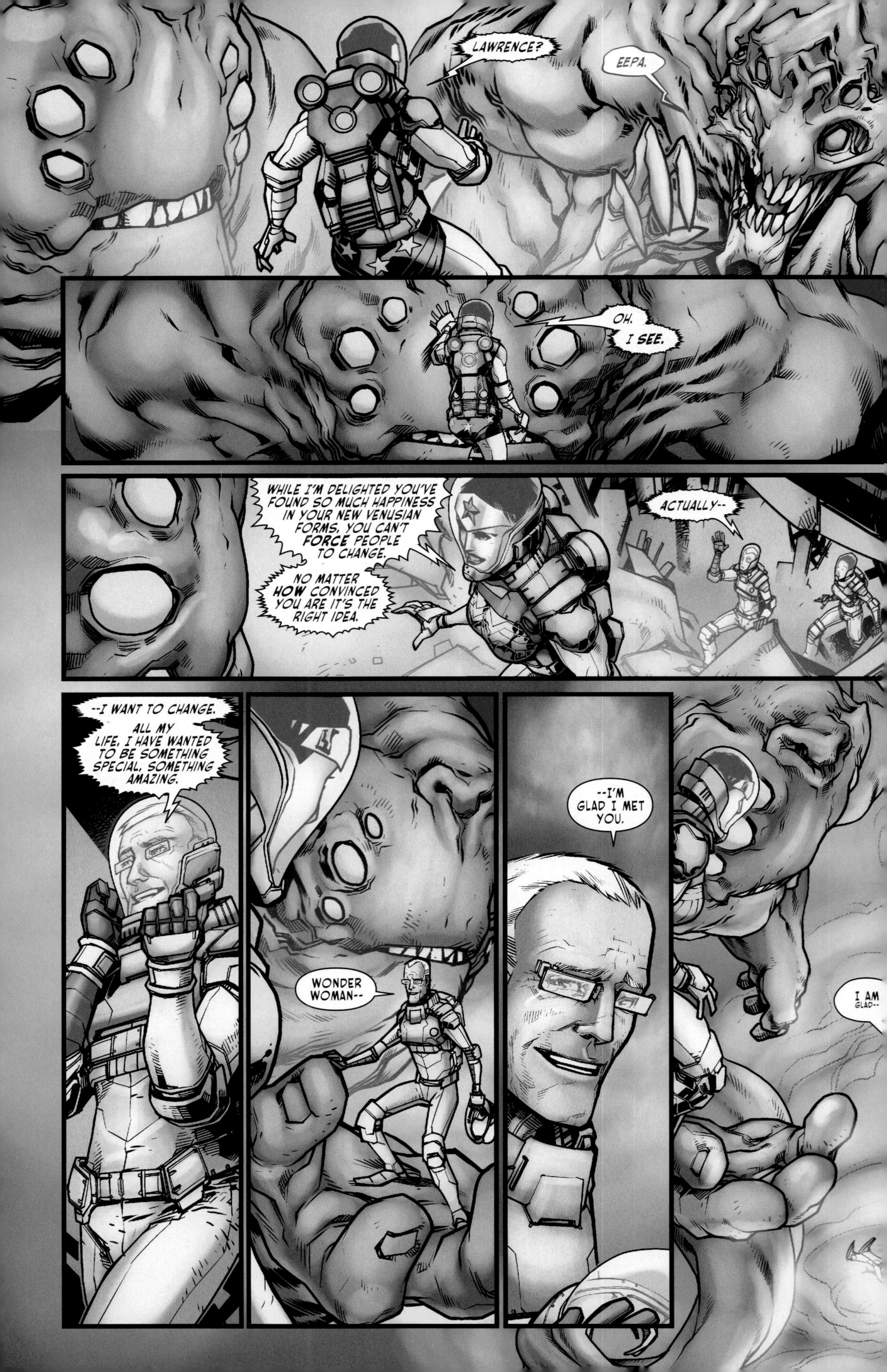
LAWRENCE?
EEPA.
OH.
I SEE.
WHILE I'M DELIGHTED YOU'VE FOUND SO MUCH HAPPINESS IN YOUR NEW VENUSIAN FORMS, YOU CAN'T FORCE PEOPLE TO CHANGE.
NO MATTER HOW CONVINCED YOU ARE IT'S THE RIGHT IDEA.
ACTUALLY--
--I WANT TO CHANGE.
ALL MY LIFE, I HAVE WANTED TO BE SOMETHING SPECIAL, SOMETHING AMAZING.
WONDER WOMAN--
--I'M GLAD I MET YOU.
I AM GLAD--

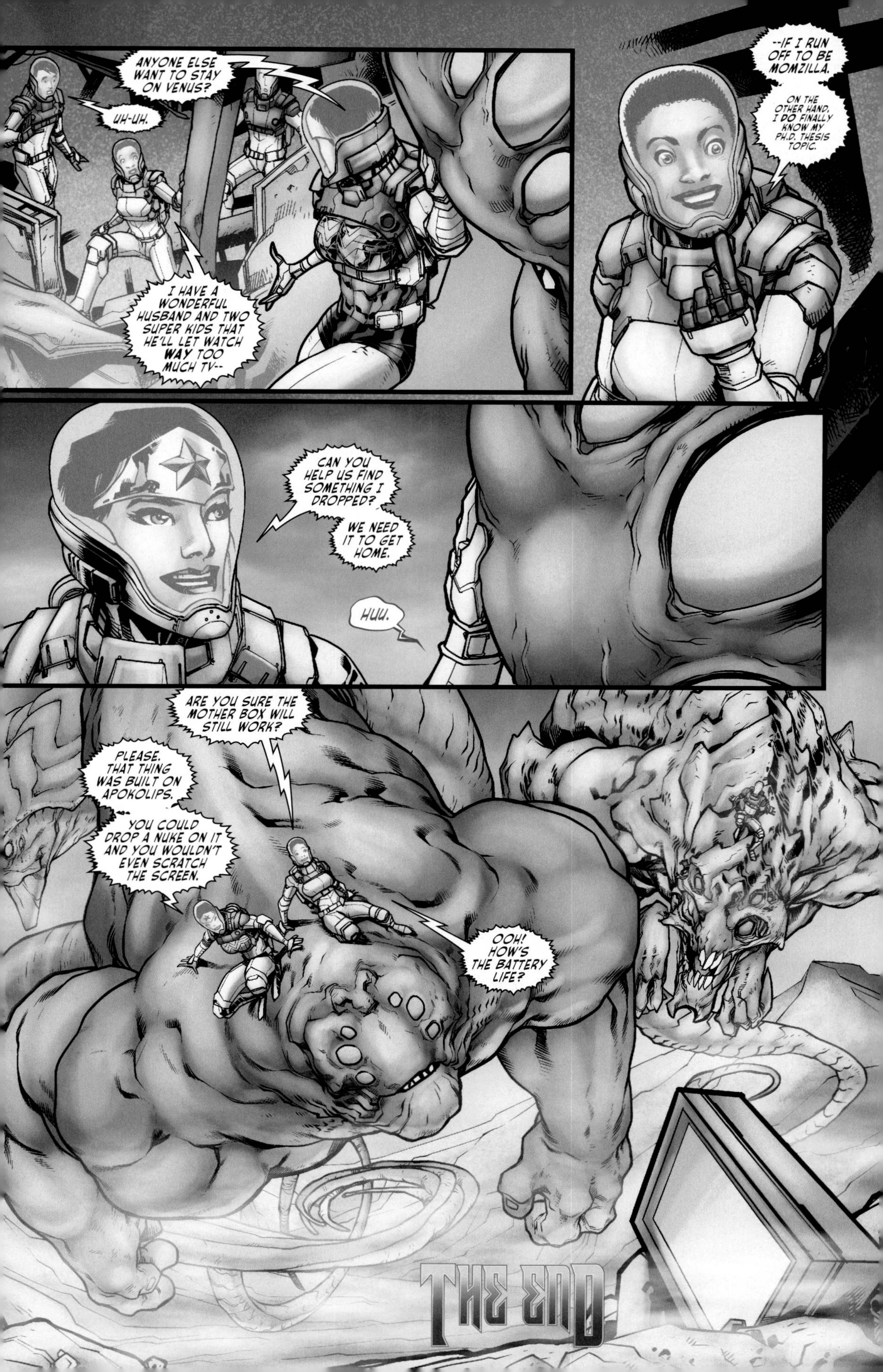
ANYONE ELSE WANT TO STAY ON VENUS?
UH-UH.
I HAVE A WONDERFUL HUSBAND AND TWO SUPER KIDS THAT HE'LL LET WATCH WAY TOO MUCH TV--
--IF I RUN OFF TO BE MOMZILLA.
ON THE OTHER HAND, I DO FINALLY KNOW MY PH.D. THESIS TOPIC.
CAN YOU HELP US FIND SOMETHING I DROPPED?
WE NEED IT TO GET HOME.
HUU.
ARE YOU SURE THE MOTHER BOX WILL STILL WORK?
PLEASE. THAT THING WAS BUILT ON APOKOLIPS.
YOU COULD DROP A NUKE ON IT AND YOU WOULDN'T EVEN SCRATCH THE SCREEN.
OOH! HOW'S THE BATTERY LIFE?
THE END

RESCUE ANGEL

AMY CHU
WRITER

BERNARD CHANG
ARTIST

WENDY BROOME
COLORIST

SAIDA TEMOFONTE
LETTERER

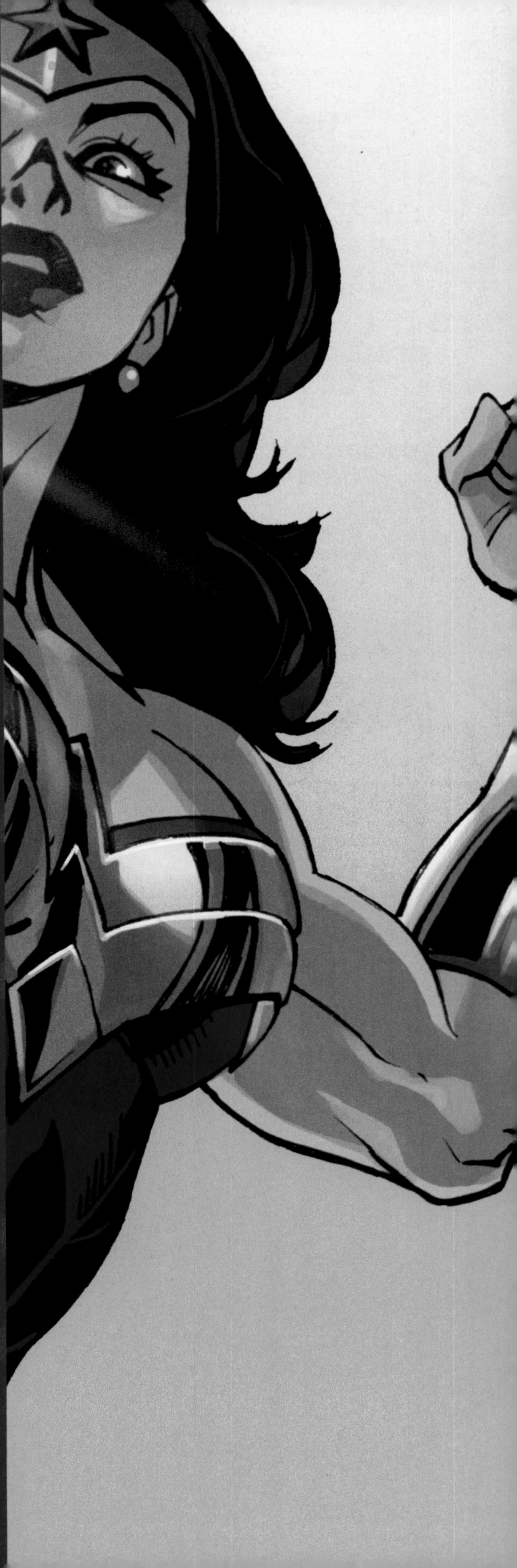

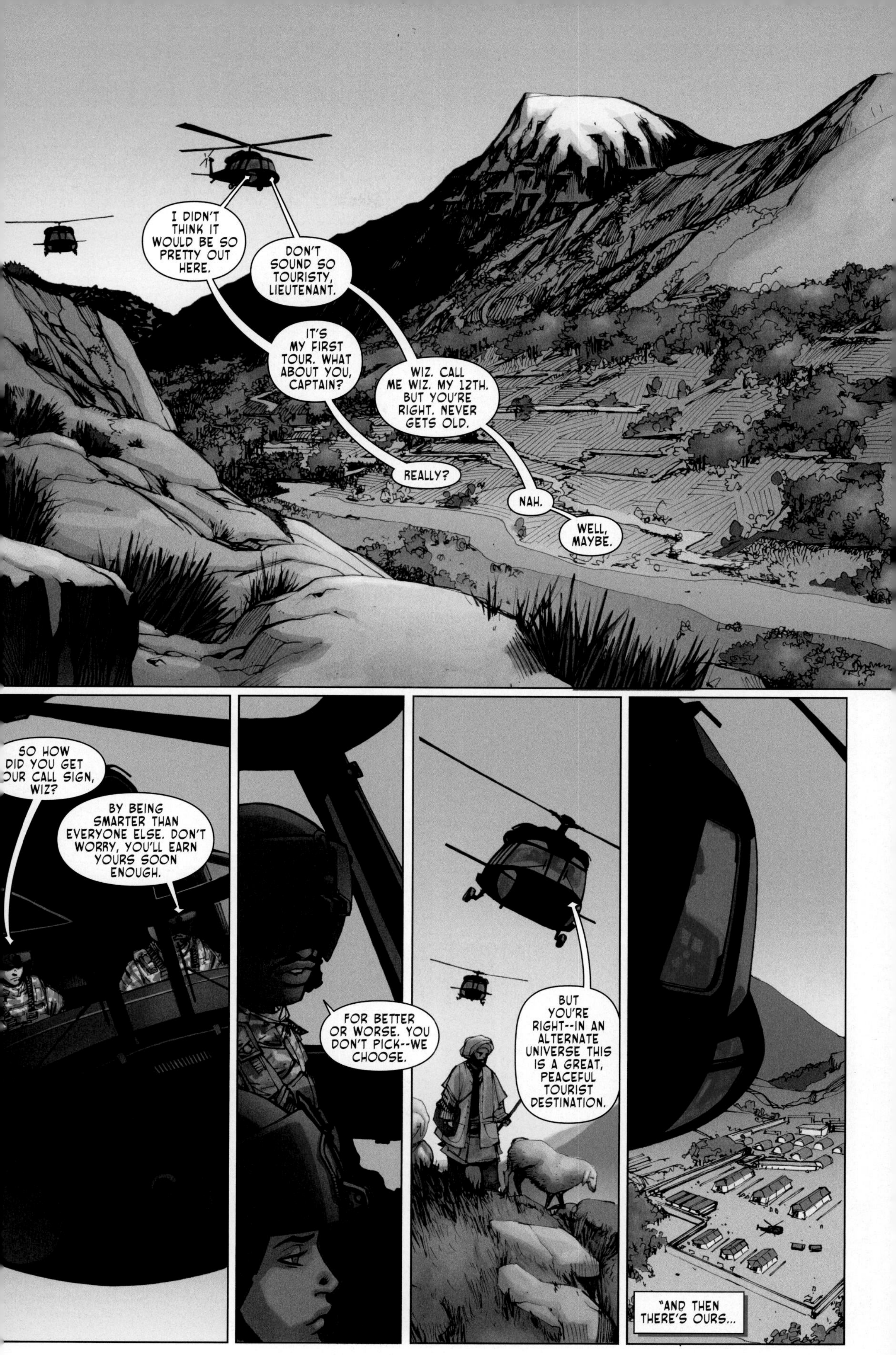
I DIDN'T THINK IT WOULD BE SO PRETTY OUT HERE.
DON'T SOUND SO TOURISTY, LIEUTENANT.
IT'S MY FIRST TOUR. WHAT ABOUT YOU, CAPTAIN?
WIZ. CALL ME WIZ. MY 12TH. BUT YOU'RE RIGHT. NEVER GETS OLD.
REALLY?
NAH.
WELL, MAYBE.
SO HOW DID YOU GET OUR CALL SIGN, WIZ?
BY BEING SMARTER THAN EVERYONE ELSE. DON'T WORRY, YOU'LL EARN YOURS SOON ENOUGH.
FOR BETTER OR WORSE. YOU DON'T PICK--WE CHOOSE.
BUT YOU'RE RIGHT--IN AN ALTERNATE UNIVERSE THIS IS A GREAT, PEACEFUL TOURIST DESTINATION.
"AND THEN THERE'S OURS...

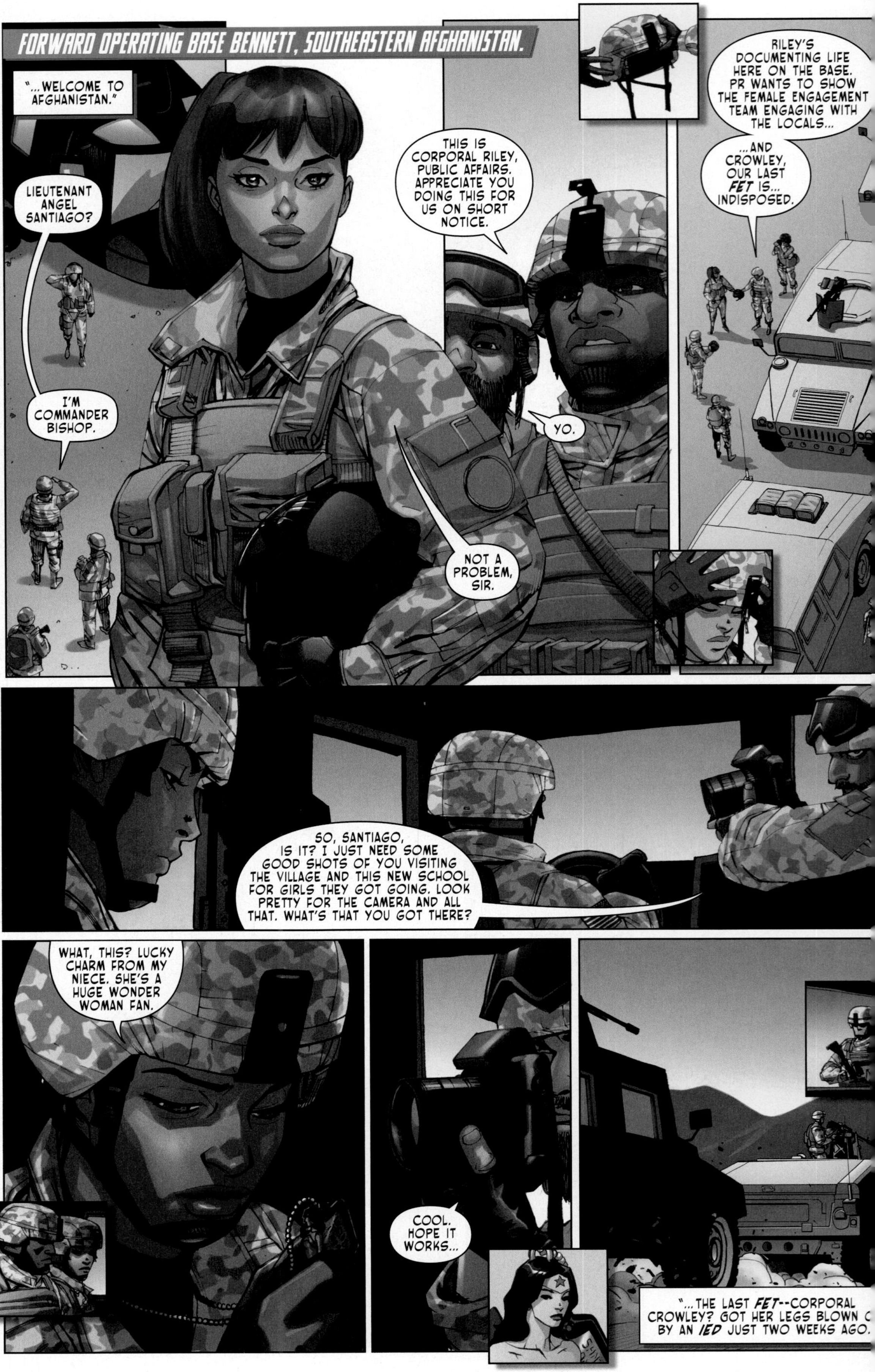
FORWARD OPERATING BASE BENNETT, SOUTHEASTERN AFGHANISTAN.
"...WELCOME TO AFGHANISTAN."
LIEUTENANT ANGEL SANTIAGO?
I'M COMMANDER BISHOP.
THIS IS CORPORAL RILEY, PUBLIC AFFAIRS. APPRECIATE YOU DOING THIS FOR US ON SHORT NOTICE.
YO.
NOT A PROBLEM, SIR.
RILEY'S DOCUMENTING LIFE HERE ON THE BASE. PR WANTS TO SHOW THE FEMALE ENGAGEMENT TEAM ENGAGING WITH THE LOCALS...
...AND CROWLEY, OUR LAST FET IS... INDISPOSED.
SO, SANTIAGO, IS IT? I JUST NEED SOME GOOD SHOTS OF YOU VISITING THE VILLAGE AND THIS NEW SCHOOL FOR GIRLS THEY GOT GOING. LOOK PRETTY FOR THE CAMERA AND ALL THAT. WHAT'S THAT YOU GOT THERE?
WHAT, THIS? LUCKY CHARM FROM MY NIECE. SHE'S A HUGE WONDER WOMAN FAN.
COOL. HOPE IT WORKS...
"...THE LAST FET--CORPORAL CROWLEY? GOT HER LEGS BLOWN O BY AN IED JUST TWO WEEKS AGO.

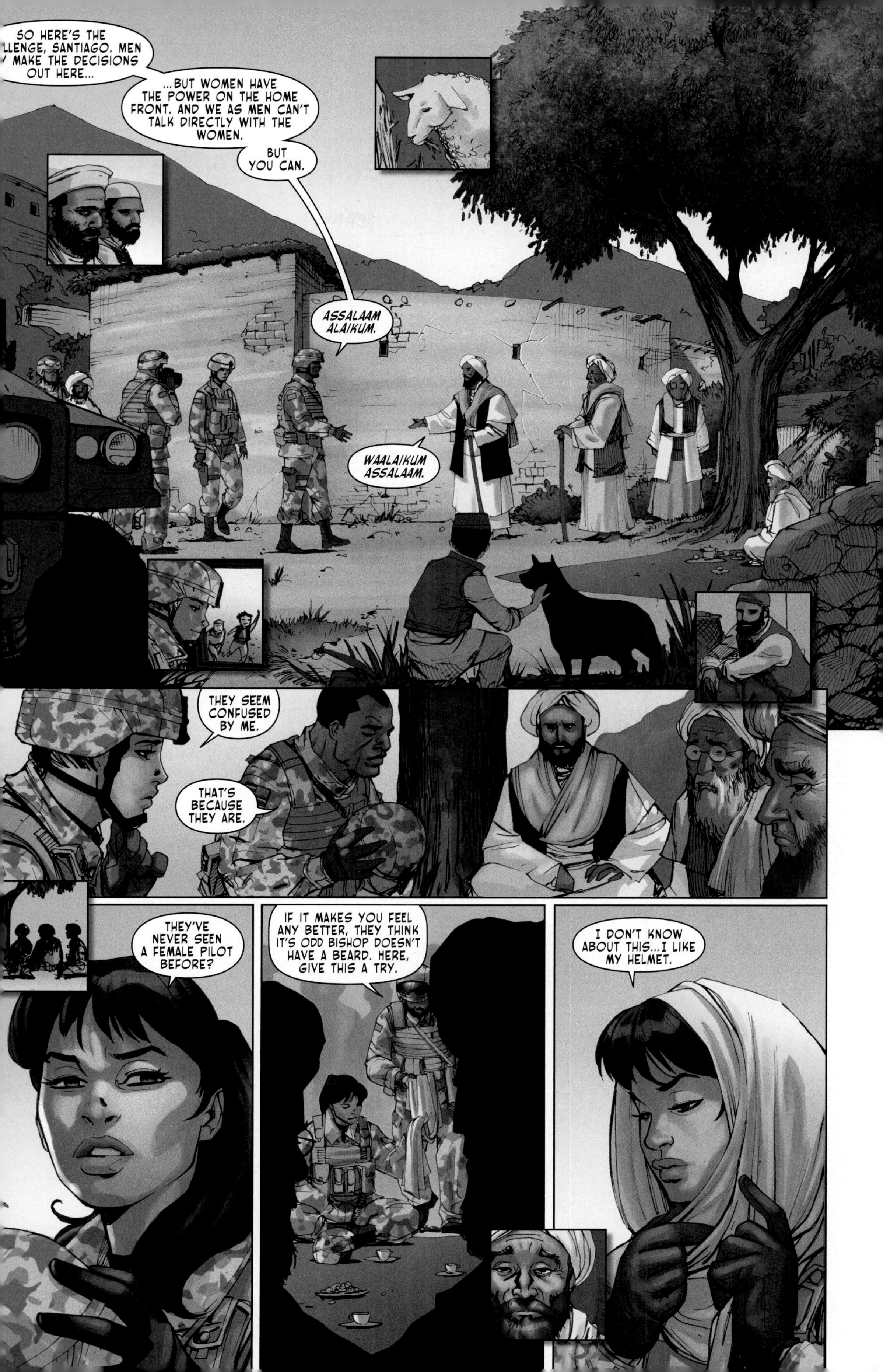
SO HERE'S THE
LLENGE, SANTIAGO. MEN
MAKE THE DECISIONS
OUT HERE...
...BUT WOMEN HAVE THE POWER ON THE HOME FRONT. AND WE AS MEN CAN'T TALK DIRECTLY WITH THE WOMEN.
BUT YOU CAN.
ASSALAAM ALAIKUM.
WAALAIKUM ASSALAAM.
THEY SEEM CONFUSED BY ME.
THAT'S BECAUSE THEY ARE.
THEY'VE NEVER SEEN A FEMALE PILOT BEFORE?
IF IT MAKES YOU FEEL ANY BETTER, THEY THINK IT'S ODD BISHOP DOESN'T HAVE A BEARD. HERE, GIVE THIS A TRY.
I DON'T KNOW ABOUT THIS...I LIKE MY HELMET.

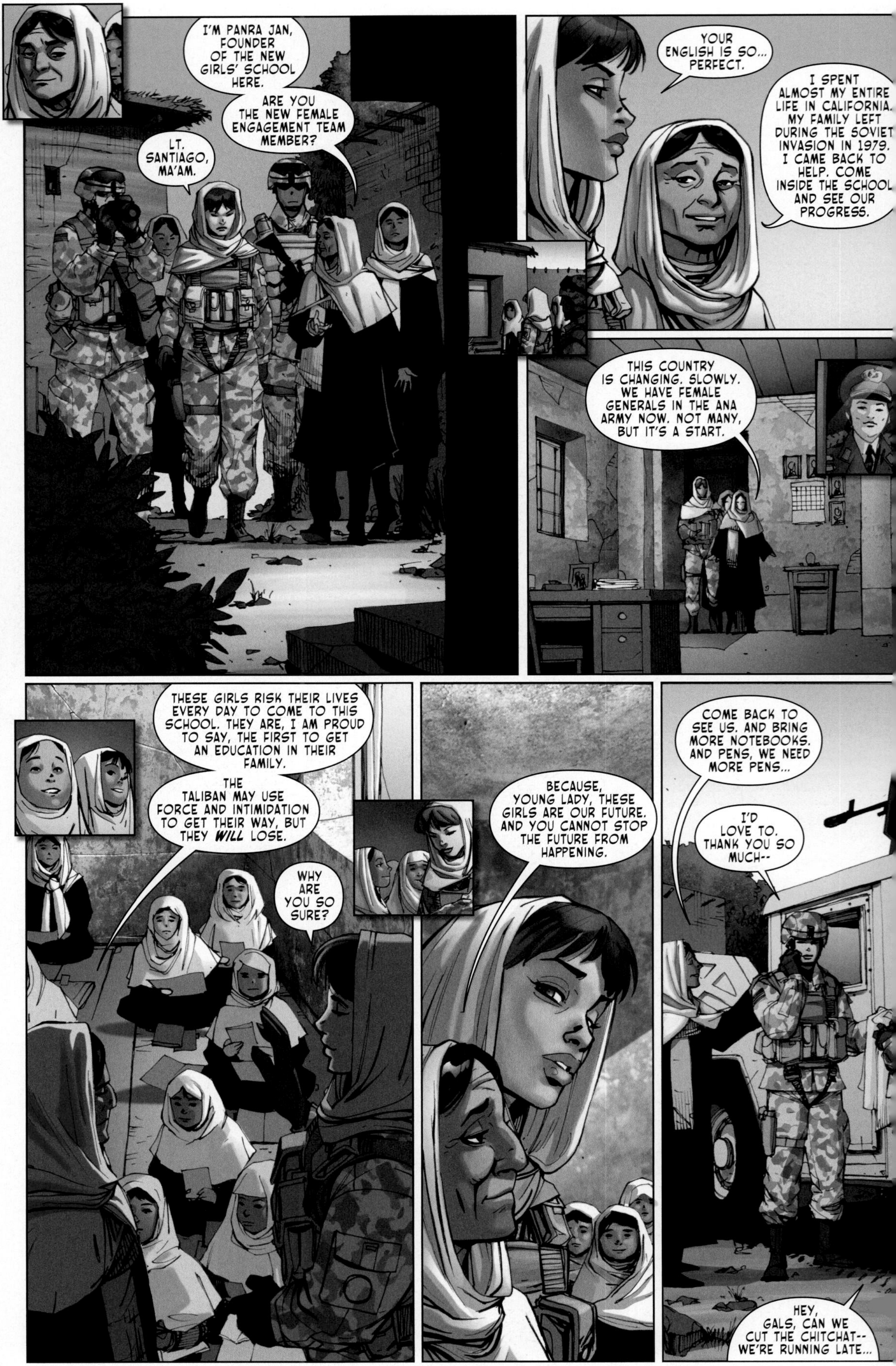
I'M PANRA JAN, FOUNDER OF THE NEW GIRLS' SCHOOL HERE.
ARE YOU THE NEW FEMALE ENGAGEMENT TEAM MEMBER?
LT. SANTIAGO, MA'AM.
YOUR ENGLISH IS SO... PERFECT.
I SPENT ALMOST MY ENTIRE LIFE IN CALIFORNIA. MY FAMILY LEFT DURING THE SOVIET INVASION IN 1979. I CAME BACK TO HELP. COME INSIDE THE SCHOOL AND SEE OUR PROGRESS.
THIS COUNTRY IS CHANGING. SLOWLY. WE HAVE FEMALE GENERALS IN THE ANA ARMY NOW. NOT MANY, BUT IT'S A START.
THESE GIRLS RISK THEIR LIVES EVERY DAY TO COME TO THIS SCHOOL. THEY ARE, I AM PROUD TO SAY, THE FIRST TO GET AN EDUCATION IN THEIR FAMILY.
THE TALIBAN MAY USE FORCE AND INTIMIDATION TO GET THEIR WAY, BUT THEY *WILL* LOSE.
WHY ARE YOU SO SURE?
BECAUSE, YOUNG LADY, THESE GIRLS ARE OUR FUTURE. AND YOU CANNOT STOP THE FUTURE FROM HAPPENING.
COME BACK TO SEE US. AND BRING MORE NOTEBOOKS. AND PENS, WE NEED MORE PENS...
I'D LOVE TO. THANK YOU SO MUCH--
HEY, GALS, CAN WE CUT THE CHITCHAT-- WE'RE RUNNING LATE...

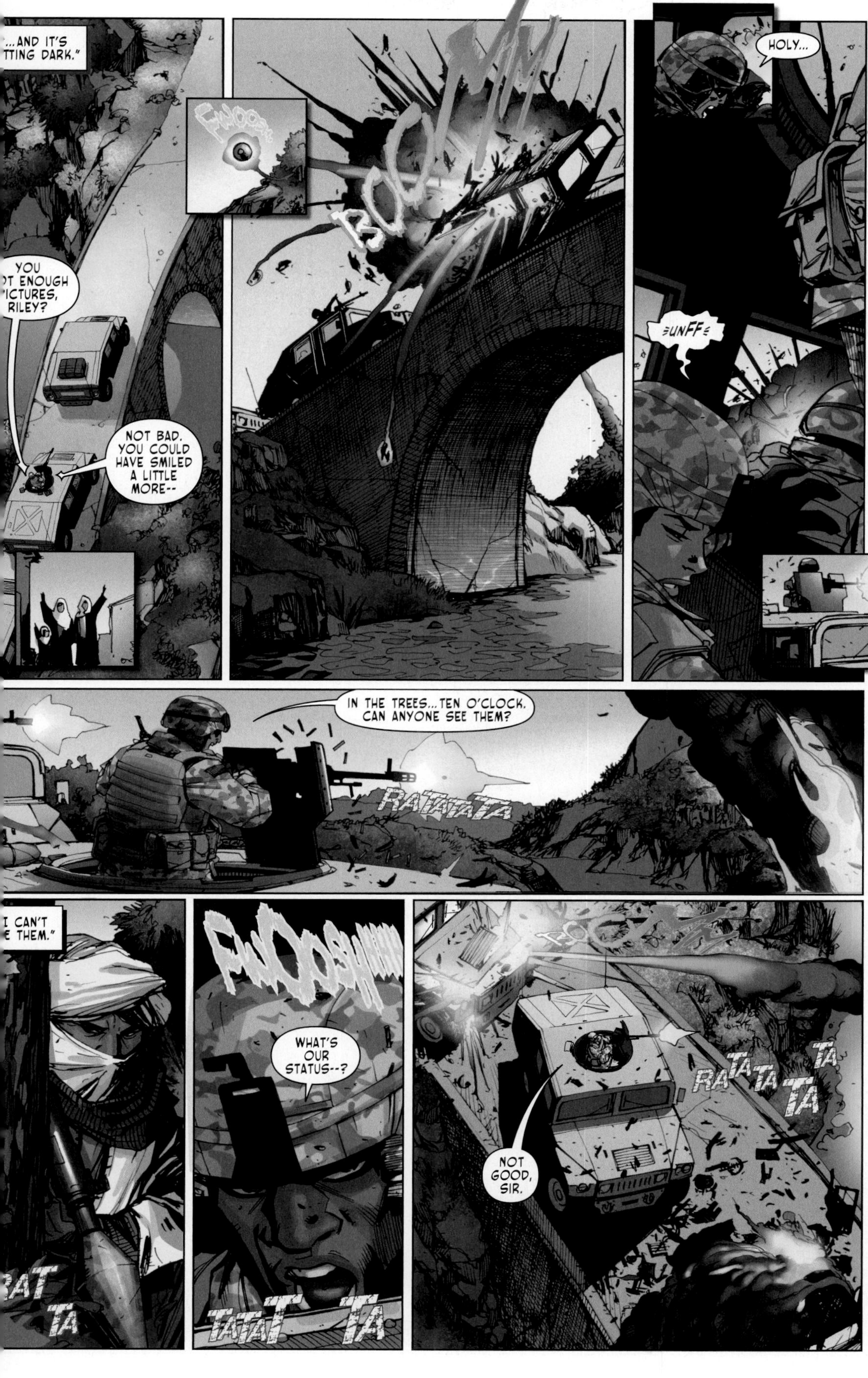

...AND IT'S
TTING DARK."
FWOOSH
BOOM
HOLY...
YOU
OT ENOUGH
PICTURES,
RILEY?
NOT BAD. YOU COULD HAVE SMILED A LITTLE MORE--
UNFF
IN THE TREES... TEN O'CLOCK. CAN ANYONE SEE THEM?
RATATATA
I CAN'T
E THEM."
RAT
TA
FWOOSH
WHAT'S OUR STATUS--?
TATAT TA
BOOM
RATATATA
TA
NOT GOOD, SIR.

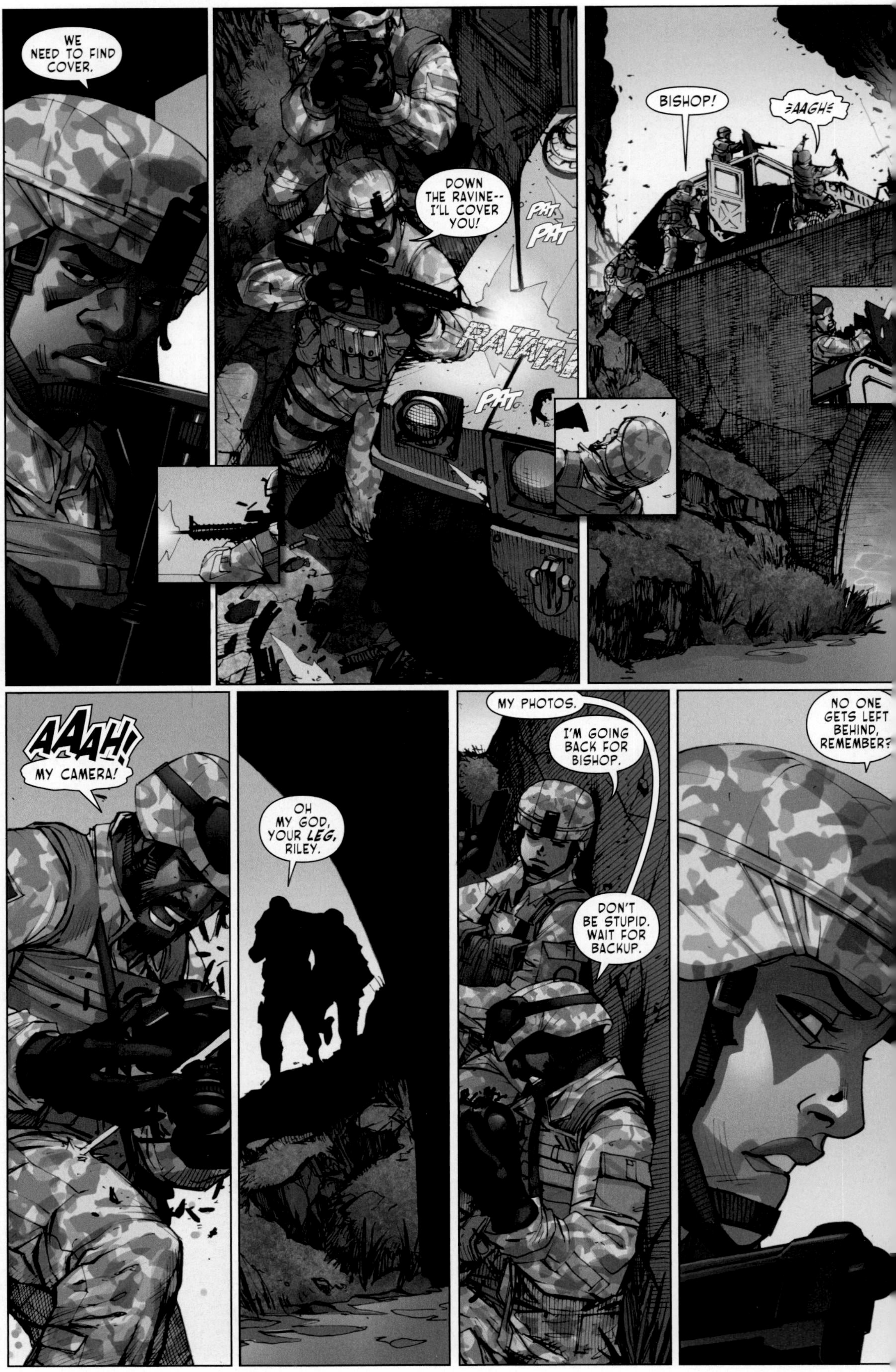
WE NEED TO FIND COVER.
DOWN THE RAVINE-- I'LL COVER YOU!
PAT
PAT
RATATAT
PAT
BISHOP!
AAGH
AAAH!
MY CAMERA!
OH MY GOD, YOUR LEG, RILEY.
MY PHOTOS.
I'M GOING BACK FOR BISHOP.
DON'T BE STUPID. WAIT FOR BACKUP.
NO ONE GETS LEFT BEHIND, REMEMBER?

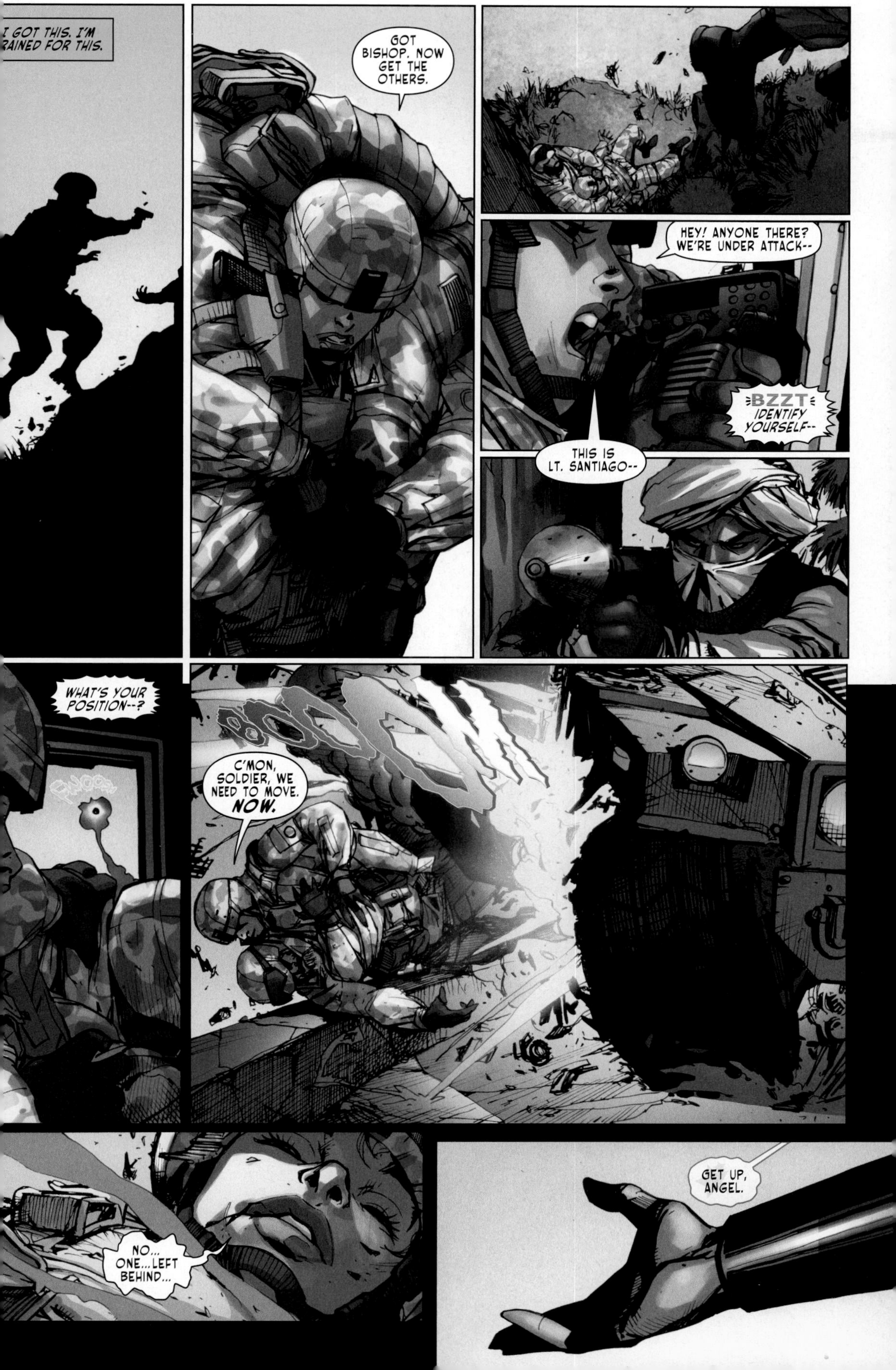
I GOT THIS. I'M TRAINED FOR THIS.
GOT BISHOP. NOW GET THE OTHERS.
HEY! ANYONE THERE? WE'RE UNDER ATTACK--
BZZT IDENTIFY YOURSELF--
THIS IS LT. SANTIAGO--
WHAT'S YOUR POSITION--?
C'MON, SOLDIER, WE NEED TO MOVE. NOW.
NO... ONE...LEFT BEHIND...
GET UP, ANGEL.

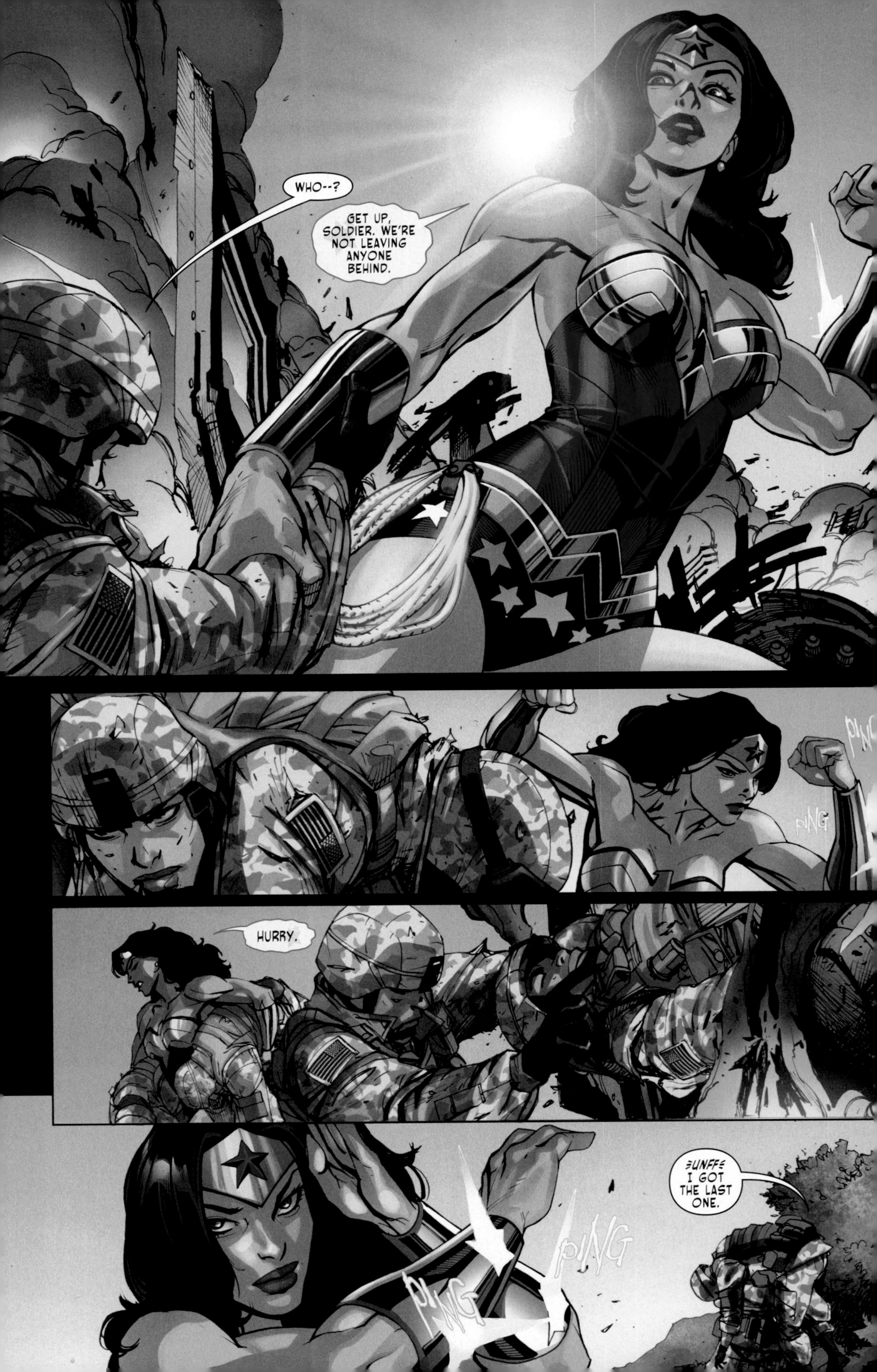
WHO--?
GET UP, SOLDIER. WE'RE NOT LEAVING ANYONE BEHIND.
PING
PING
HURRY.
PING
PING
UNFF
I GOT THE LAST ONE.

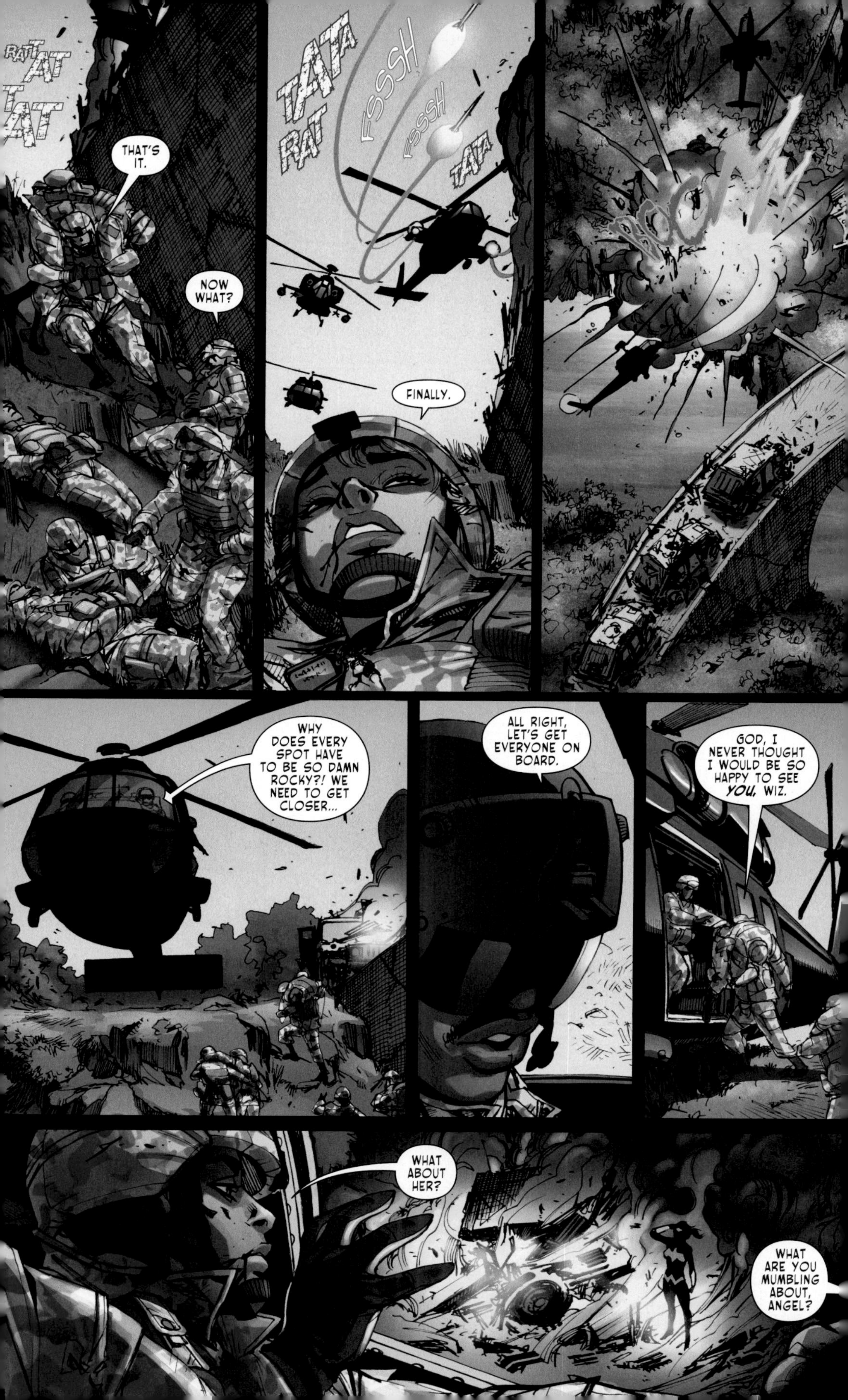
RATTAT TAT
THAT'S IT.
NOW WHAT?
TATA RAT
FSSSH
FSSSH
TATA
FINALLY.
BOOM
WHY DOES EVERY SPOT HAVE TO BE SO DAMN ROCKY?! WE NEED TO GET CLOSER...
ALL RIGHT, LET'S GET EVERYONE ON BOARD.
GOD, I NEVER THOUGHT I WOULD BE SO HAPPY TO SEE *YOU*, WIZ.
WHAT ABOUT HER?
WHAT ARE YOU MUMBLING ABOUT, ANGEL?

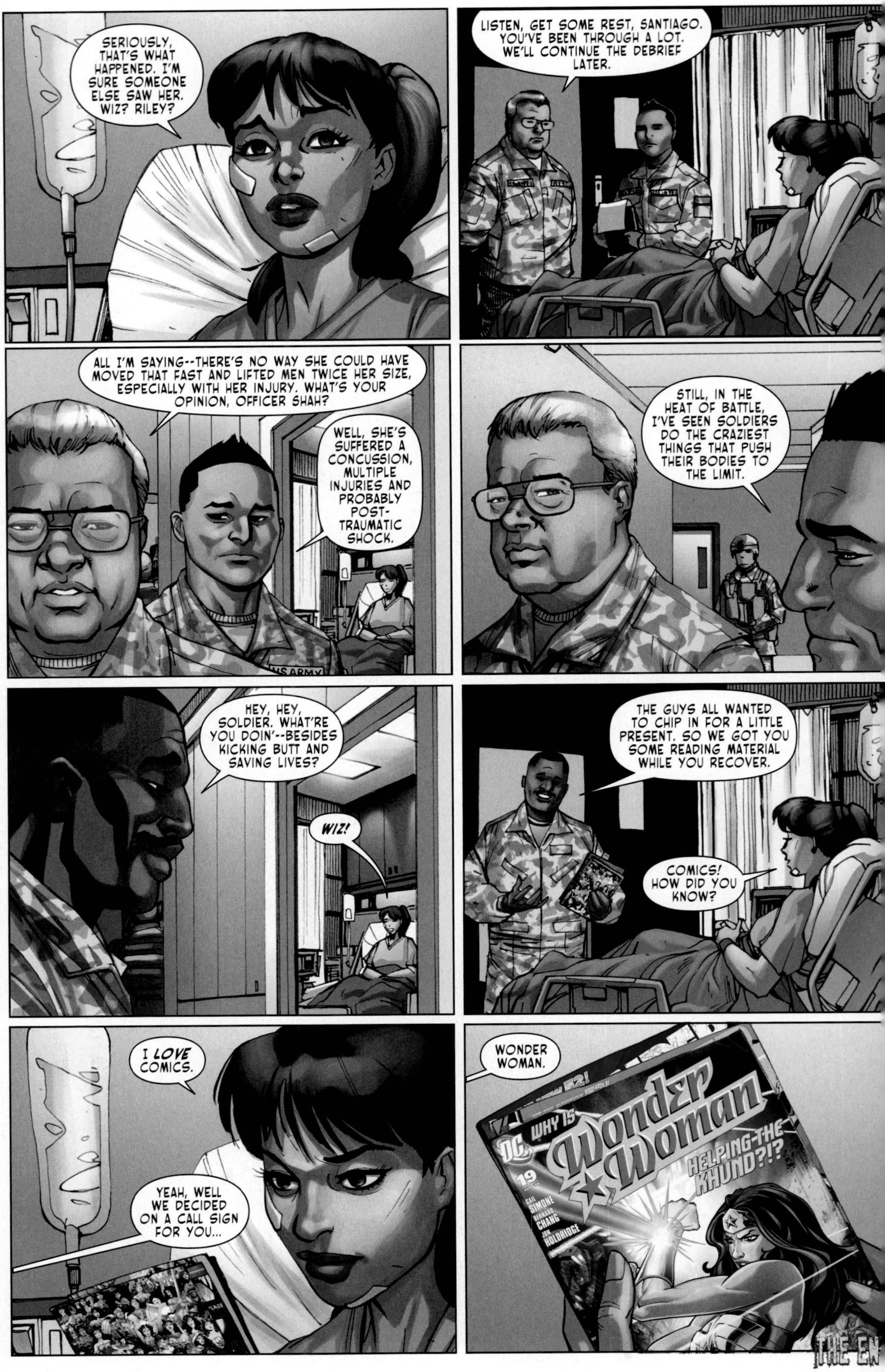
SERIOUSLY, THAT'S WHAT HAPPENED. I'M SURE SOMEONE ELSE SAW HER. WIZ? RILEY?
LISTEN, GET SOME REST, SANTIAGO. YOU'VE BEEN THROUGH A LOT. WE'LL CONTINUE THE DEBRIEF LATER.
ALL I'M SAYING--THERE'S NO WAY SHE COULD HAVE MOVED THAT FAST AND LIFTED MEN TWICE HER SIZE, ESPECIALLY WITH HER INJURY. WHAT'S YOUR OPINION, OFFICER SHAH?
WELL, SHE'S SUFFERED A CONCUSSION, MULTIPLE INJURIES AND PROBABLY POST-TRAUMATIC SHOCK.
US ARMY
STILL, IN THE HEAT OF BATTLE, I'VE SEEN SOLDIERS DO THE CRAZIEST THINGS THAT PUSH THEIR BODIES TO THE LIMIT.
HEY, HEY, SOLDIER. WHAT'RE YOU DOIN'--BESIDES KICKING BUTT AND SAVING LIVES?
WIZ!
THE GUYS ALL WANTED TO CHIP IN FOR A LITTLE PRESENT. SO WE GOT YOU SOME READING MATERIAL WHILE YOU RECOVER.
COMICS! HOW DID YOU KNOW?
I LOVE COMICS.
YEAH, WELL WE DECIDED ON A CALL SIGN FOR YOU...
WONDER WOMAN.
DC
19
WHY IS Wonder Woman HELPING THE KHUND?!?
GAIL SIMONE
BERNARD CHANG
JON HOLDRIDGE
THE EN

SABOTAGE IS IN THE STARS

HEATHER NUHFER
WRITER

RYAN BENJAMIN
ARTIST

SAIDA TEMOFONTE
LETTERER

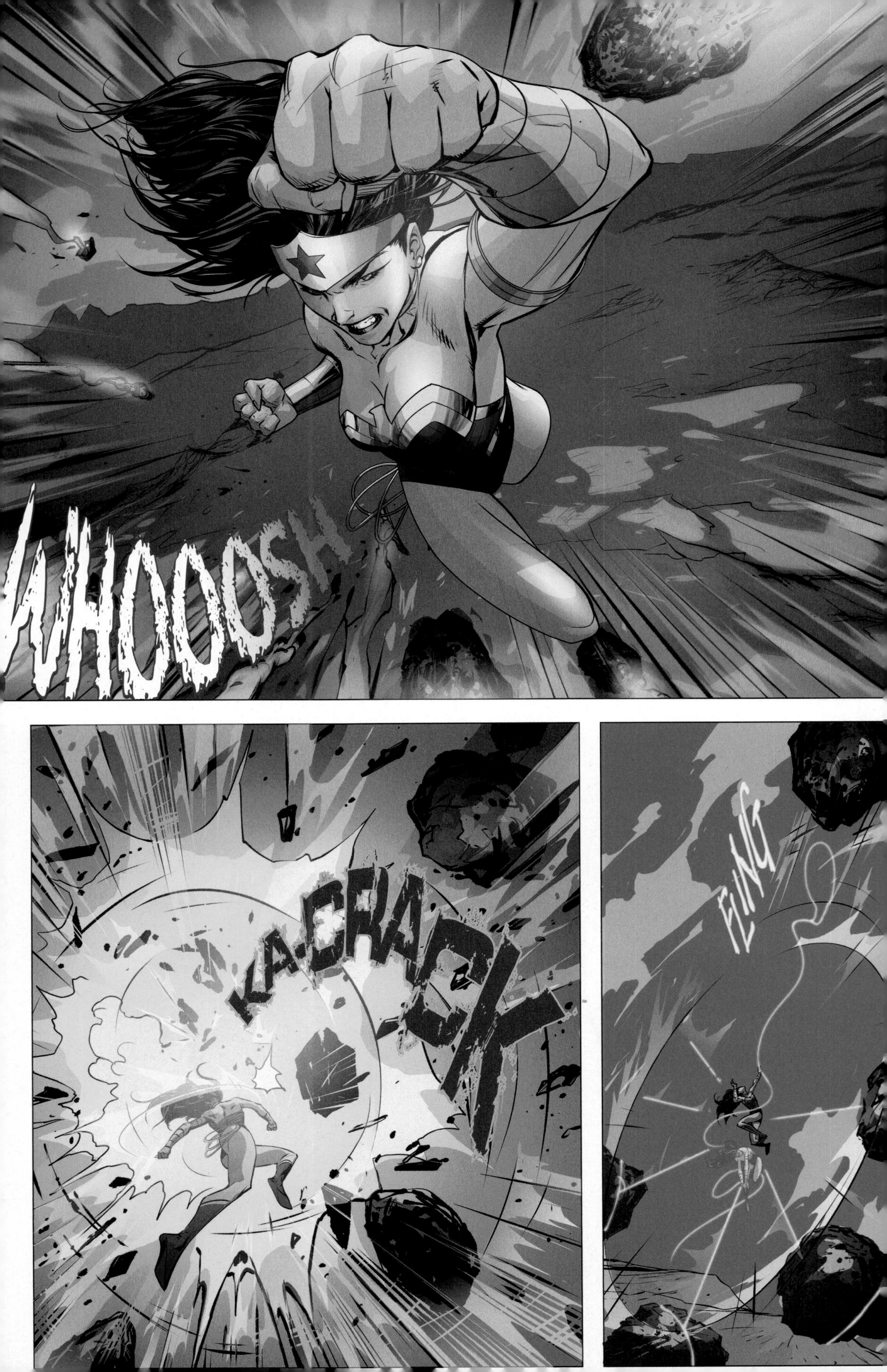
WHOOOSH
KA-CRACK
FLING

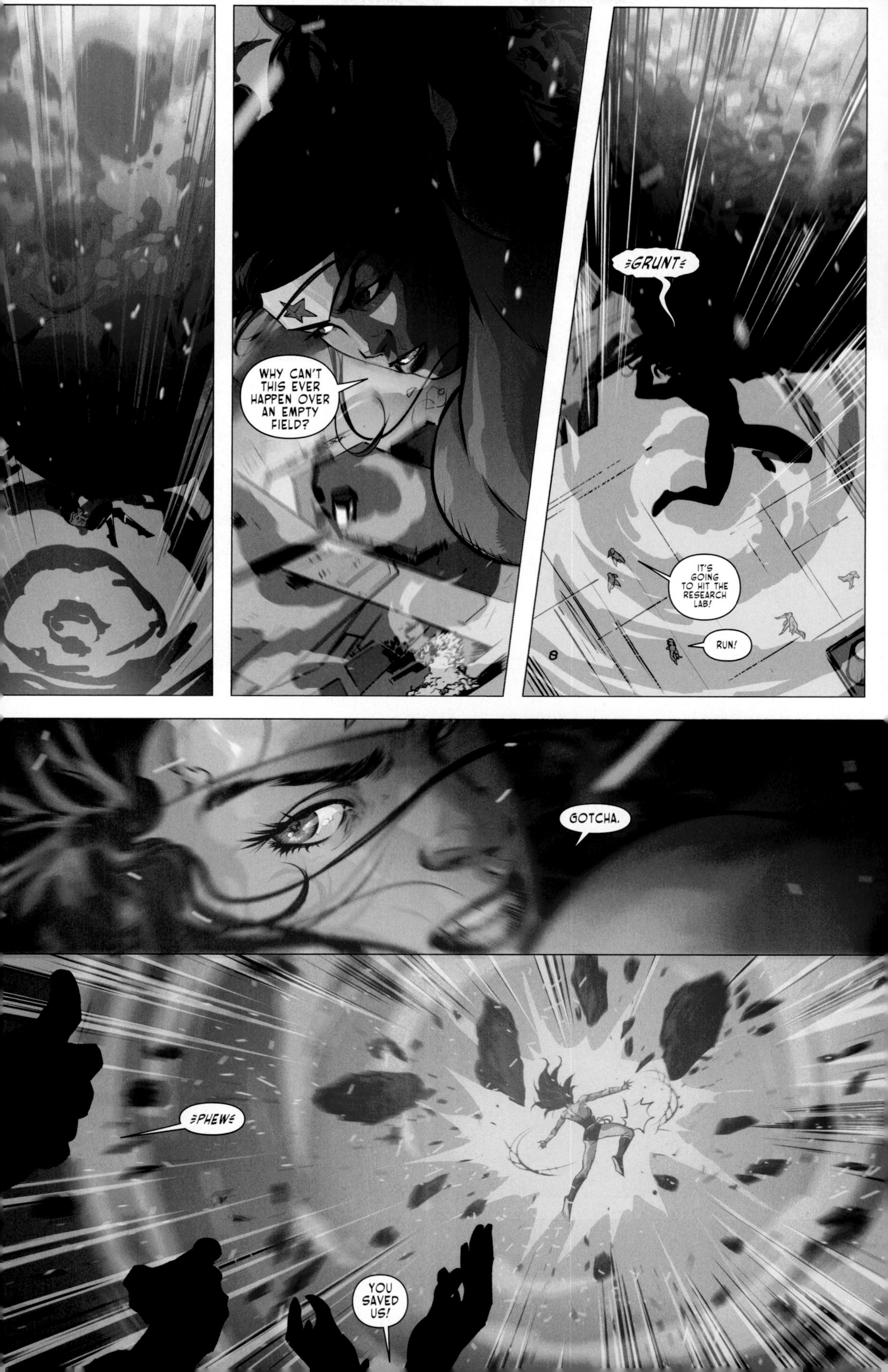
WHY CAN'T THIS EVER HAPPEN OVER AN EMPTY FIELD?
GRUNT
IT'S GOING TO HIT THE RESEARCH LAB!
RUN!
GOTCHA.
PHEW
YOU SAVED US!

THANK YOU
WONDER WOMAN

WITHOUT YOU, WONDER WOMAN, OUR RESEARCH LAB WOULD HAVE BEEN DESTROYED ALONG WITH MANY YEARS' WORTH OF INVALUABLE PROGRESS ON OUR SPACECROPS PROGRAM...

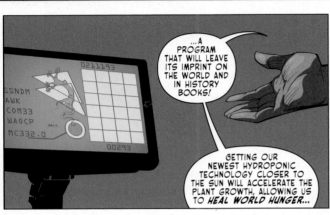

...A PROGRAM THAT WILL LEAVE ITS IMPRINT ON THE WORLD AND IN HISTORY BOOKS!

GETTING OUR NEWEST HYDROPONIC TECHNOLOGY CLOSER TO THE SUN WILL ACCELERATE THE PLANT GROWTH, ALLOWING US TO *HEAL WORLD HUNGER*...

...AND PROVE TO THE WORLD THAT *INDIA'S TECHNOLOGY* IS INFERIOR TO *NONE!*

HEAR THAT, LEXCORP?!

CAPTAIN CHAWLA, OUR MOST REVERED AND EXPERIENCED ASTRONAUT, WILL ALSO BE MAKING HISTORY AS THE FIRST FEMALE TO COMMAND A MISSION OF THIS CALIBER!

THANK YOU FOR ALL OF YOUR WORK.

I SHOULD BE THANKING YOU. YOU'VE SAVED THE WORLD IN MORE THAN ONE WAY TODAY.

IT IS MY HONOR TO HELP PROTECT ALL INHABITANTS OF EARTH THE BEST I CAN, CAPTAIN.

EXCEPT MAYBE HIM...

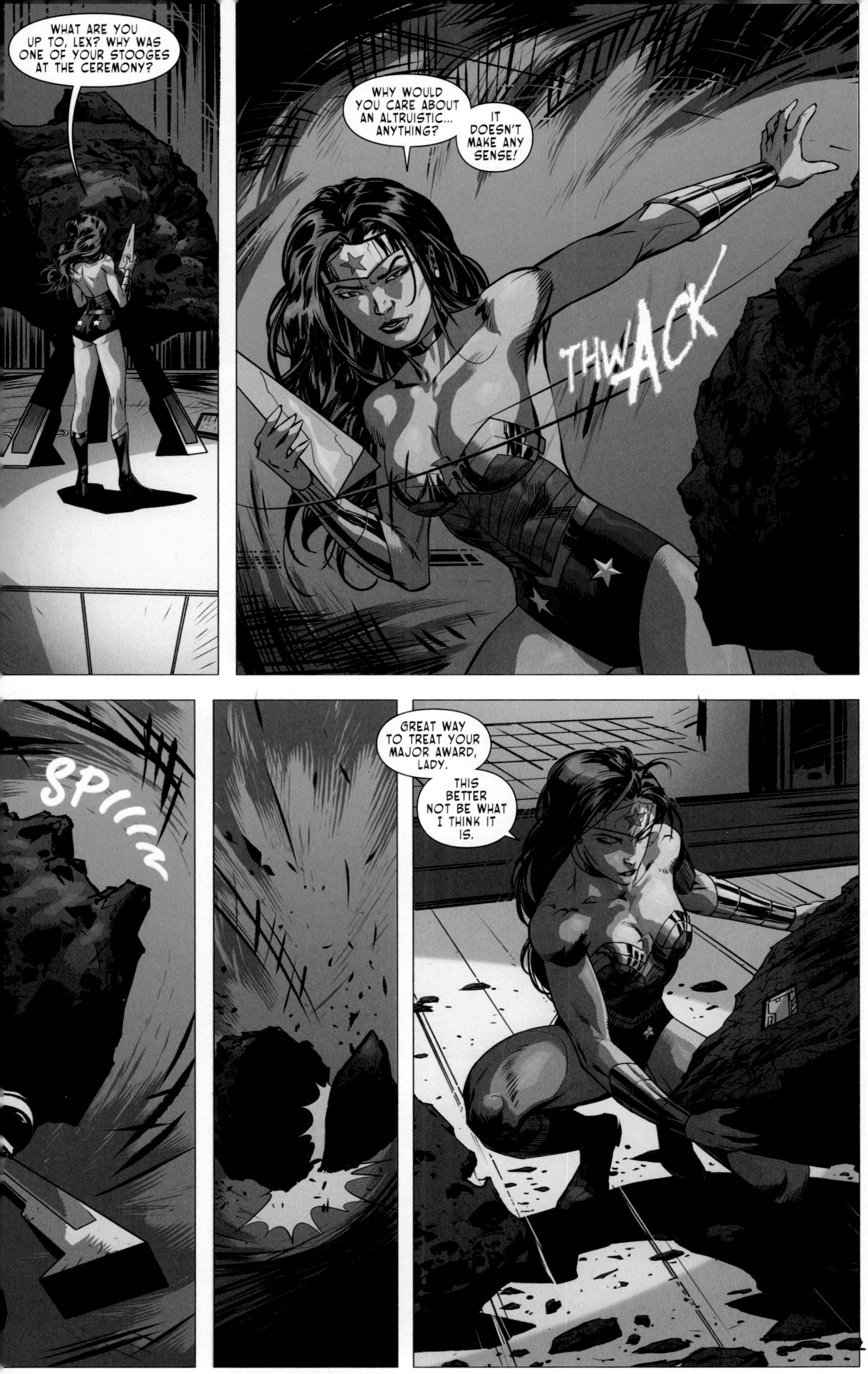
WHAT ARE YOU UP TO, LEX? WHY WAS ONE OF YOUR STOOGES AT THE CEREMONY?
WHY WOULD YOU CARE ABOUT AN ALTRUISTIC... ANYTHING?
IT DOESN'T MAKE ANY SENSE!
THWACK
SPIIIN
GREAT WAY TO TREAT YOUR MAJOR AWARD, LADY.
THIS BETTER NOT BE WHAT I THINK IT IS.

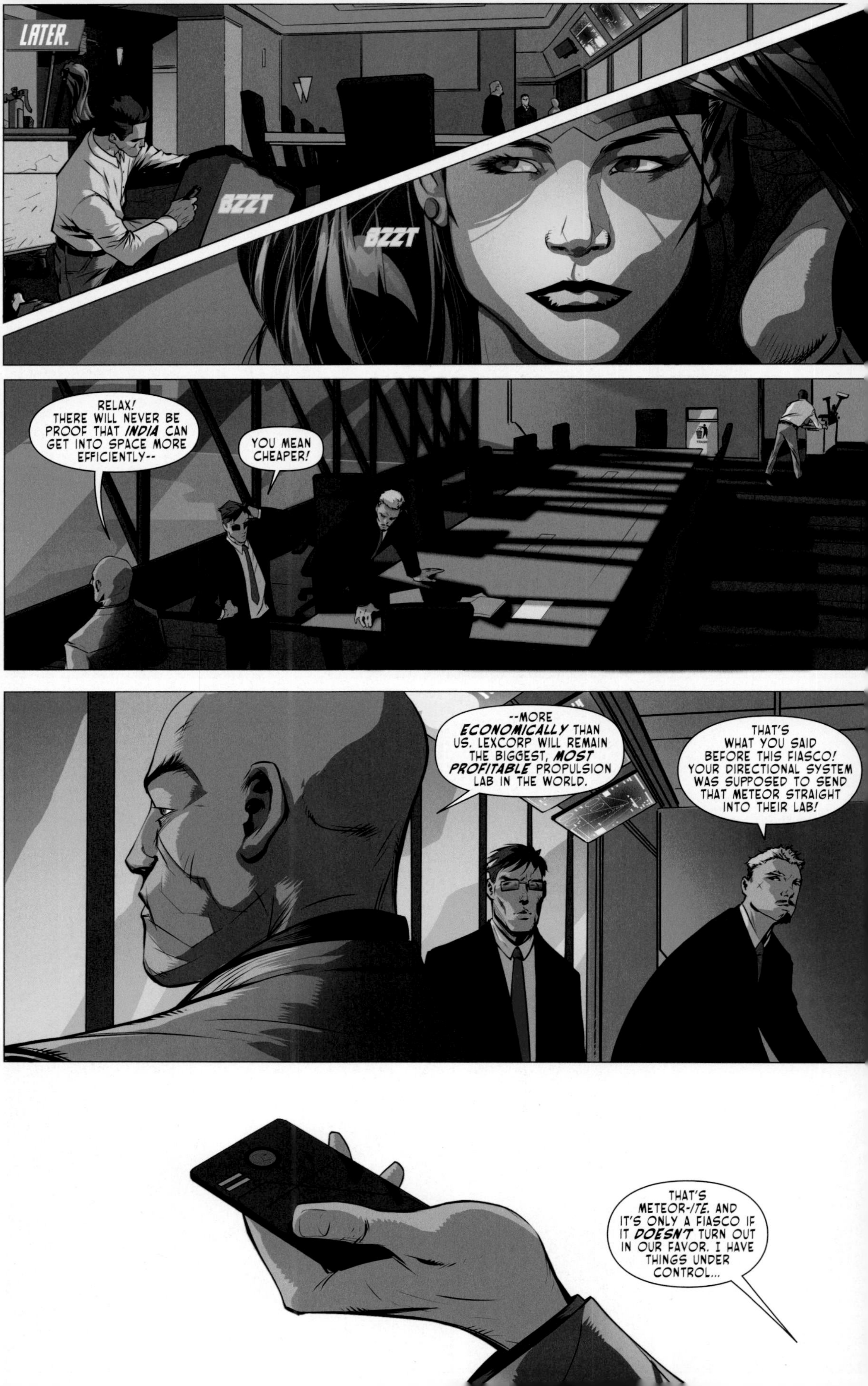
LATER.
BZZT
BZZT
RELAX! THERE WILL NEVER BE PROOF THAT INDIA CAN GET INTO SPACE MORE EFFICIENTLY--
YOU MEAN CHEAPER!
--MORE ECONOMICALLY THAN US. LEXCORP WILL REMAIN THE BIGGEST, MOST PROFITABLE PROPULSION LAB IN THE WORLD.
THAT'S WHAT YOU SAID BEFORE THIS FIASCO! YOUR DIRECTIONAL SYSTEM WAS SUPPOSED TO SEND THAT METEOR STRAIGHT INTO THEIR LAB!
THAT'S METEOR-ITE. AND IT'S ONLY A FIASCO IF IT DOESN'T TURN OUT IN OUR FAVOR. I HAVE THINGS UNDER CONTROL...

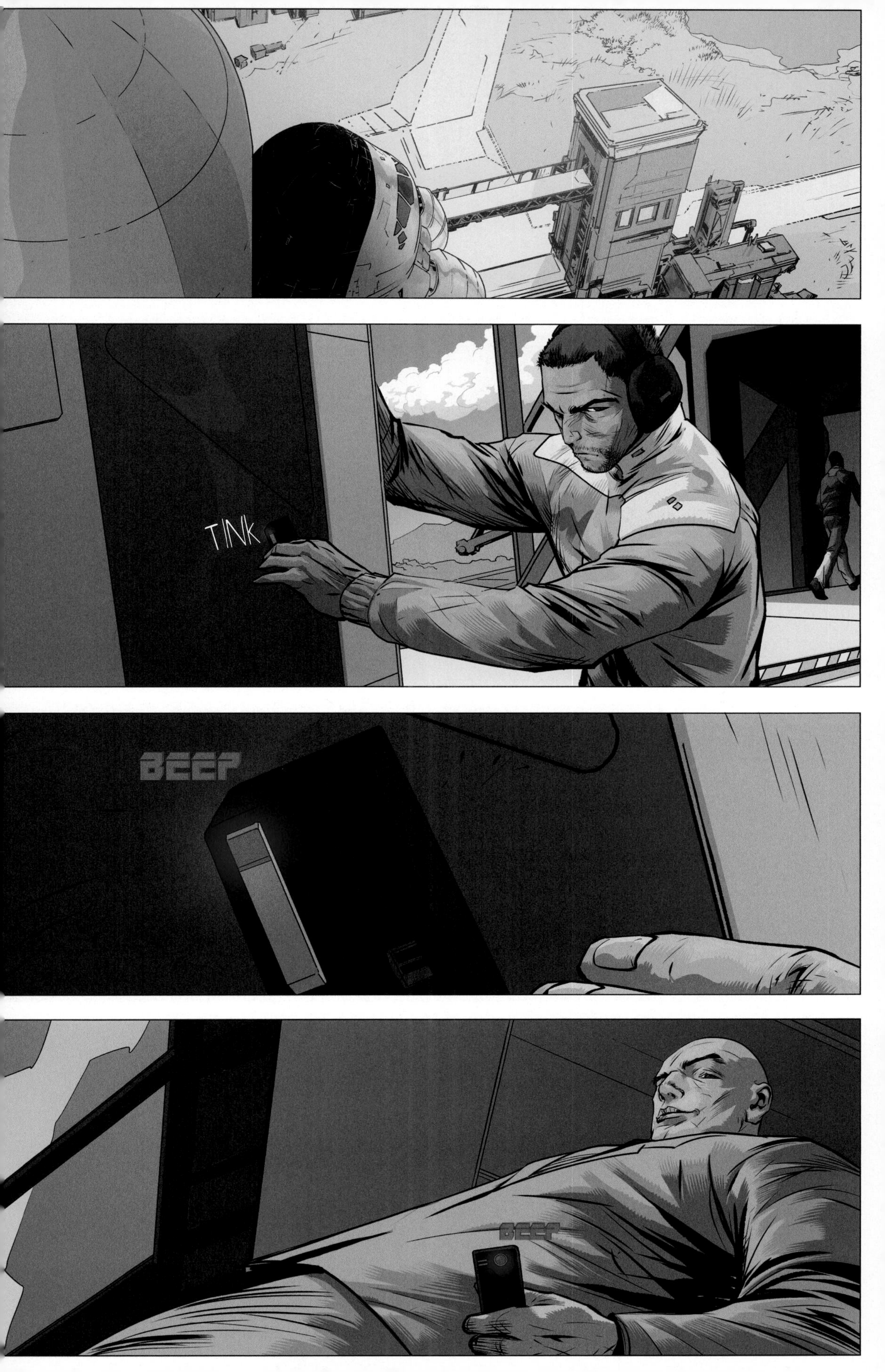
TINK
BEEP
BEEP

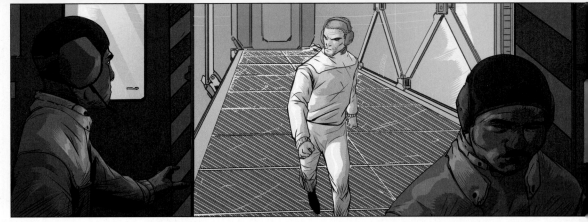

READY FOR COUNTDOWN, CAPTAIN CHAWLA.

ROGER THAT. MORE THAN YOU'LL EVER KNOW.

IN FIVE... FOUR...THREE...

....TWO... ONE...

WHAT ABOUT WONDER WOMAN?

OH, I'VE GOT SOMETHING *VERY* SPECIAL ARRANGED FOR HER.

AND I'LL BE READY.

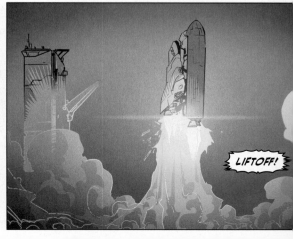

LIFTOFF!

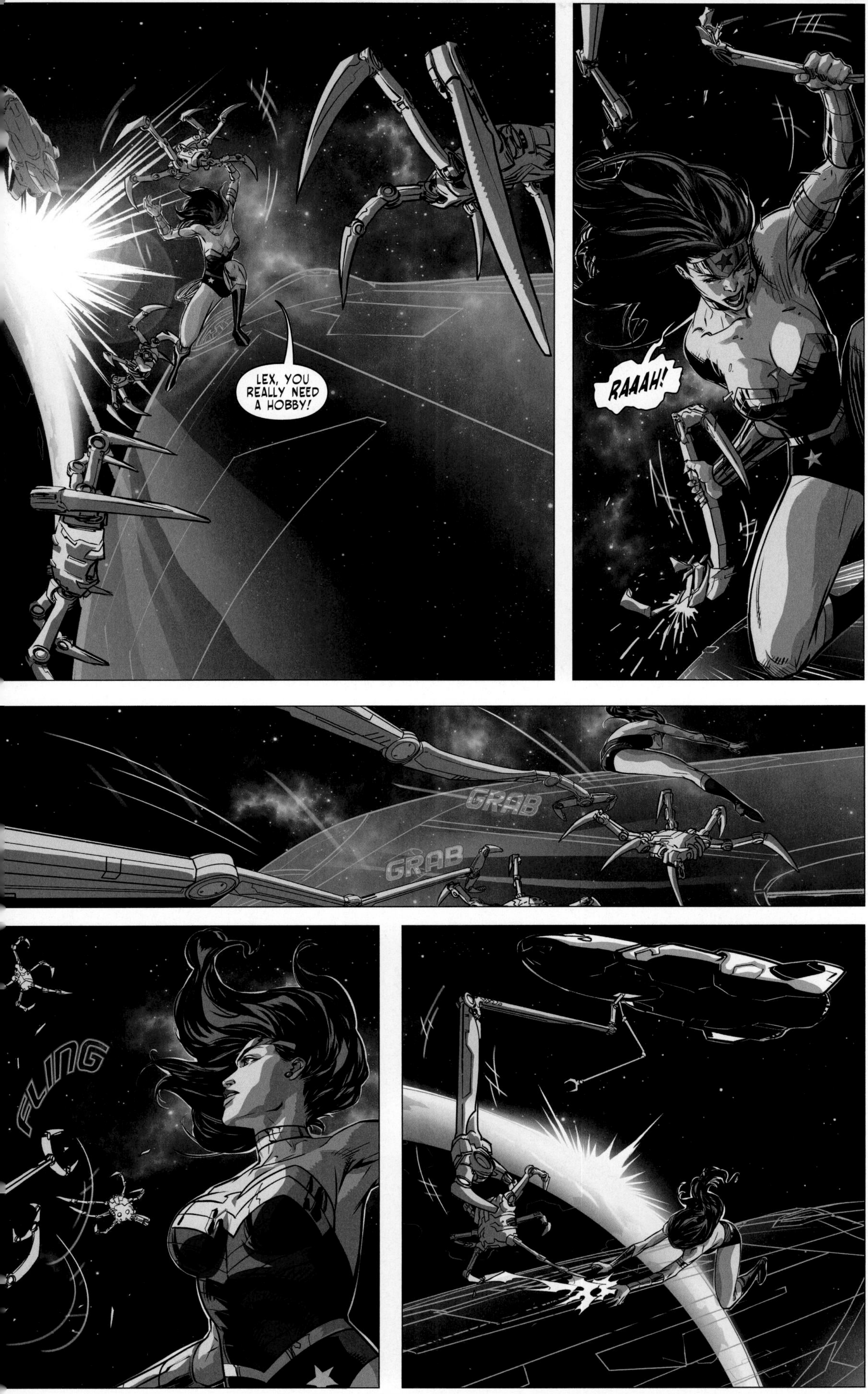
LEX, YOU REALLY NEED A HOBBY!
RAAAH!
GRAB
GRAB
FLING

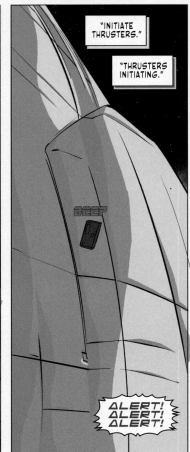

A GOOD DEED TO START THE TRIP.

NOW, LET'S GET GOING. SET COORDINATES.

COORDINATES SET.

"INITIATE THRUSTERS."

"THRUSTERS INITIATING."

CAPTAIN, THE SHIP IS CHANGING OUR COORDINATES. I CAN'T STOP IT! IT'S SENDING US *TOO CLOSE* TO THE SUN! WE'LL BURN UP!

CONTROL? CAN YOU HEAR ME? CAPTAIN CHAWLA TO CONTROL!

LOOKS LIKE WE'RE ON OUR OWN...

ALERT! ALERT! ALERT!

...OR NOT!

CAPTAIN, WE'VE REGAINED CONTROL OF THE SHIP. BUT WE'VE LOST OUR FLIGHT PLAN!

THEY MADE ME CAPTAIN FOR A REASON. I CAN HANDLE THIS BIRD.

IT'S ALL UP TO YOU NOW.

I HAVE A BOARD MEETING T CRASH...

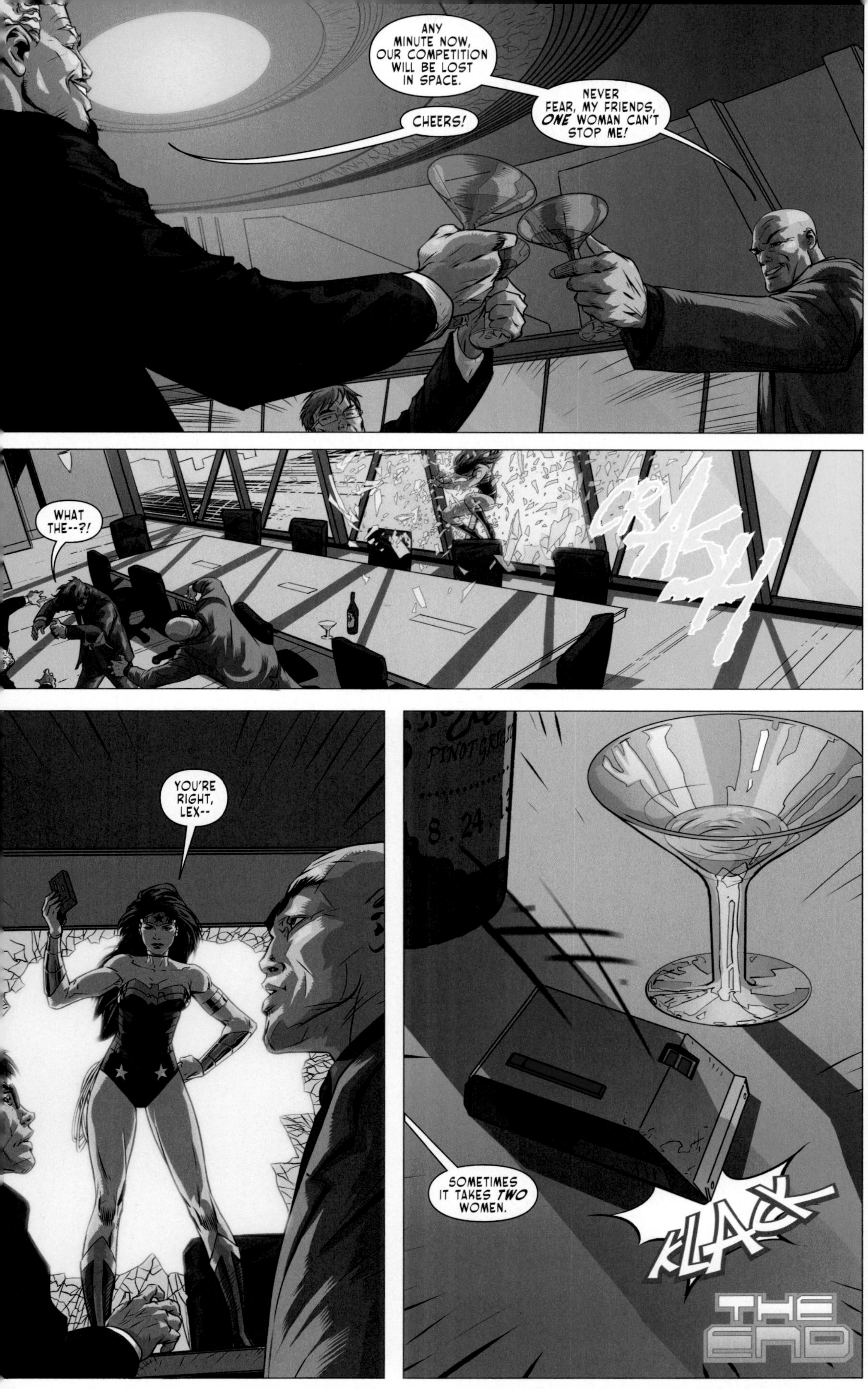
ANY MINUTE NOW, OUR COMPETITION WILL BE LOST IN SPACE.
CHEERS!
NEVER FEAR, MY FRIENDS, *ONE* WOMAN CAN'T STOP ME!
WHAT THE--?!
CRASH
YOU'RE RIGHT, LEX--
PINOT GRIGIO
SOMETIMES IT TAKES *TWO* WOMEN.
KLACK
THE END

WONDER WORLD

JAMES TYNION IV
WRITER

NOELLE STEVENSON
ARTIST

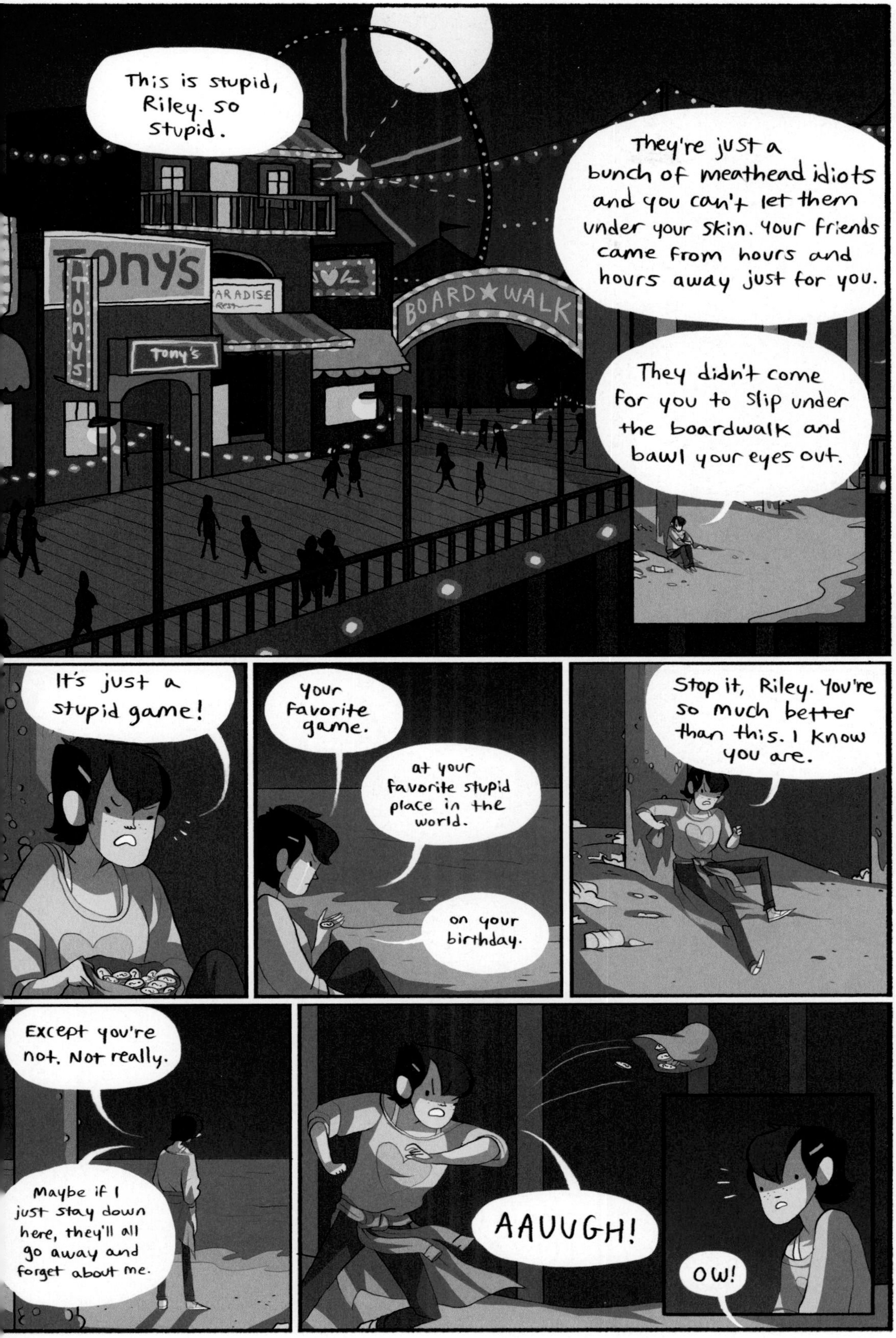
This is stupid, Riley. So stupid.
TONY'S
TONY'S
Tony's
PARADISE
BOARD★WALK
They're just a bunch of meathead idiots and you can't let them under your skin. Your friends came from hours and hours away just for you.
They didn't come for you to slip under the boardwalk and bawl your eyes out.
It's just a stupid game!
Your favorite game.
at your favorite stupid place in the world.
on your birthday.
Stop it, Riley. You're so much better than this. I know you are.
Except you're not. Not really.
Maybe if I just stay down here, they'll all go away and forget about me.
AAUUGH!
OW!

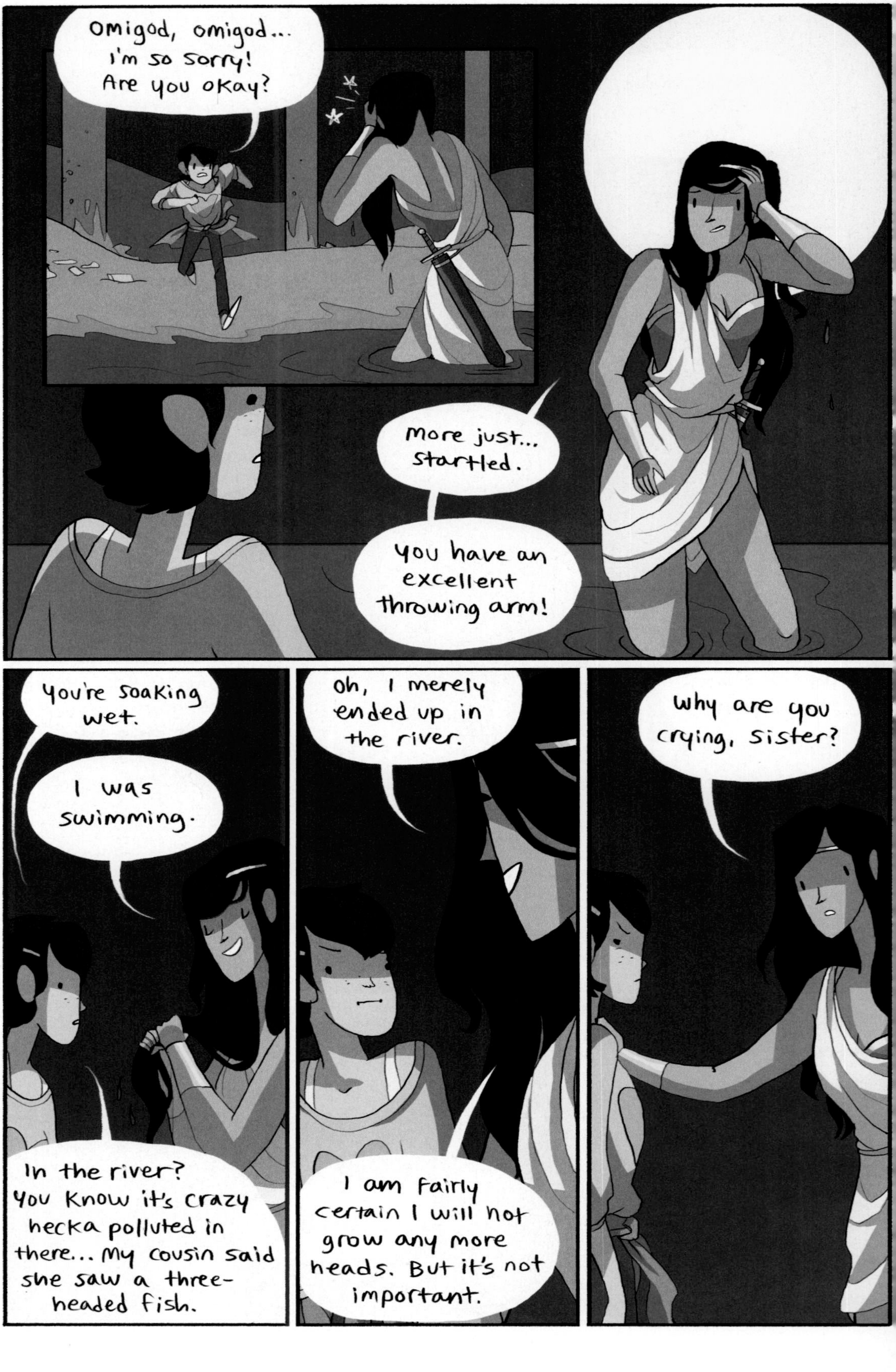
Omigod, omigod... I'm so sorry! Are you okay?
More just... startled.
You have an excellent throwing arm!
You're soaking wet.
I was swimming.
In the river? You know it's crazy hecka polluted in there... My cousin said she saw a three-headed fish.
Oh, I merely ended up in the river.
I am fairly certain I will not grow any more heads. But it's not important.
Why are you crying, sister?

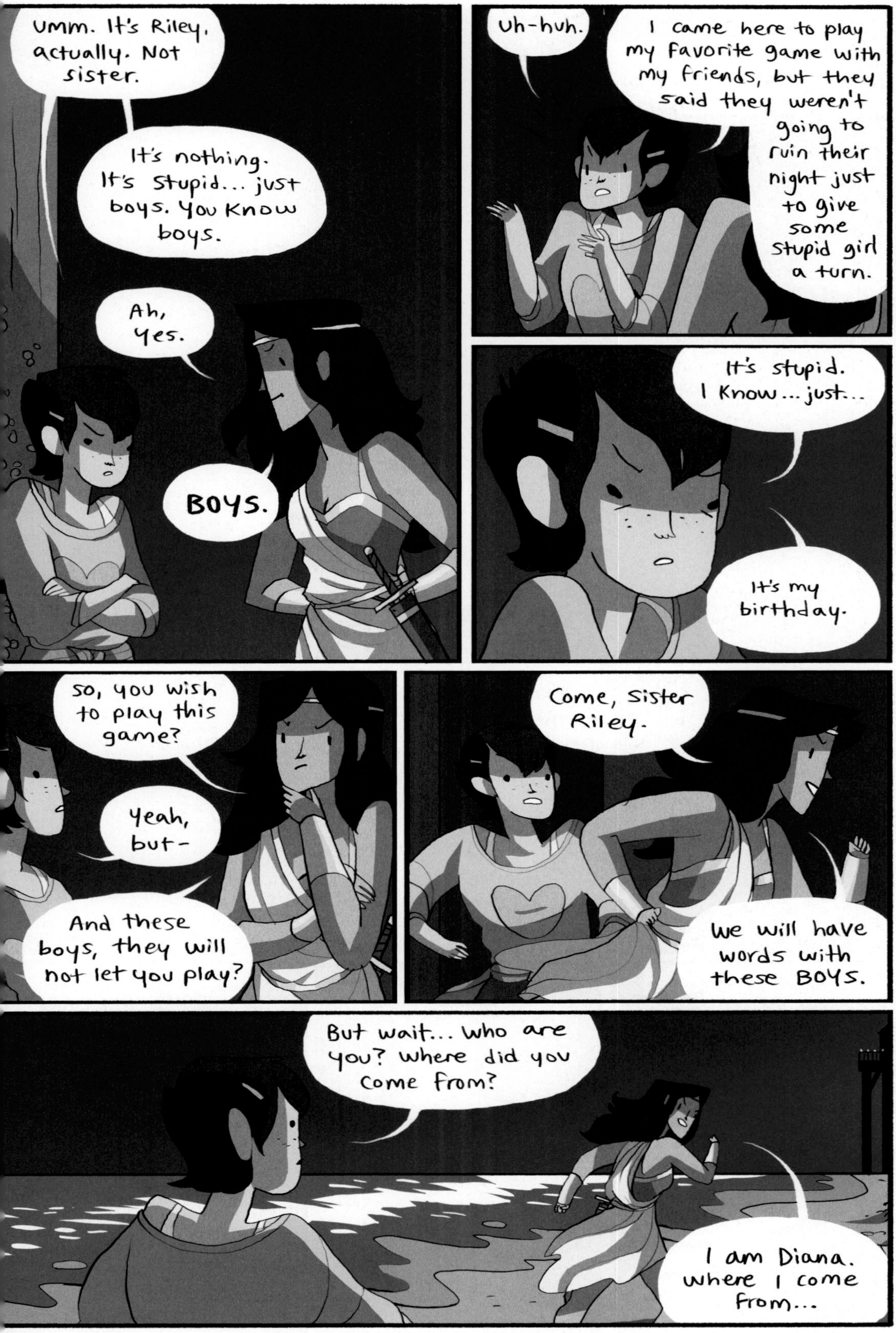
Umm. It's Riley, actually. Not sister.
It's nothing. It's stupid... just boys. You know boys.
Ah, yes.
BOYS.
Uh-huh.
I came here to play my favorite game with my friends, but they said they weren't going to ruin their night just to give some stupid girl a turn.
It's stupid. I know... just...
It's my birthday.
So, you wish to play this game?
Yeah, but-
And these boys, they will not let you play?
Come, Sister Riley.
We will have words with these BOYS.
But wait... who are you? Where did you come from?
I am Diana. Where I come from...

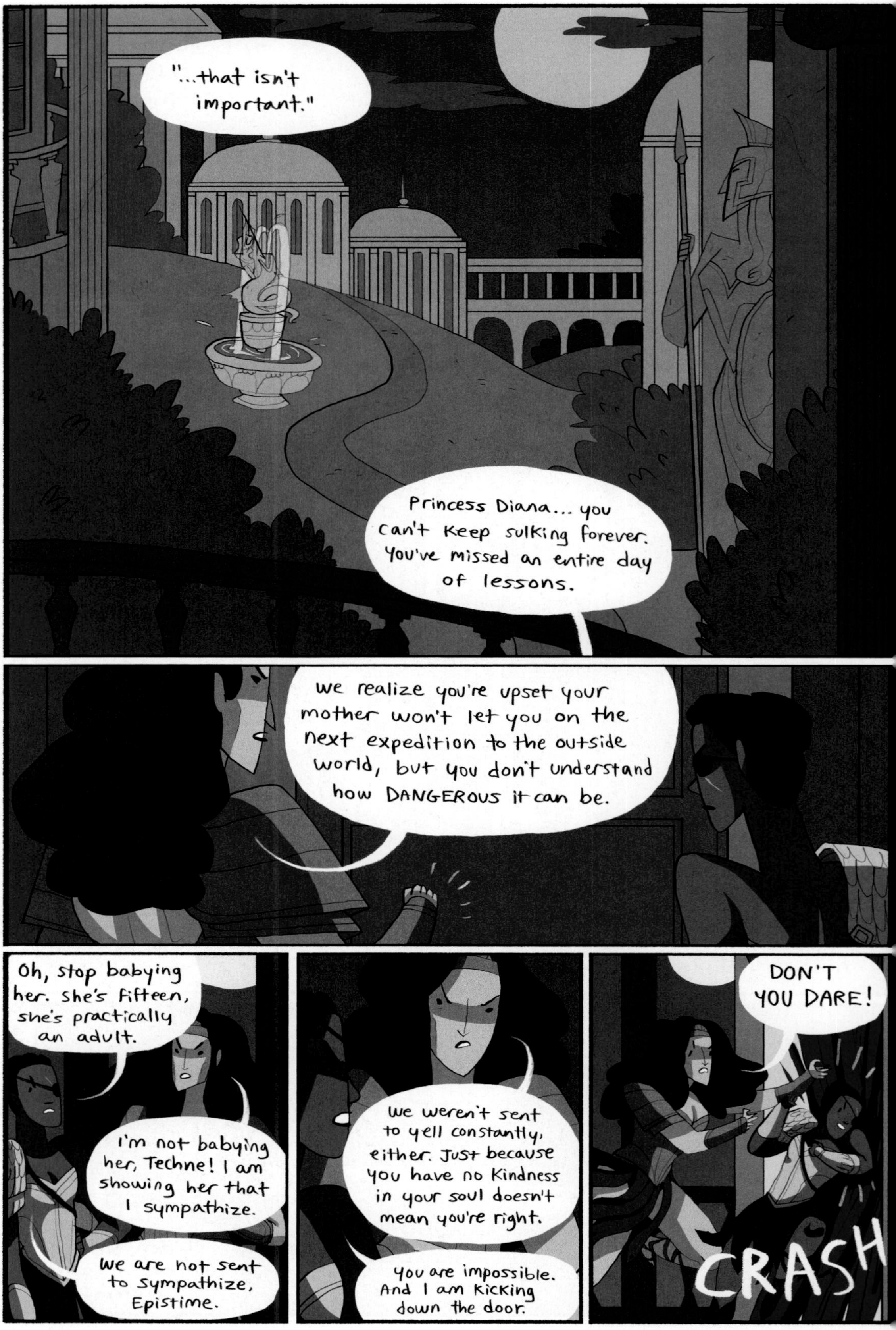
"...that isn't important."
Princess Diana... you can't keep sulking forever. You've missed an entire day of lessons.
We realize you're upset your mother won't let you on the next expedition to the outside world, but you don't understand how DANGEROUS it can be.
Oh, stop babying her. She's fifteen, she's practically an adult.
I'm not babying her, Techne! I am showing her that I sympathize.
We are not sent to sympathize, Epistime.
We weren't sent to yell constantly, either. Just because you have no kindness in your soul doesn't mean you're right.
You are impossible. And I am kicking down the door.
DON'T YOU DARE!
CRASH

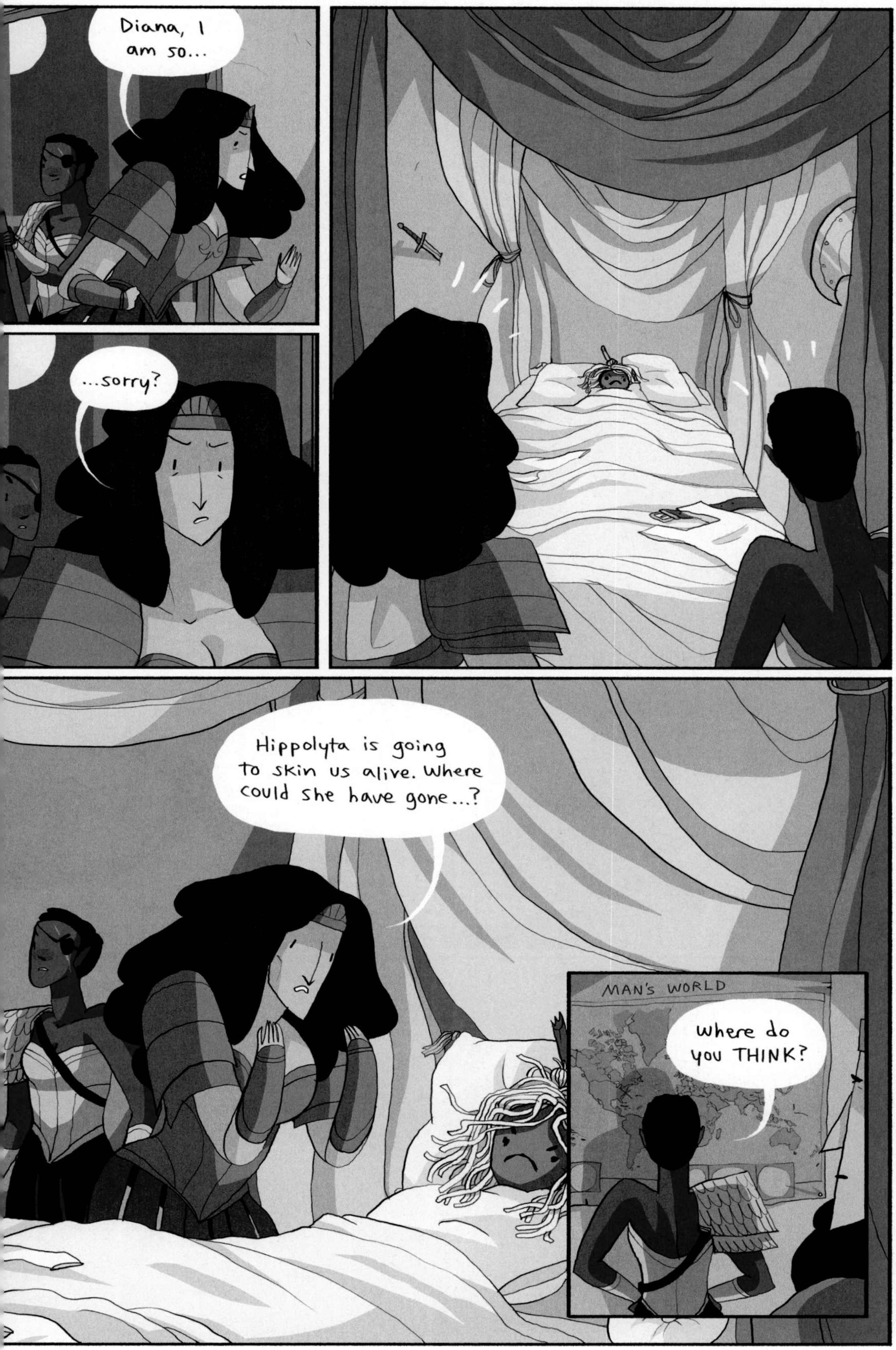
Diana, I am so...
...sorry?
Hippolyta is going to skin us alive. Where could she have gone...?
MAN'S WORLD
Where do you THINK?

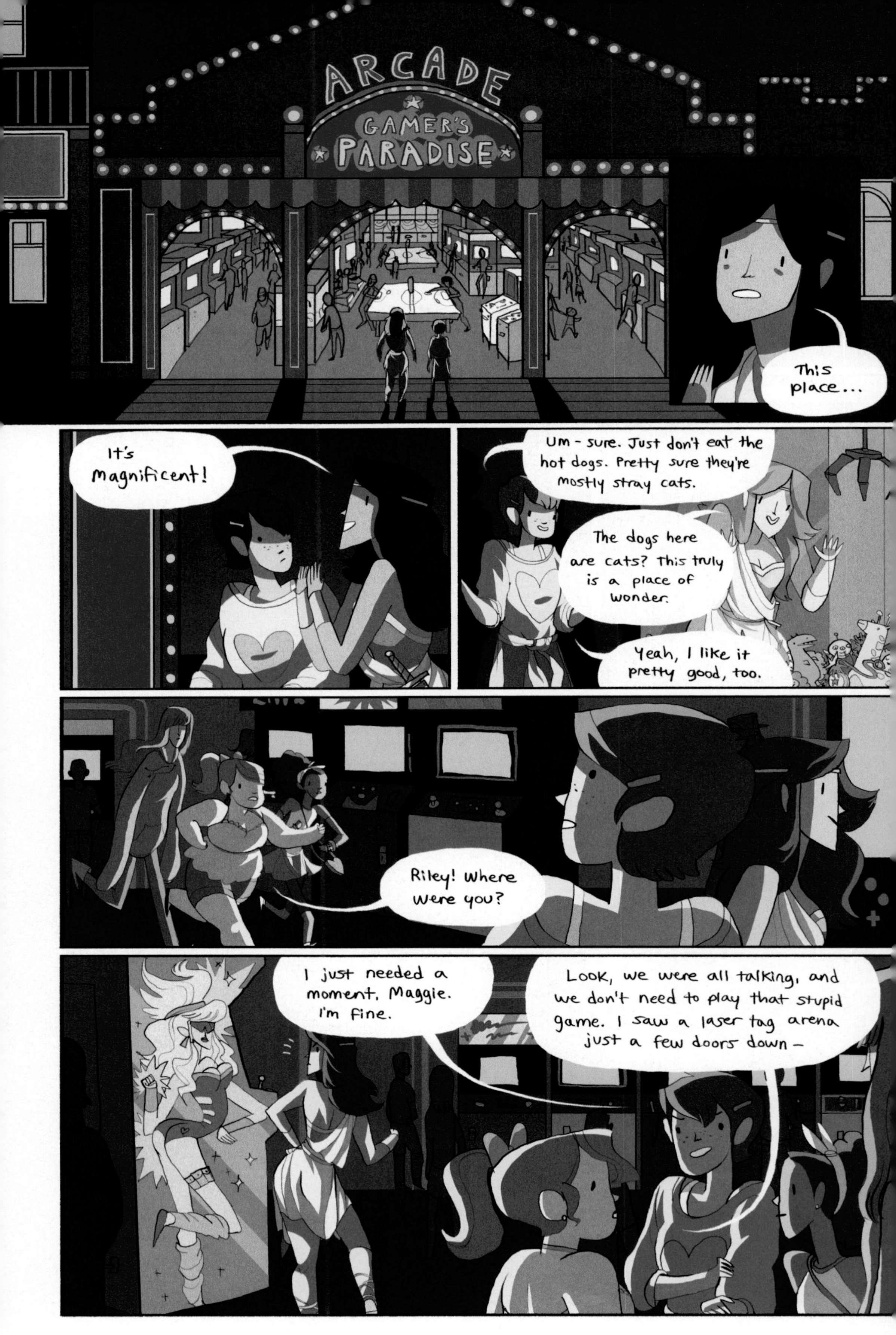
ARCADE
GAMER'S PARADISE
This place...
It's magnificent!
Um - sure. Just don't eat the hot dogs. Pretty sure they're mostly stray cats.
The dogs here are cats? This truly is a place of wonder.
Yeah, I like it pretty good, too.
Riley! Where were you?
I just needed a moment, Maggie. I'm fine.
Look, we were all talking, and we don't need to play that stupid game. I saw a laser tag arena just a few doors down -

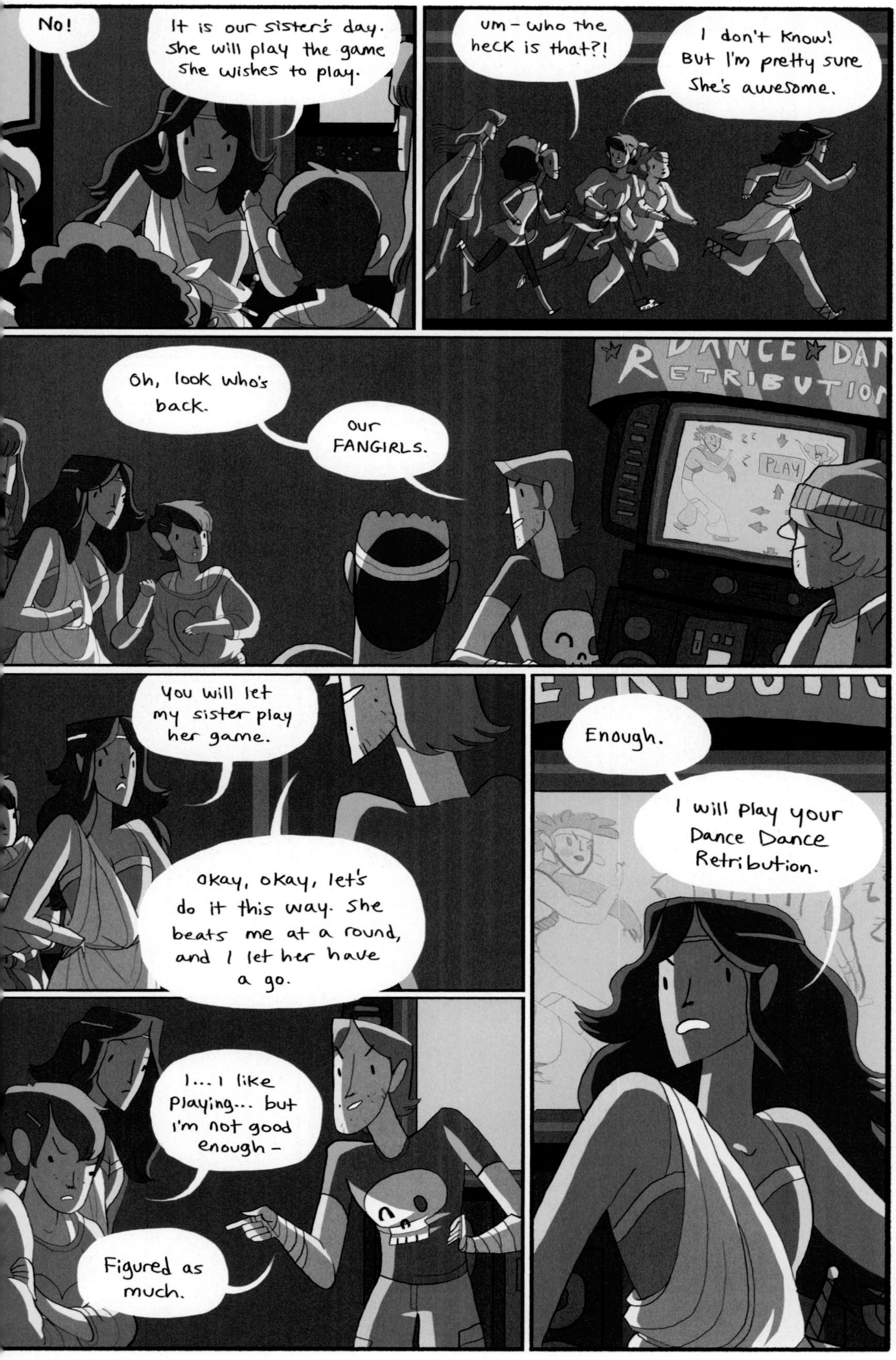
No!
It is our sister's day. She will play the game she wishes to play.
Um - who the heck is that?!
I don't know! But I'm pretty sure she's awesome.
DANCE DANCE RETRIBUTION
PLAY
Oh, look who's back.
Our FANGIRLS.
You will let my sister play her game.
Okay, okay, let's do it this way. She beats me at a round, and I let her have a go.
I... I like playing... but I'm not good enough -
Figured as much.
Enough.
I will play your Dance Dance Retribution.

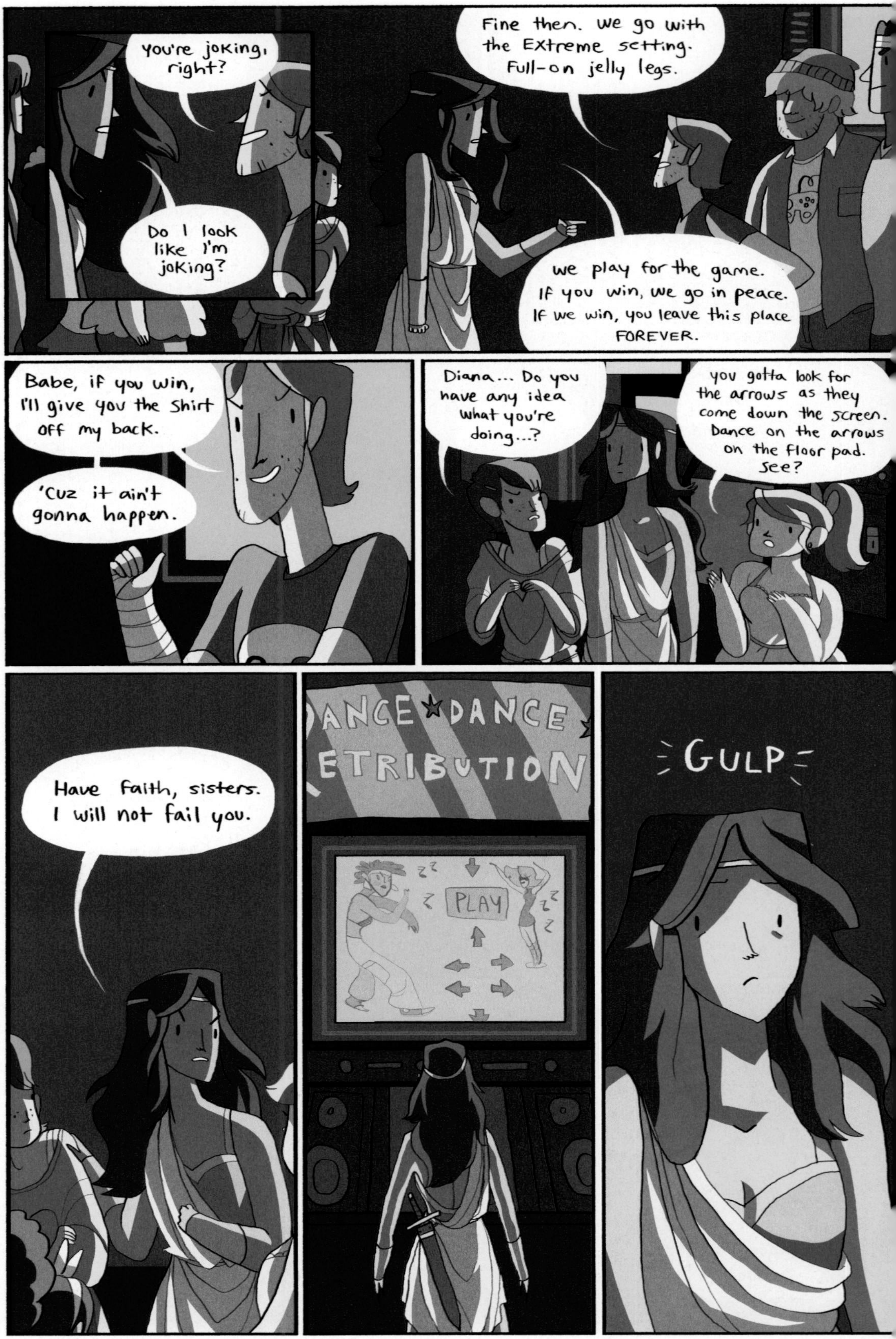
You're joking, right?
Do I look like I'm joking?
Fine then. We go with the Extreme setting. Full-on jelly legs.
We play for the game. If you win, we go in peace. If we win, you leave this place FOREVER.
Babe, if you win, I'll give you the shirt off my back.
'Cuz it ain't gonna happen.
Diana... Do you have any idea what you're doing...?
You gotta look for the arrows as they come down the screen. Dance on the arrows on the floor pad. See?
Have faith, sisters. I will not fail you.
DANCE DANCE RETRIBUTION
PLAY
GULP

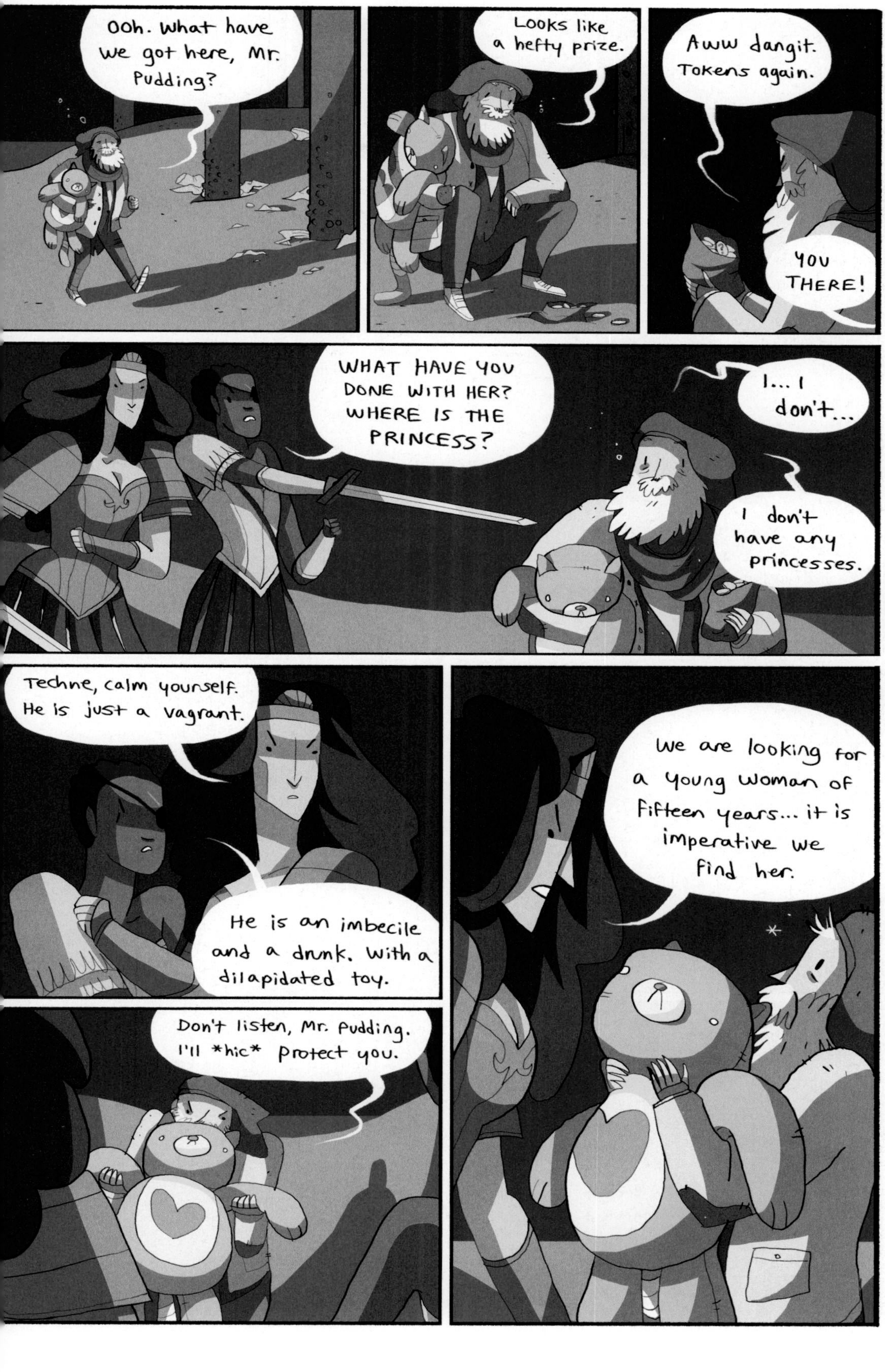
Ooh. What have we got here, Mr. Pudding?
Looks like a hefty prize.
Aww dangit. Tokens again.
YOU THERE!
WHAT HAVE YOU DONE WITH HER? WHERE IS THE PRINCESS?
I... I don't...
I don't have any princesses.
Techne, calm yourself. He is just a vagrant.
He is an imbecile and a drunk. With a dilapidated toy.
Don't listen, Mr. Pudding. I'll *hic* protect you.
We are looking for a young woman of fifteen years... it is imperative we find her.

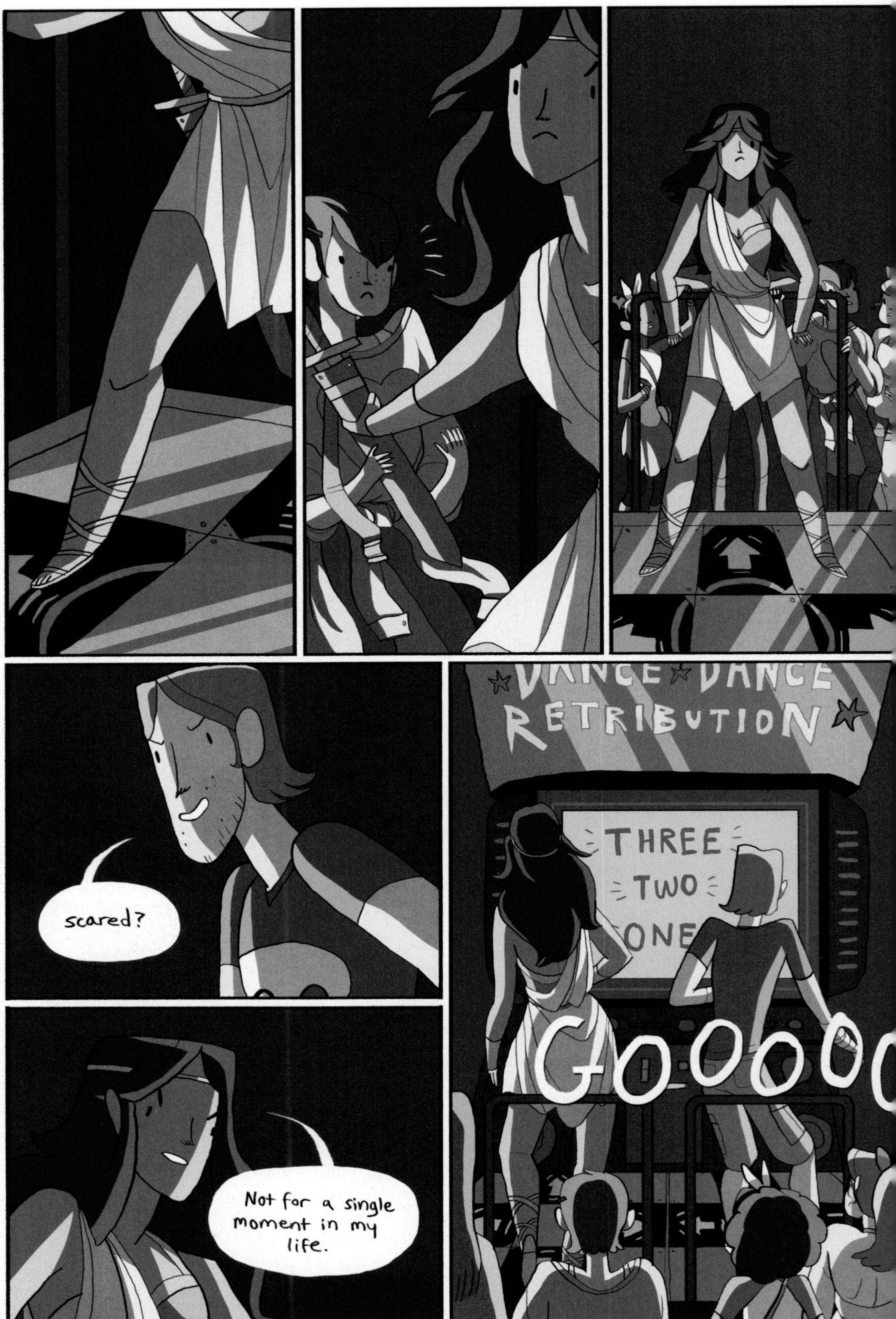
DANCE DANCE RETRIBUTION
scared?
THREE
TWO
ONE
Not for a single moment in my life.
GOOOOO

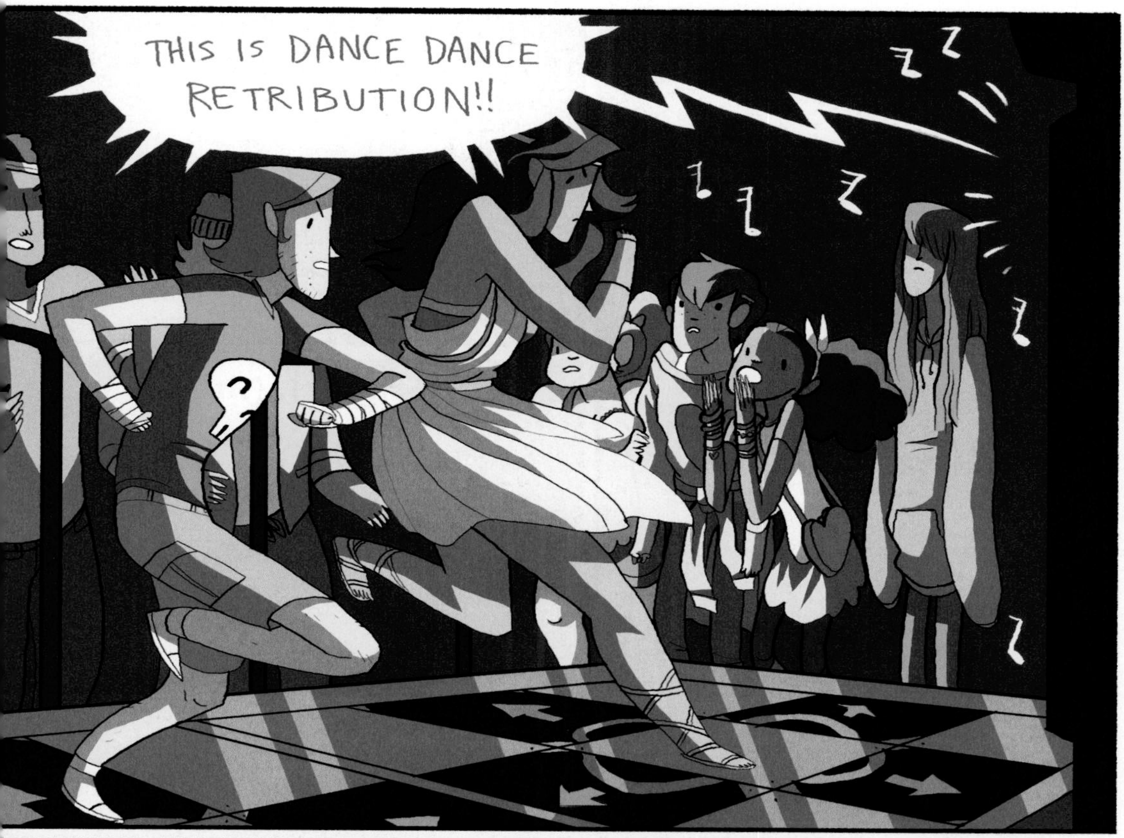
THIS IS DANCE DANCE RETRIBUTION!!
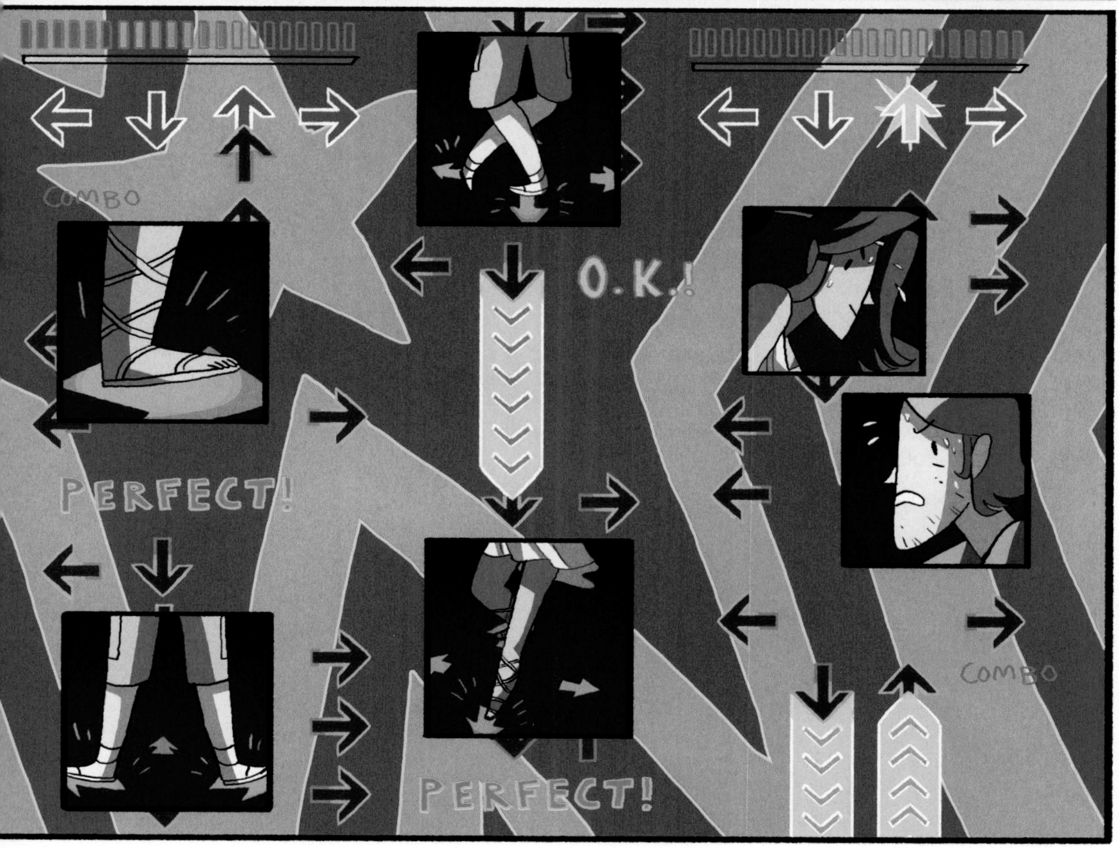
COMBO
O.K.!
PERFECT!
COMBO
PERFECT!

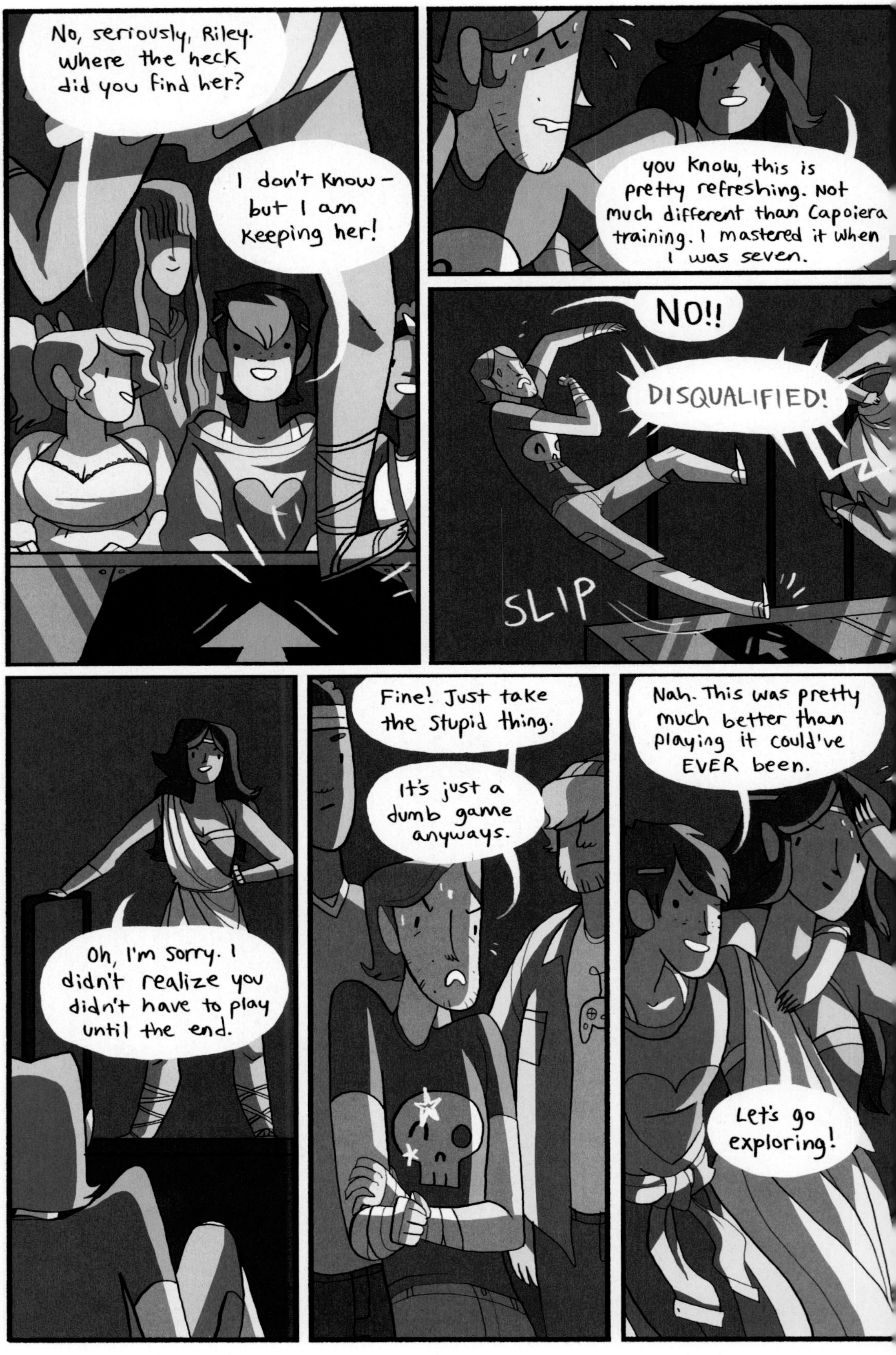
No, seriously, Riley. where the heck did you find her?
I don't know - but I am keeping her!
you know, this is pretty refreshing. Not much different than Capoiera training. I mastered it when I was seven.
NO!!
DISQUALIFIED!
SLIP
Oh, I'm sorry. I didn't realize you didn't have to play until the end.
Fine! Just take the stupid thing.
It's just a dumb game anyways.
Nah. This was pretty much better than playing it could've EVER been.
Let's go exploring!

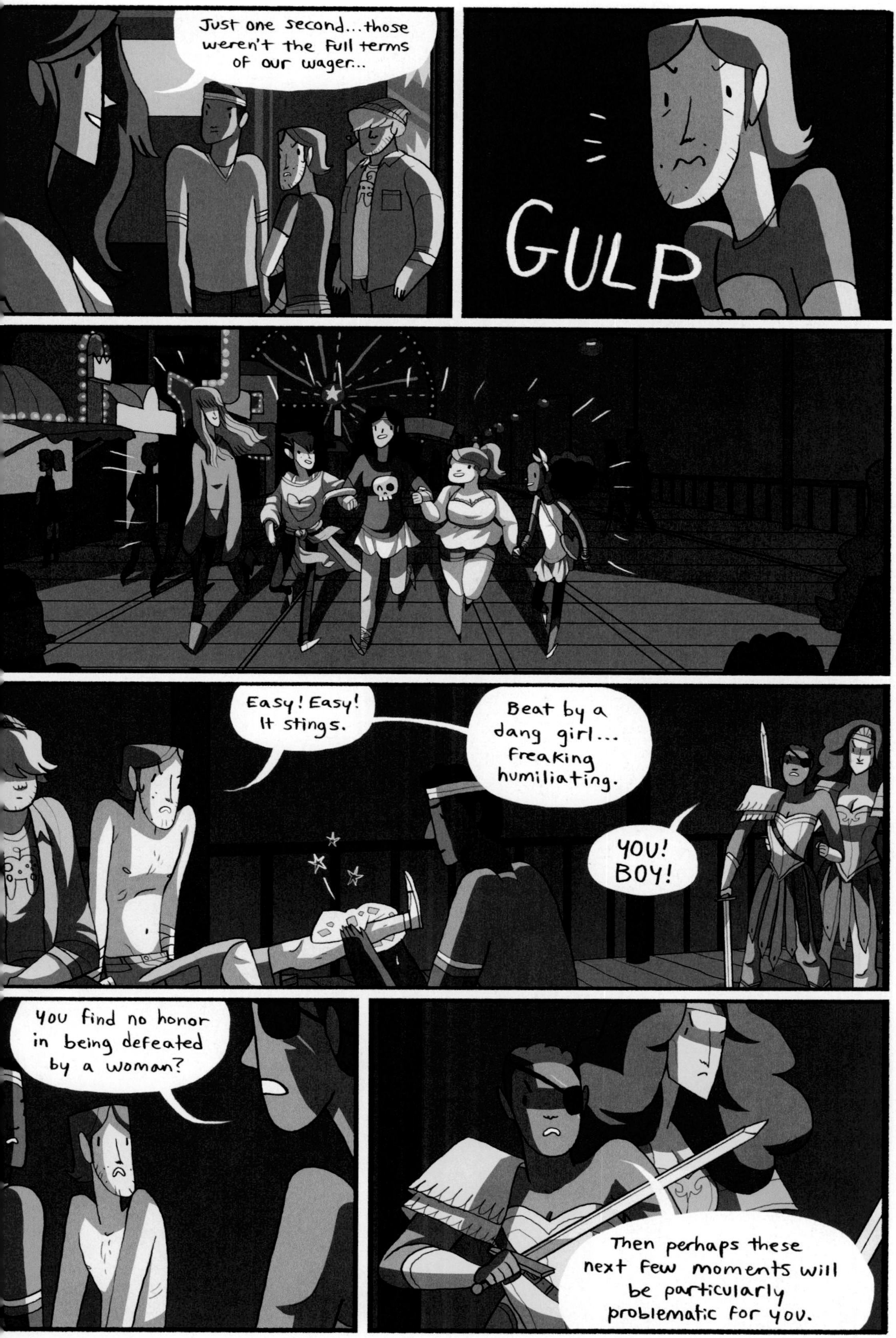
Just one second...those weren't the full terms of our wager...
GULP
Easy! Easy! It stings.
Beat by a dang girl... freaking humiliating.
YOU! BOY!
You find no honor in being defeated by a woman?
Then perhaps these next few moments will be particularly problematic for you.

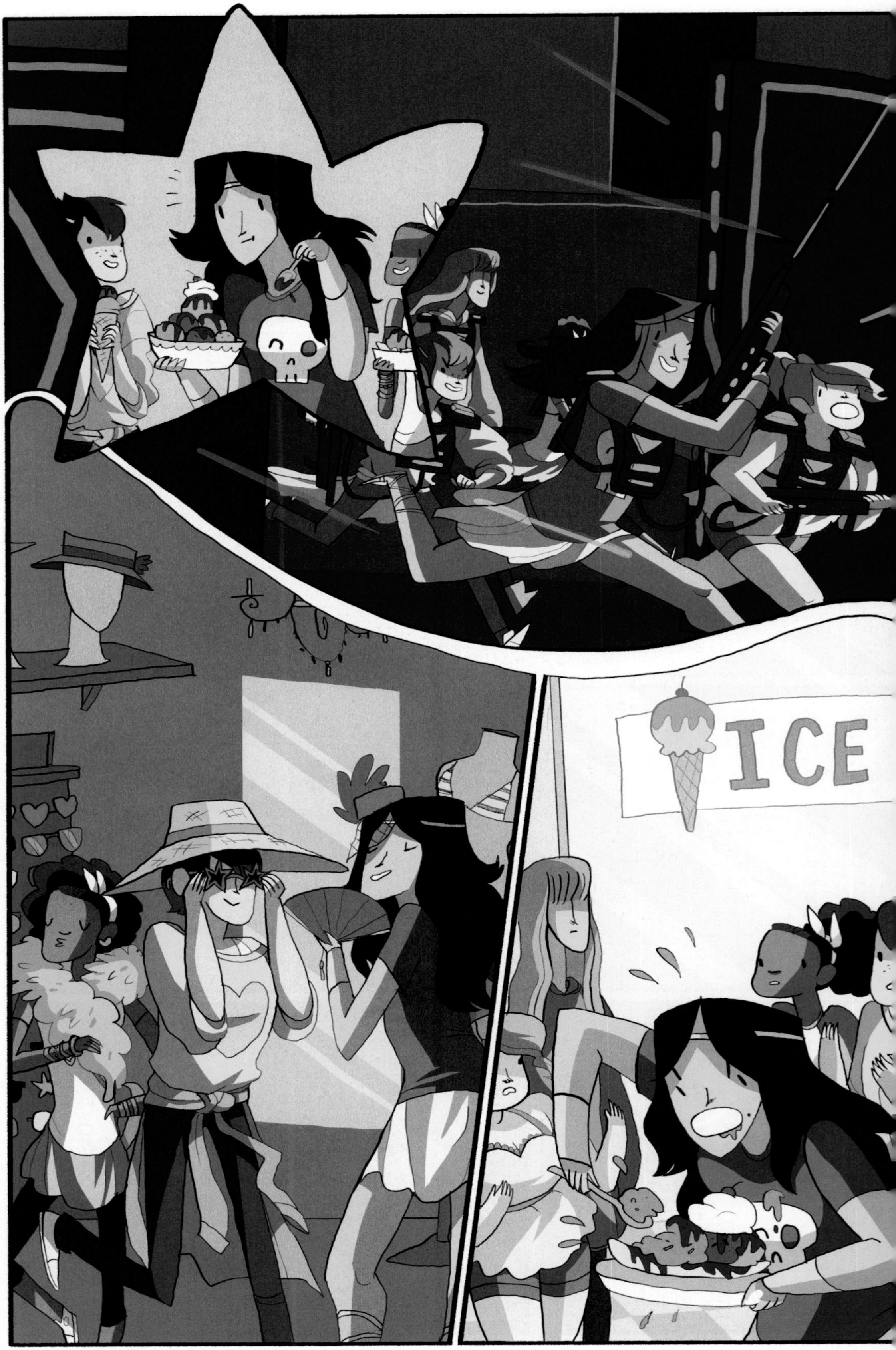
ICE

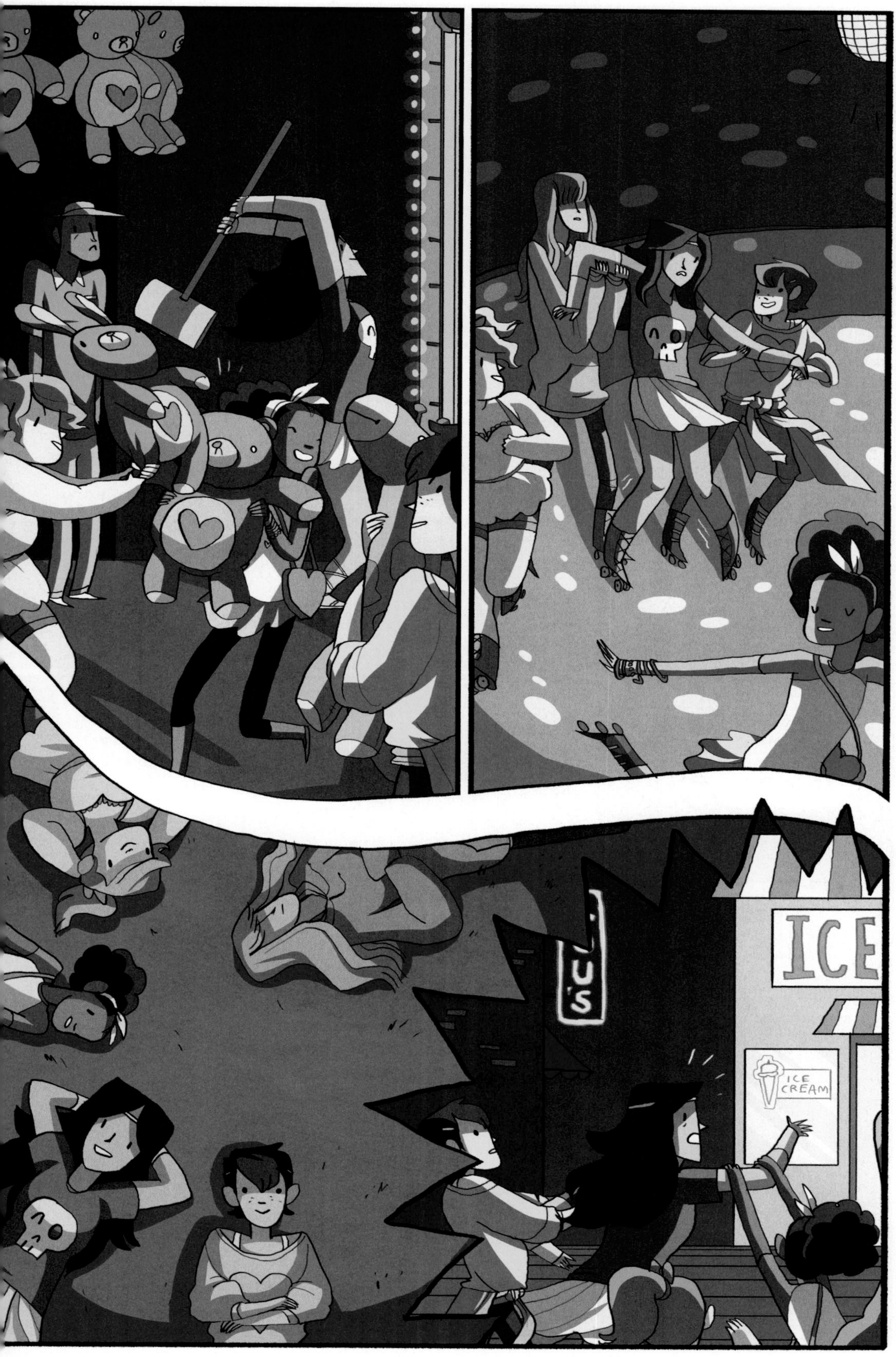
ICE
ICE CREAM

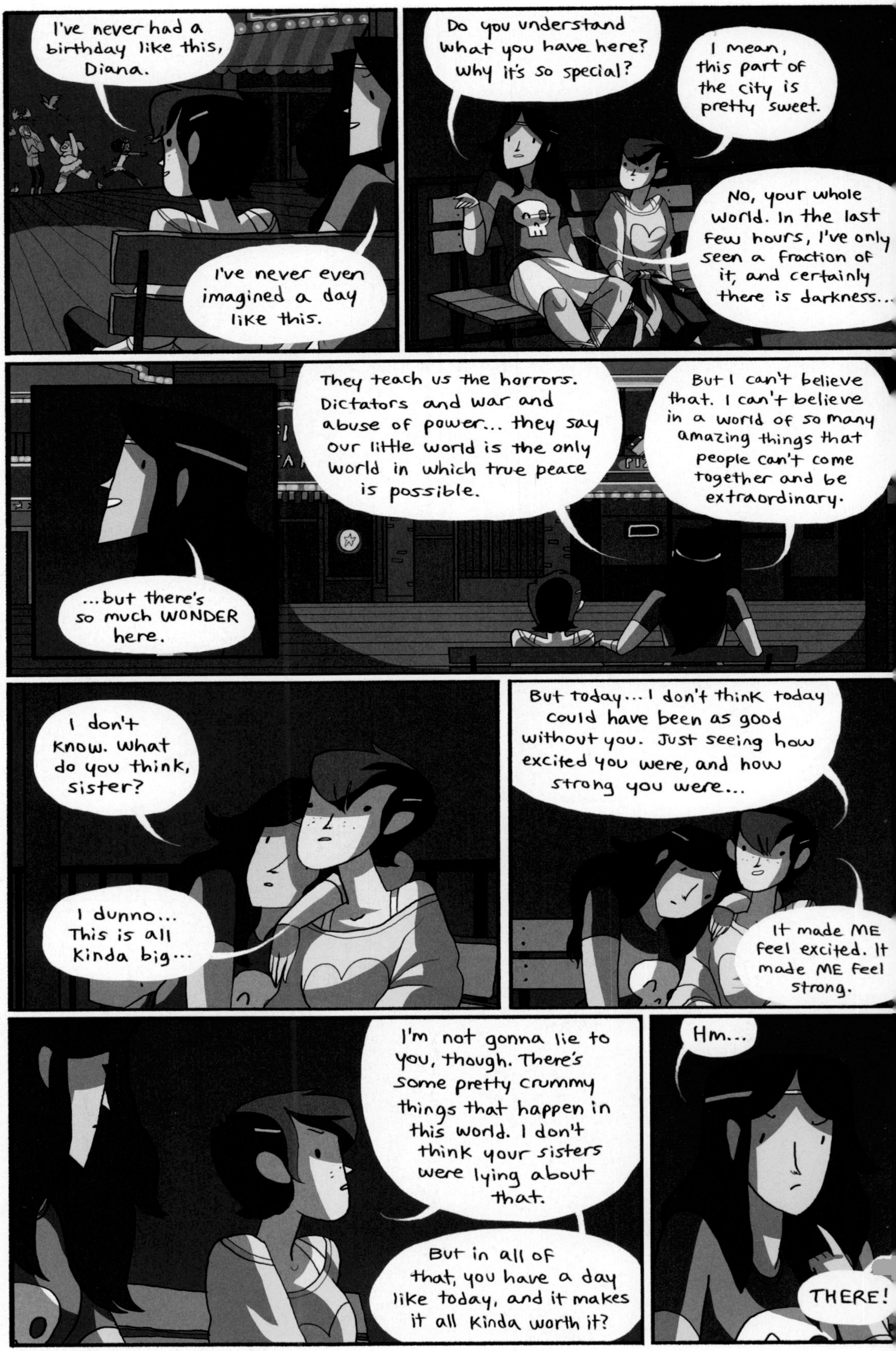
I've never had a birthday like this, Diana.
I've never even imagined a day like this.
Do you understand what you have here? Why it's so special?
I mean, this part of the city is pretty sweet.
No, your whole world. In the last few hours, I've only seen a fraction of it, and certainly there is darkness...
...but there's so much WONDER here.
They teach us the horrors. Dictators and war and abuse of power... they say our little world is the only world in which true peace is possible.
But I can't believe that. I can't believe in a world of so many amazing things that people can't come together and be extraordinary.
I don't know. What do you think, sister?
I dunno... This is all kinda big...
But today... I don't think today could have been as good without you. Just seeing how excited you were, and how strong you were...
It made ME feel excited. It made ME feel strong.
I'm not gonna lie to you, though. There's some pretty crummy things that happen in this world. I don't think your sisters were lying about that.
But in all of that, you have a day like today, and it makes it all kinda worth it?
Hm...
THERE!

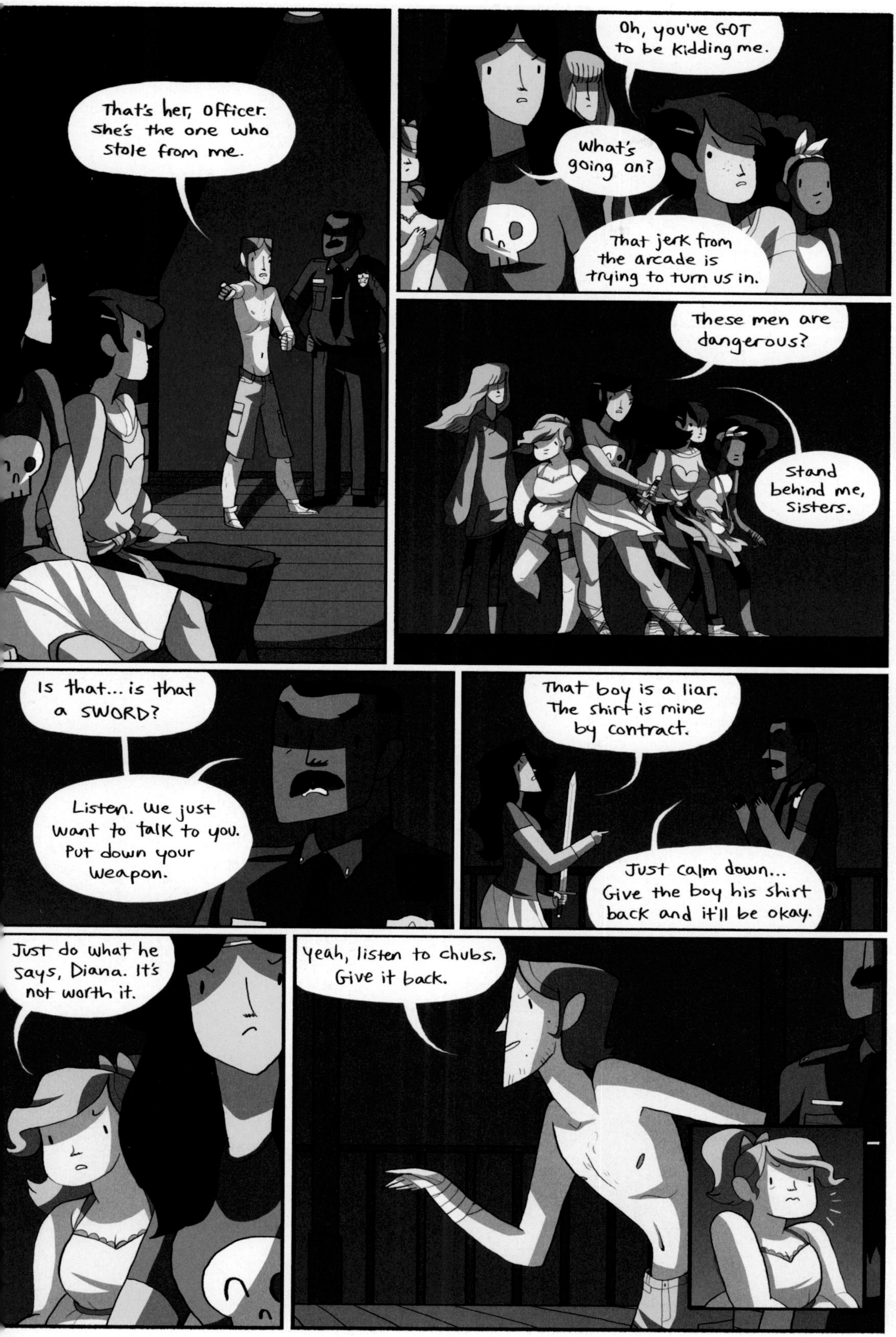
That's her, Officer. She's the one who stole from me.
Oh, you've GOT to be kidding me.
What's going on?
That jerk from the arcade is trying to turn us in.
These men are dangerous?
Stand behind me, Sisters.
Is that... is that a SWORD?
Listen. We just want to talk to you. Put down your weapon.
That boy is a liar. The shirt is mine by contract.
Just calm down... Give the boy his shirt back and it'll be okay.
Just do what he says, Diana. It's not worth it.
Yeah, listen to chubs. Give it back.

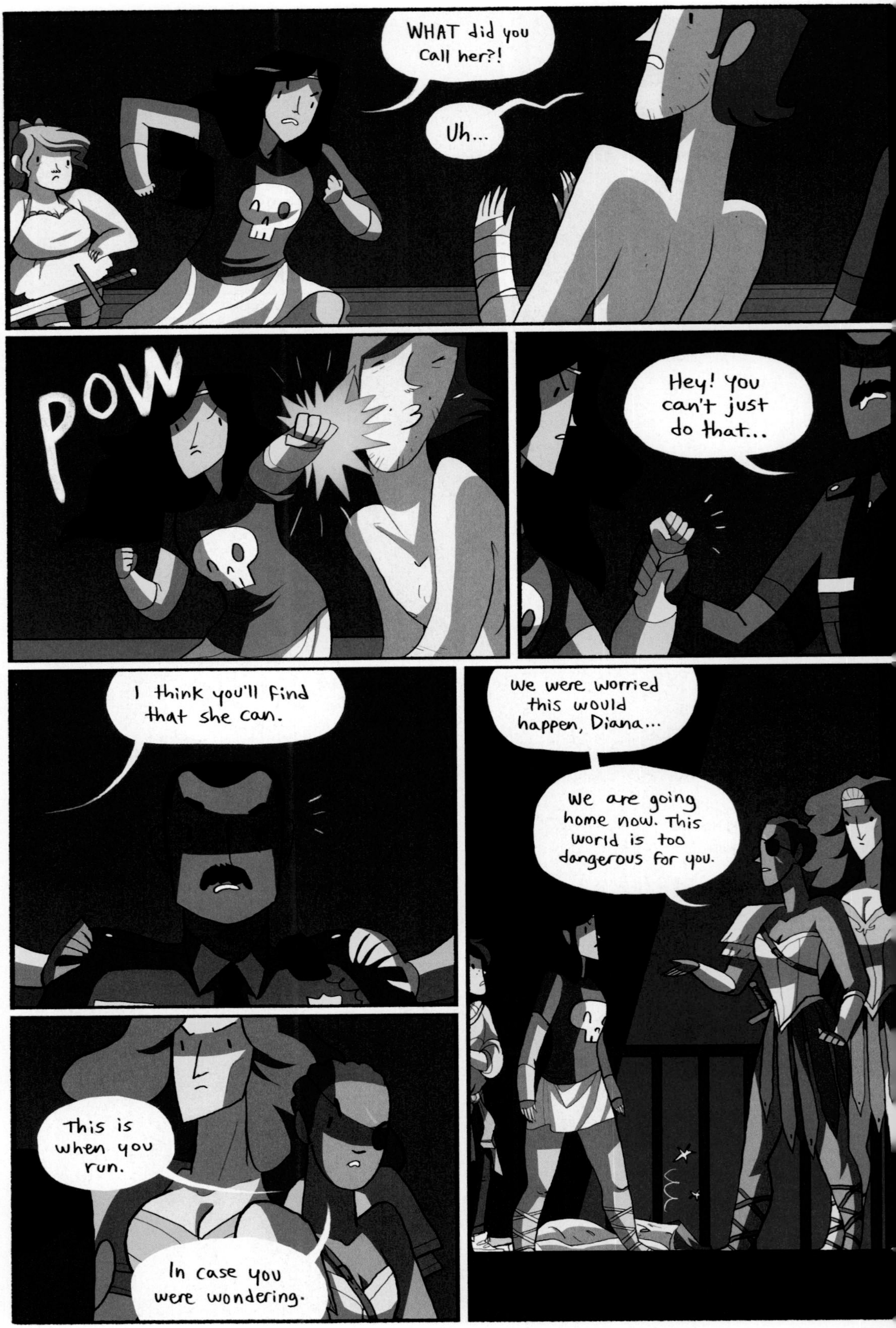
WHAT did you call her?!
Uh...
POW
Hey! You can't just do that...
I think you'll find that she can.
We were worried this would happen, Diana...
We are going home now. This world is too dangerous for you.
This is when you run.
In case you were wondering.

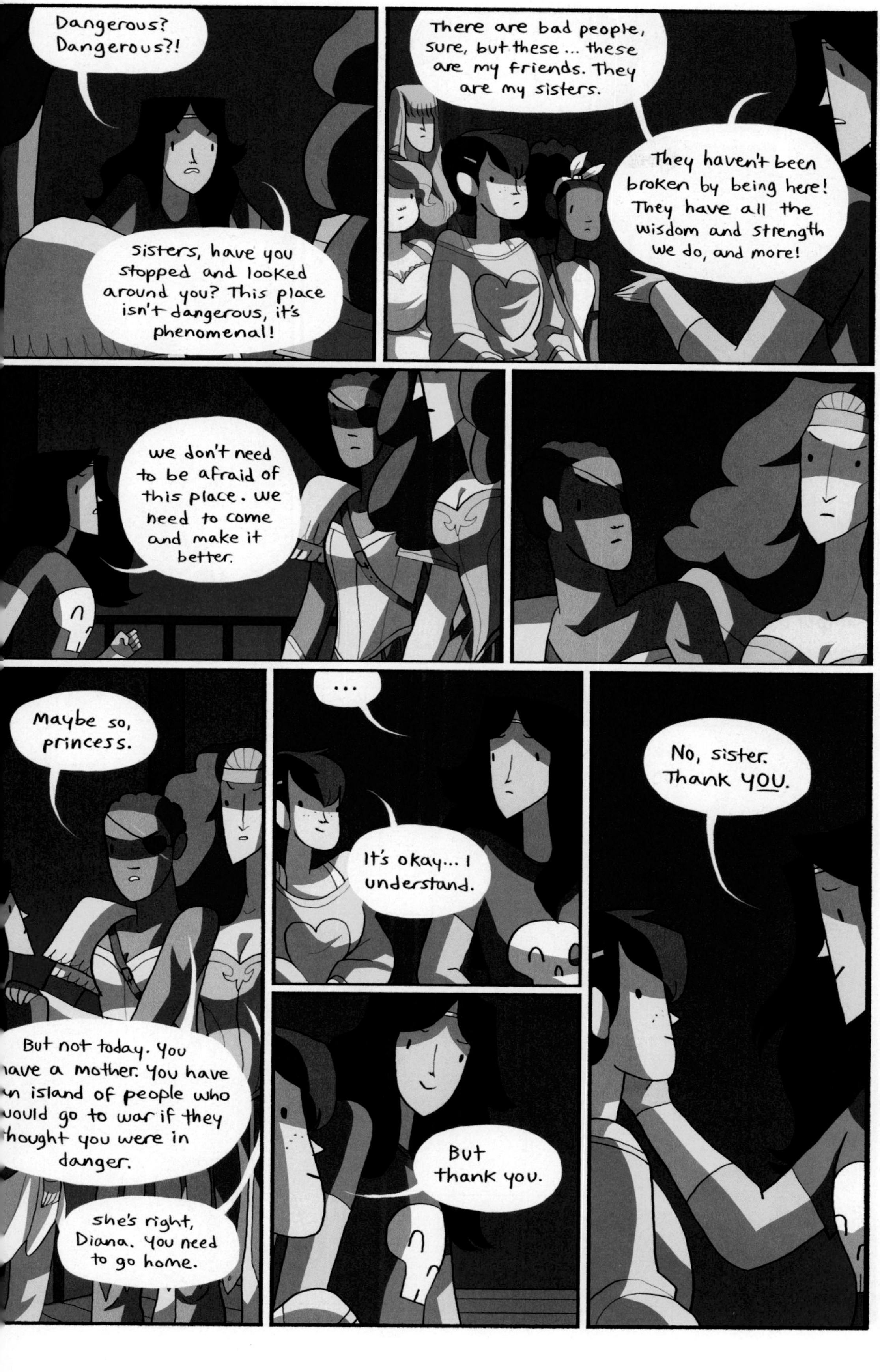
Dangerous? Dangerous?!
Sisters, have you stopped and looked around you? This place isn't dangerous, it's phenomenal!
There are bad people, sure, but these ... these are my friends. They are my sisters.
They haven't been broken by being here! They have all the wisdom and strength we do, and more!
We don't need to be afraid of this place. We need to come and make it better.
Maybe so, princess.
But not today. You have a mother. You have an island of people who would go to war if they thought you were in danger.
She's right, Diana. You need to go home.
...
It's okay... I understand.
But thank you.
No, sister. Thank YOU.

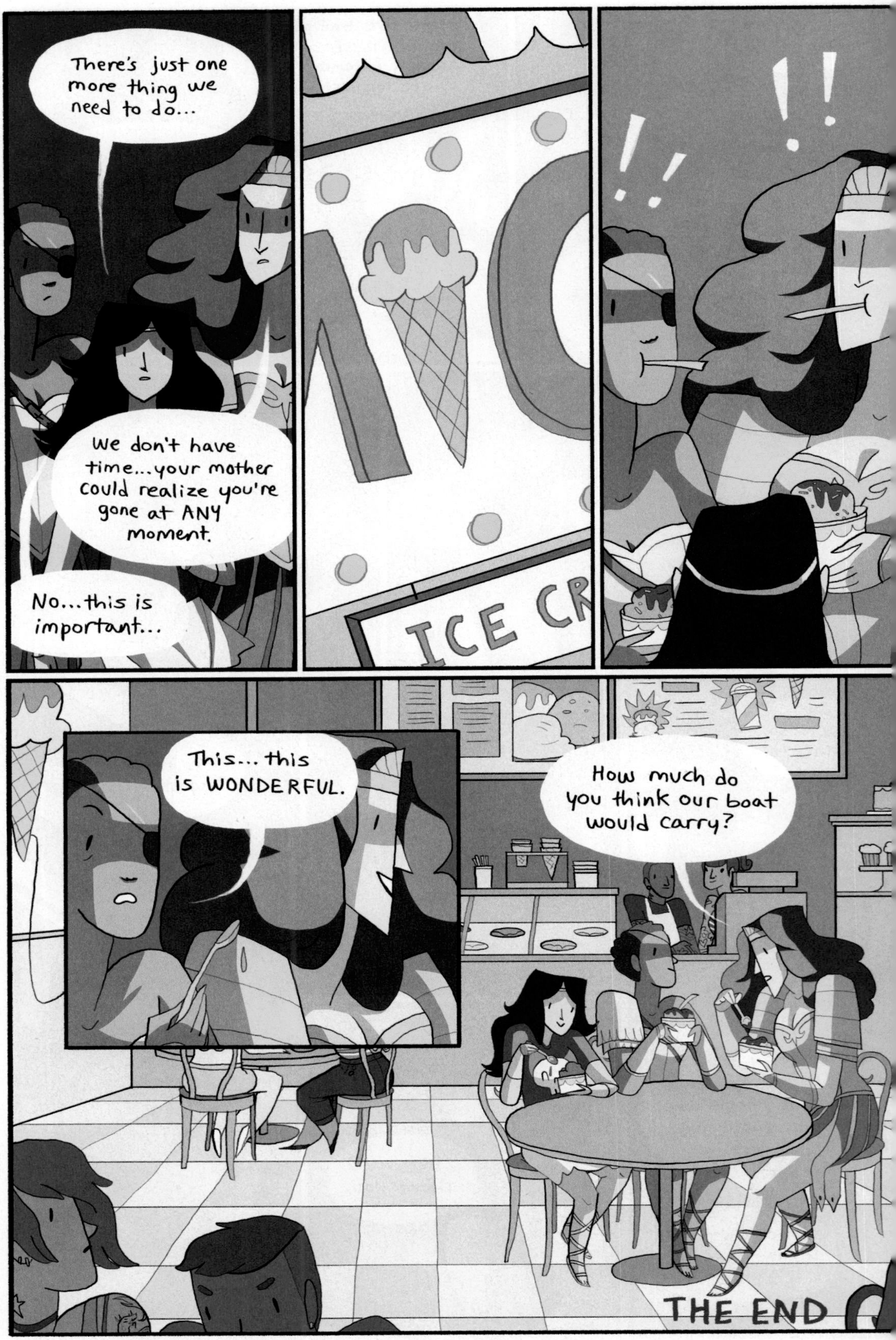
There's just one more thing we need to do...
We don't have time...your mother could realize you're gone at ANY moment.
No...this is important...
ICE CR
!!
!!
This... this is WONDERFUL.
How much do you think our boat would carry?
THE END

THE PROBLEM WITH CATS

LAUREN BEUKES
WRITER

MIKE MAIHACK
ARTIST

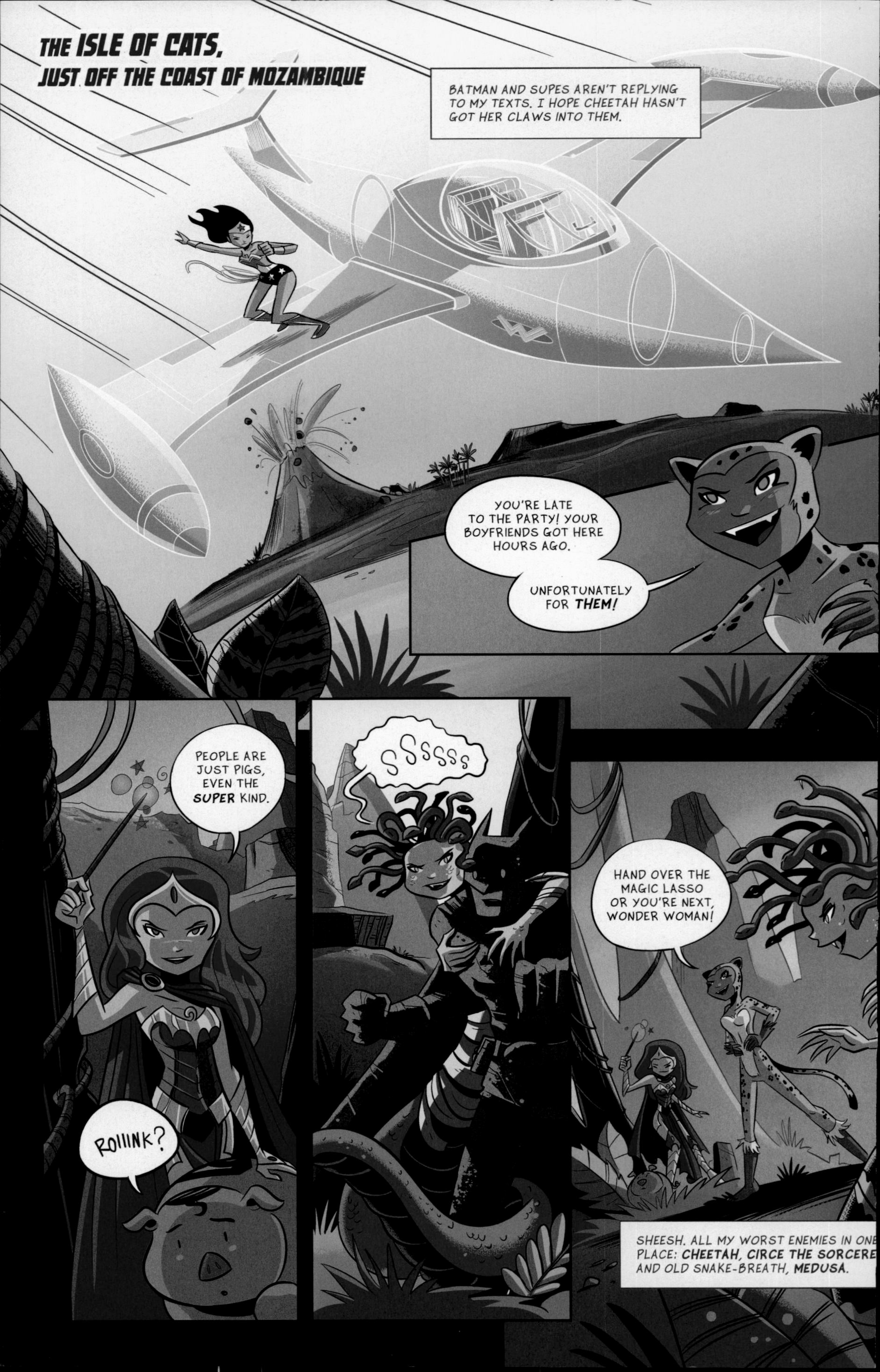
THE ISLE OF CATS,
JUST OFF THE COAST OF MOZAMBIQUE
BATMAN AND SUPES AREN'T REPLYING TO MY TEXTS. I HOPE CHEETAH HASN'T GOT HER CLAWS INTO THEM.
YOU'RE LATE TO THE PARTY! YOUR BOYFRIENDS GOT HERE HOURS AGO.
UNFORTUNATELY FOR THEM!
PEOPLE ARE JUST PIGS, EVEN THE SUPER KIND.
ROIIINK?
SSSSSS
HAND OVER THE MAGIC LASSO OR YOU'RE NEXT, WONDER WOMAN!
SHEESH. ALL MY WORST ENEMIES IN ONE PLACE: CHEETAH, CIRCE THE SORCERE AND OLD SNAKE-BREATH, MEDUSA.

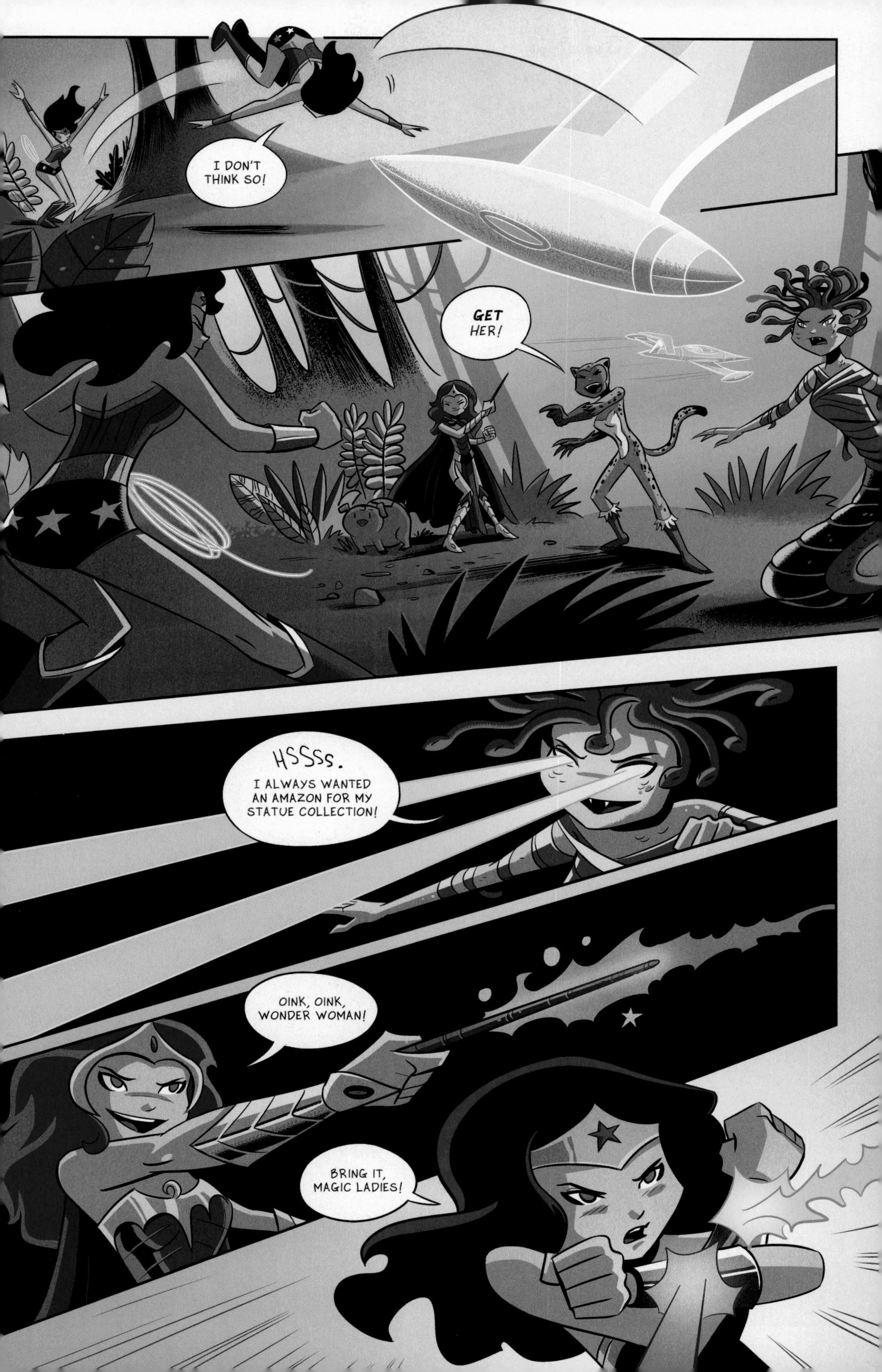
I DON'T THINK SO!
GET HER!
HSSSS. I ALWAYS WANTED AN AMAZON FOR MY STATUE COLLECTION!
OINK, OINK, WONDER WOMAN!
BRING IT, MAGIC LADIES!

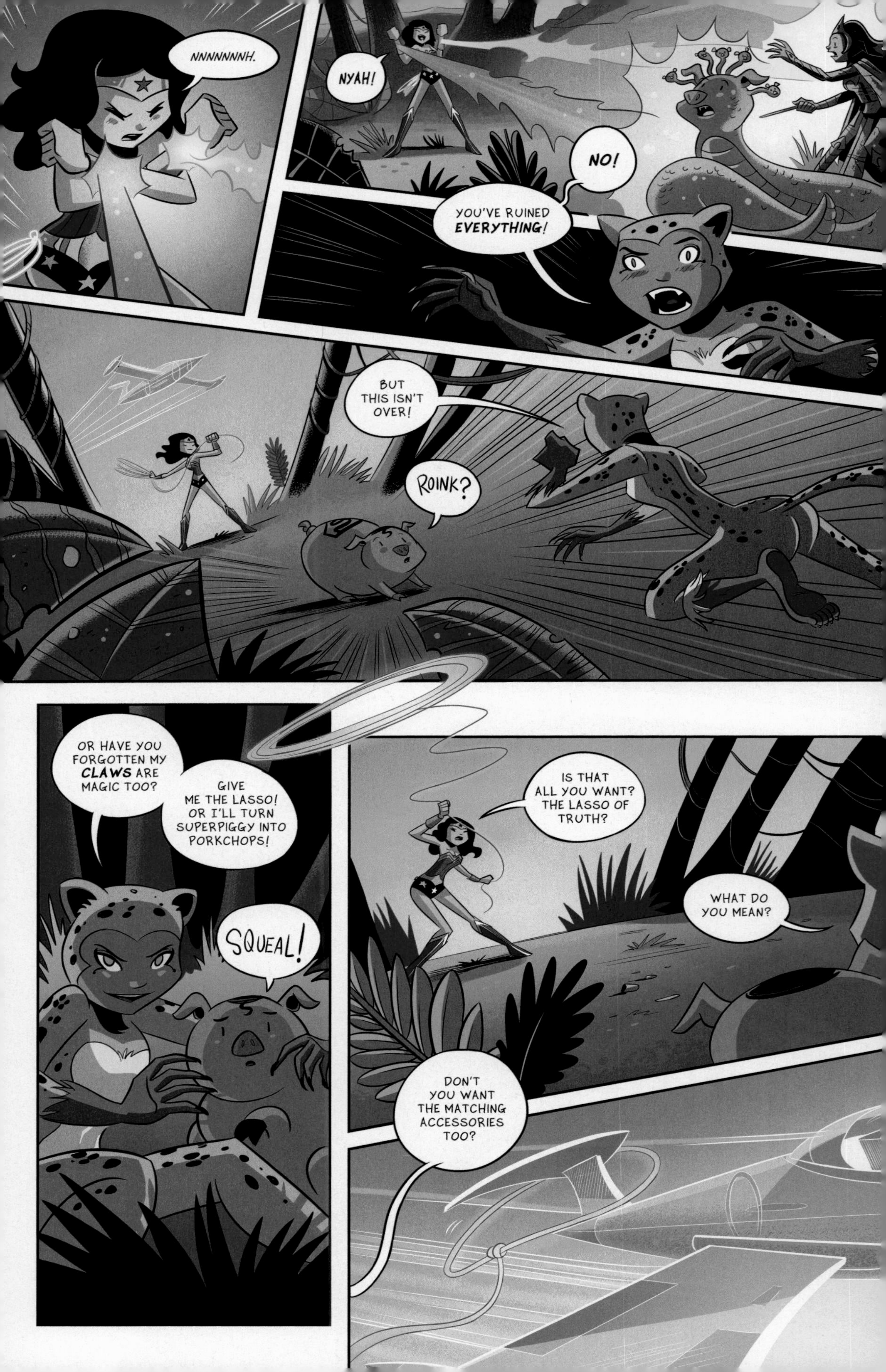
NNNNNNNH.
NYAH!
NO!
YOU'VE RUINED **EVERYTHING**!
BUT THIS ISN'T OVER!
ROINK?
OR HAVE YOU FORGOTTEN MY **CLAWS** ARE MAGIC TOO?
GIVE ME THE LASSO! OR I'LL TURN SUPERPIGGY INTO PORKCHOPS!
SQUEAL!
IS THAT ALL YOU WANT? THE LASSO OF TRUTH?
WHAT DO YOU MEAN?
DON'T YOU WANT THE MATCHING ACCESSORIES TOO?

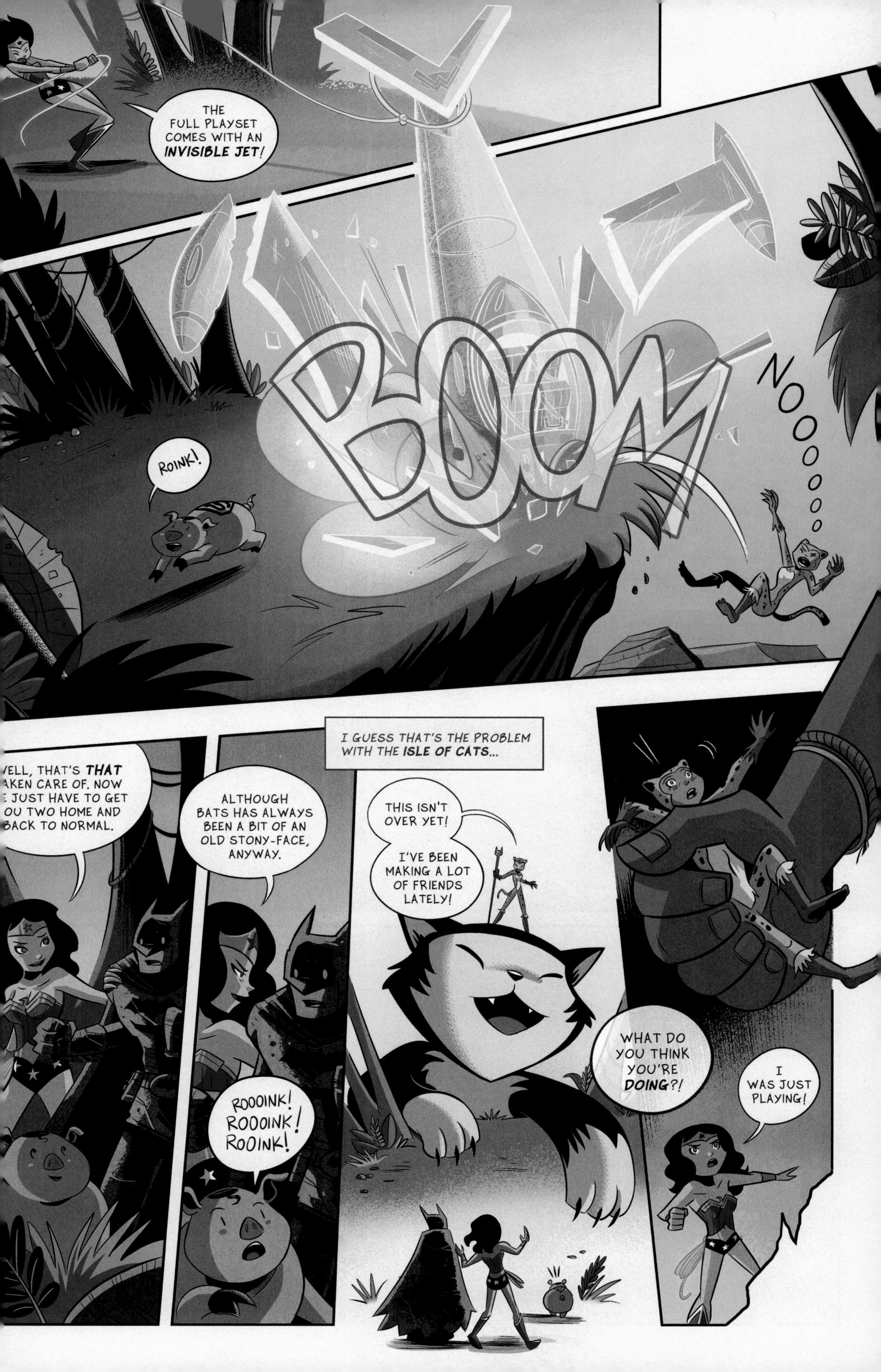

THE FULL PLAYSET COMES WITH AN INVISIBLE JET!
BOOM
NOOOOOOOO
ROINK!
WELL, THAT'S THAT TAKEN CARE OF. NOW WE JUST HAVE TO GET YOU TWO HOME AND BACK TO NORMAL.
ALTHOUGH BATS HAS ALWAYS BEEN A BIT OF AN OLD STONY-FACE, ANYWAY.
ROOOINK! ROOOINK! ROOINK!
I GUESS THAT'S THE PROBLEM WITH THE ISLE OF CATS...
THIS ISN'T OVER YET!
I'VE BEEN MAKING A LOT OF FRIENDS LATELY!
WHAT DO YOU THINK YOU'RE DOING?!
I WAS JUST PLAYING!

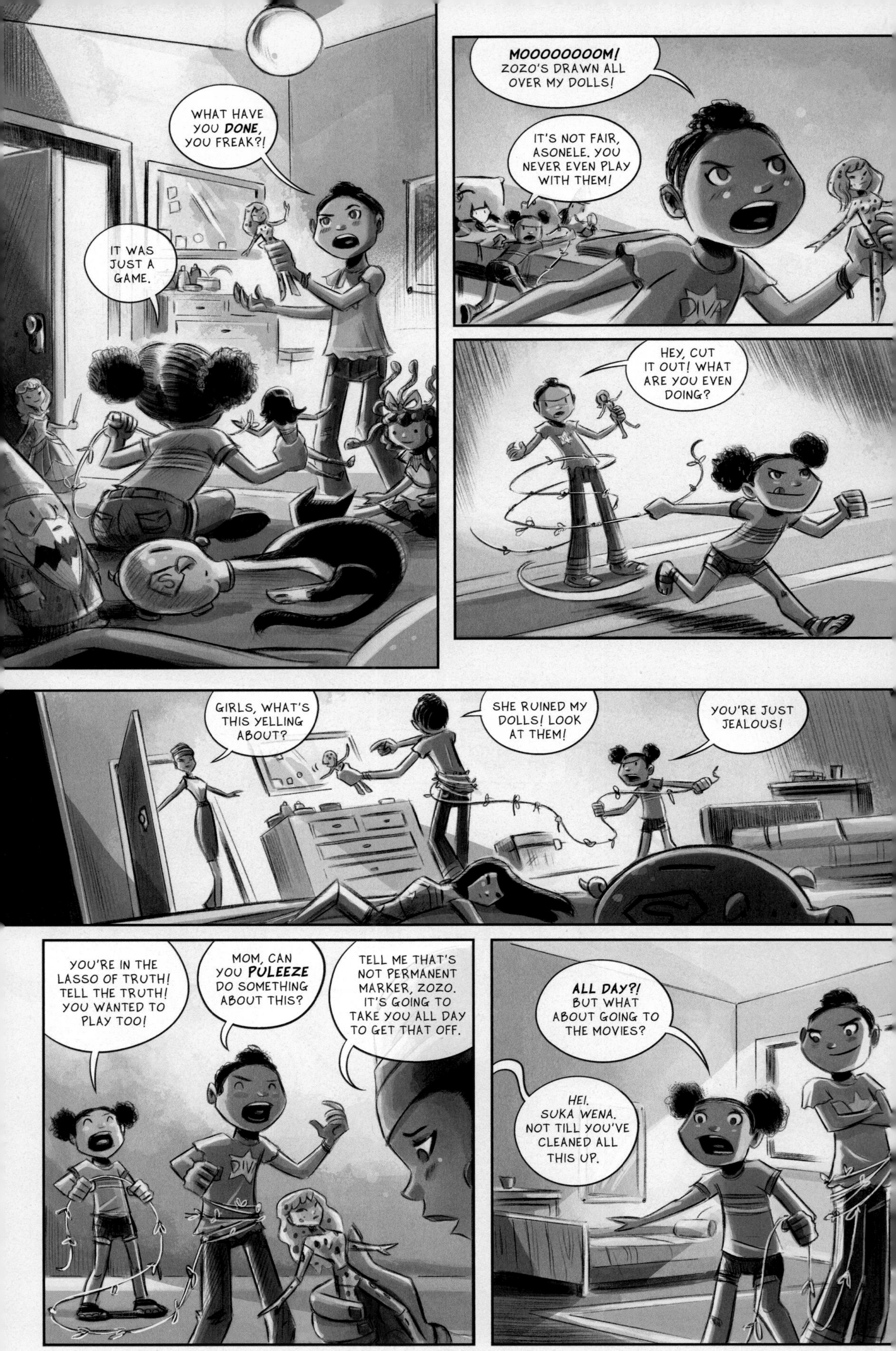
WHAT HAVE YOU **DONE**, YOU FREAK?!
IT WAS JUST A GAME.
MOOOOOOOOM! ZOZO'S DRAWN ALL OVER MY DOLLS!
IT'S NOT FAIR, ASONELE. YOU NEVER EVEN PLAY WITH THEM!
HEY, CUT IT OUT! WHAT ARE YOU EVEN DOING?
GIRLS, WHAT'S THIS YELLING ABOUT?
SHE RUINED MY DOLLS! LOOK AT THEM!
YOU'RE JUST JEALOUS!
YOU'RE IN THE LASSO OF TRUTH! TELL THE TRUTH! YOU WANTED TO PLAY TOO!
MOM, CAN YOU **PULEEZE** DO SOMETHING ABOUT THIS?
TELL ME THAT'S NOT PERMANENT MARKER, ZOZO. IT'S GOING TO TAKE YOU ALL DAY TO GET THAT OFF.
ALL DAY?! BUT WHAT ABOUT GOING TO THE MOVIES?
HEI. SUKA WENA. NOT TILL YOU'VE CLEANED ALL THIS UP.
DIVA

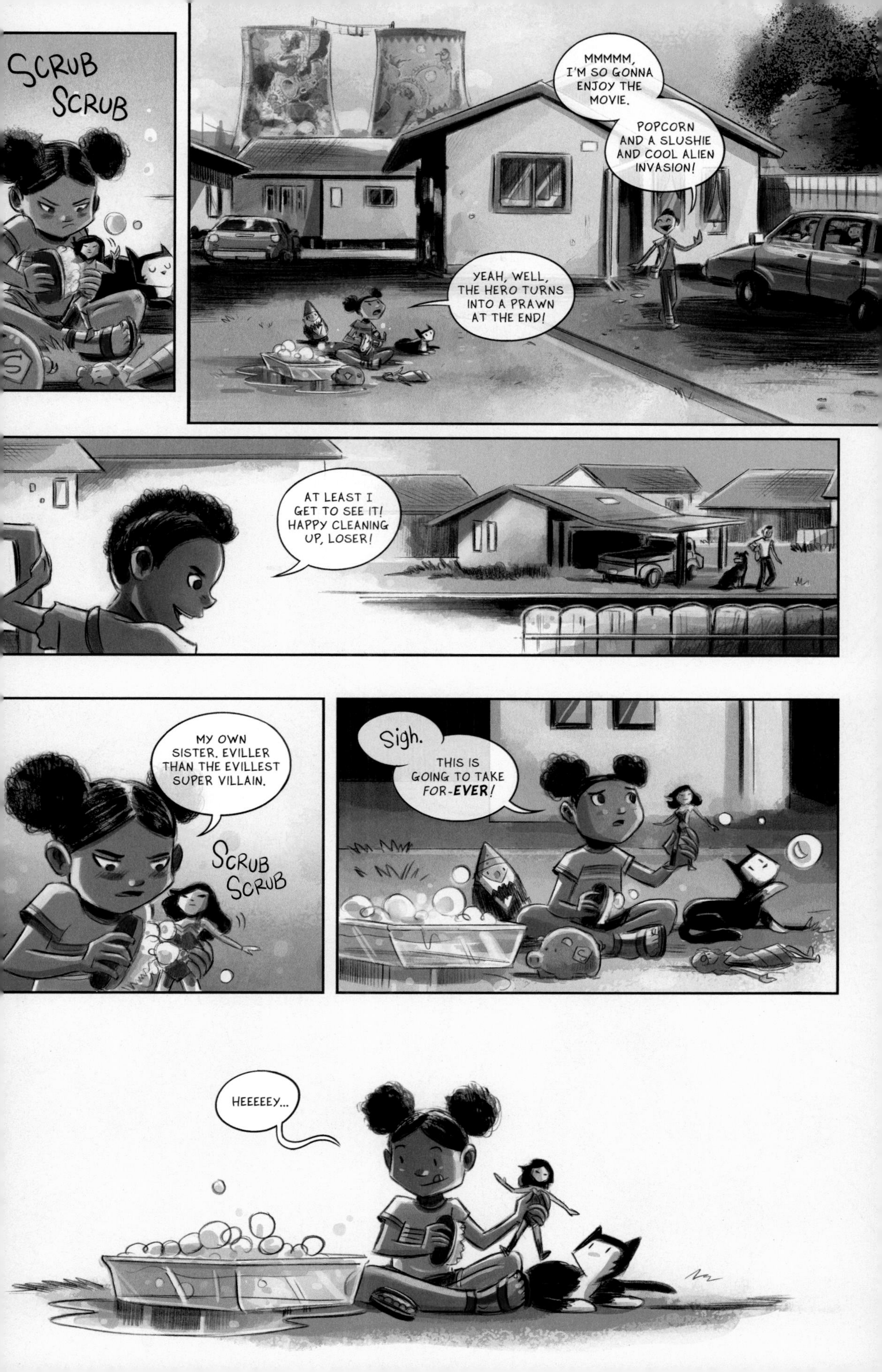
SCRUB
SCRUB
MMMMM, I'M SO GONNA ENJOY THE MOVIE.
POPCORN AND A SLUSHIE AND COOL ALIEN INVASION!
YEAH, WELL, THE HERO TURNS INTO A PRAWN AT THE END!
AT LEAST I GET TO SEE IT! HAPPY CLEANING UP, LOSER!
MY OWN SISTER. EVILLER THAN THE EVILLEST SUPER VILLAIN.
SCRUB
SCRUB
Sigh.
THIS IS GOING TO TAKE FOR-**EVER**!
HEEEEEY...

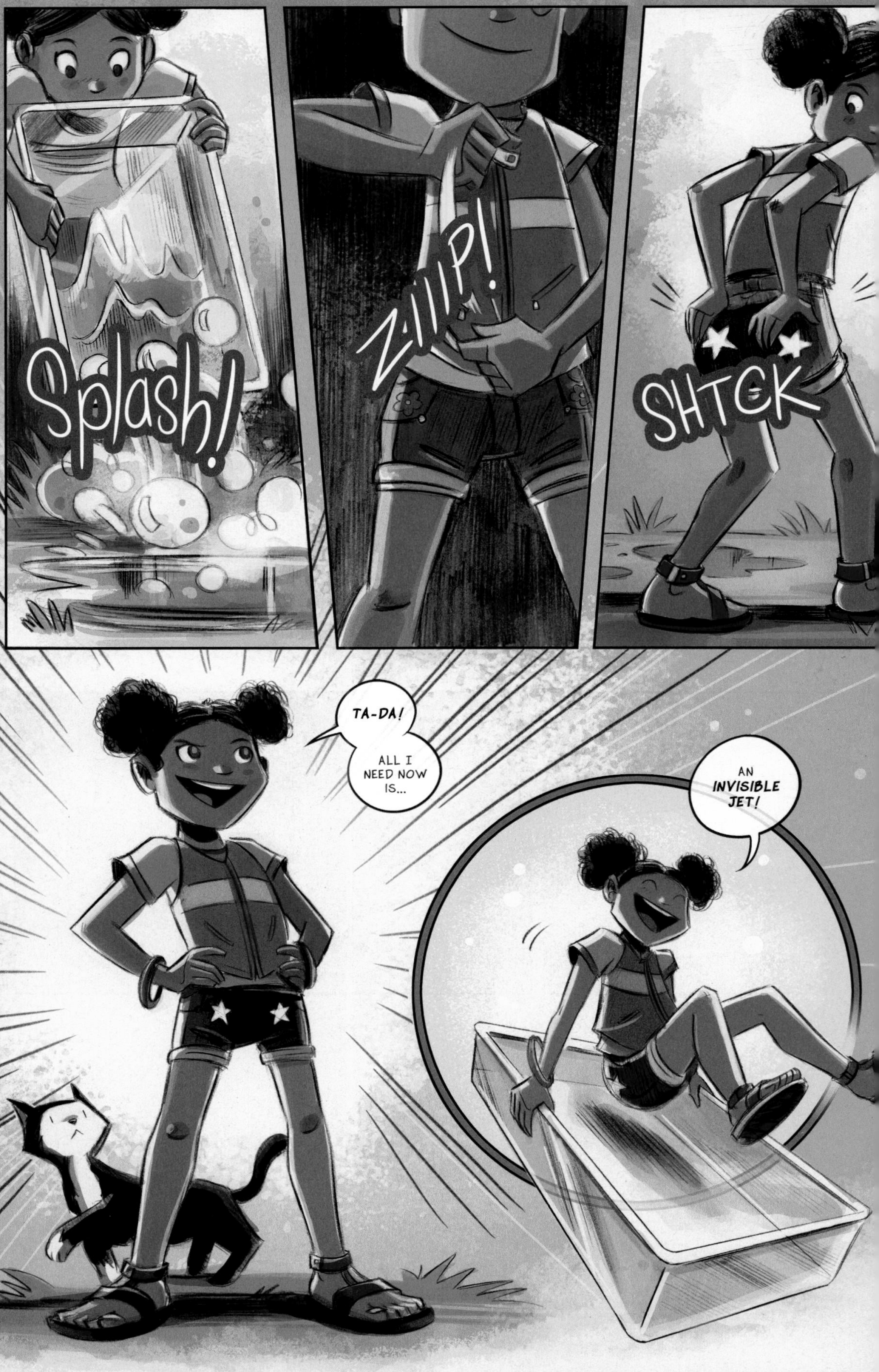

Splash!
ZIIIP!
SHTCK
TA-DA!
ALL I NEED NOW IS...
AN INVISIBLE JET!

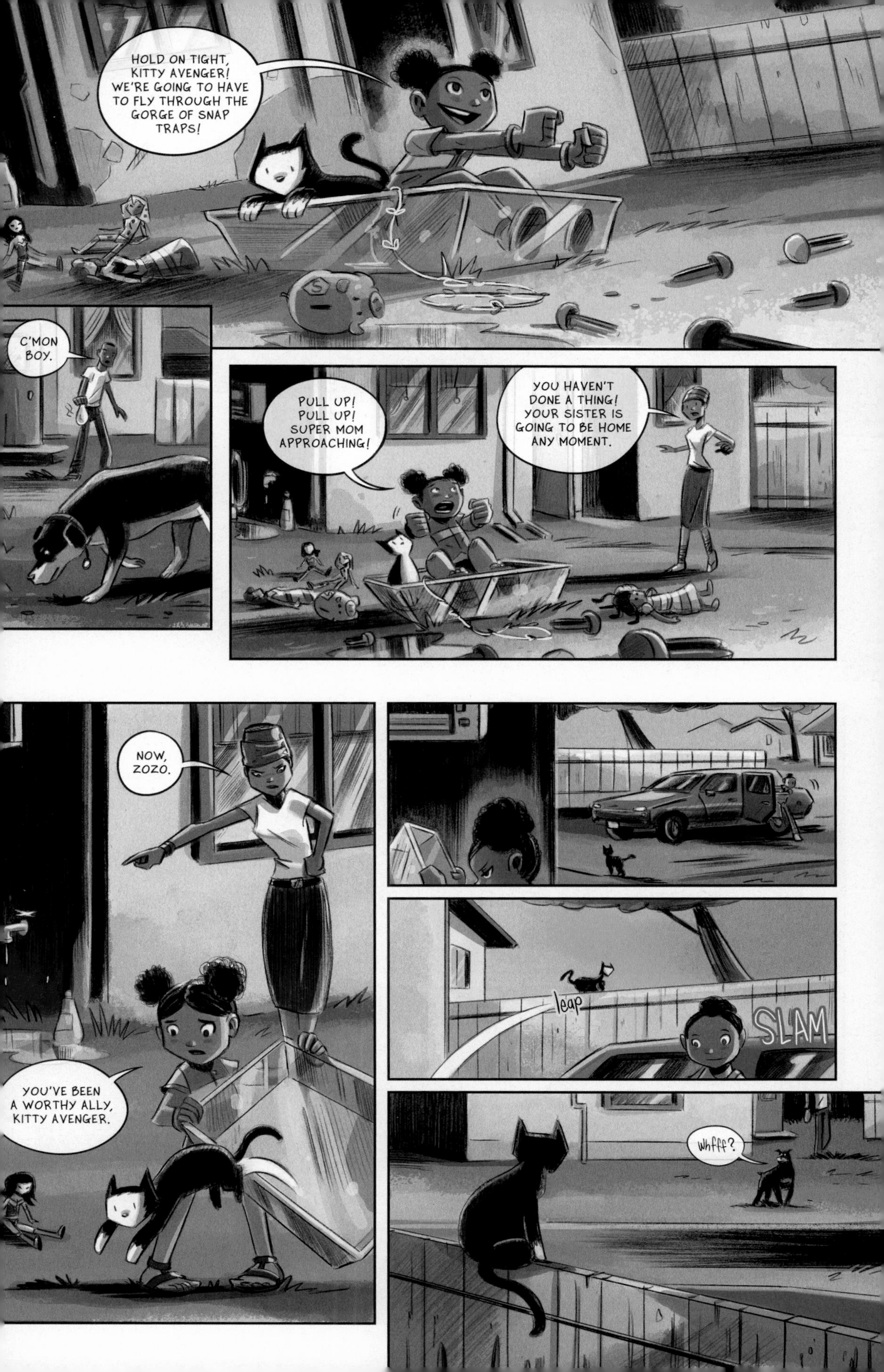
HOLD ON TIGHT, KITTY AVENGER! WE'RE GOING TO HAVE TO FLY THROUGH THE GORGE OF SNAP TRAPS!
C'MON BOY.
PULL UP! PULL UP! SUPER MOM APPROACHING!
YOU HAVEN'T DONE A THING! YOUR SISTER IS GOING TO BE HOME ANY MOMENT.
NOW, ZOZO.
YOU'VE BEEN A WORTHY ALLY, KITTY AVENGER.
leap
SLAM
Whfff?

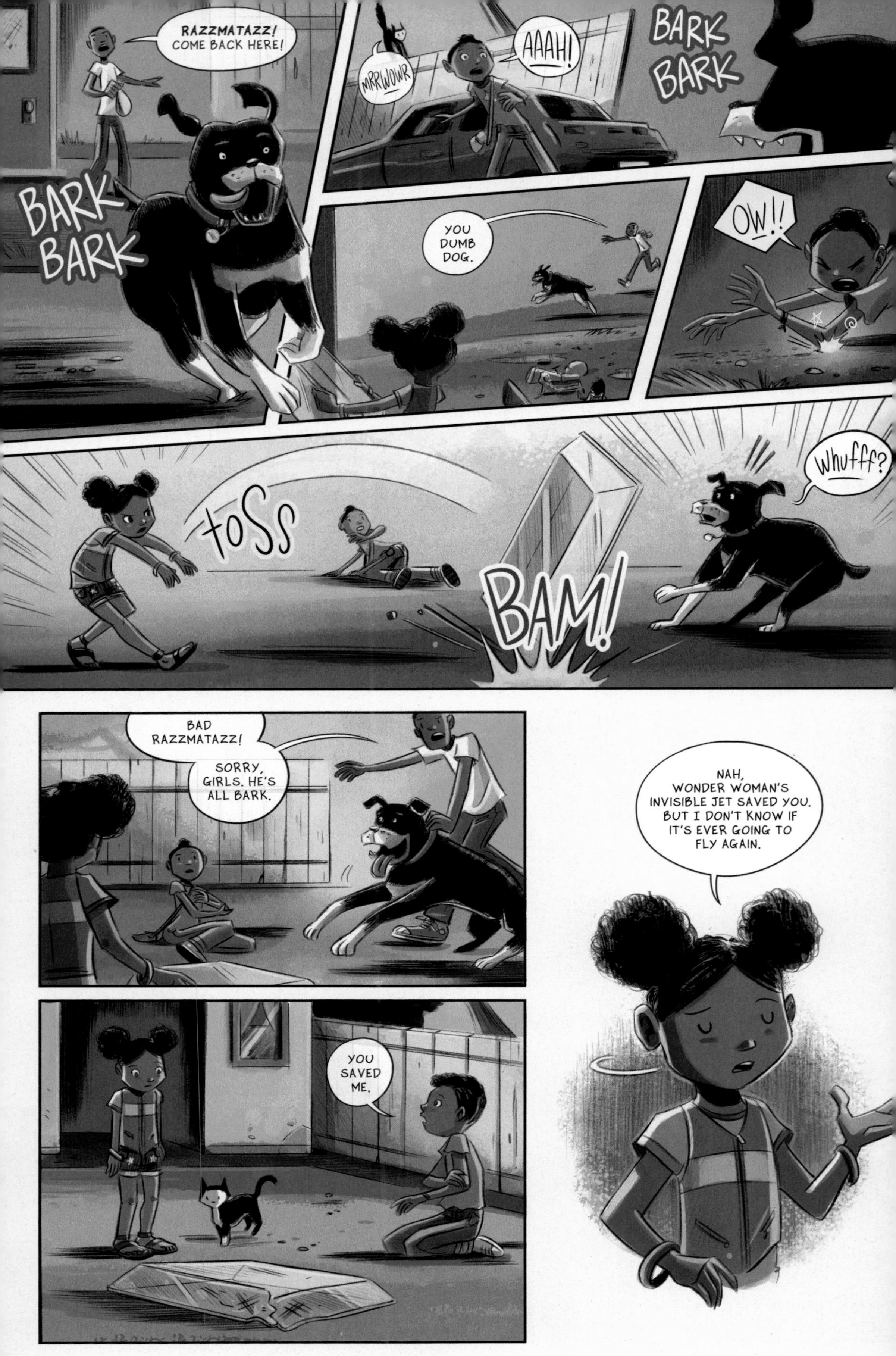
RAZZMATAZZ! COME BACK HERE!
BARK BARK
MRRWOWR
AAAH!
BARK BARK
YOU DUMB DOG.
OW!!
TOSS
Whufff?
BAM!
BAD RAZZMATAZZ!
SORRY, GIRLS. HE'S ALL BARK.
YOU SAVED ME.
NAH, WONDER WOMAN'S INVISIBLE JET SAVED YOU. BUT I DON'T KNOW IF IT'S EVER GOING TO FLY AGAIN.

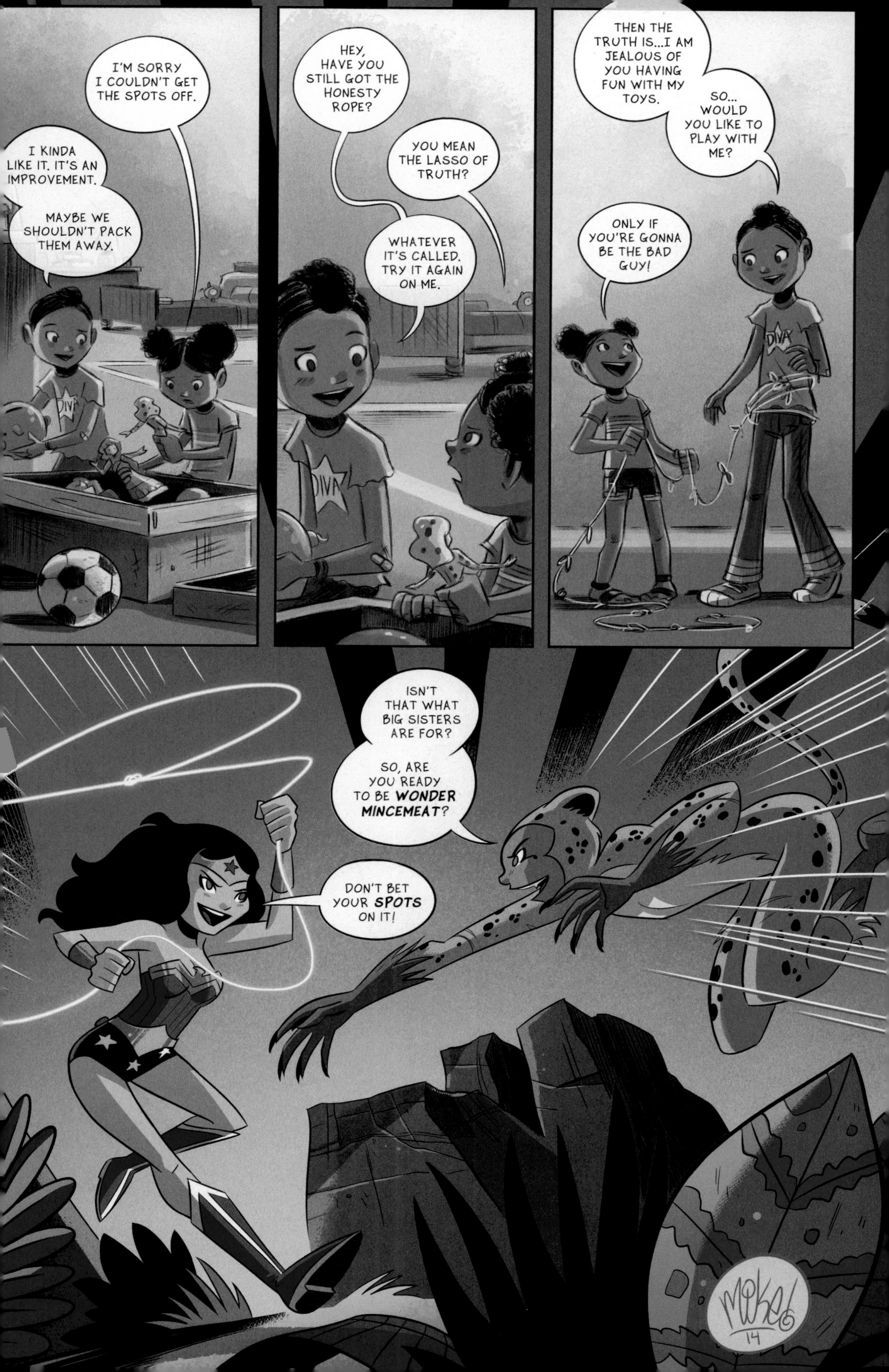
I'M SORRY I COULDN'T GET THE SPOTS OFF.
I KINDA LIKE IT. IT'S AN IMPROVEMENT.
MAYBE WE SHOULDN'T PACK THEM AWAY.
DIVA
HEY, HAVE YOU STILL GOT THE HONESTY ROPE?
YOU MEAN THE LASSO OF TRUTH?
WHATEVER IT'S CALLED. TRY IT AGAIN ON ME.
DIVA
THEN THE TRUTH IS...I AM JEALOUS OF YOU HAVING FUN WITH MY TOYS.
SO... WOULD YOU LIKE TO PLAY WITH ME?
ONLY IF YOU'RE GONNA BE THE BAD GUY!
DIVA
ISN'T THAT WHAT BIG SISTERS ARE FOR?
SO, ARE YOU READY TO BE **WONDER MINCEMEAT**?
DON'T BET YOUR **SPOTS** ON IT!

GIRLS' DAY OUT

CECIL CASTELLUCCI
WRITER

CHRIS SPROUSE
PENCILLER

KARL STORY
INKER

JORDIE BELLAIRE
COLORIST

TODD KLEIN
LETTERER

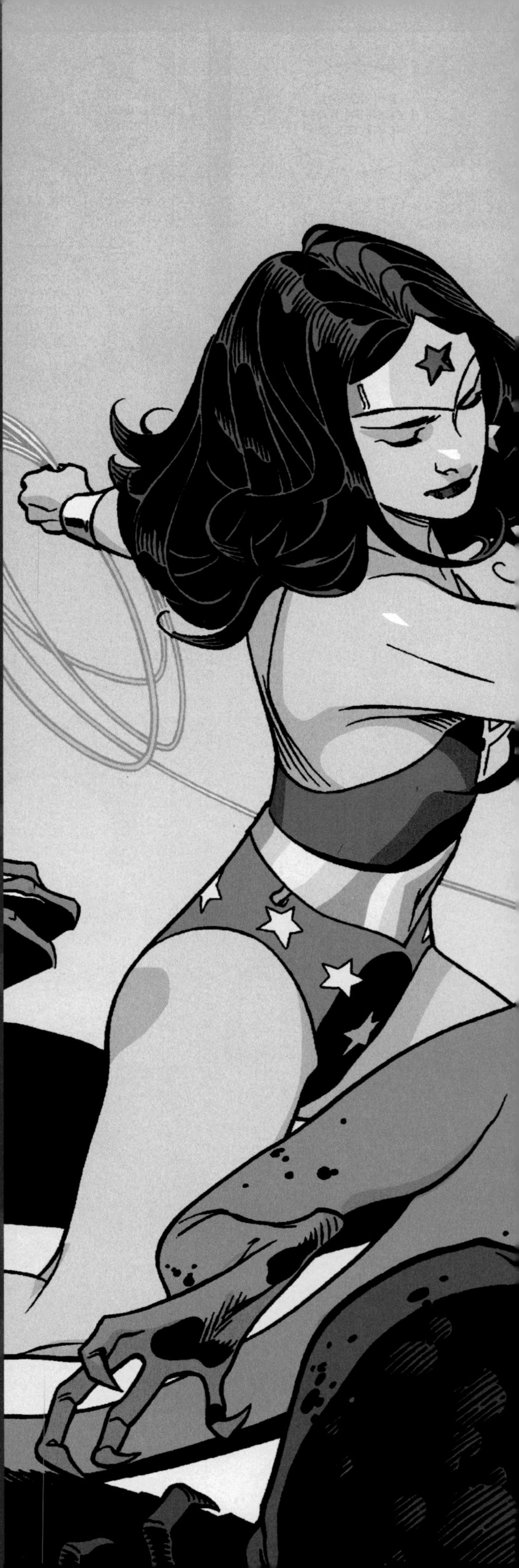

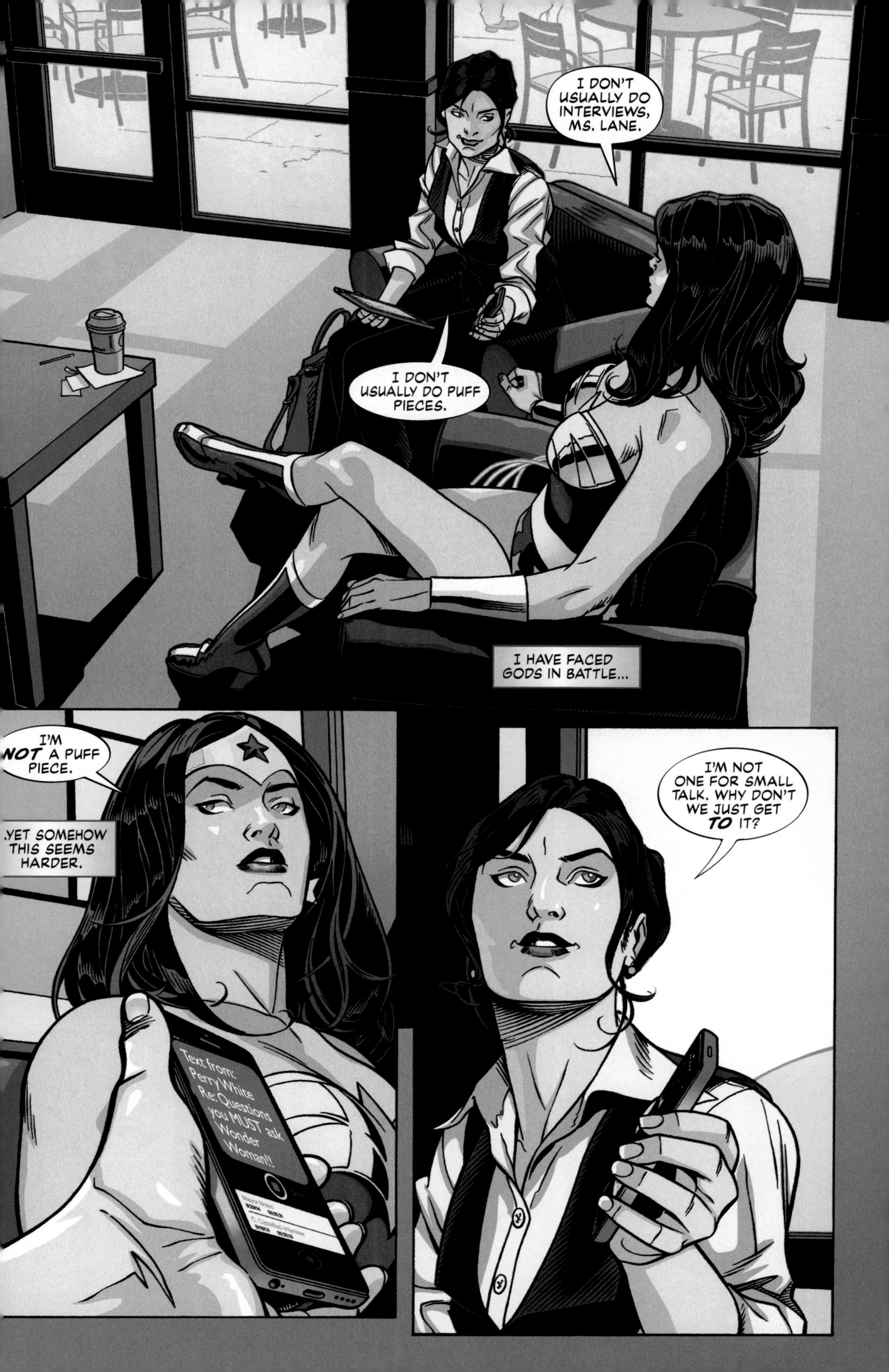
I DON'T USUALLY DO INTERVIEWS, MS. LANE.
I DON'T USUALLY DO PUFF PIECES.
I HAVE FACED GODS IN BATTLE...
I'M NOT A PUFF PIECE.
.YET SOMEHOW THIS SEEMS HARDER.
Text from: Perry White Re: Questions you MUST ask Wonder Woman!!
I'M NOT ONE FOR SMALL TALK. WHY DON'T WE JUST GET TO IT?

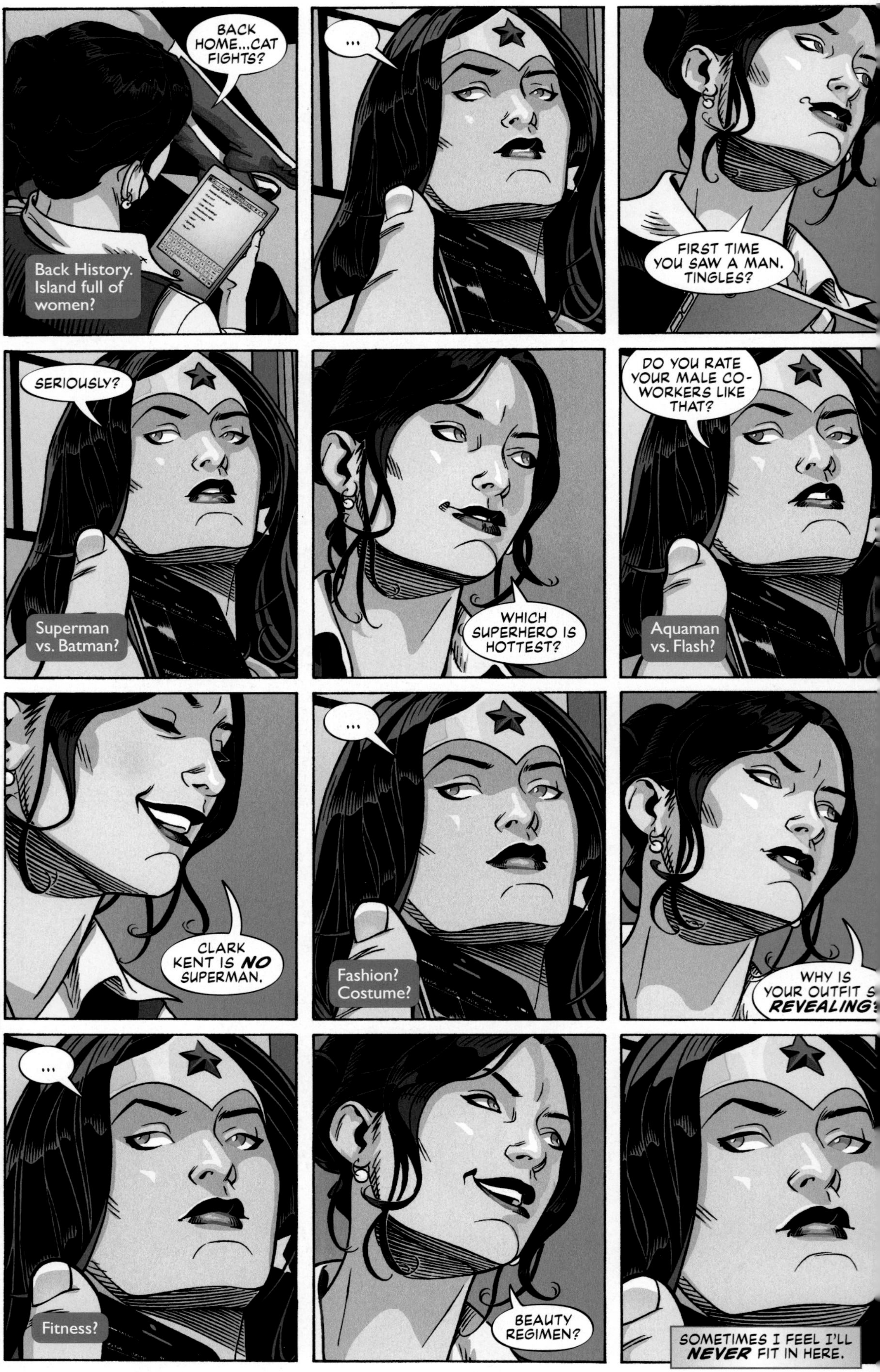

BACK HOME...CAT FIGHTS?
Back History. Island full of women?
...
FIRST TIME YOU SAW A MAN. TINGLES?
SERIOUSLY?
Superman vs. Batman?
WHICH SUPERHERO IS HOTTEST?
DO YOU RATE YOUR MALE CO-WORKERS LIKE THAT?
Aquaman vs. Flash?
CLARK KENT IS **NO** SUPERMAN.
...
Fashion? Costume?
WHY IS YOUR OUTFIT S
REVEALING
...
Fitness?
BEAUTY REGIMEN?
SOMETIMES I FEEL I'LL **NEVER** FIT IN HERE.

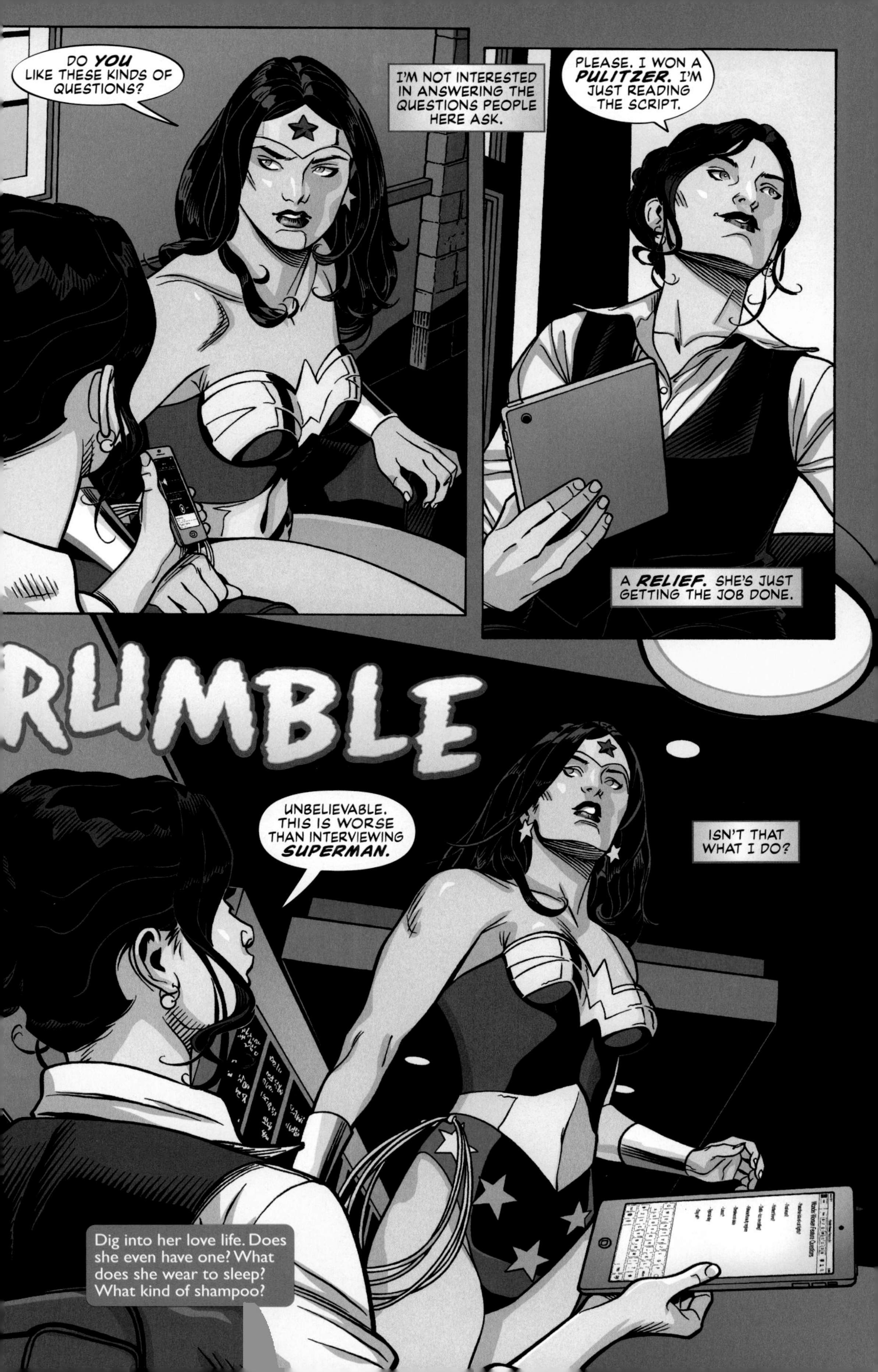
DO YOU LIKE THESE KINDS OF QUESTIONS?
I'M NOT INTERESTED IN ANSWERING THE QUESTIONS PEOPLE HERE ASK.
PLEASE. I WON A PULITZER. I'M JUST READING THE SCRIPT.
A RELIEF. SHE'S JUST GETTING THE JOB DONE.
RUMBLE
UNBELIEVABLE. THIS IS WORSE THAN INTERVIEWING SUPERMAN.
ISN'T THAT WHAT I DO?
Dig into her love life. Does she even have one? What does she wear to sleep? What kind of shampoo?

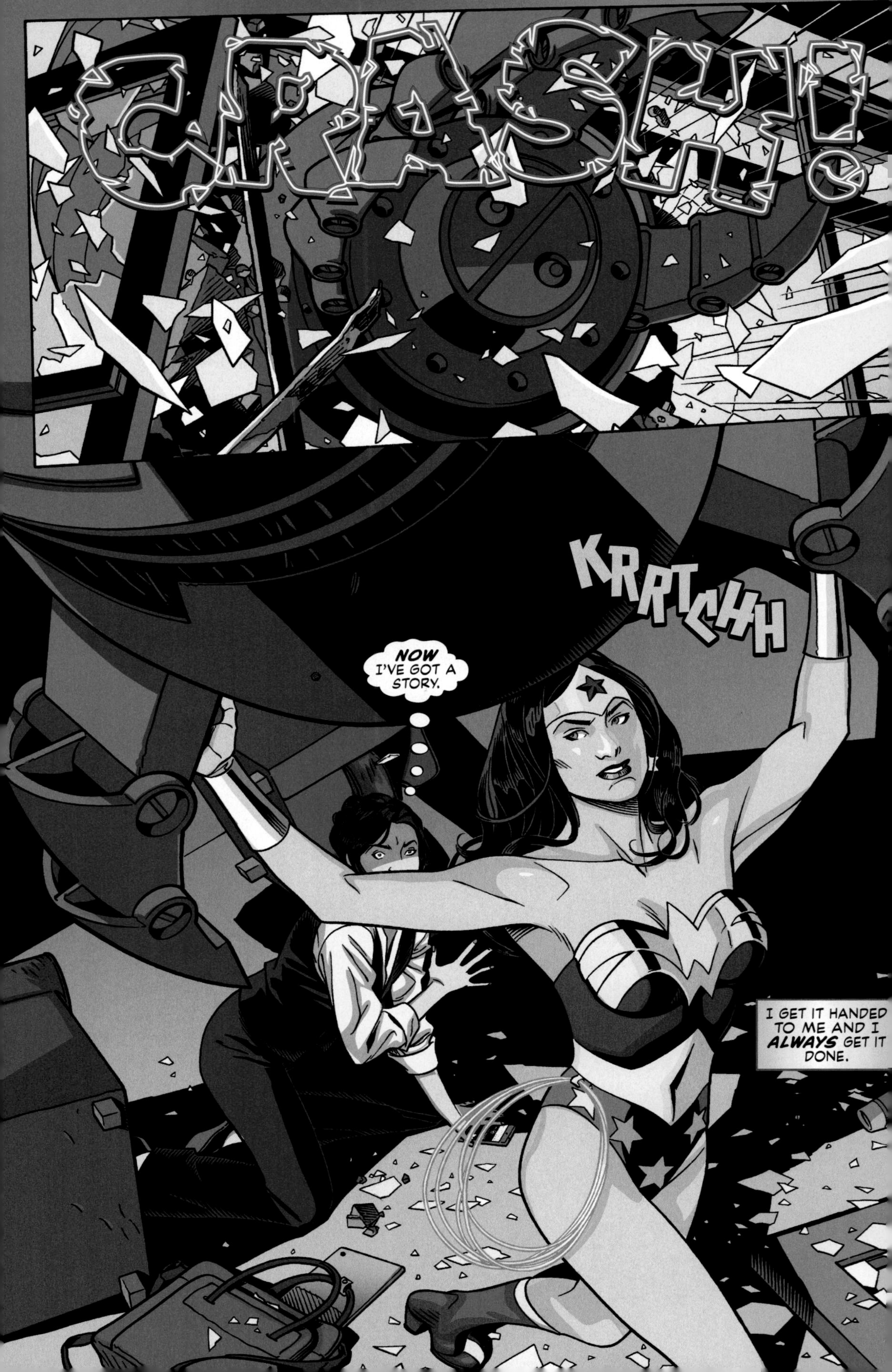
CRASH!
KRRTCHH
NOW I'VE GOT A STORY.
I GET IT HANDED TO ME AND I ALWAYS GET IT DONE.

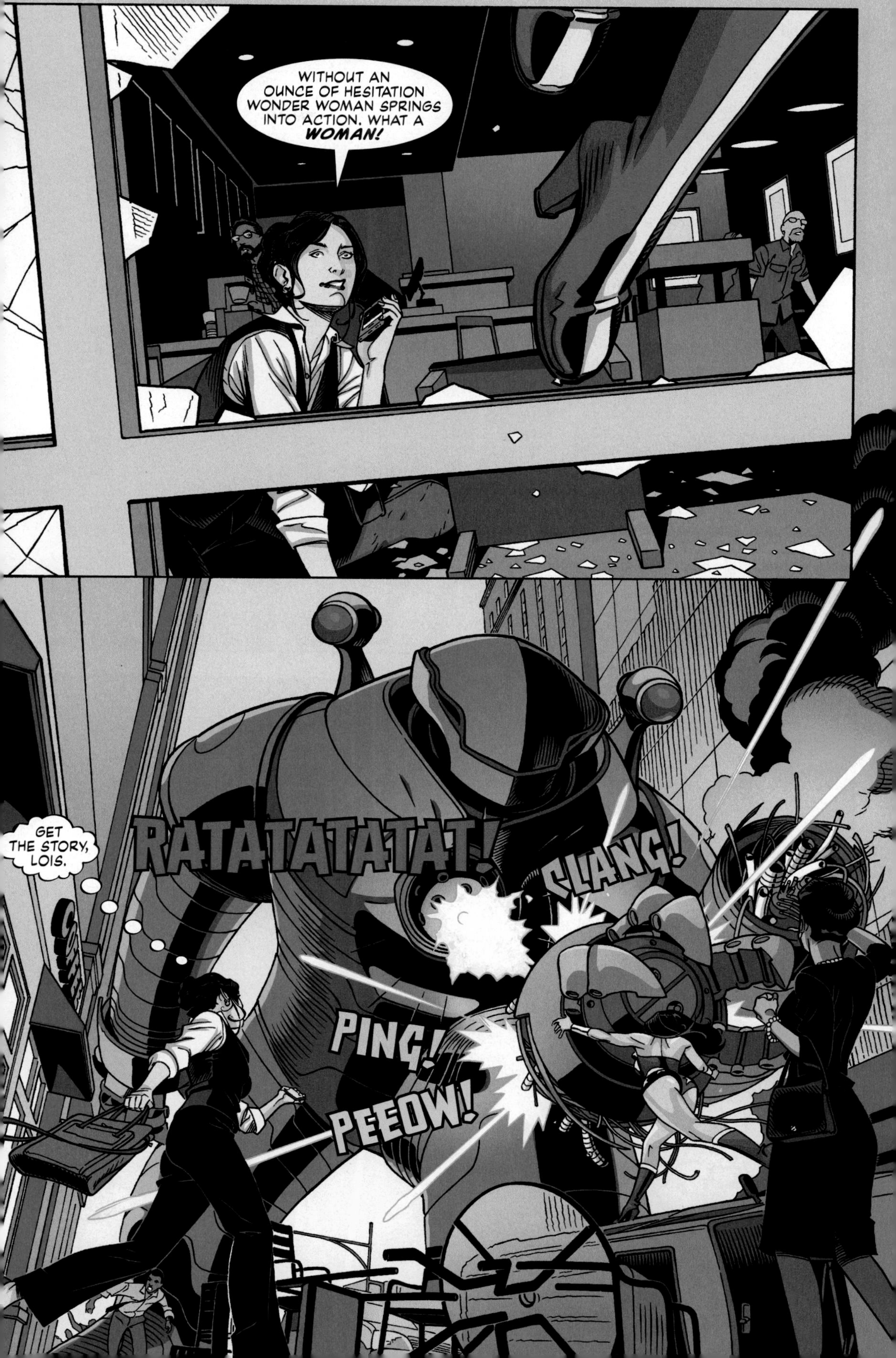
WITHOUT AN OUNCE OF HESITATION WONDER WOMAN SPRINGS INTO ACTION. WHAT A **WOMAN!**
GET THE STORY, LOIS.
RATATATATAT!
CLANG!
PING!
PEEOW!

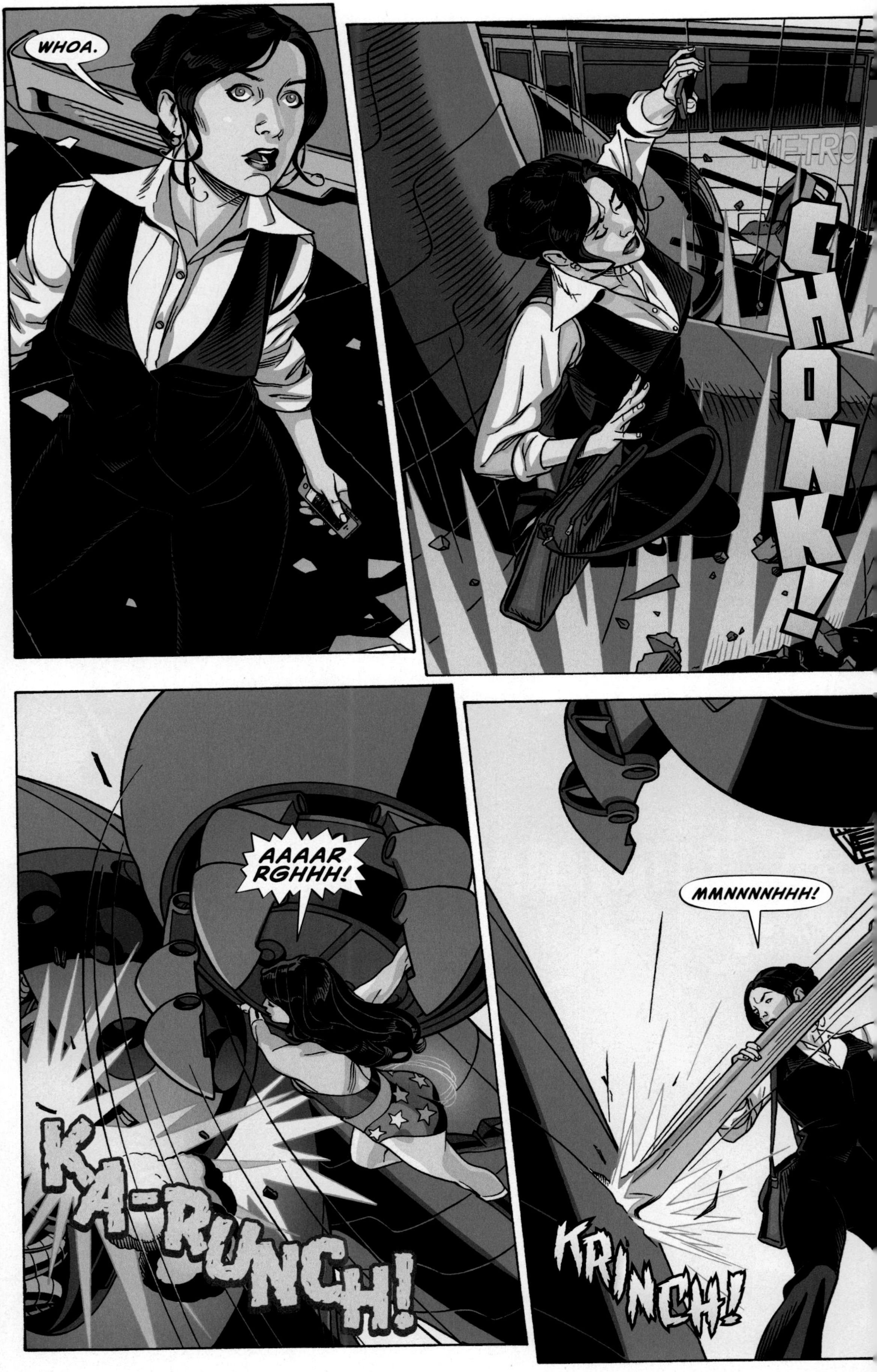
WHOA.
CHONK!
AAAAR RGHHH!
KA-RUNCH!
MMNNNNHHH!
KRINCH!

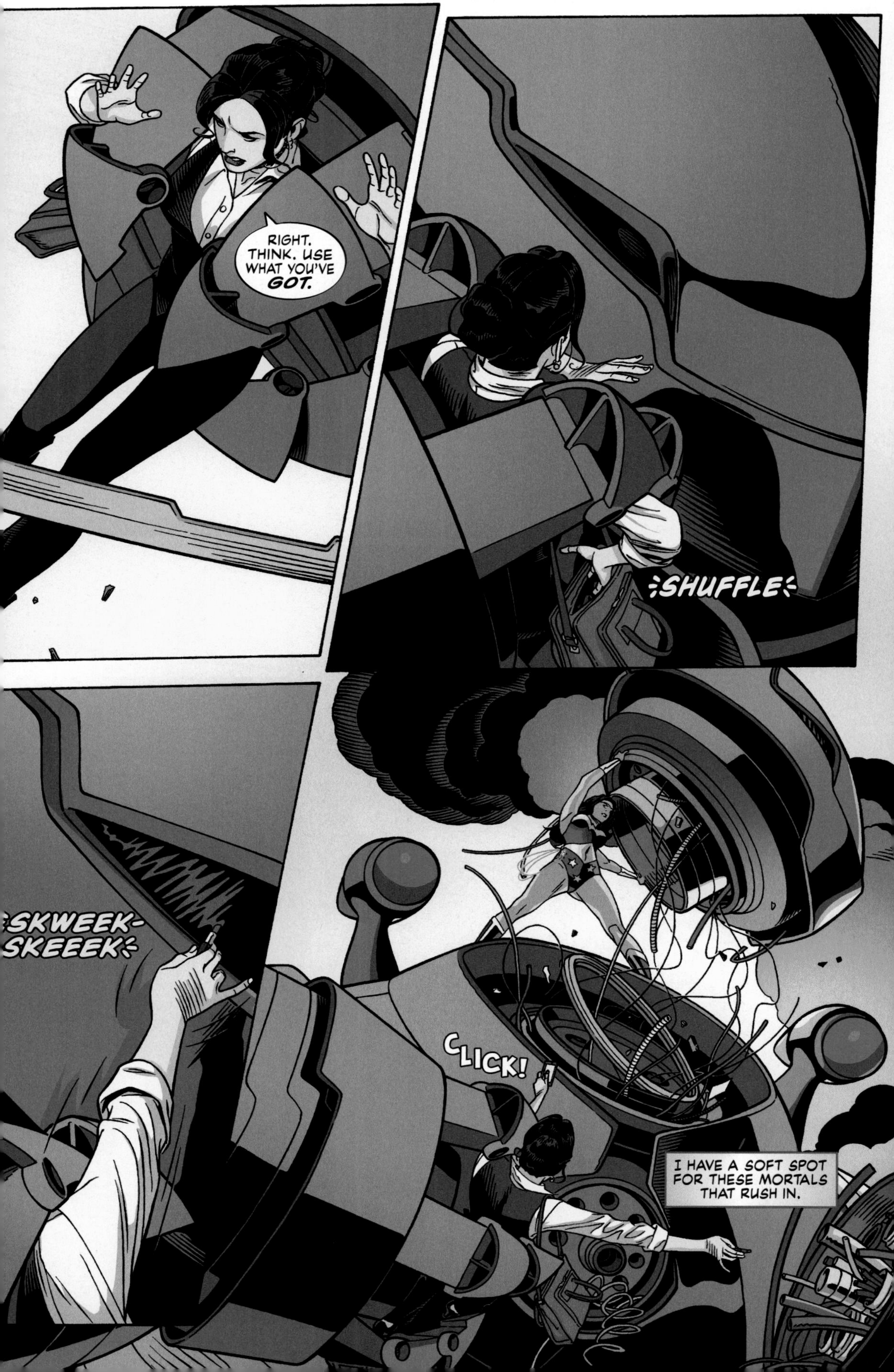
RIGHT. THINK. USE WHAT YOU'VE GOT.
SHUFFLE
SKWEEK-SKEEEK
CLICK!
I HAVE A SOFT SPOT FOR THESE MORTALS THAT RUSH IN.

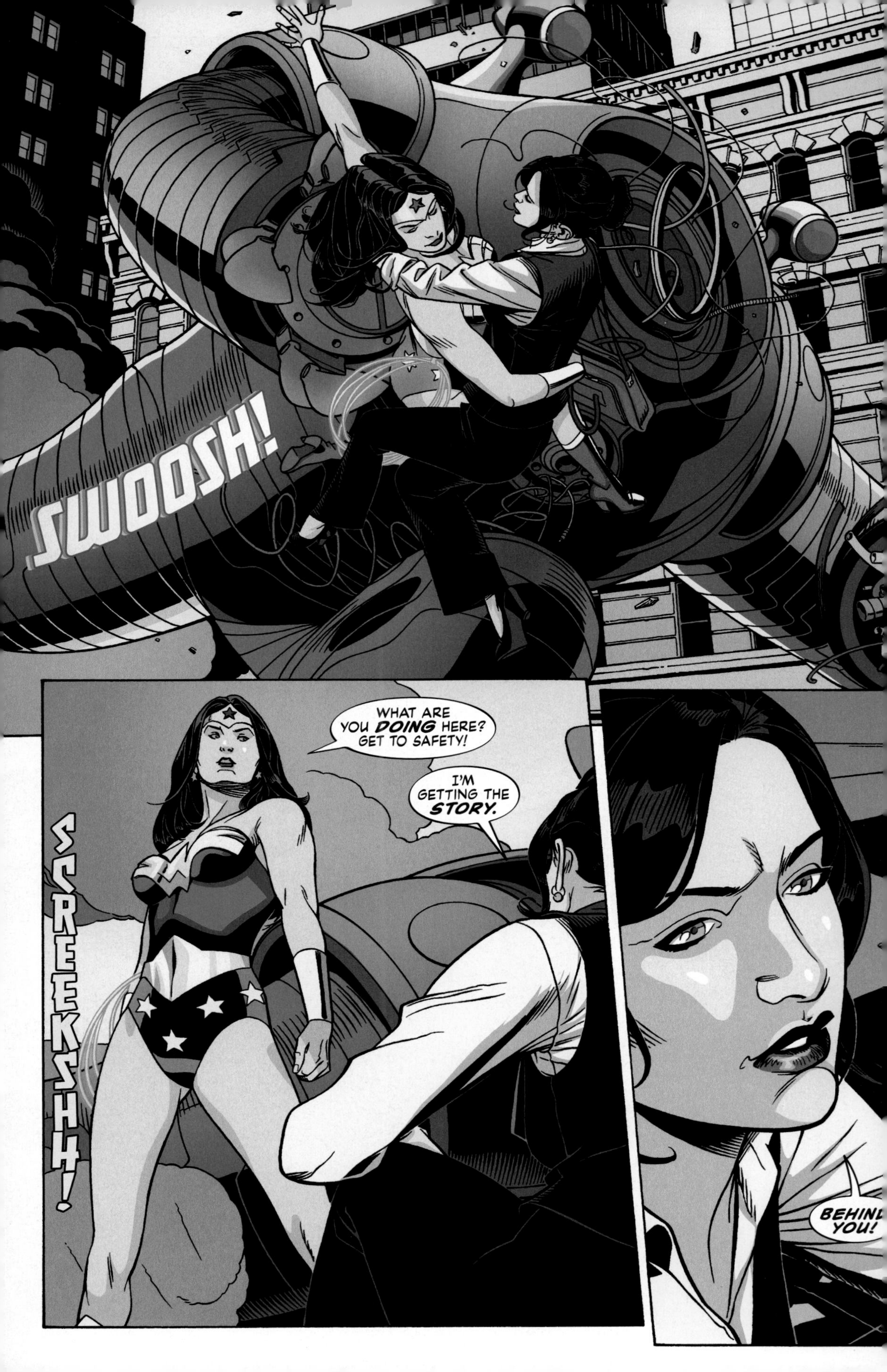
SWOOSH!
WHAT ARE YOU DOING HERE? GET TO SAFETY!
I'M GETTING THE STORY.
SCREEKSHH!
BEHIND YOU!

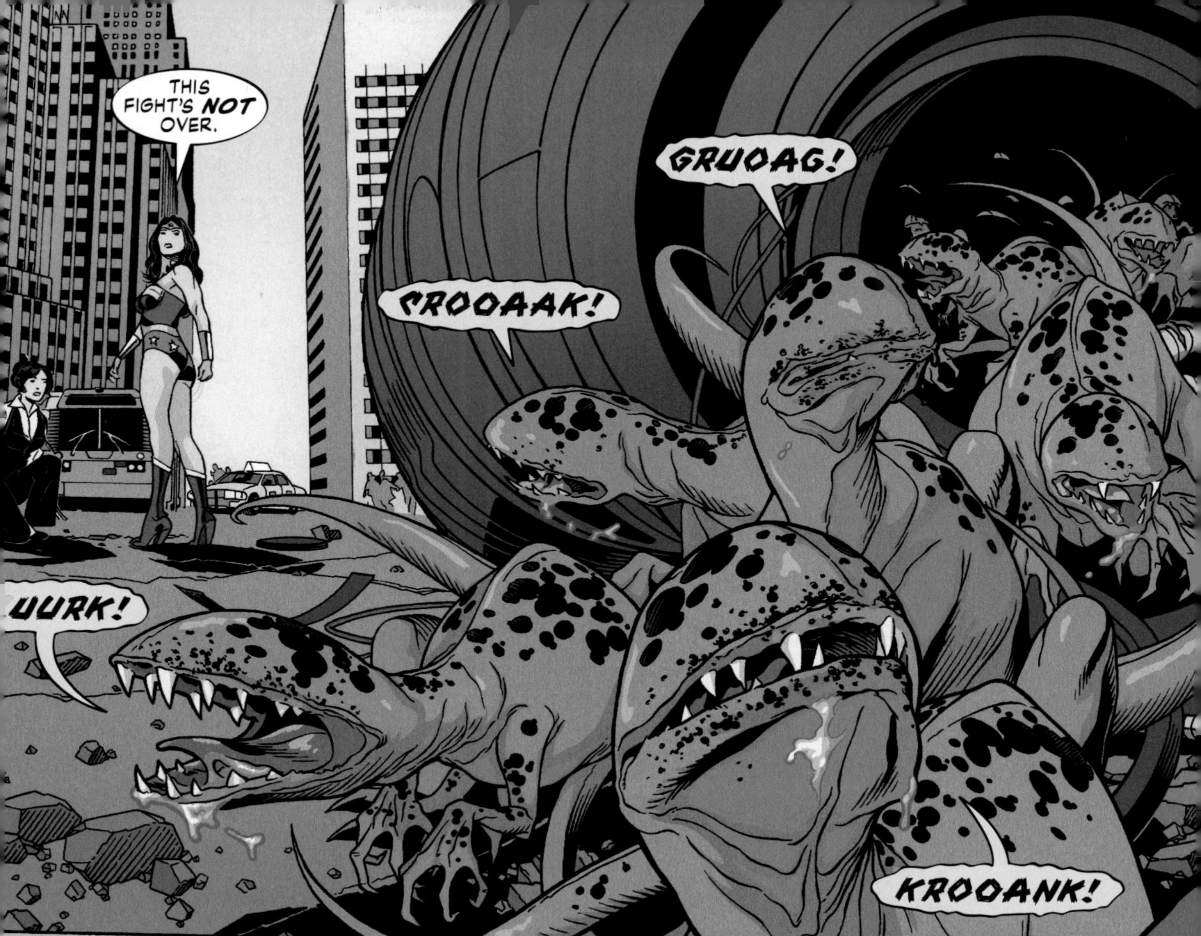
THIS FIGHT'S NOT OVER.
GRUOAG!
CROOAAK!
UURK!
KROOANK!

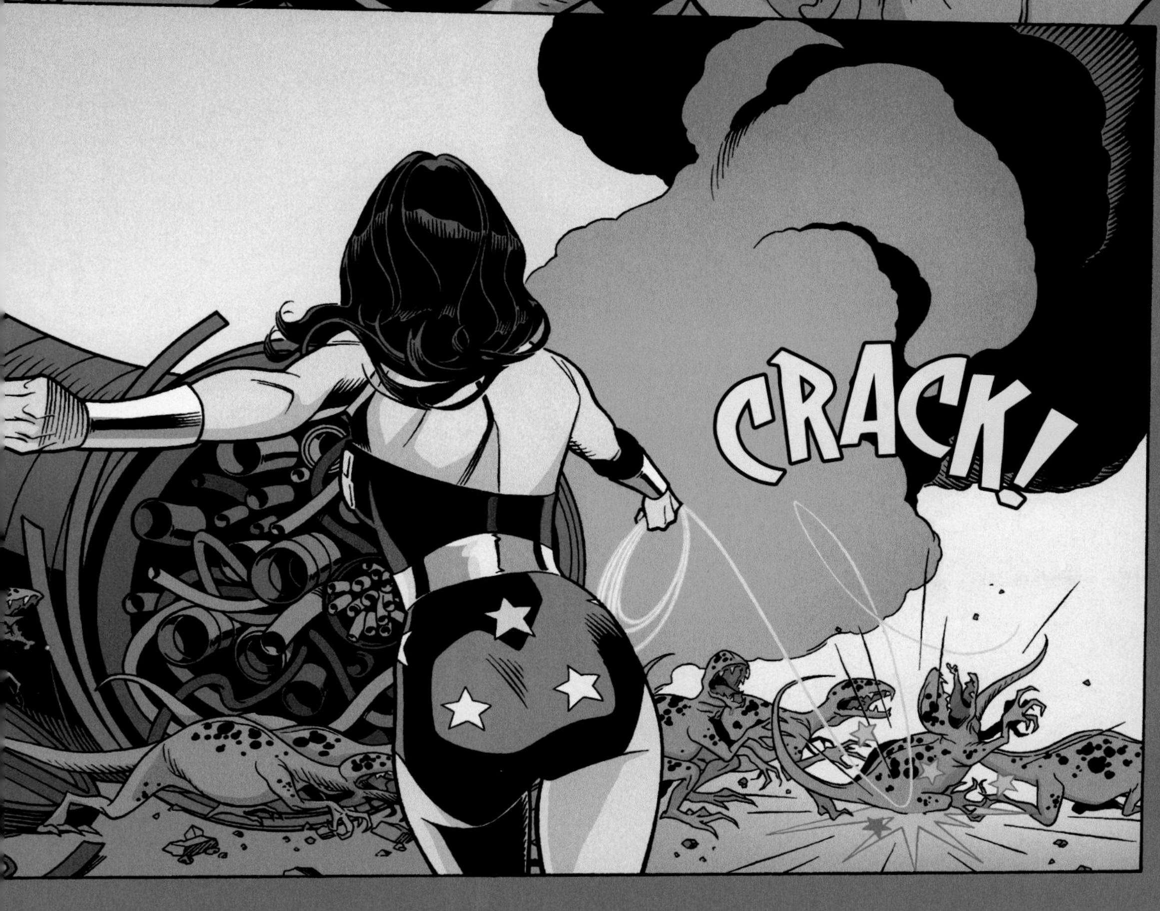
CRACK!

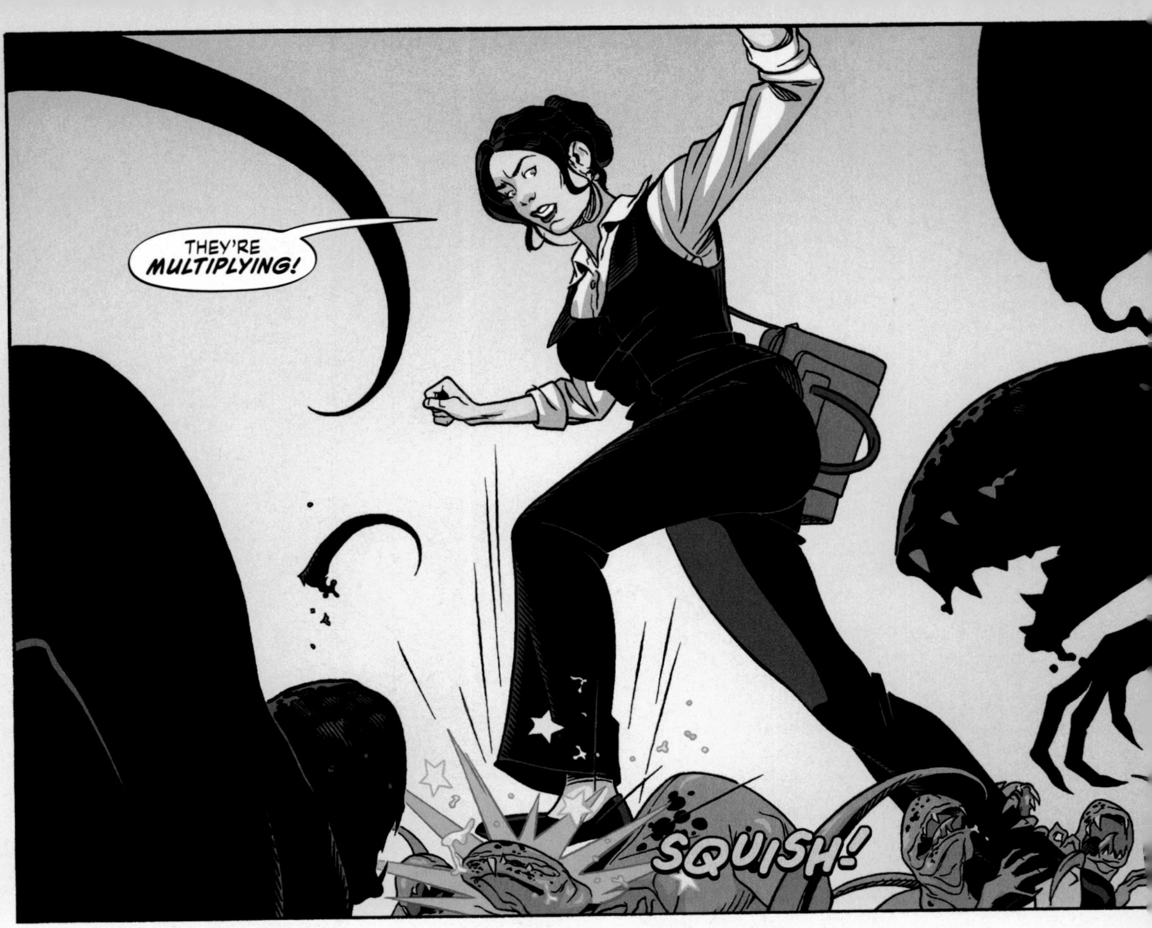
THEY'RE MULTIPLYING!
SQUISH!

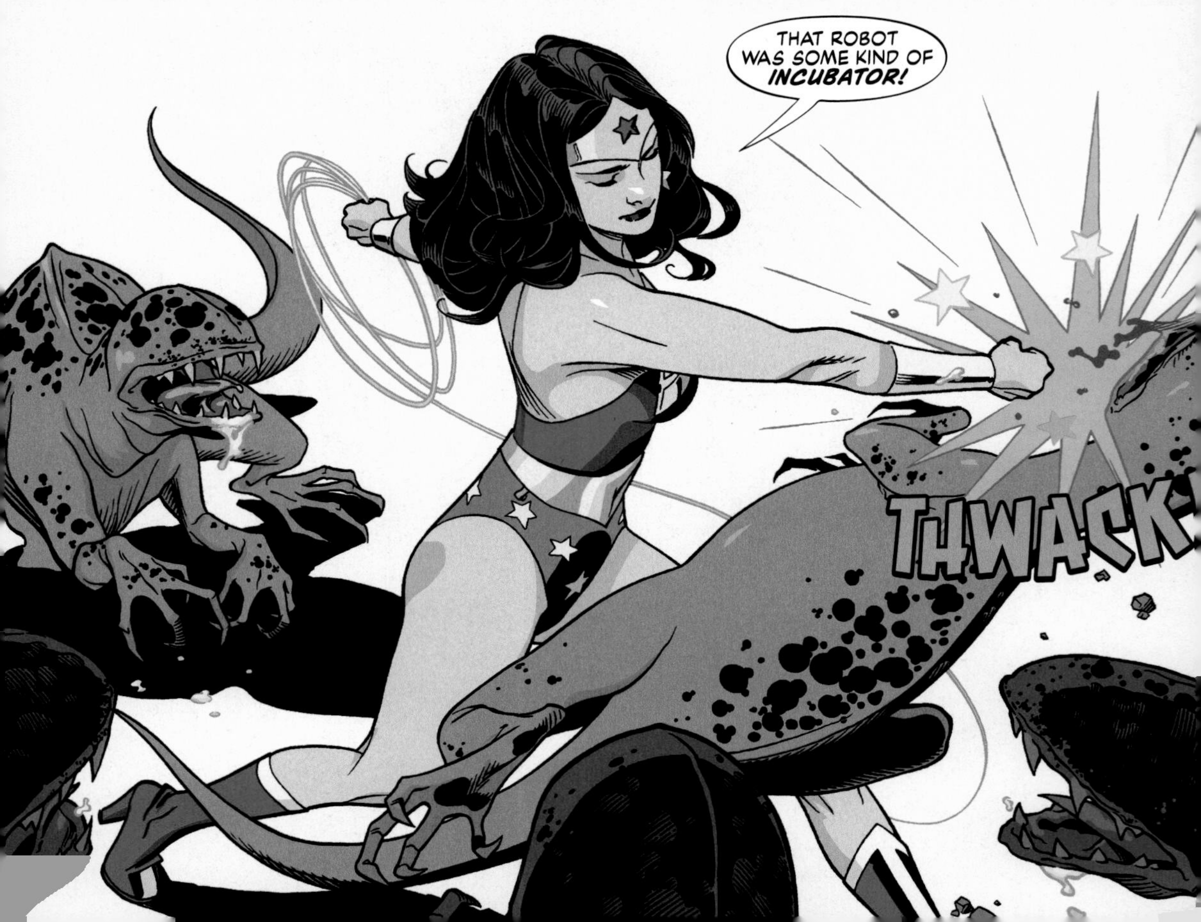
THAT ROBOT WAS SOME KIND OF INCUBATOR!
THWACK

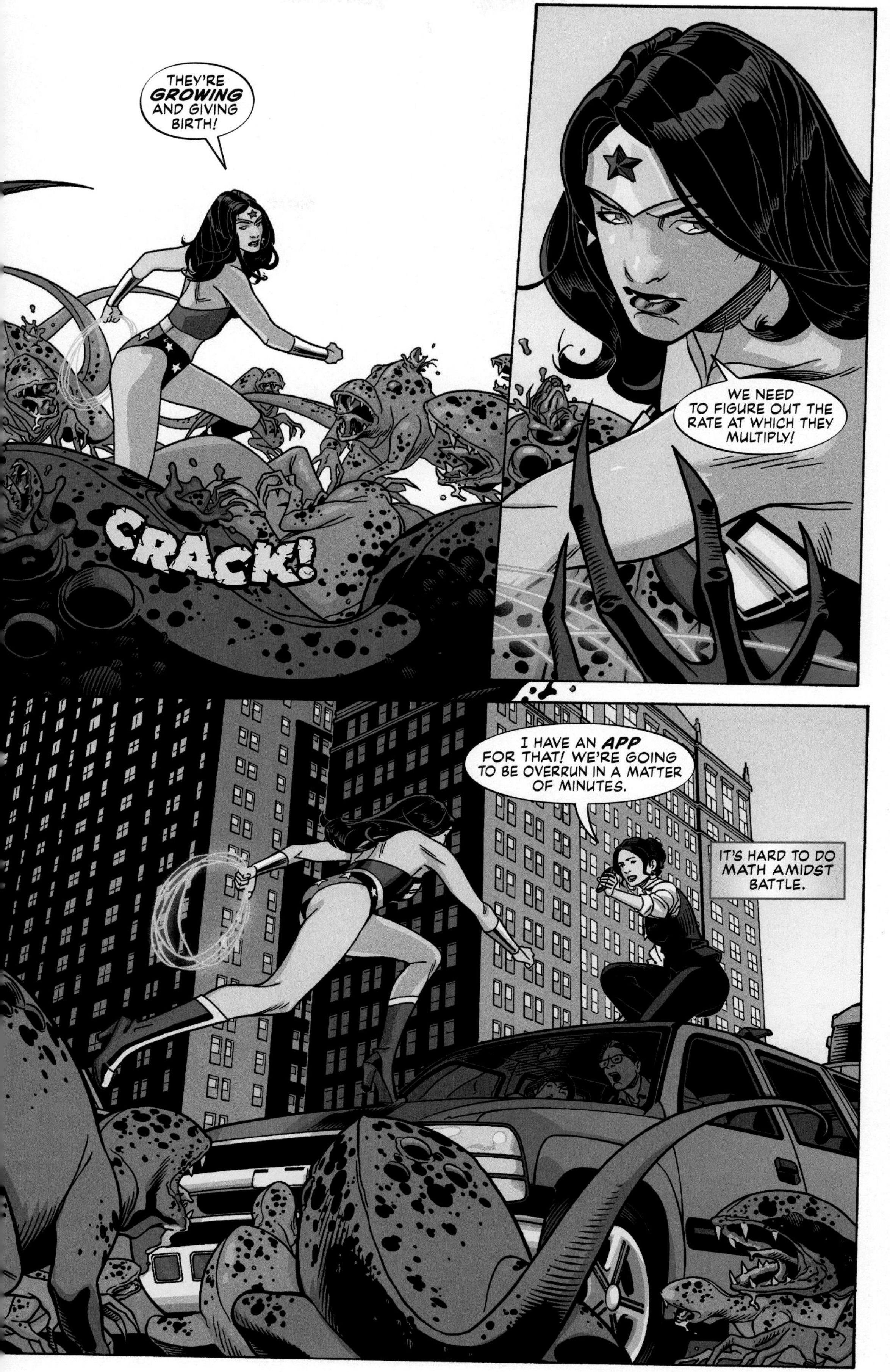
THEY'RE GROWING AND GIVING BIRTH!
CRACK!
WE NEED TO FIGURE OUT THE RATE AT WHICH THEY MULTIPLY!
I HAVE AN APP FOR THAT! WE'RE GOING TO BE OVERRUN IN A MATTER OF MINUTES.
IT'S HARD TO DO MATH AMIDST BATTLE.

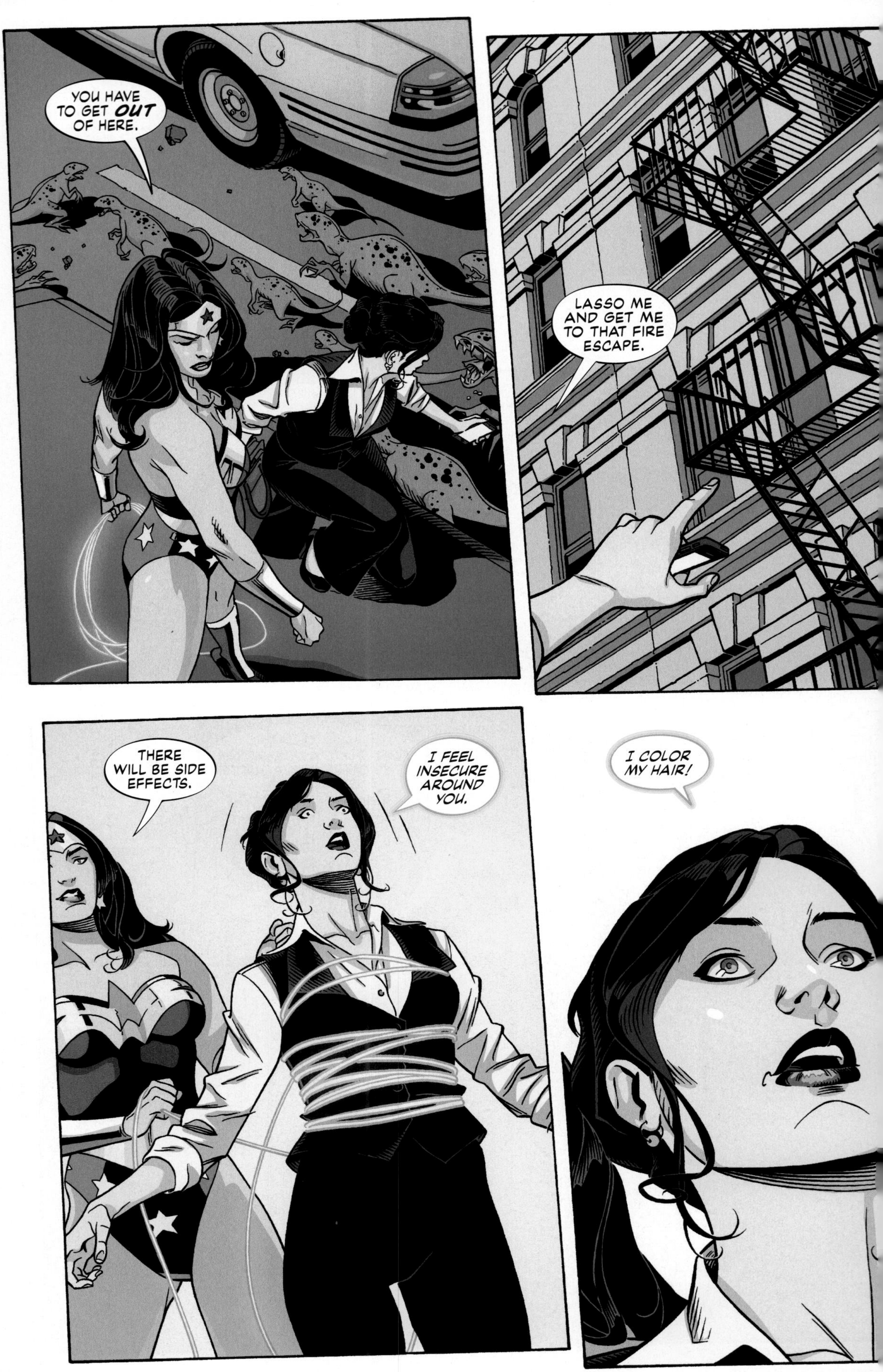
YOU HAVE TO GET OUT OF HERE.
LASSO ME AND GET ME TO THAT FIRE ESCAPE.
THERE WILL BE SIDE EFFECTS.
I FEEL INSECURE AROUND YOU.
I COLOR MY HAIR!

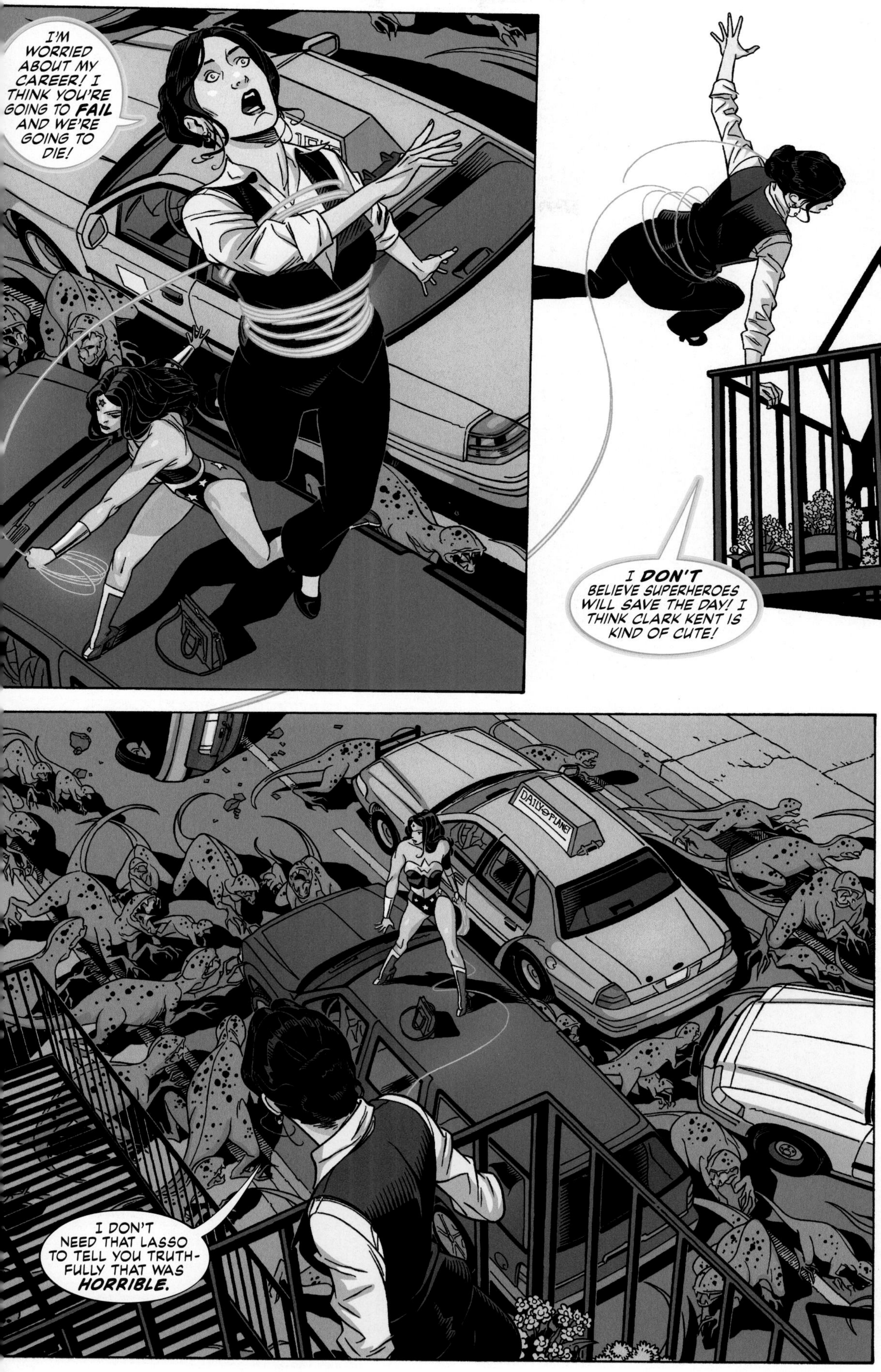
I'M WORRIED ABOUT MY CAREER! I THINK YOU'RE GOING TO **FAIL** AND WE'RE GOING TO DIE!
I **DON'T** BELIEVE SUPERHEROES WILL SAVE THE DAY! I THINK CLARK KENT IS KIND OF CUTE!
DAILY PLANET
I DON'T NEED THAT LASSO TO TELL YOU TRUTH-FULLY THAT WAS **HORRIBLE**.

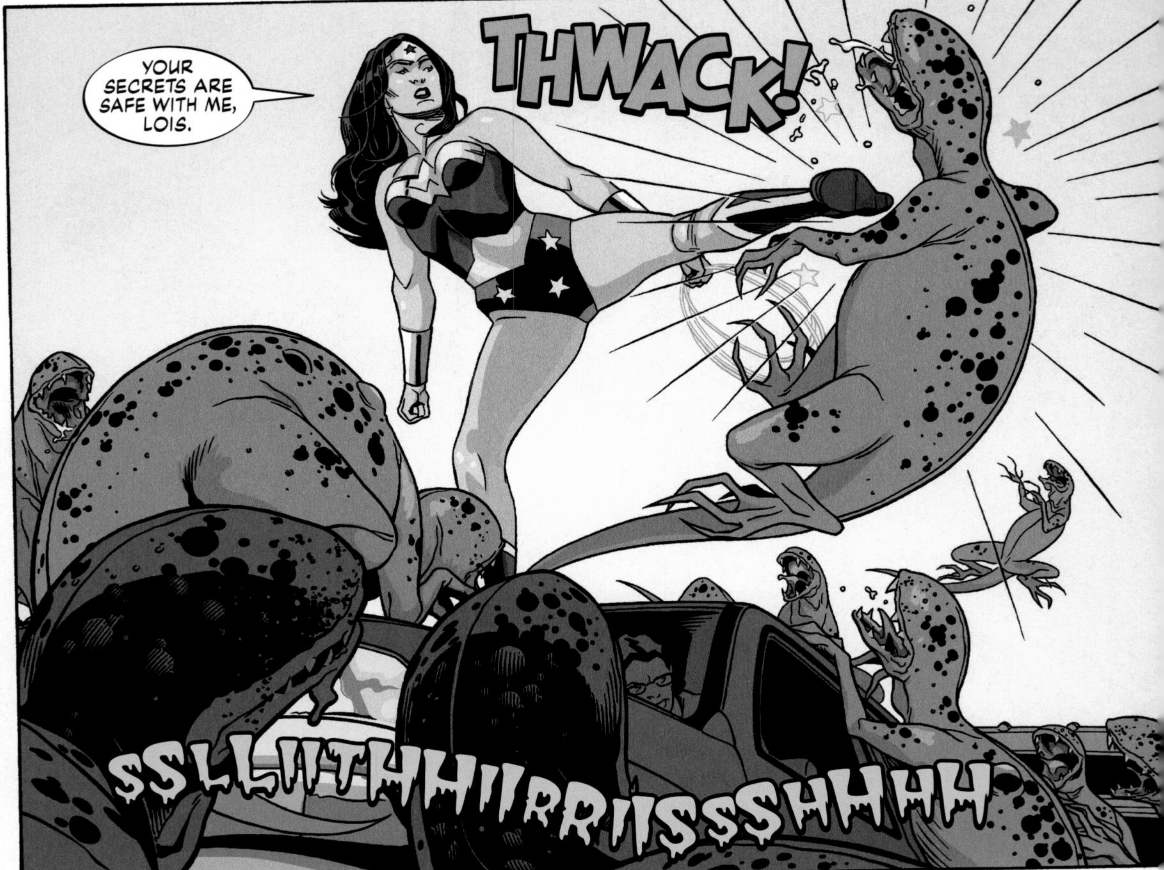
YOUR SECRETS ARE SAFE WITH ME, LOIS.
THWACK!
SSLLIITHHIIRRIISSSSHHHH

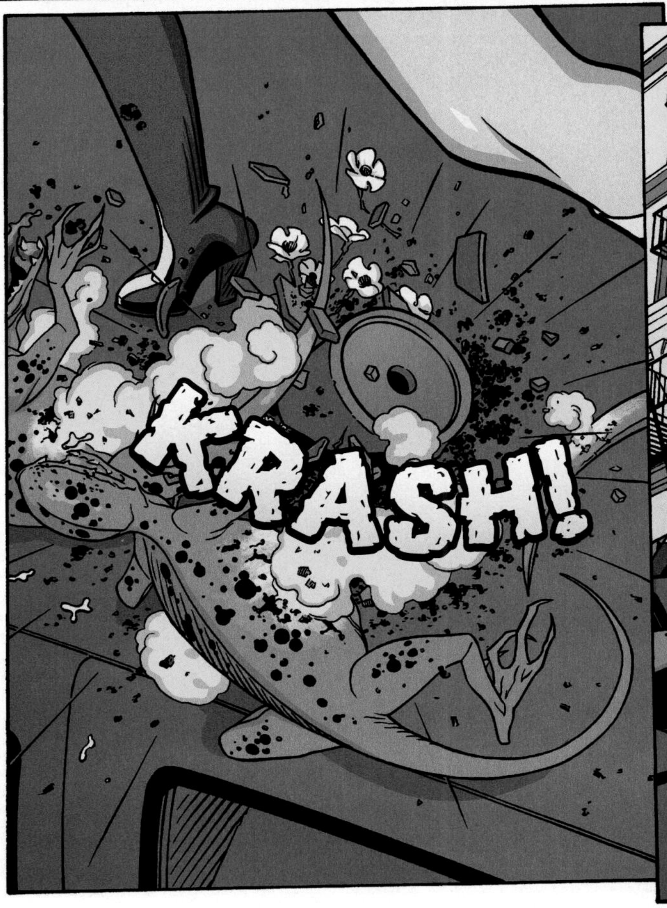
KRASH!

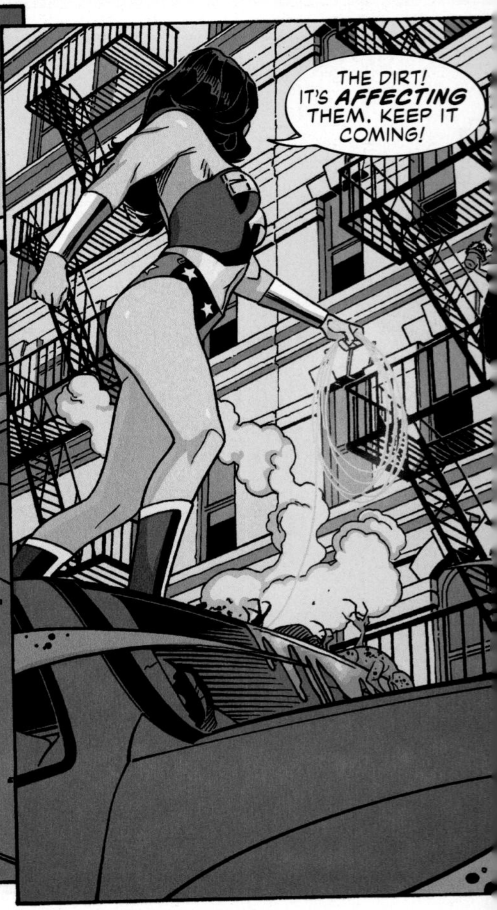
THE DIRT! IT'S *AFFECTING* THEM. KEEP IT COMING!

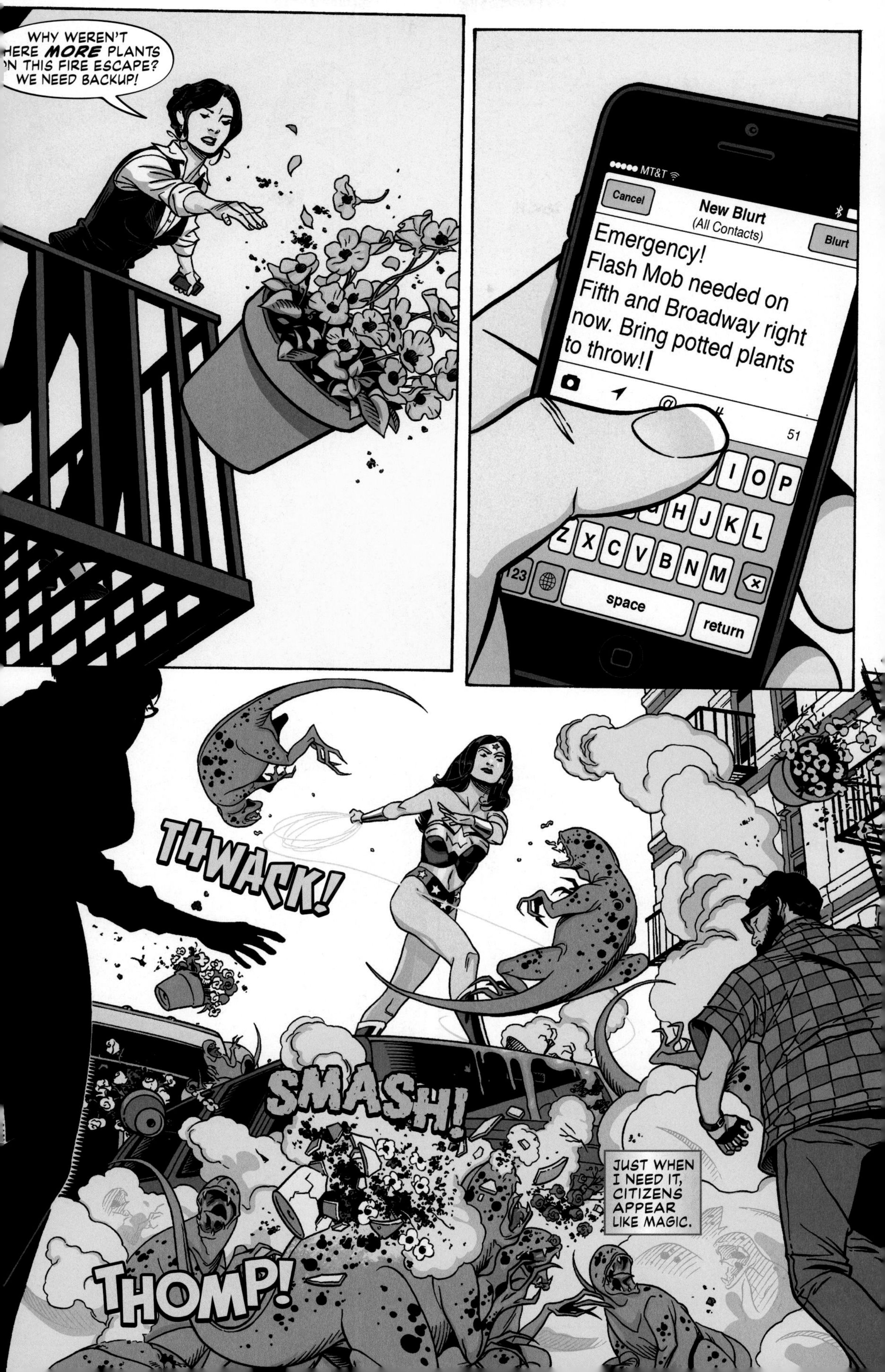
WHY WEREN'T
HERE MORE PLANTS
'N THIS FIRE ESCAPE?
WE NEED BACKUP!
MT&T
Cancel
New Blurt
(All Contacts)
Blurt
Emergency!
Flash Mob needed on
Fifth and Broadway right
now. Bring potted plants
to throw!!
51
space
return
THWACK!
SMASH!
JUST WHEN
I NEED IT,
CITIZENS
APPEAR
LIKE MAGIC.
THOMP!

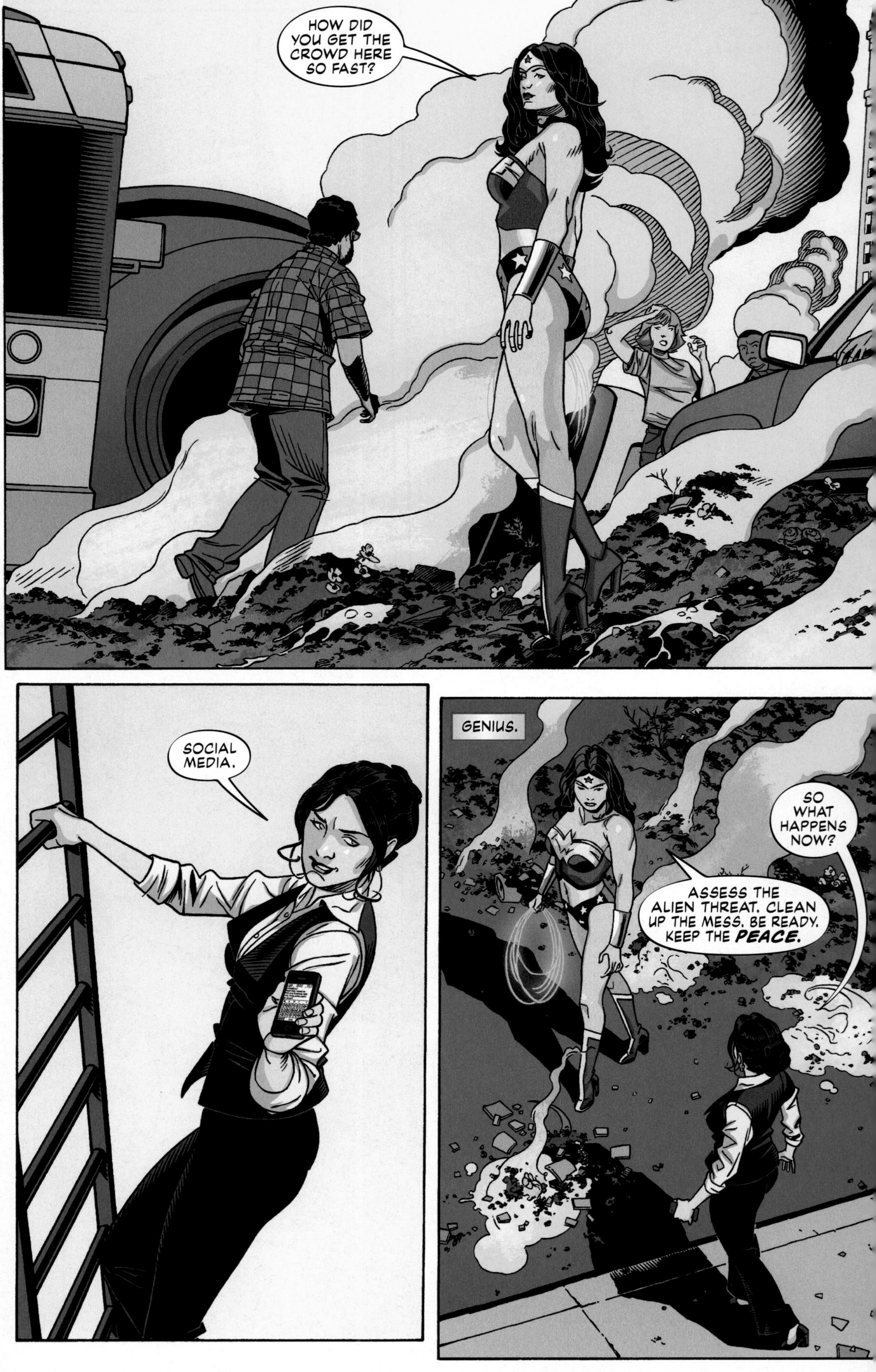
HOW DID YOU GET THE CROWD HERE SO FAST?
SOCIAL MEDIA.
GENIUS.
SO WHAT HAPPENS NOW?
ASSESS THE ALIEN THREAT. CLEAN UP THE MESS. BE READY. KEEP THE **PEACE.**

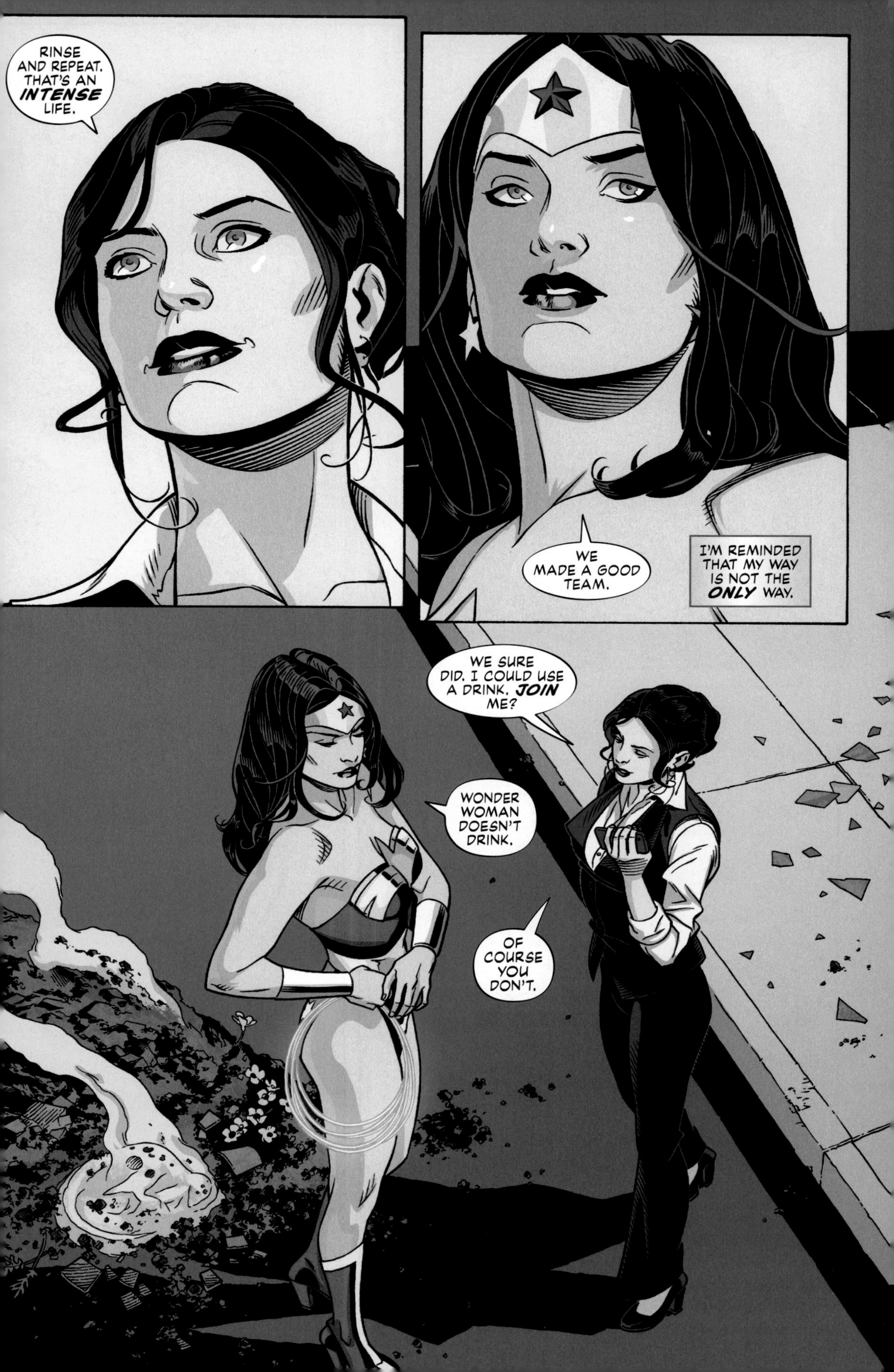
RINSE AND REPEAT. THAT'S AN *INTENSE* LIFE.
WE MADE A GOOD TEAM.
I'M REMINDED THAT MY WAY IS NOT THE *ONLY* WAY.
WE SURE DID. I COULD USE A DRINK. *JOIN* ME?
WONDER WOMAN DOESN'T DRINK.
OF COURSE YOU DON'T.

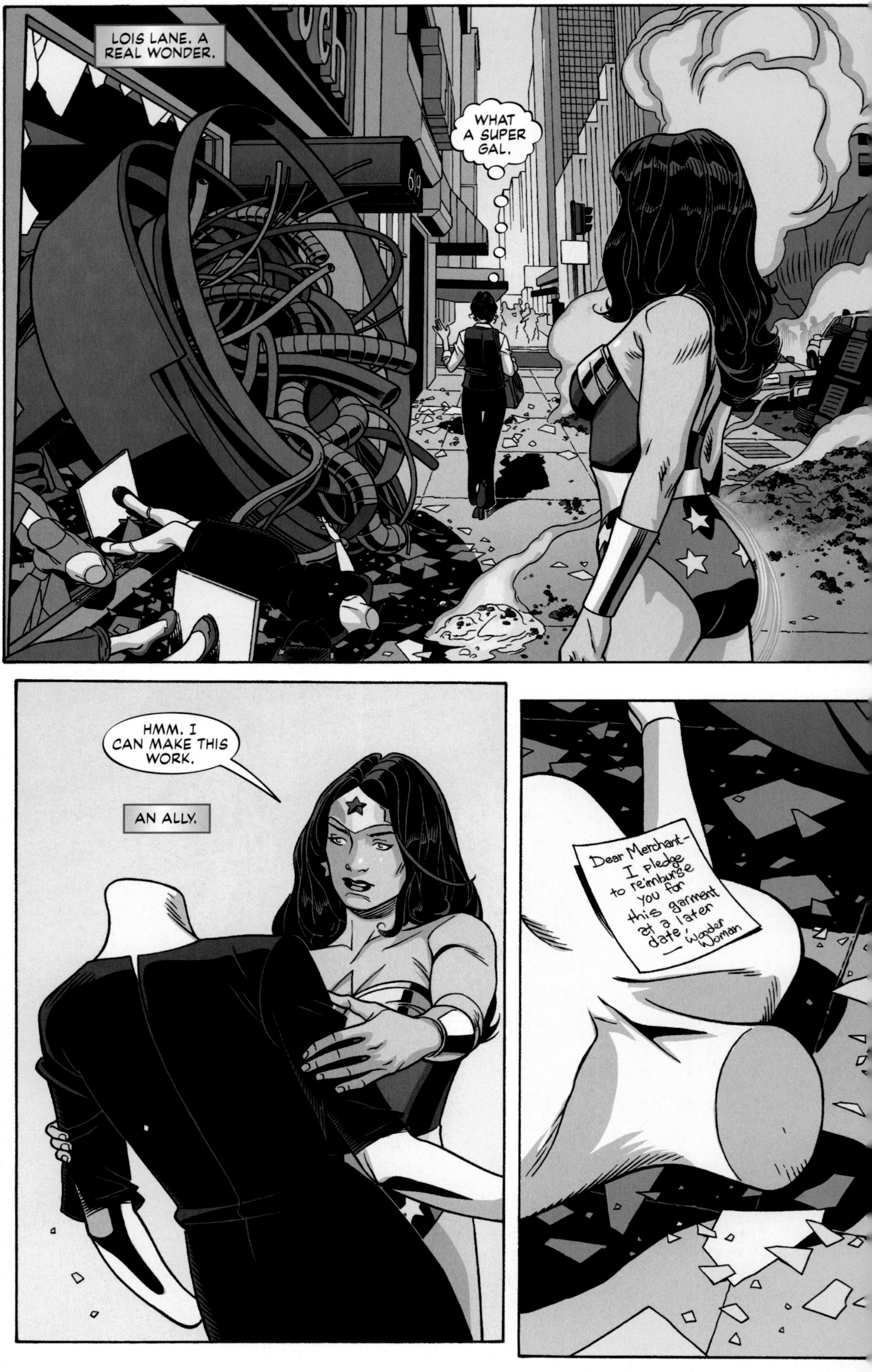
LOIS LANE. A REAL WONDER.
WHAT A SUPER GAL.
619
HMM. I CAN MAKE THIS WORK.
AN ALLY.
Dear Merchant- I pledge to reimburse you for this garment at a later date, — Wonder Woman

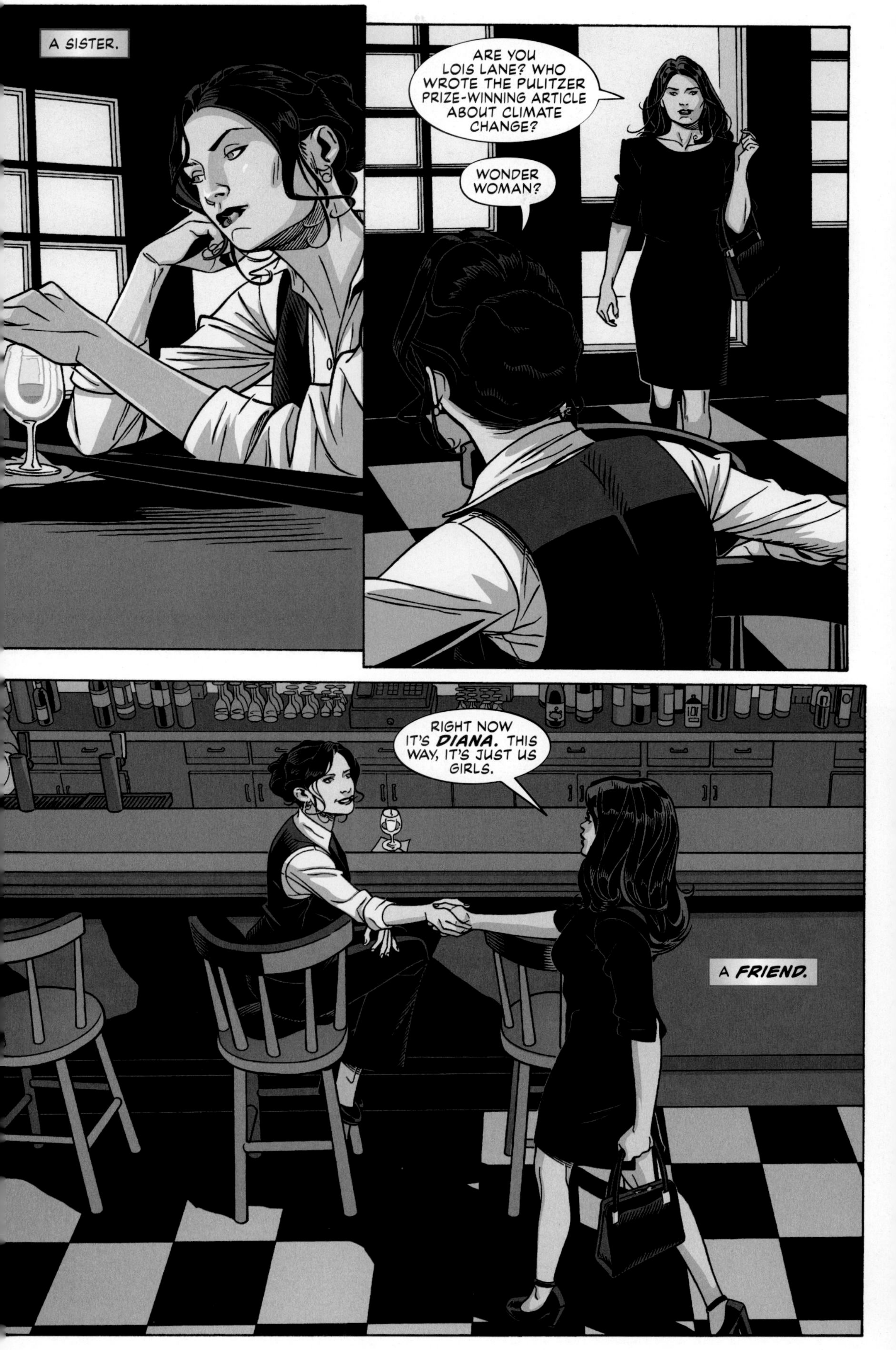
A SISTER.
ARE YOU LOIS LANE? WHO WROTE THE PULITZER PRIZE-WINNING ARTICLE ABOUT CLIMATE CHANGE?
WONDER WOMAN?
RIGHT NOW IT'S **DIANA.** THIS WAY, IT'S JUST US GIRLS.
A **FRIEND.**

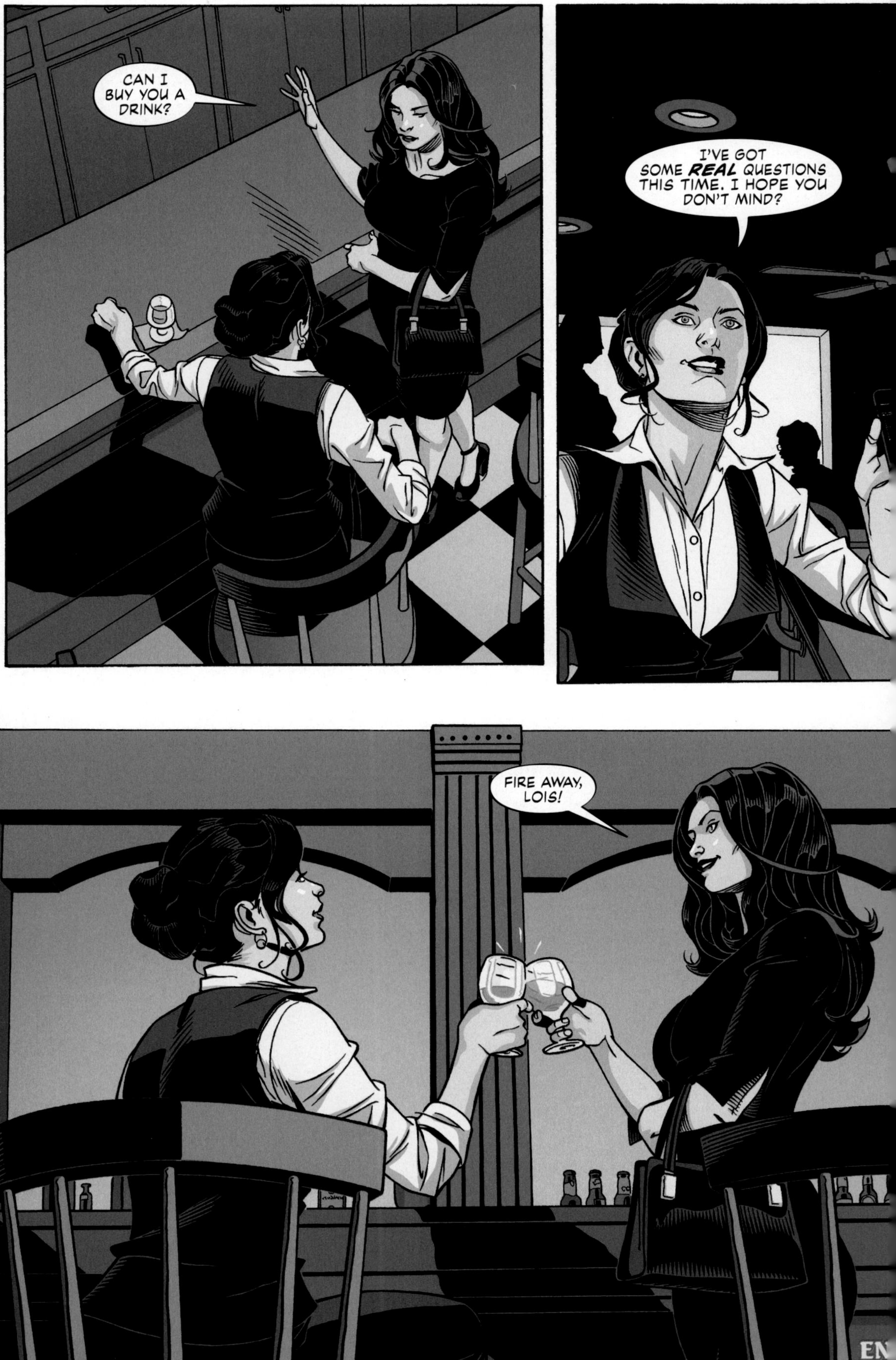
CAN I BUY YOU A DRINK?
I'VE GOT SOME REAL QUESTIONS THIS TIME. I HOPE YOU DON'T MIND?
FIRE AWAY, LOIS!

⭐ VIP

SARA RYAN
WRITER

CHRISTIAN DUCE
ARTIST

WENDY BROOME
COLORIST

SAIDA TEMOFONTE
LETTERER

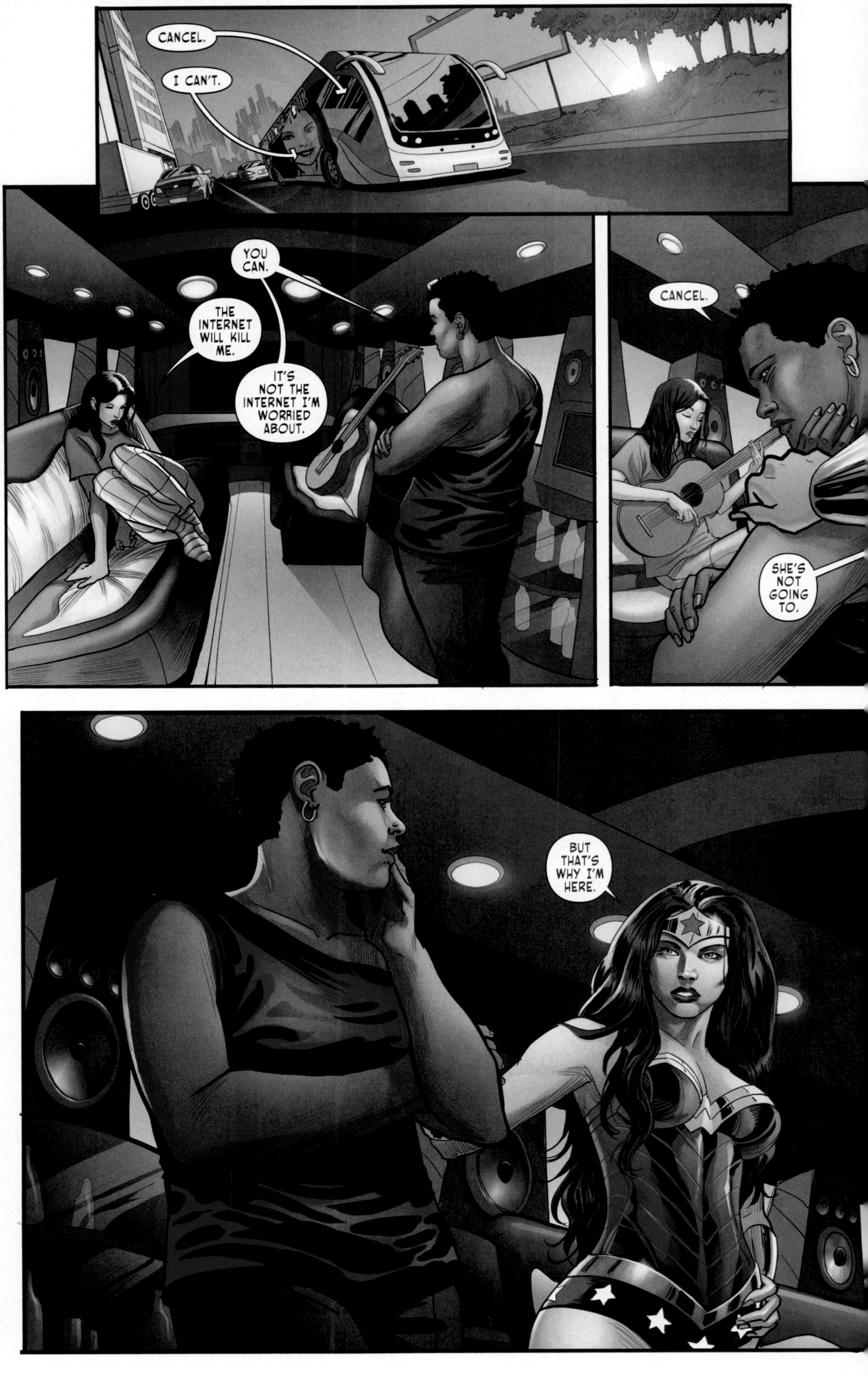
CANCEL.
I CAN'T.
YOU CAN.
THE INTERNET WILL KILL ME.
IT'S NOT THE INTERNET I'M WORRIED ABOUT.
CANCEL.
SHE'S NOT GOING TO.
BUT THAT'S WHY I'M HERE.

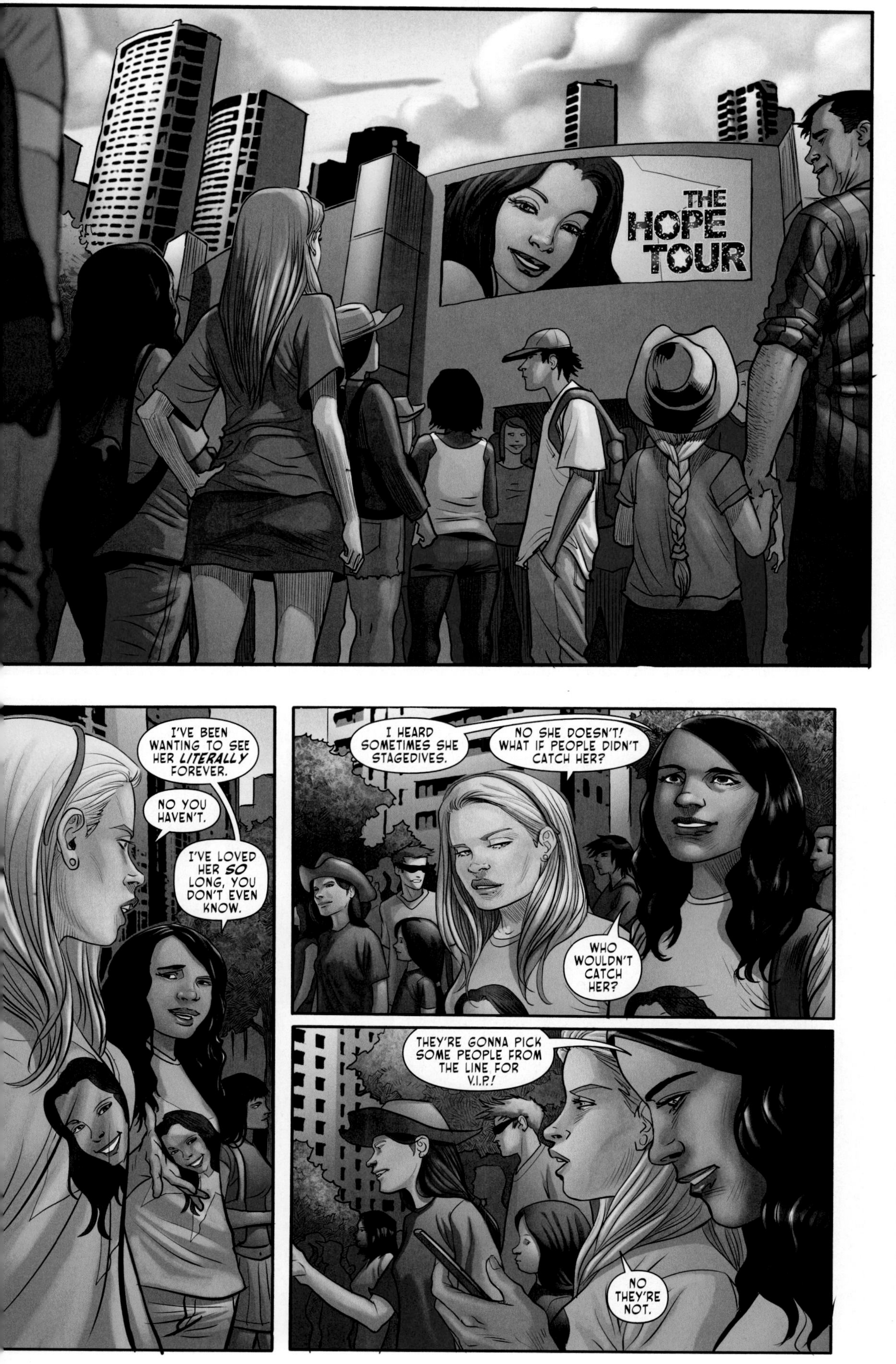
THE HOPE TOUR
I'VE BEEN WANTING TO SEE HER LITERALLY FOREVER.
NO YOU HAVEN'T.
I'VE LOVED HER SO LONG, YOU DON'T EVEN KNOW.
I HEARD SOMETIMES SHE STAGEDIVES.
NO SHE DOESN'T! WHAT IF PEOPLE DIDN'T CATCH HER?
WHO WOULDN'T CATCH HER?
THEY'RE GONNA PICK SOME PEOPLE FROM THE LINE FOR V.I.P.!
NO THEY'RE NOT.

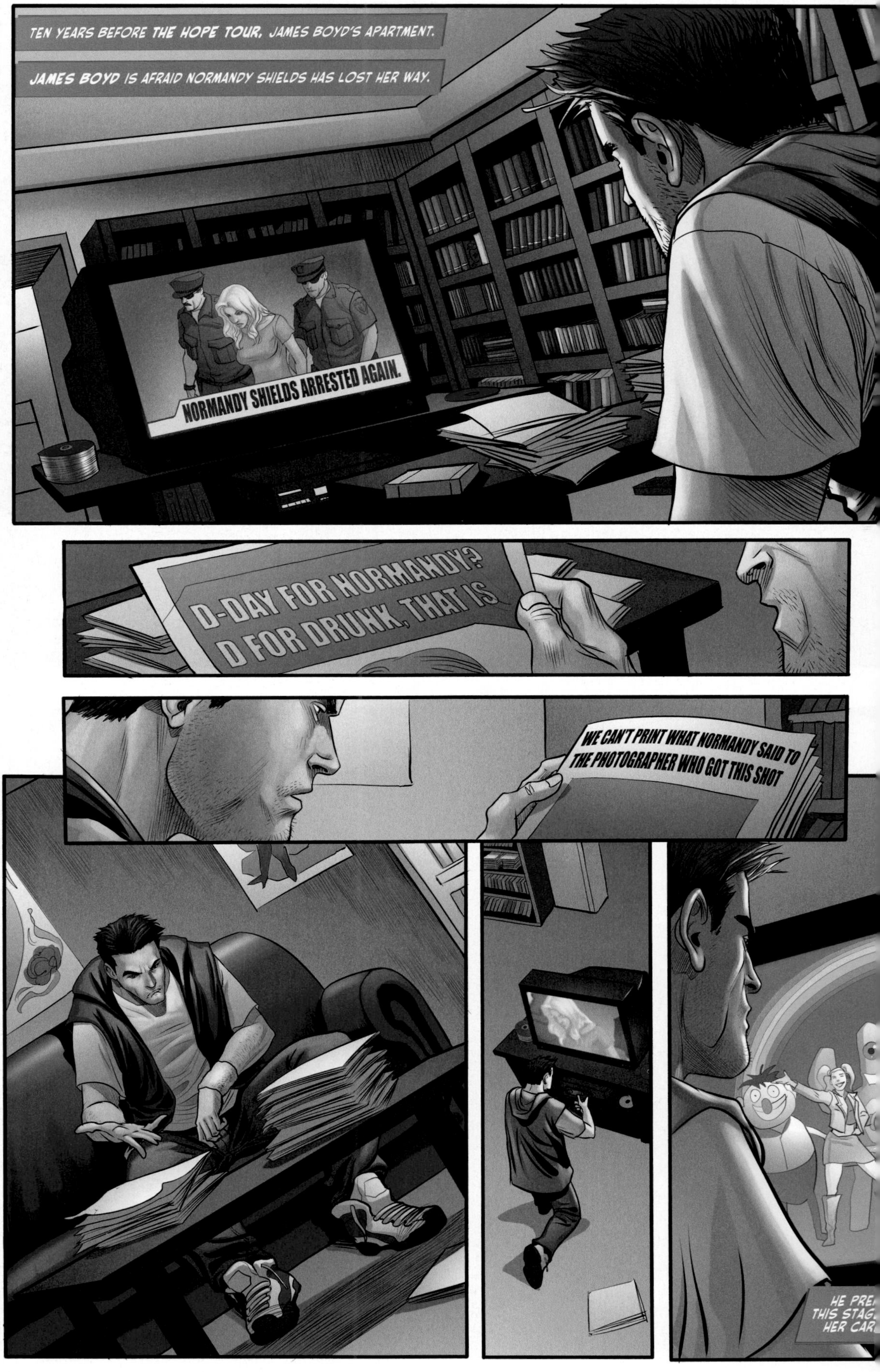

TEN YEARS BEFORE THE HOPE TOUR, JAMES BOYD'S APARTMENT.
JAMES BOYD IS AFRAID NORMANDY SHIELDS HAS LOST HER WAY.
NORMANDY SHIELDS ARRESTED AGAIN.
D-DAY FOR NORMANDY? D FOR DRUNK, THAT IS
WE CAN'T PRINT WHAT NORMANDY SAID TO THE PHOTOGRAPHER WHO GOT THIS SHOT

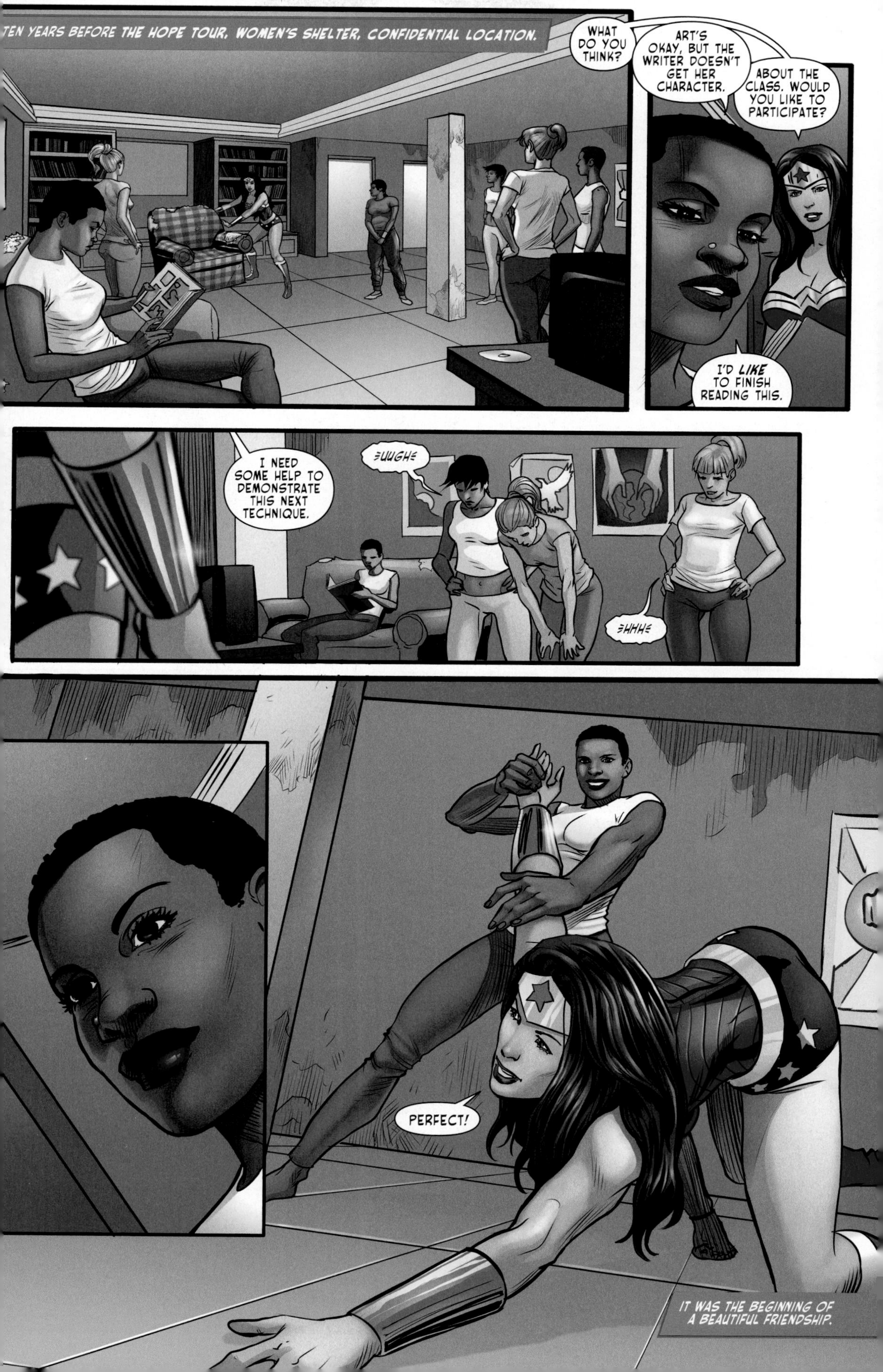
TEN YEARS BEFORE THE HOPE TOUR, WOMEN'S SHELTER, CONFIDENTIAL LOCATION.
WHAT DO YOU THINK?
ART'S OKAY, BUT THE WRITER DOESN'T GET HER CHARACTER.
ABOUT THE CLASS. WOULD YOU LIKE TO PARTICIPATE?
I'D LIKE TO FINISH READING THIS.
I NEED SOME HELP TO DEMONSTRATE THIS NEXT TECHNIQUE.
UUGH
HHH
PERFECT!
IT WAS THE BEGINNING OF A BEAUTIFUL FRIENDSHIP.

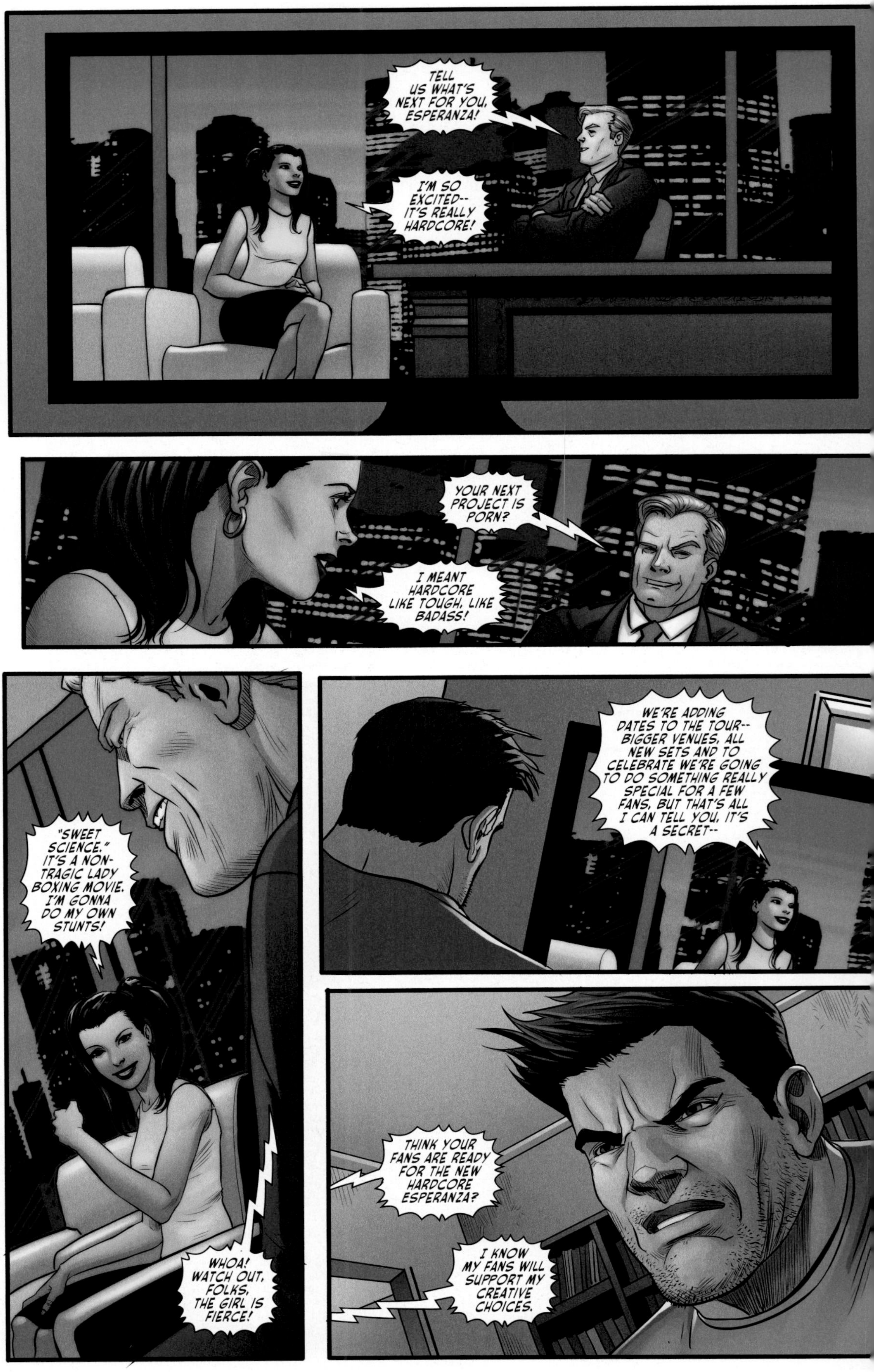
TELL US WHAT'S NEXT FOR YOU, ESPERANZA!
I'M SO EXCITED-- IT'S REALLY HARDCORE!
YOUR NEXT PROJECT IS PORN?
I MEANT HARDCORE LIKE TOUGH, LIKE BADASS!
"SWEET SCIENCE." IT'S A NON-TRAGIC LADY BOXING MOVIE. I'M GONNA DO MY OWN STUNTS!
WHOA! WATCH OUT, FOLKS, THE GIRL IS FIERCE!
WE'RE ADDING DATES TO THE TOUR-- BIGGER VENUES, ALL NEW SETS AND TO CELEBRATE WE'RE GOING TO DO SOMETHING REALLY SPECIAL FOR A FEW FANS, BUT THAT'S ALL I CAN TELL YOU, IT'S A SECRET--
THINK YOUR FANS ARE READY FOR THE NEW HARDCORE ESPERANZA?
I KNOW MY FANS WILL SUPPORT MY CREATIVE CHOICES.

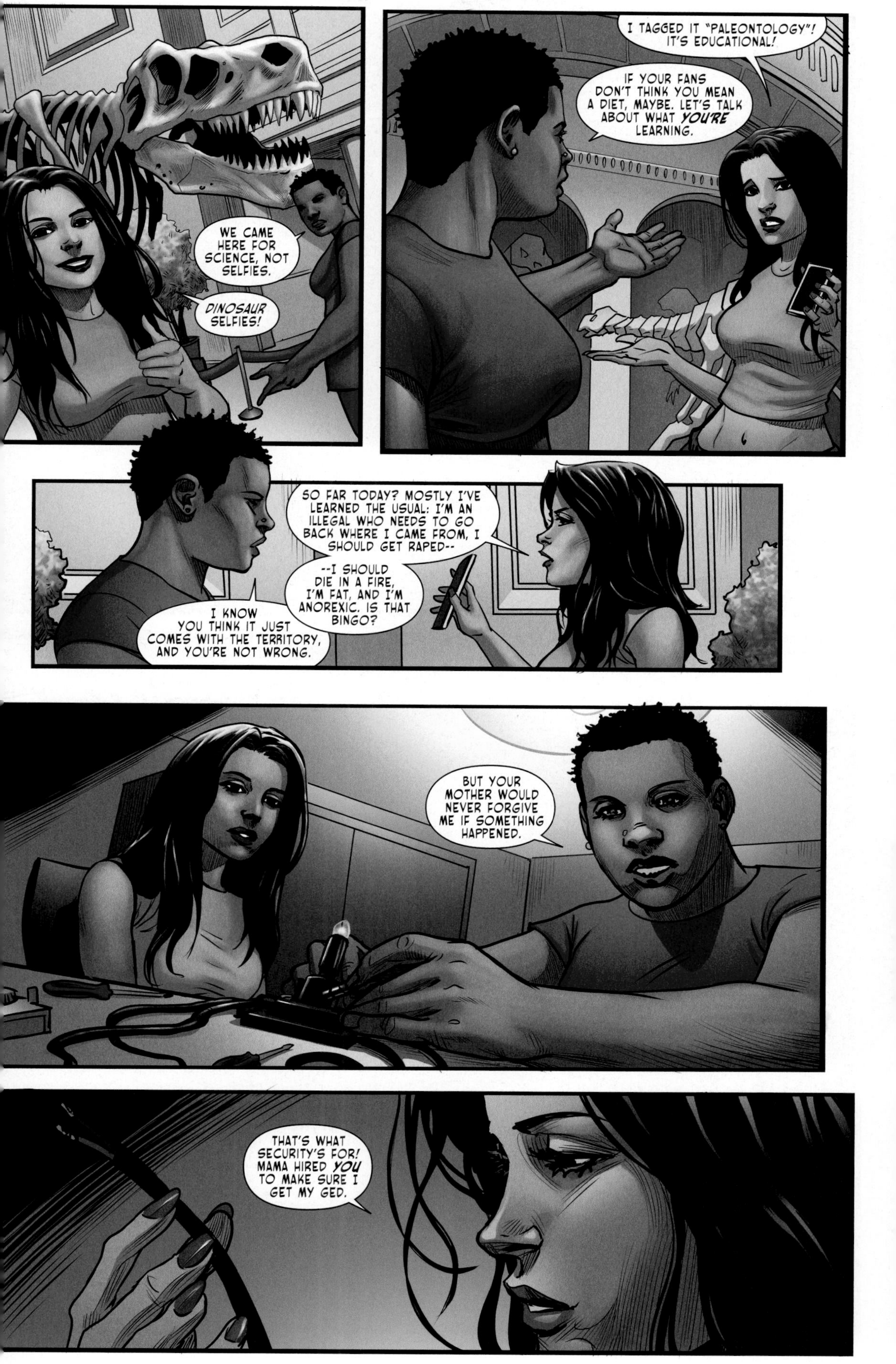
WE CAME HERE FOR SCIENCE, NOT SELFIES.
DINOSAUR SELFIES!
I TAGGED IT "PALEONTOLOGY"! IT'S EDUCATIONAL!
IF YOUR FANS DON'T THINK YOU MEAN A DIET, MAYBE. LET'S TALK ABOUT WHAT YOU'RE LEARNING.
SO FAR TODAY? MOSTLY I'VE LEARNED THE USUAL: I'M AN ILLEGAL WHO NEEDS TO GO BACK WHERE I CAME FROM, I SHOULD GET RAPED--
--I SHOULD DIE IN A FIRE, I'M FAT, AND I'M ANOREXIC. IS THAT BINGO?
I KNOW YOU THINK IT JUST COMES WITH THE TERRITORY, AND YOU'RE NOT WRONG.
BUT YOUR MOTHER WOULD NEVER FORGIVE ME IF SOMETHING HAPPENED.
THAT'S WHAT SECURITY'S FOR! MAMA HIRED YOU TO MAKE SURE I GET MY GED.

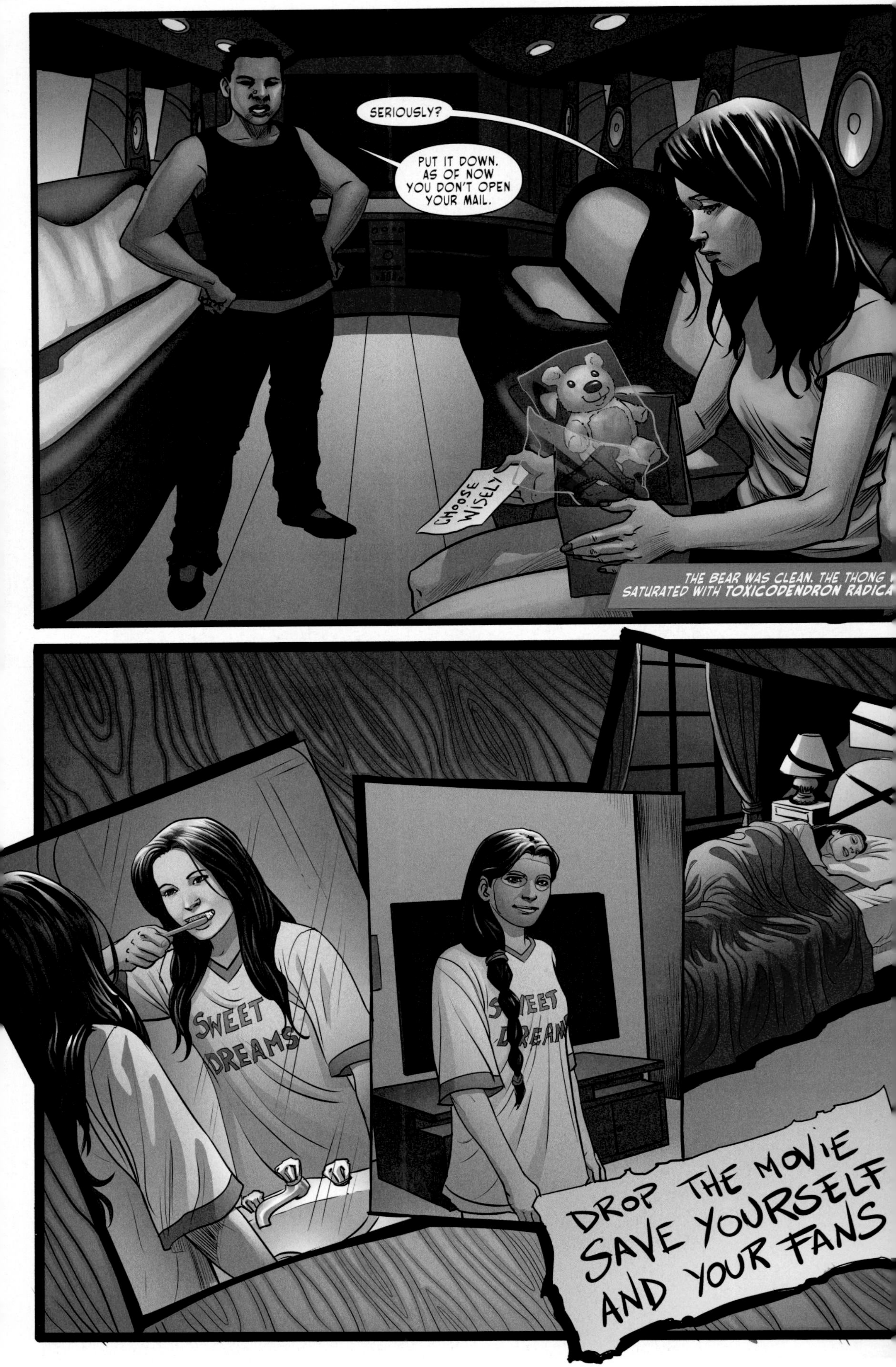
SERIOUSLY?
PUT IT DOWN. AS OF NOW YOU DON'T OPEN YOUR MAIL.
CHOOSE WISELY
THE BEAR WAS CLEAN. THE THONG
SATURATED WITH TOXICODENDRON RADICA
SWEET DREAMS
SWEET DREAMS
DROP THE MOVIE
SAVE YOURSELF
AND YOUR FANS

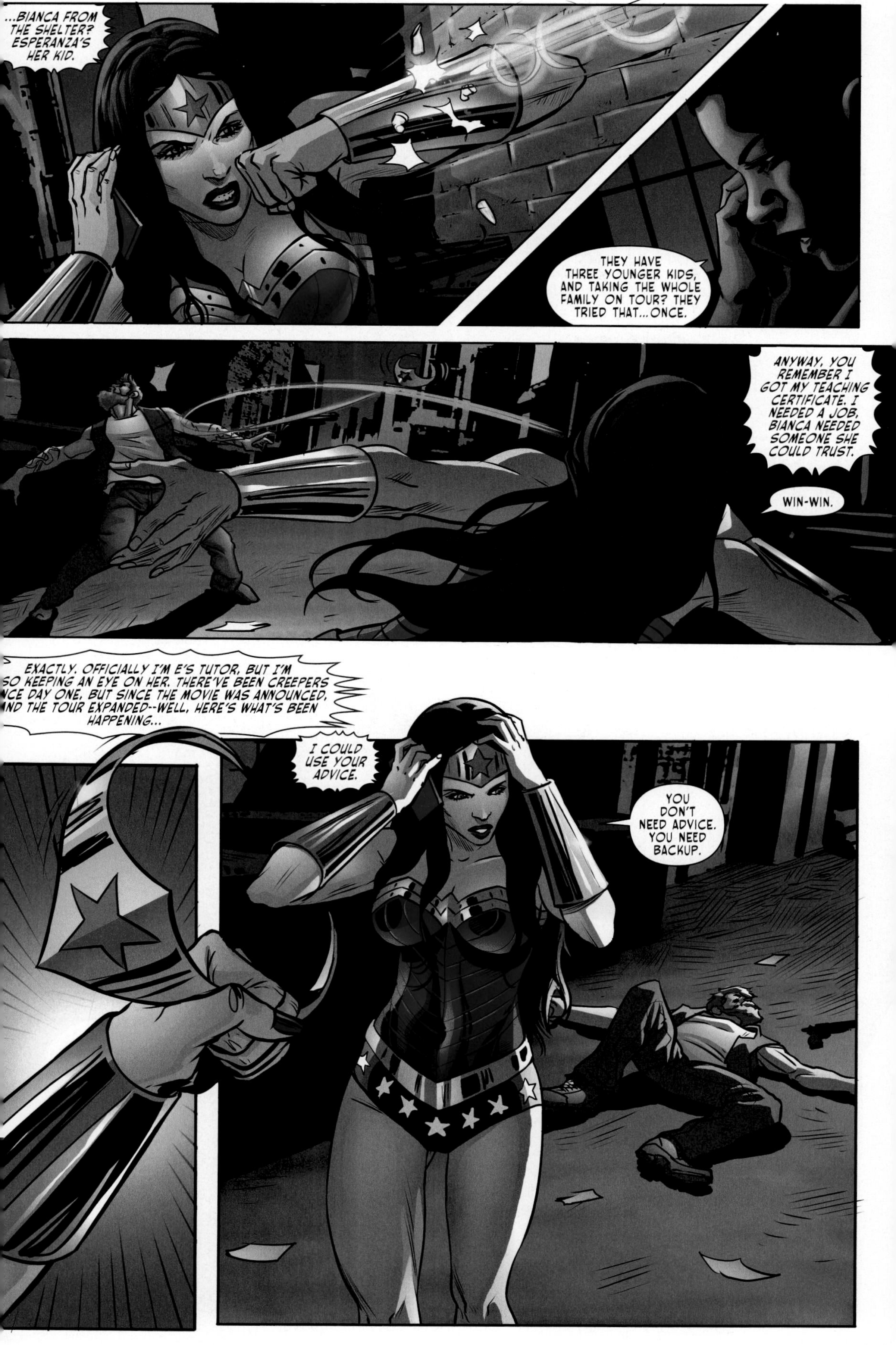
...BIANCA FROM THE SHELTER? ESPERANZA'S HER KID.
THEY HAVE THREE YOUNGER KIDS, AND TAKING THE WHOLE FAMILY ON TOUR? THEY TRIED THAT...ONCE.
ANYWAY, YOU REMEMBER I GOT MY TEACHING CERTIFICATE. I NEEDED A JOB, BIANCA NEEDED SOMEONE SHE COULD TRUST.
WIN-WIN.
EXACTLY. OFFICIALLY I'M E'S TUTOR, BUT I'M SO KEEPING AN EYE ON HER. THERE'VE BEEN CREEPERS NCE DAY ONE, BUT SINCE THE MOVIE WAS ANNOUNCED, AND THE TOUR EXPANDED--WELL, HERE'S WHAT'S BEEN HAPPENING...
I COULD USE YOUR ADVICE.
YOU DON'T NEED ADVICE. YOU NEED BACKUP.

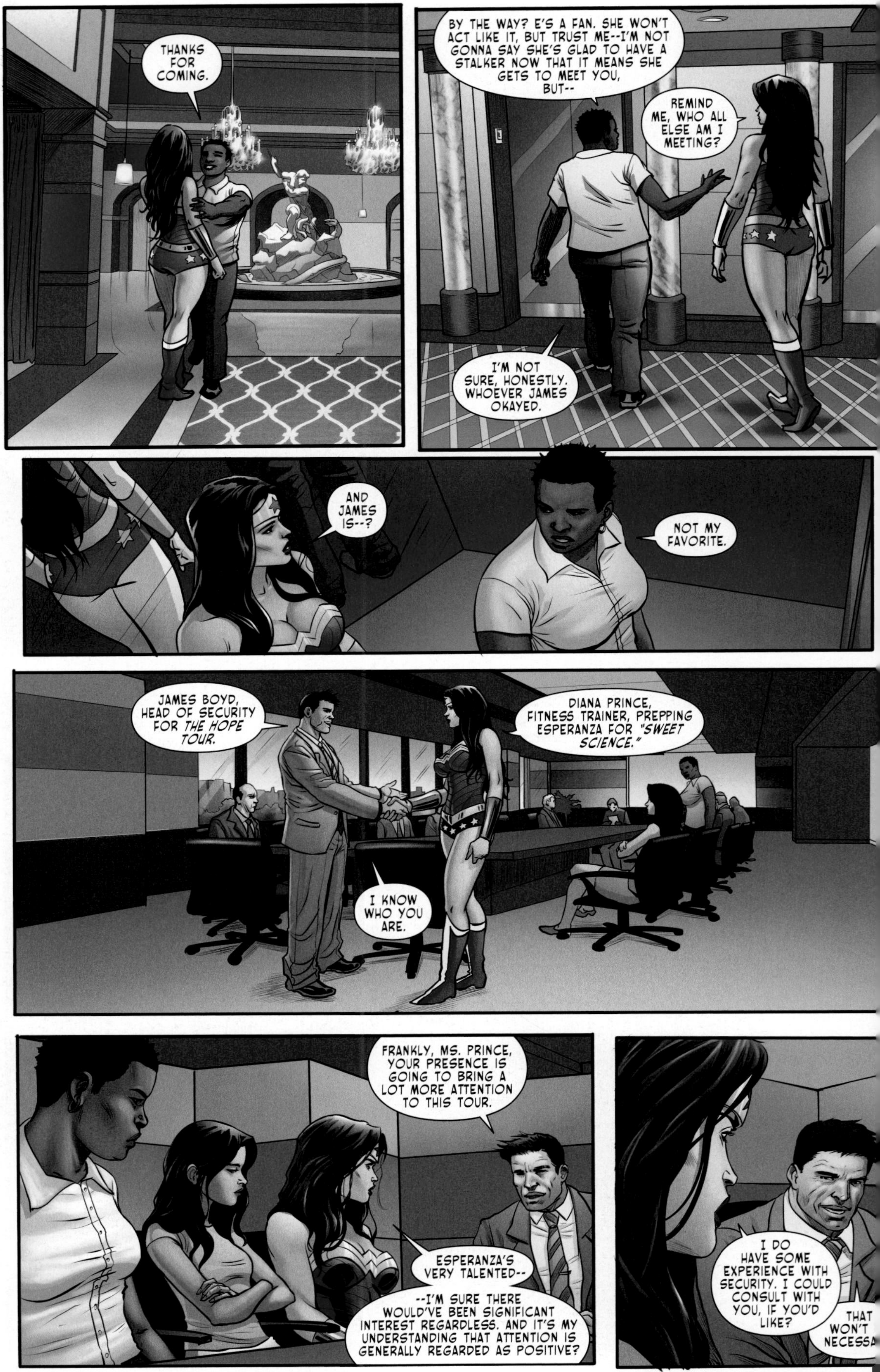
THANKS FOR COMING.
BY THE WAY? E'S A FAN. SHE WON'T ACT LIKE IT, BUT TRUST ME--I'M NOT GONNA SAY SHE'S GLAD TO HAVE A STALKER NOW THAT IT MEANS SHE GETS TO MEET YOU, BUT--
REMIND ME, WHO ALL ELSE AM I MEETING?
I'M NOT SURE, HONESTLY. WHOEVER JAMES OKAYED.
AND JAMES IS--?
NOT MY FAVORITE.
JAMES BOYD, HEAD OF SECURITY FOR THE HOPE TOUR.
DIANA PRINCE, FITNESS TRAINER, PREPPING ESPERANZA FOR "SWEET SCIENCE."
I KNOW WHO YOU ARE.
FRANKLY, MS. PRINCE, YOUR PRESENCE IS GOING TO BRING A LOT MORE ATTENTION TO THIS TOUR.
ESPERANZA'S VERY TALENTED--
--I'M SURE THERE WOULD'VE BEEN SIGNIFICANT INTEREST REGARDLESS. AND IT'S MY UNDERSTANDING THAT ATTENTION IS GENERALLY REGARDED AS POSITIVE?
I DO HAVE SOME EXPERIENCE WITH SECURITY. I COULD CONSULT WITH YOU, IF YOU'D LIKE?

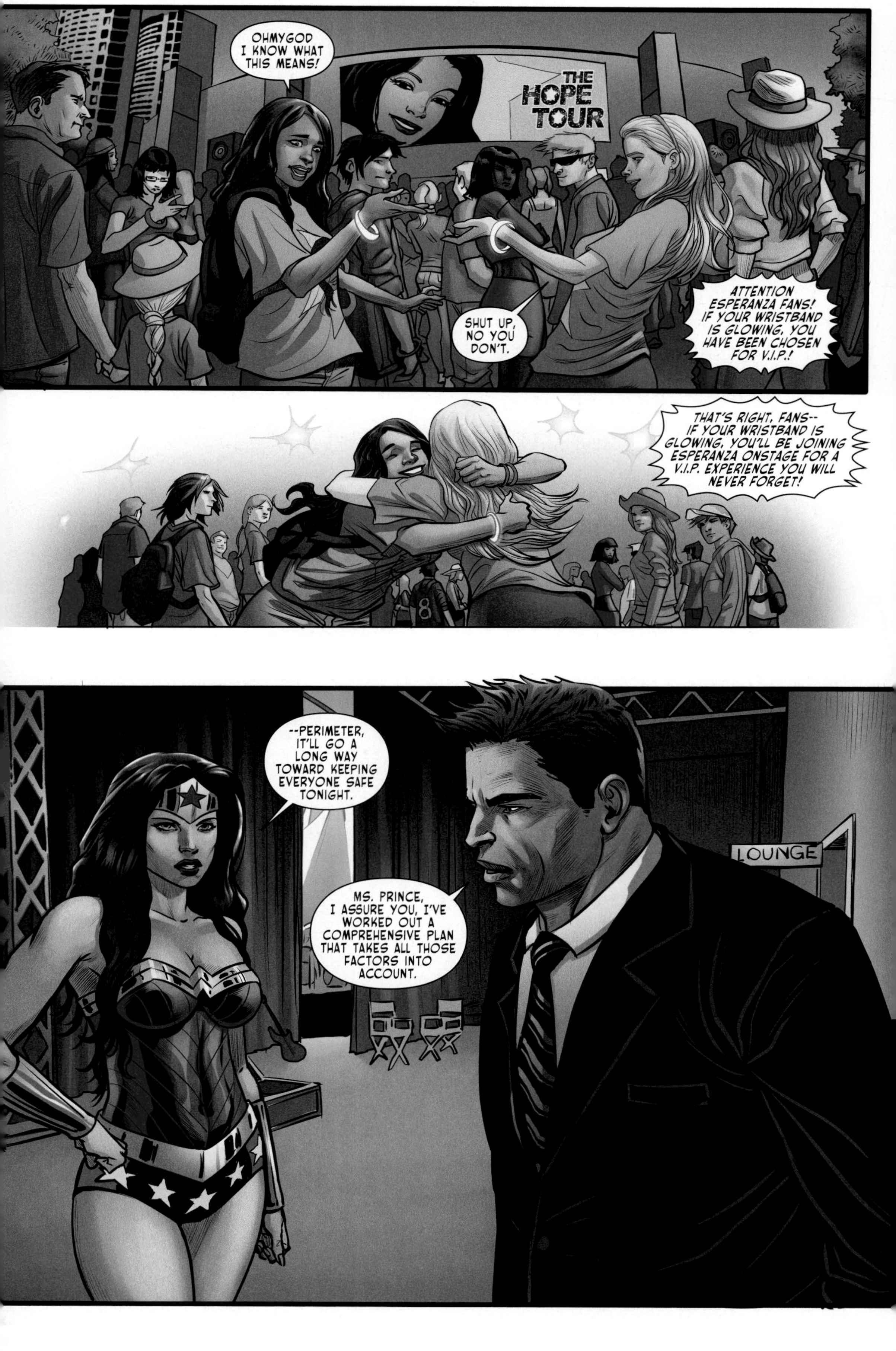
OHMYGOD I KNOW WHAT THIS MEANS!
THE HOPE TOUR
SHUT UP, NO YOU DON'T.
ATTENTION ESPERANZA FANS! IF YOUR WRISTBAND IS GLOWING, YOU HAVE BEEN CHOSEN FOR V.I.P.!
THAT'S RIGHT, FANS-- IF YOUR WRISTBAND IS GLOWING, YOU'LL BE JOINING ESPERANZA ONSTAGE FOR A V.I.P. EXPERIENCE YOU WILL NEVER FORGET!
--PERIMETER, IT'LL GO A LONG WAY TOWARD KEEPING EVERYONE SAFE TONIGHT.
MS. PRINCE, I ASSURE YOU, I'VE WORKED OUT A COMPREHENSIVE PLAN THAT TAKES ALL THOSE FACTORS INTO ACCOUNT.
LOUNGE

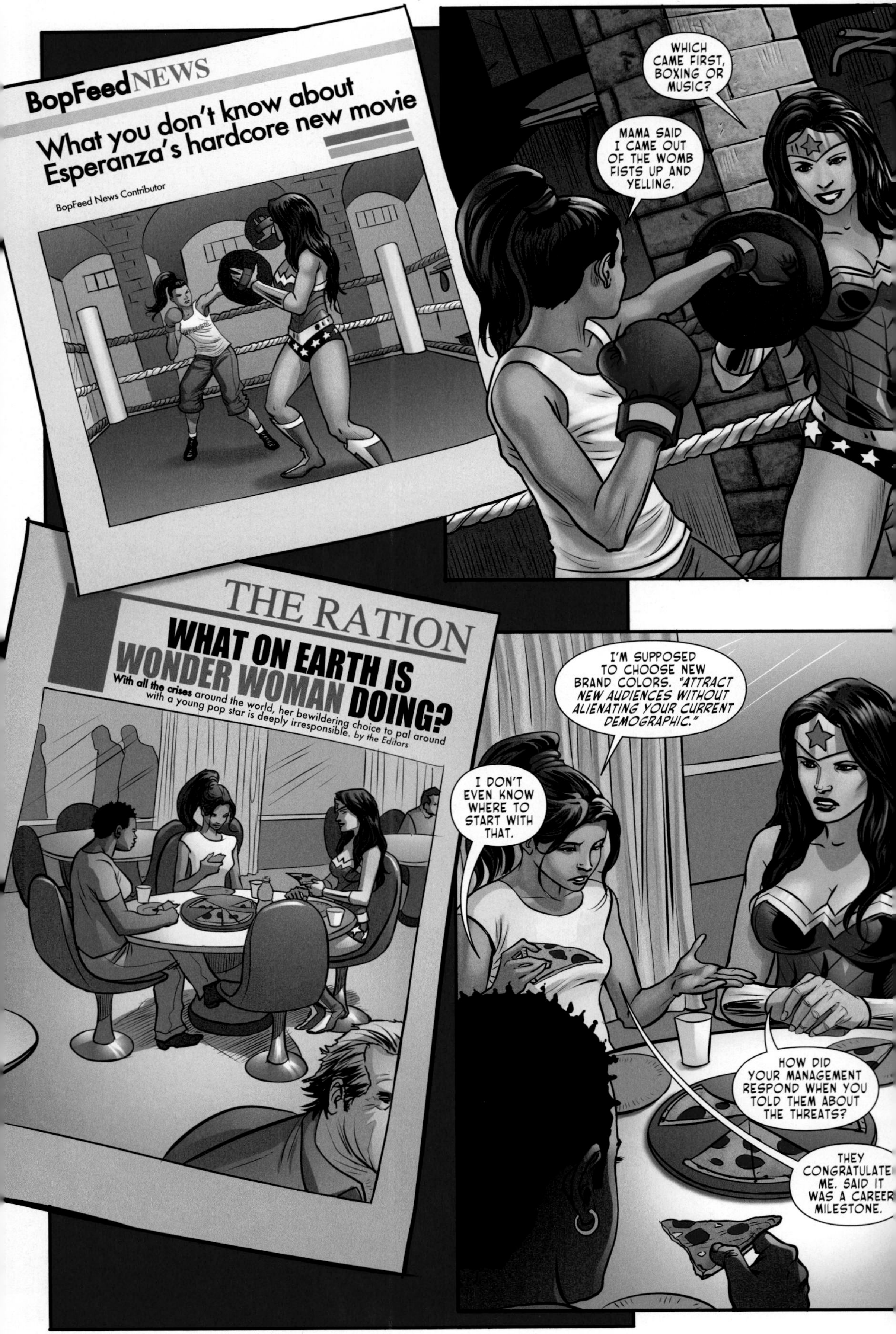
BopFeed NEWS
What you don't know about Esperanza's hardcore new movie
BopFeed News Contributor
WHICH CAME FIRST, BOXING OR MUSIC?
MAMA SAID I CAME OUT OF THE WOMB FISTS UP AND YELLING.
THE RATION
WHAT ON EARTH IS WONDER WOMAN DOING?
With all the crises around the world, her bewildering choice to pal around with a young pop star is deeply irresponsible. by the Editors
I'M SUPPOSED TO CHOOSE NEW BRAND COLORS. "ATTRACT NEW AUDIENCES WITHOUT ALIENATING YOUR CURRENT DEMOGRAPHIC."
I DON'T EVEN KNOW WHERE TO START WITH THAT.
HOW DID YOUR MANAGEMENT RESPOND WHEN YOU TOLD THEM ABOUT THE THREATS?
THEY CONGRATULATE ME. SAID IT WAS A CAREER MILESTONE.

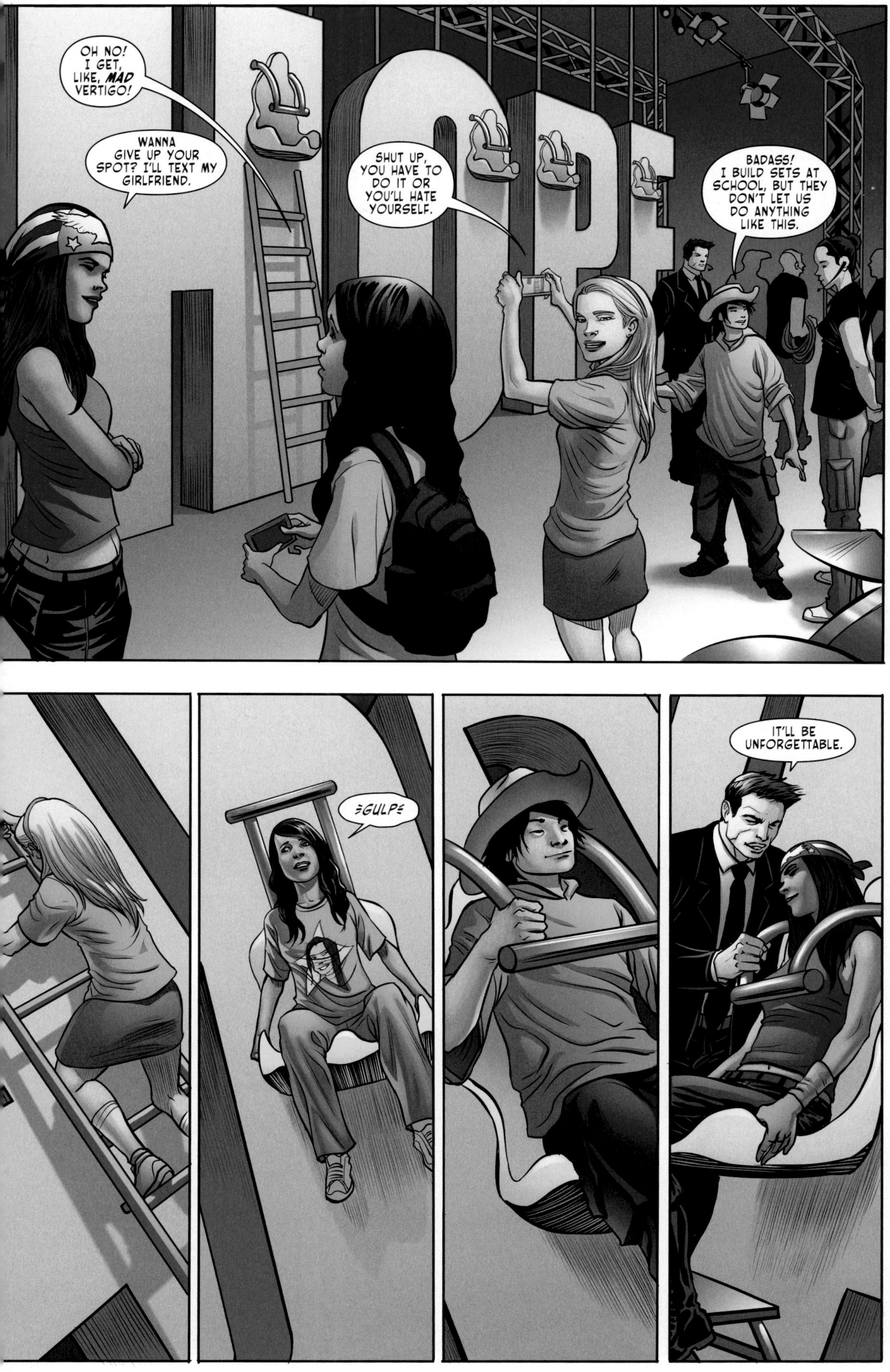

OH NO! I GET, LIKE, *MAD* VERTIGO!
WANNA GIVE UP YOUR SPOT? I'LL TEXT MY GIRLFRIEND.
SHUT UP, YOU HAVE TO DO IT OR YOU'LL HATE YOURSELF.
BADASS! I BUILD SETS AT SCHOOL, BUT THEY DON'T LET US DO ANYTHING LIKE THIS.
GULP
IT'LL BE UNFORGETTABLE.

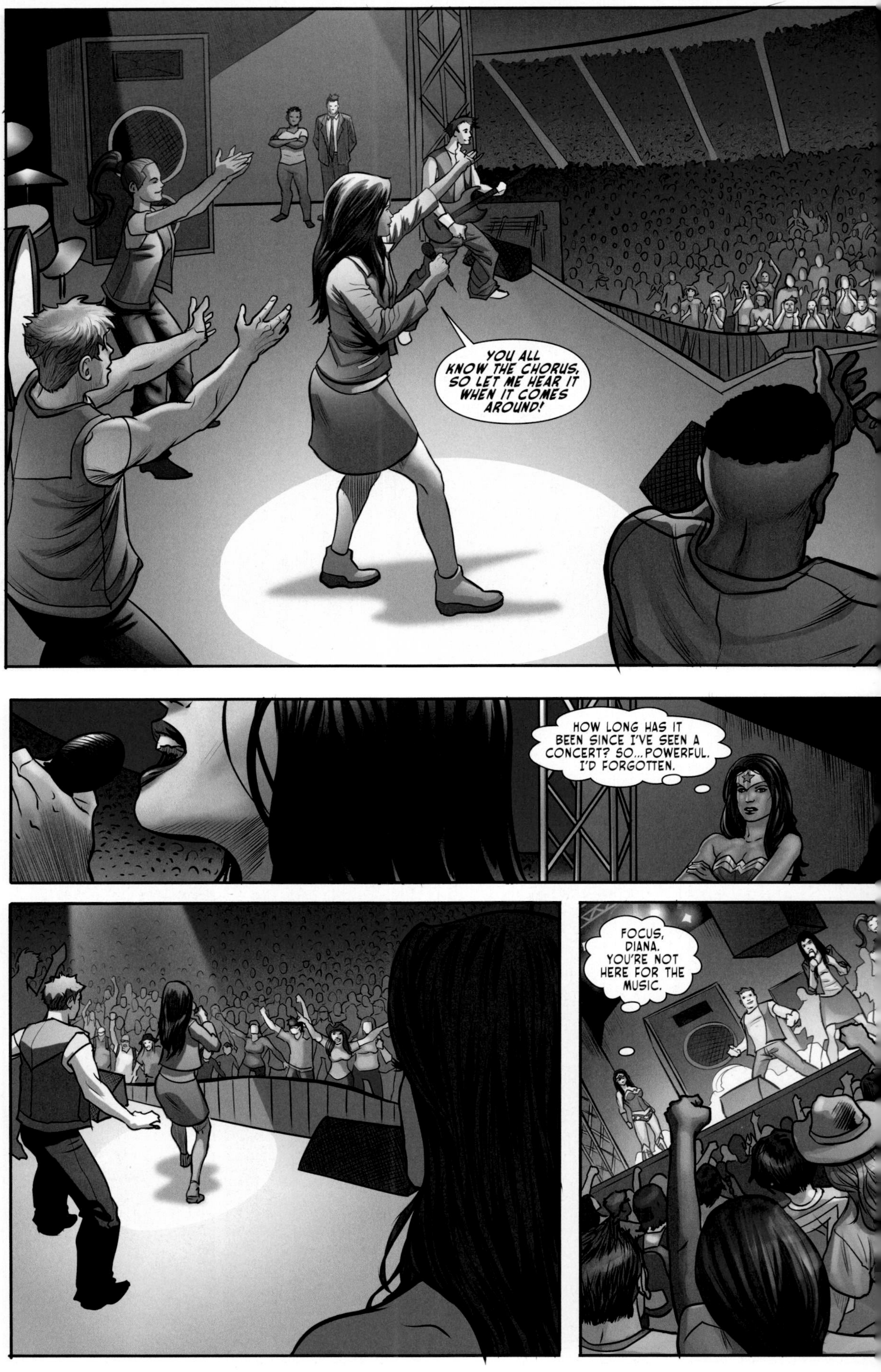
YOU ALL KNOW THE CHORUS, SO LET ME HEAR IT WHEN IT COMES AROUND!
HOW LONG HAS IT BEEN SINCE I'VE SEEN A CONCERT? SO...POWERFUL. I'D FORGOTTEN.
FOCUS, DIANA. YOU'RE NOT HERE FOR THE MUSIC.

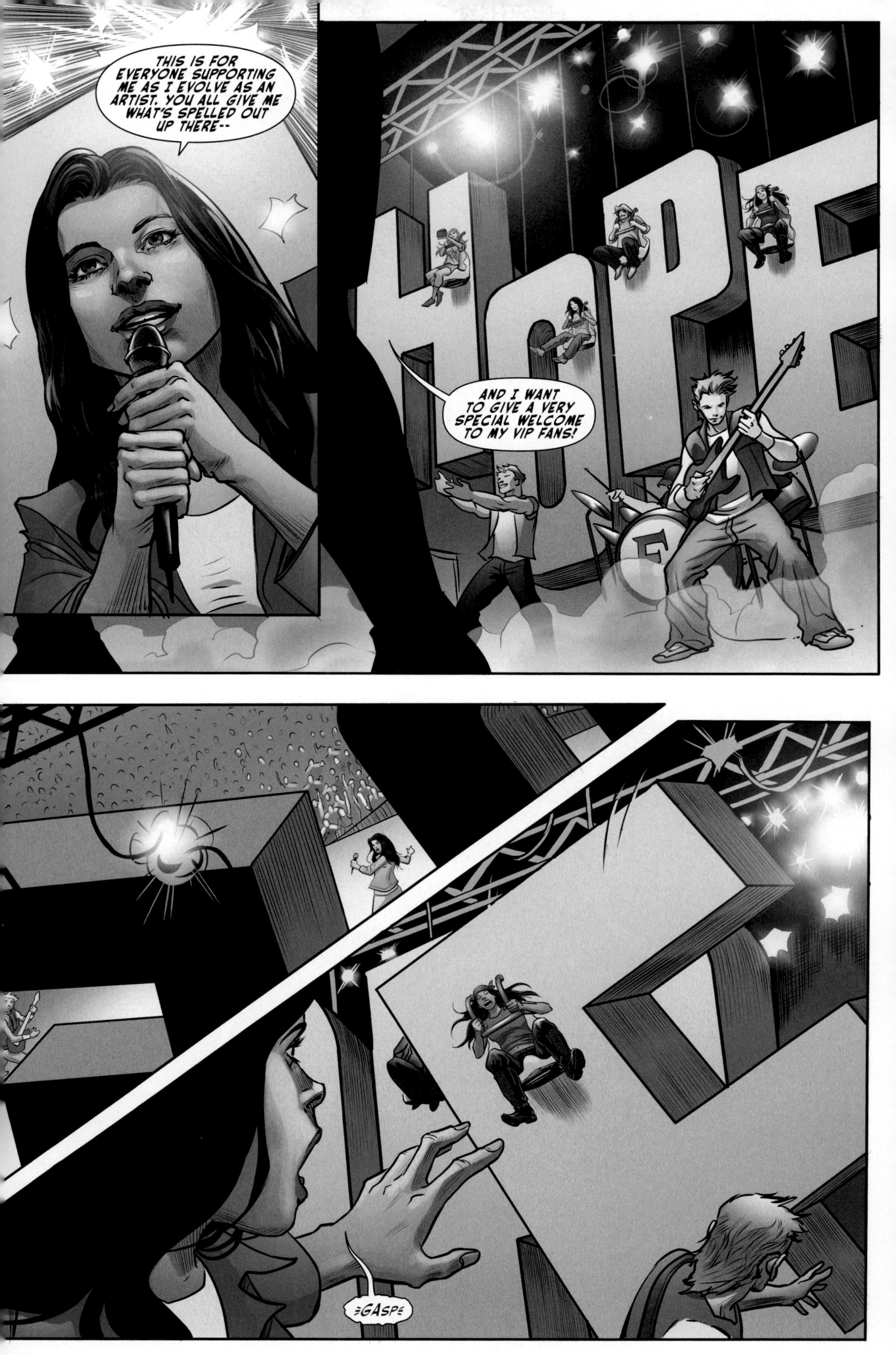

THIS IS FOR EVERYONE SUPPORTING ME AS I EVOLVE AS AN ARTIST. YOU ALL GIVE ME WHAT'S SPELLED OUT UP THERE--
AND I WANT TO GIVE A VERY SPECIAL WELCOME TO MY VIP FANS!
GASP

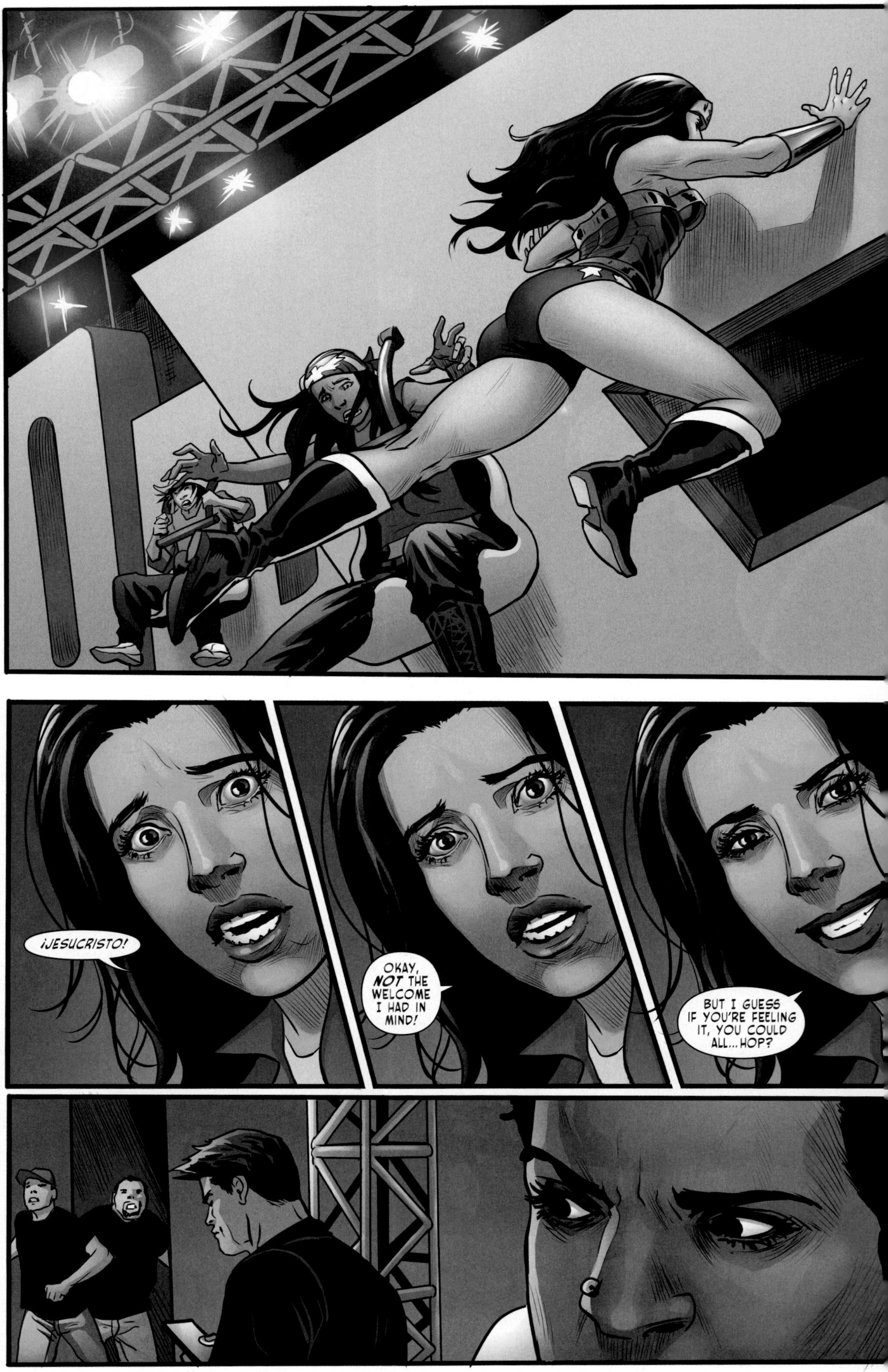
¡JESUCRISTO!
OKAY, NOT THE WELCOME I HAD IN MIND!
BUT I GUESS IF YOU'RE FEELING IT, YOU COULD ALL... HOP?

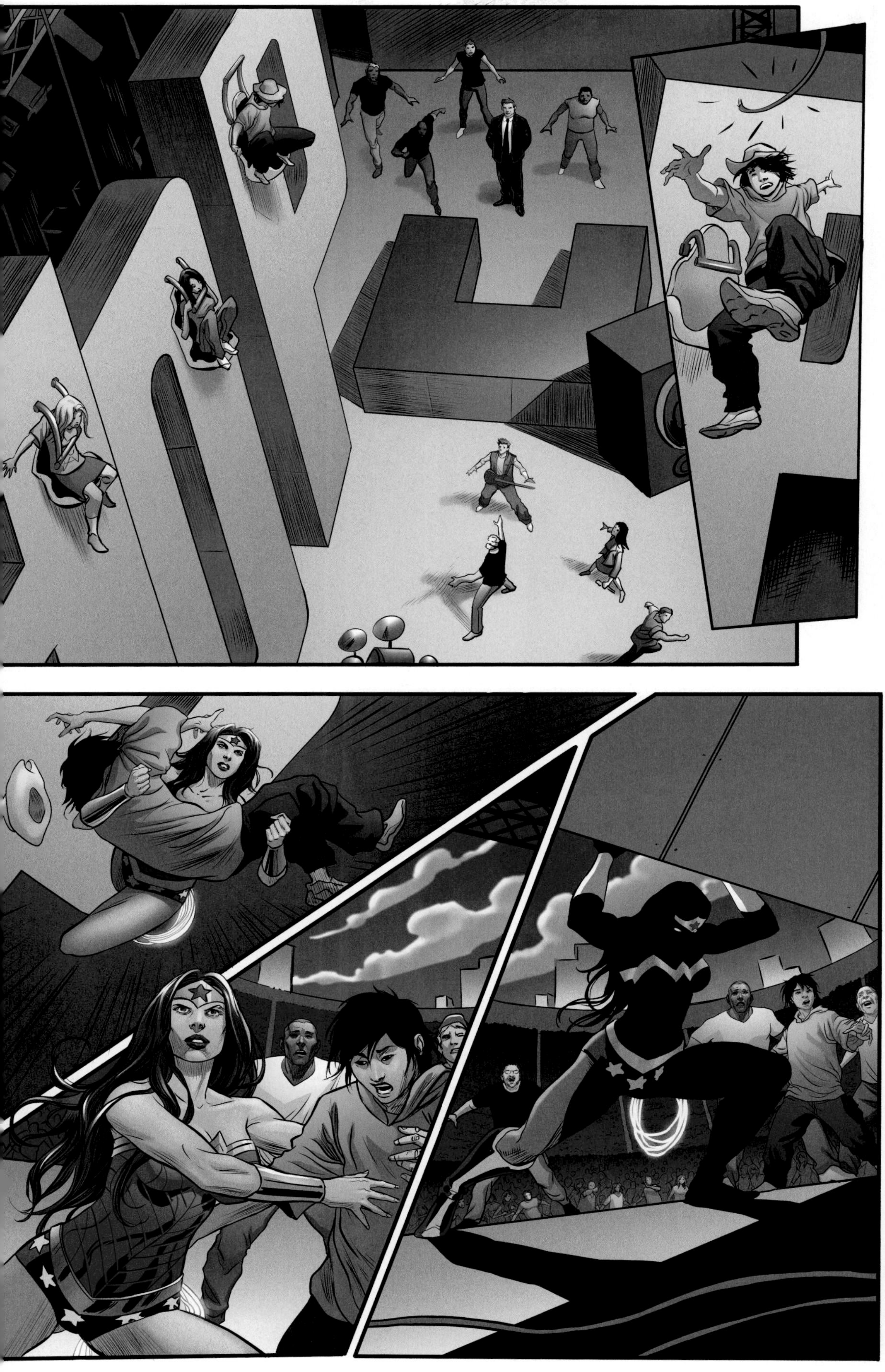

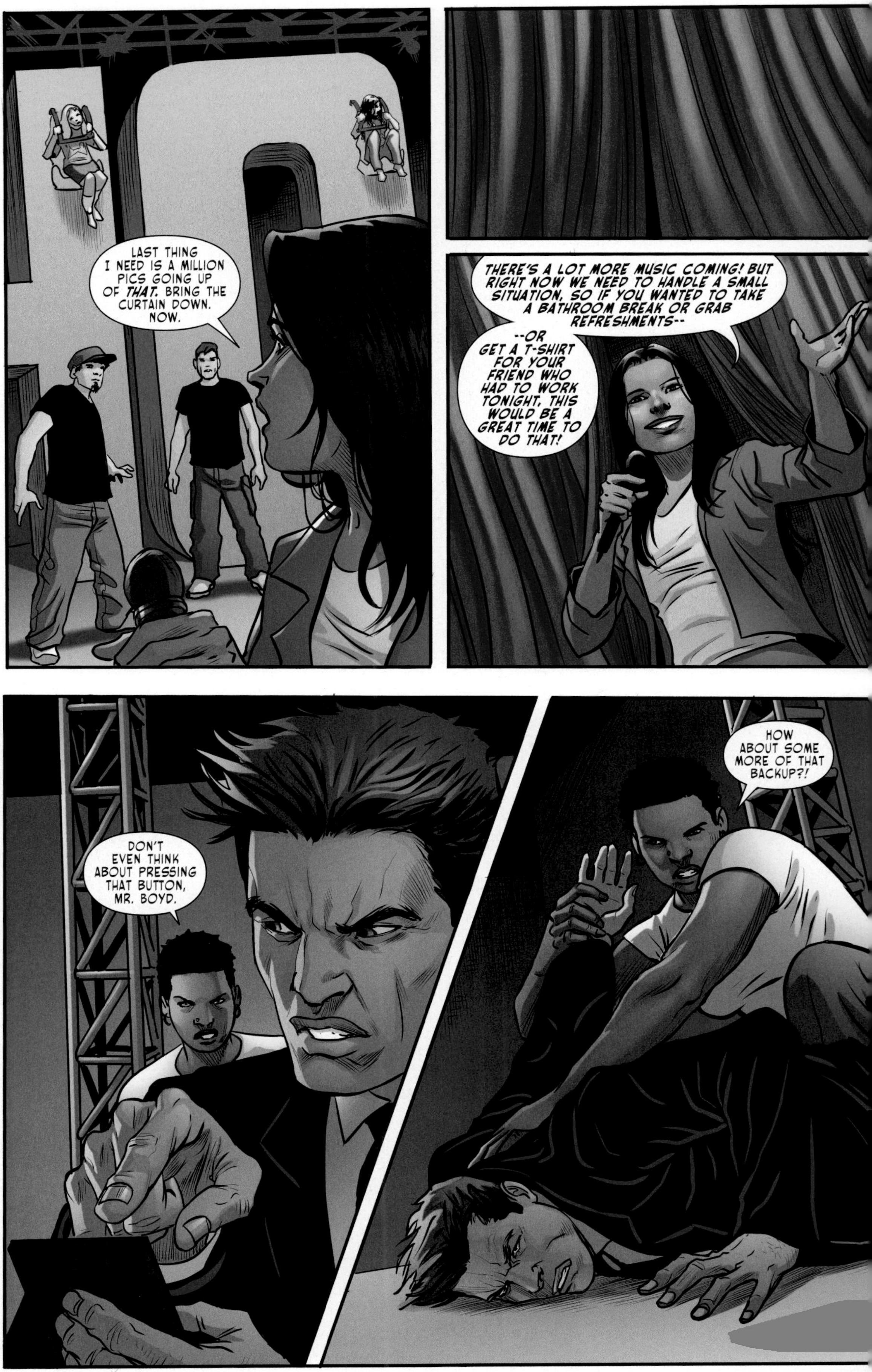
LAST THING I NEED IS A MILLION PICS GOING UP OF *THAT*. BRING THE CURTAIN DOWN. NOW.
THERE'S A LOT MORE MUSIC COMING! BUT RIGHT NOW WE NEED TO HANDLE A SMALL SITUATION, SO IF YOU WANTED TO TAKE A BATHROOM BREAK OR GRAB REFRESHMENTS--
--OR GET A T-SHIRT FOR YOUR FRIEND WHO HAD TO WORK TONIGHT, THIS WOULD BE A GREAT TIME TO DO THAT!
DON'T EVEN THINK ABOUT PRESSING THAT BUTTON, MR. BOYD.
HOW ABOUT SOME MORE OF THAT BACKUP?!

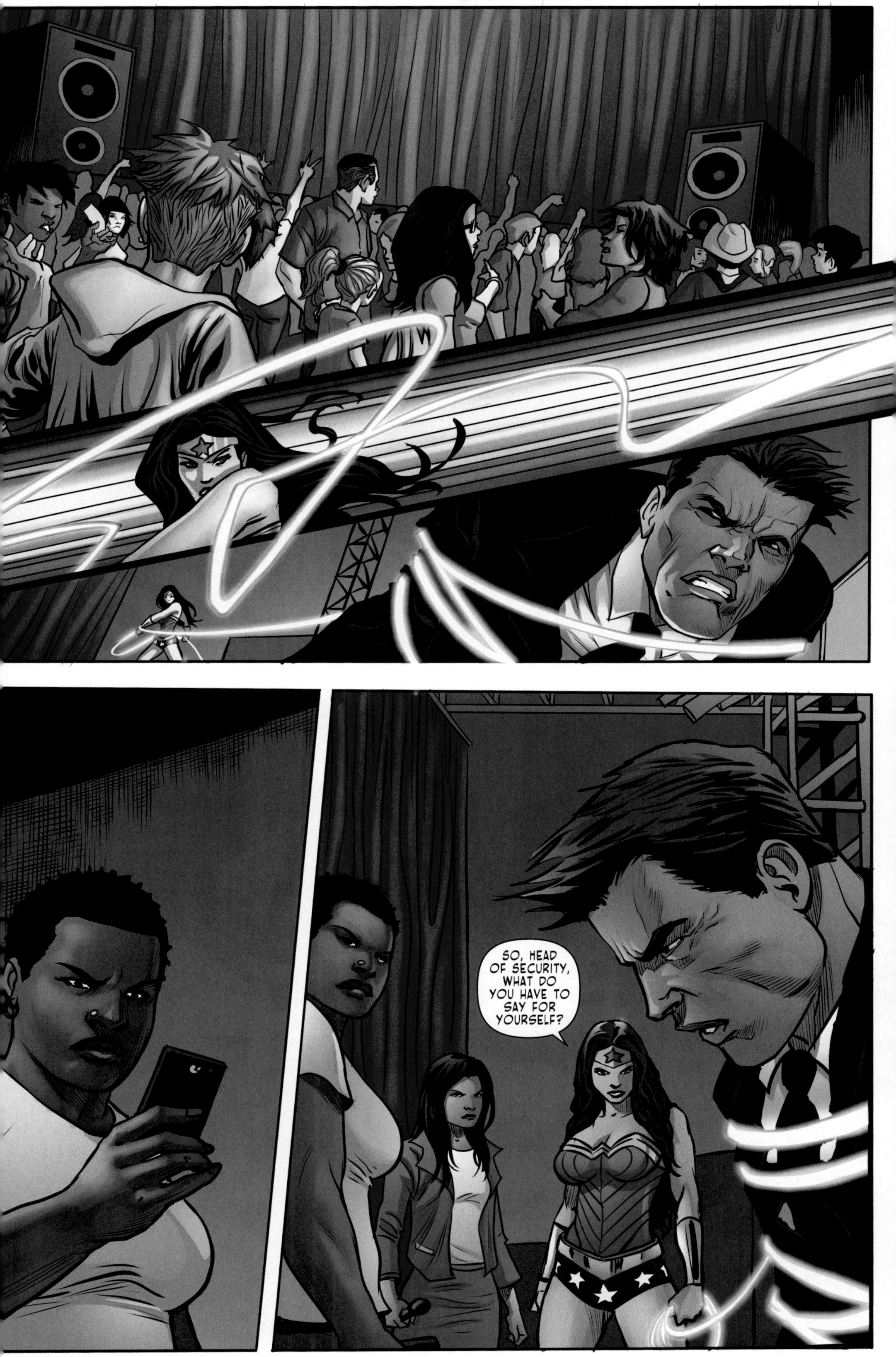
SO, HEAD OF SECURITY, WHAT DO YOU HAVE TO SAY FOR YOURSELF?

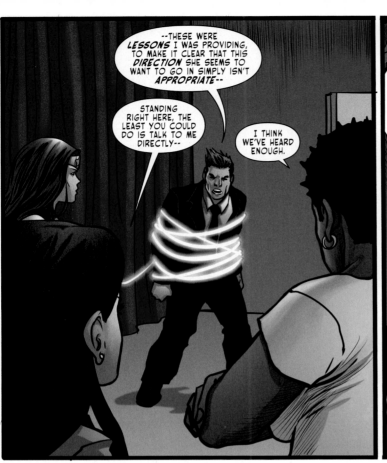

--THESE WERE *LESSONS* I WAS PROVIDING, TO MAKE IT CLEAR THAT THIS *DIRECTION* SHE SEEMS TO WANT TO GO IN SIMPLY ISN'T *APPROPRIATE*--

STANDING RIGHT HERE, THE LEAST YOU COULD DO IS TALK TO ME *DIRECTLY*--

I THINK WE'VE HEARD ENOUGH.

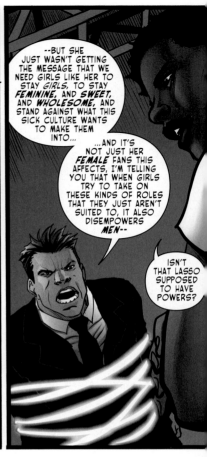

--BUT SHE JUST WASN'T GETTING THE MESSAGE THAT WE NEED GIRLS LIKE HER TO STAY *GIRLS*, TO STAY *FEMININE*, AND *SWEET*, AND *WHOLESOME*, AND STAND AGAINST WHAT THIS SICK CULTURE WANTS TO MAKE THEM INTO...

...AND IT'S NOT JUST HER *FEMALE* FANS THIS AFFECTS, I'M TELLING YOU THAT WHEN GIRLS TRY TO TAKE ON THESE KINDS OF ROLES THAT THEY JUST AREN'T SUITED TO, IT ALSO DISEMPOWERS *MEN*--

ISN'T THAT LASSO SUPPOSED TO HAVE POWERS?

THE LASSO COMPELS TRUTH, BUT IT CAN'T STOP MANSPLAINING.

I KNOW WHAT *WILL.*

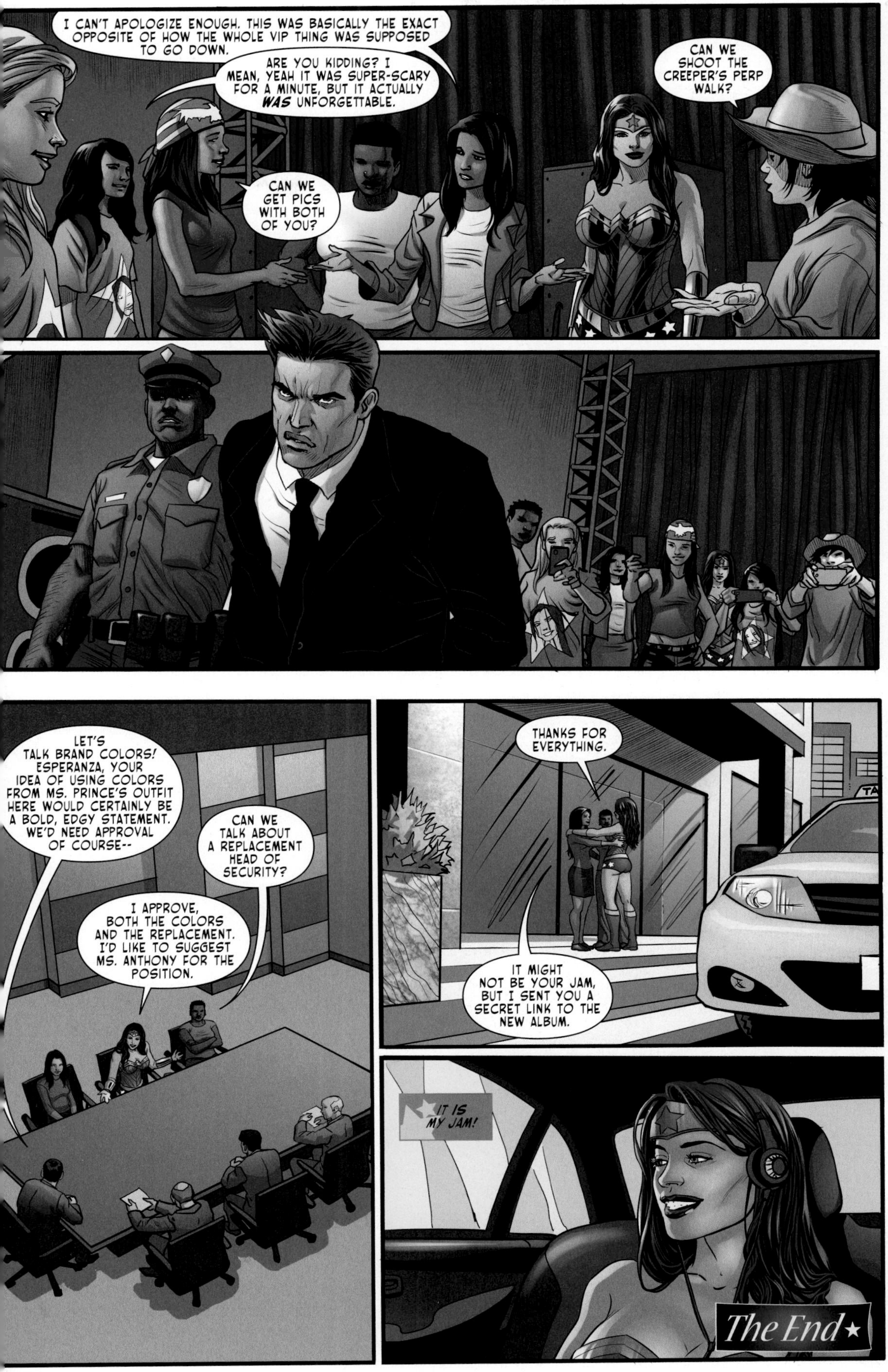
I CAN'T APOLOGIZE ENOUGH. THIS WAS BASICALLY THE EXACT OPPOSITE OF HOW THE WHOLE VIP THING WAS SUPPOSED TO GO DOWN.
ARE YOU KIDDING? I MEAN, YEAH IT WAS SUPER-SCARY FOR A MINUTE, BUT IT ACTUALLY WAS UNFORGETTABLE.
CAN WE GET PICS WITH BOTH OF YOU?
CAN WE SHOOT THE CREEPER'S PERP WALK?
LET'S TALK BRAND COLORS! ESPERANZA, YOUR IDEA OF USING COLORS FROM MS. PRINCE'S OUTFIT HERE WOULD CERTAINLY BE A BOLD, EDGY STATEMENT. WE'D NEED APPROVAL OF COURSE--
CAN WE TALK ABOUT A REPLACEMENT HEAD OF SECURITY?
I APPROVE, BOTH THE COLORS AND THE REPLACEMENT. I'D LIKE TO SUGGEST MS. ANTHONY FOR THE POSITION.
THANKS FOR EVERYTHING.
IT MIGHT NOT BE YOUR JAM, BUT I SENT YOU A SECRET LINK TO THE NEW ALBUM.
IT IS MY JAM!
The End

CASUALTIES
OF WAR

AARON LOPRESTI
WRITER and ARTIST

HI-FI
COLORIST

SAIDA TEMOFONTE
LETTERER

CASUALTIES OF WAR

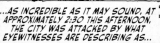

...AS INCREDIBLE AS IT MAY SOUND, AT APPROXIMATELY 2:30 THIS AFTERNOON, THE CITY WAS ATTACKED BY WHAT EYEWITNESSES ARE DESCRIBING AS...

...A DRAGON. THE ASSAULT BEGAN AT THE EDGE OF THE CITY ON THE UPPER WEST SIDE, AND THE CREATURE RAPIDLY MOVED THROUGH THE HEART OF THE CITY, LEAVING DEATH AND DESTRUCTION IN ITS WAKE.

AUTHORITIES ARE REPORTING SEVERAL FATALITIES, AND MANY MORE INJURED. REPORTEDLY, THE CREATURE HAS BURROWED ITS WAY UNDERNEATH THE ROADWAY...

...AT THE INTERSECTION OF WASHINGTON BLVD AND 5TH AVENUE IN THE HEART OF MIDTOWN.

THE AREA HAS BEEN BLOCKED OFF AND EVACUATED AS AUTHORITIES AWAIT THE ARRIVAL OF THE NATIONAL GUARD.

IN THE INTERIM, THERE IS NO CLEAR WORD ON A PLAN OF ACTION TO COMBAT THE CREATURE-- AND AUTHORITIES ARE AT A LOSS AS TO WHO OR WHAT CAN STOP IT.

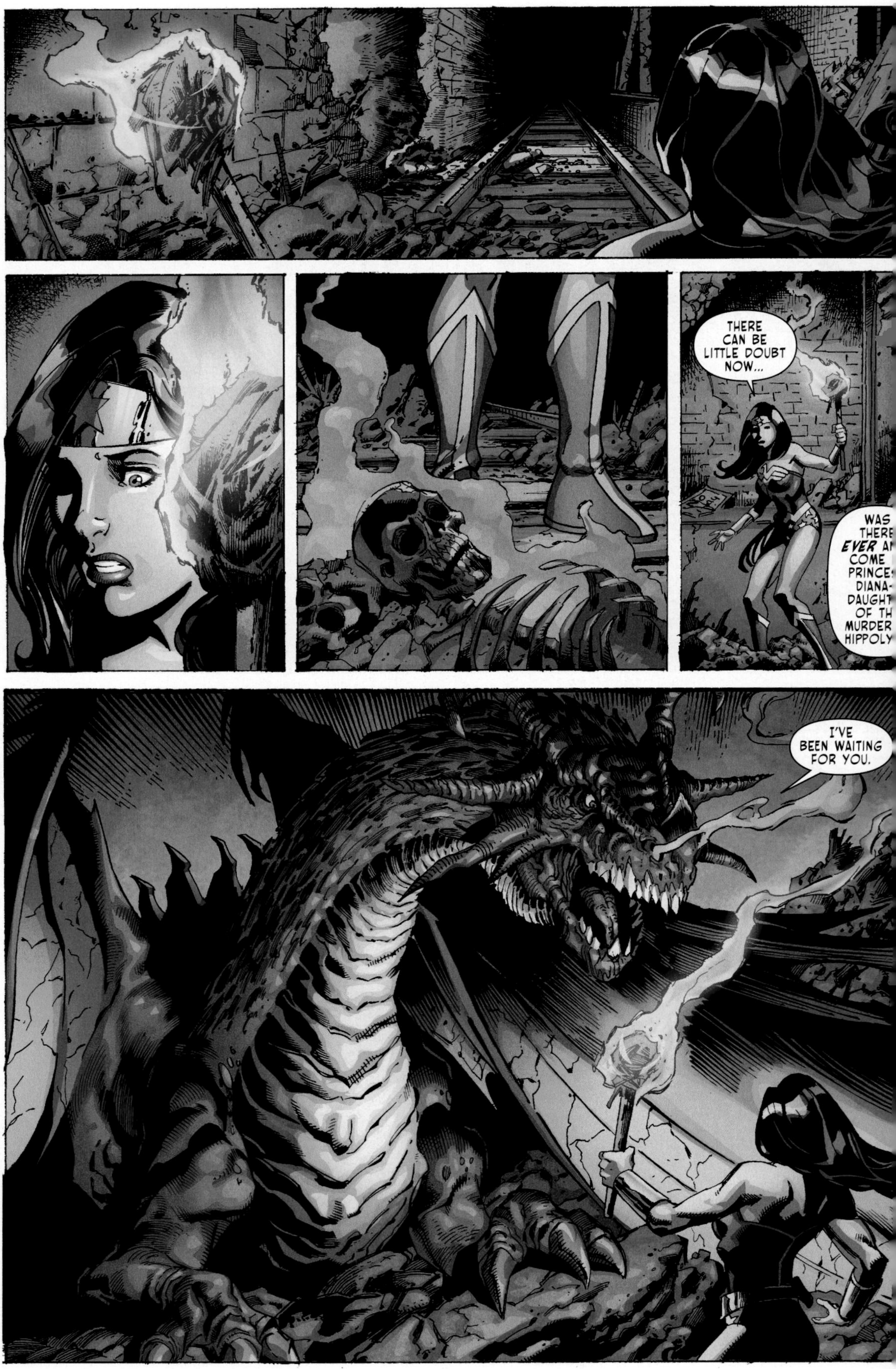

THERE CAN BE LITTLE DOUBT NOW...
WAS THERE *EVER* A COME PRINCE DIANA- DAUGHT OF TH MURDER HIPPOLY
I'VE BEEN WAITING FOR YOU.

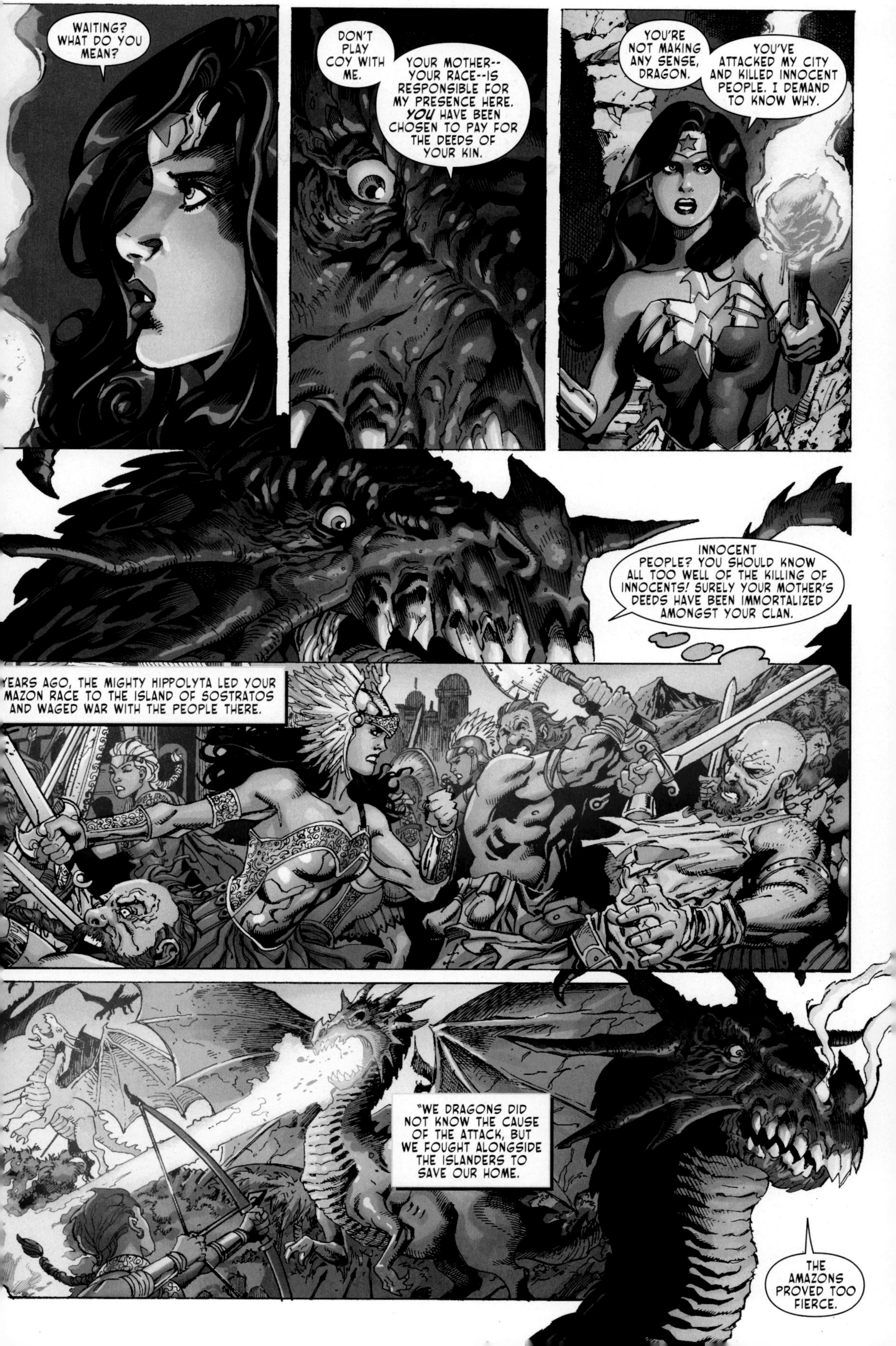
WAITING? WHAT DO YOU MEAN?
DON'T PLAY COY WITH ME.
YOUR MOTHER-- YOUR RACE--IS RESPONSIBLE FOR MY PRESENCE HERE. YOU HAVE BEEN CHOSEN TO PAY FOR THE DEEDS OF YOUR KIN.
YOU'RE NOT MAKING ANY SENSE, DRAGON.
YOU'VE ATTACKED MY CITY AND KILLED INNOCENT PEOPLE. I DEMAND TO KNOW WHY.
INNOCENT PEOPLE? YOU SHOULD KNOW ALL TOO WELL OF THE KILLING OF INNOCENTS! SURELY YOUR MOTHER'S DEEDS HAVE BEEN IMMORTALIZED AMONGST YOUR CLAN.
YEARS AGO, THE MIGHTY HIPPOLYTA LED YOUR AMAZON RACE TO THE ISLAND OF SOSTRATOS AND WAGED WAR WITH THE PEOPLE THERE.
"WE DRAGONS DID NOT KNOW THE CAUSE OF THE ATTACK, BUT WE FOUGHT ALONGSIDE THE ISLANDERS TO SAVE OUR HOME.
THE AMAZONS PROVED TOO FIERCE.

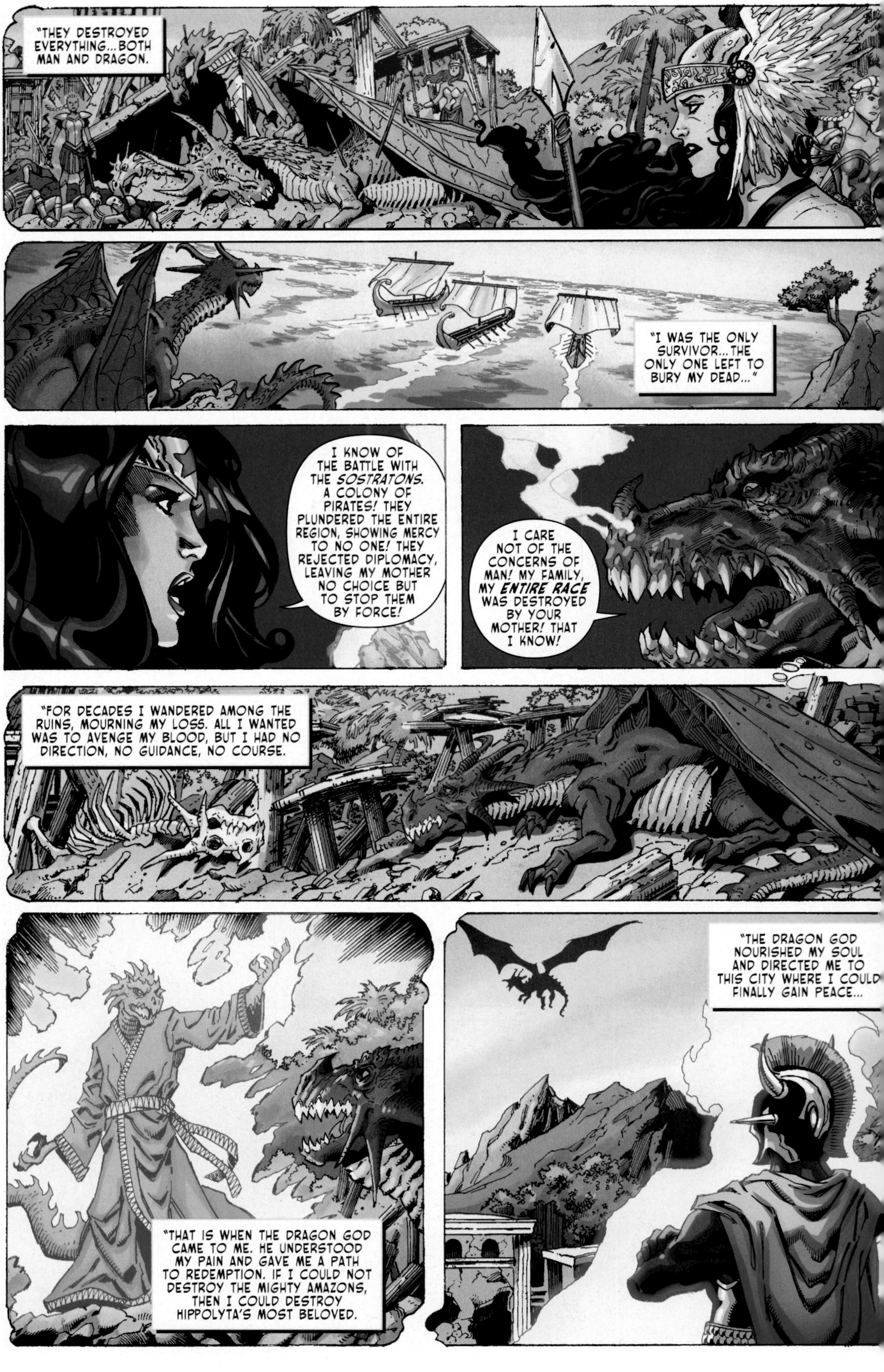
"THEY DESTROYED EVERYTHING...BOTH MAN AND DRAGON.
"I WAS THE ONLY SURVIVOR...THE ONLY ONE LEFT TO BURY MY DEAD..."
I KNOW OF THE BATTLE WITH THE *SOSTRATONS.* A COLONY OF PIRATES! THEY PLUNDERED THE ENTIRE REGION, SHOWING MERCY TO NO ONE! THEY REJECTED DIPLOMACY, LEAVING MY MOTHER NO CHOICE BUT TO STOP THEM BY FORCE!
I CARE NOT OF THE CONCERNS OF MAN! MY FAMILY, MY ***ENTIRE RACE*** WAS DESTROYED BY YOUR MOTHER! THAT I KNOW!
"FOR DECADES I WANDERED AMONG THE RUINS, MOURNING MY LOSS. ALL I WANTED WAS TO AVENGE MY BLOOD, BUT I HAD NO DIRECTION, NO GUIDANCE, NO COURSE.
"THAT IS WHEN THE DRAGON GOD CAME TO ME. HE UNDERSTOOD MY PAIN AND GAVE ME A PATH TO REDEMPTION. IF I COULD NOT DESTROY THE MIGHTY AMAZONS, THEN I COULD DESTROY HIPPOLYTA'S MOST BELOVED.
"THE DRAGON GOD NOURISHED MY SOUL AND DIRECTED ME TO THIS CITY WHERE I COULD FINALLY GAIN PEACE...

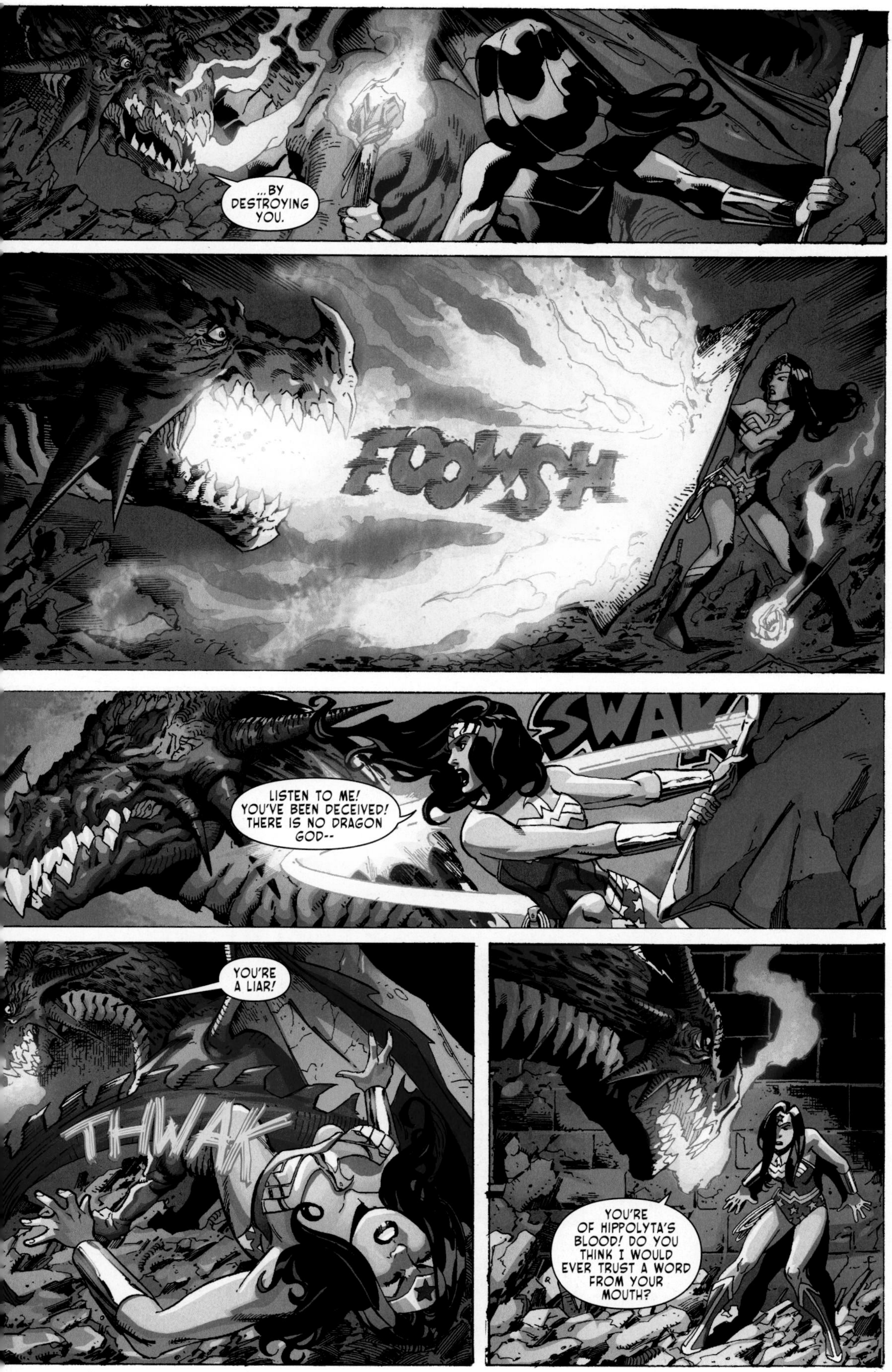

...BY DESTROYING YOU.
FOOSH
SWAK
LISTEN TO ME! YOU'VE BEEN DECEIVED! THERE IS NO DRAGON GOD--
YOU'RE A LIAR!
THWAK
YOU'RE OF HIPPOLYTA'S BLOOD! DO YOU THINK I WOULD EVER TRUST A WORD FROM YOUR MOUTH?

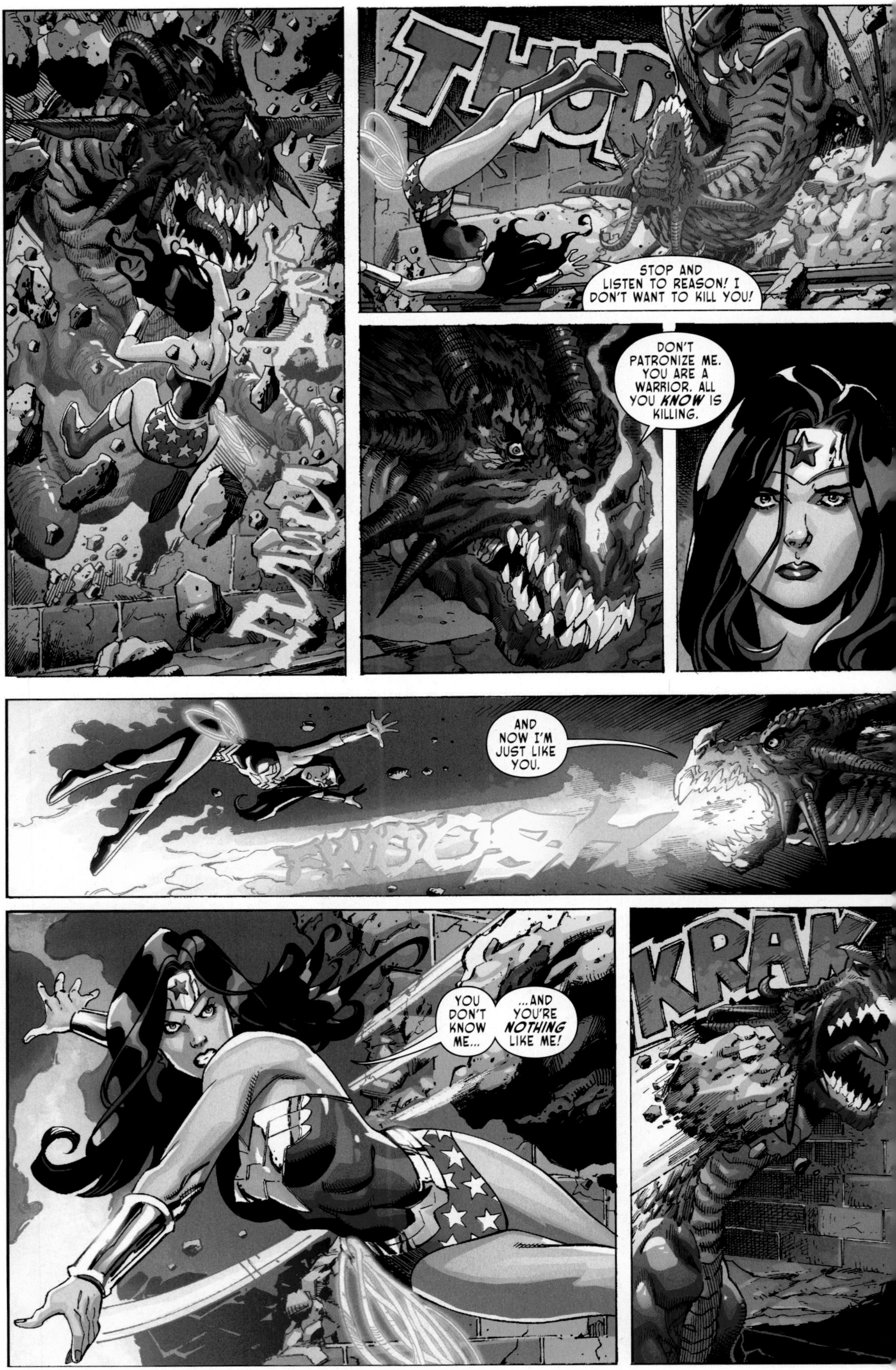
THUD
STOP AND LISTEN TO REASON! I DON'T WANT TO KILL YOU!
DON'T PATRONIZE ME. YOU ARE A WARRIOR. ALL YOU *KNOW* IS KILLING.
AND NOW I'M JUST LIKE YOU.
YOU DON'T KNOW ME...
...AND YOU'RE *NOTHING* LIKE ME!
KRAK

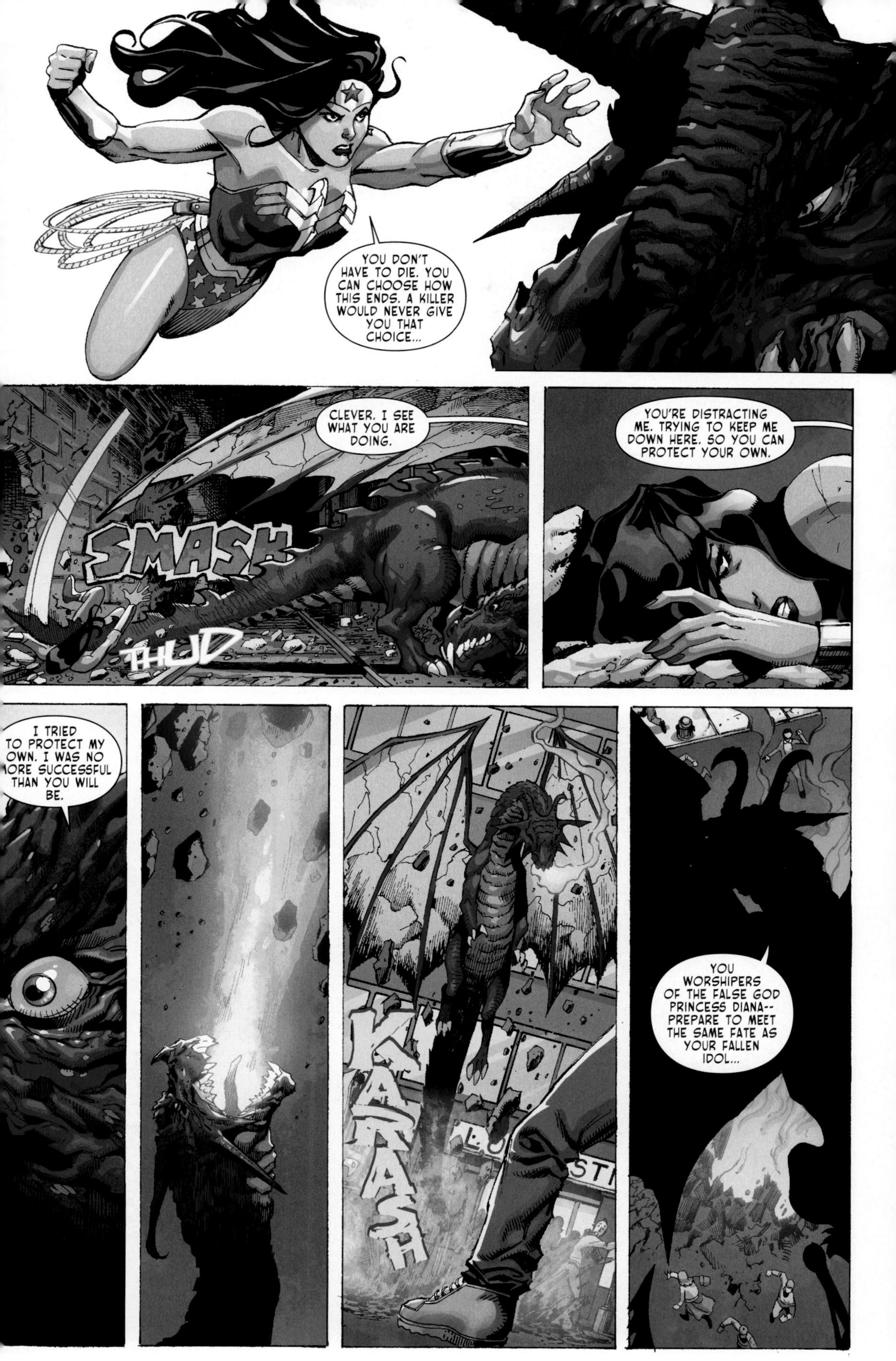
YOU DON'T HAVE TO DIE. YOU CAN CHOOSE HOW THIS ENDS. A KILLER WOULD NEVER GIVE YOU THAT CHOICE...
CLEVER. I SEE WHAT YOU ARE DOING.
SMASH
THUD
YOU'RE DISTRACTING ME. TRYING TO KEEP ME DOWN HERE. SO YOU CAN PROTECT YOUR OWN.
I TRIED TO PROTECT MY OWN. I WAS NO MORE SUCCESSFUL THAN YOU WILL BE.
KARASH
YOU WORSHIPERS OF THE FALSE GOD PRINCESS DIANA-- PREPARE TO MEET THE SAME FATE AS YOUR FALLEN IDOL...

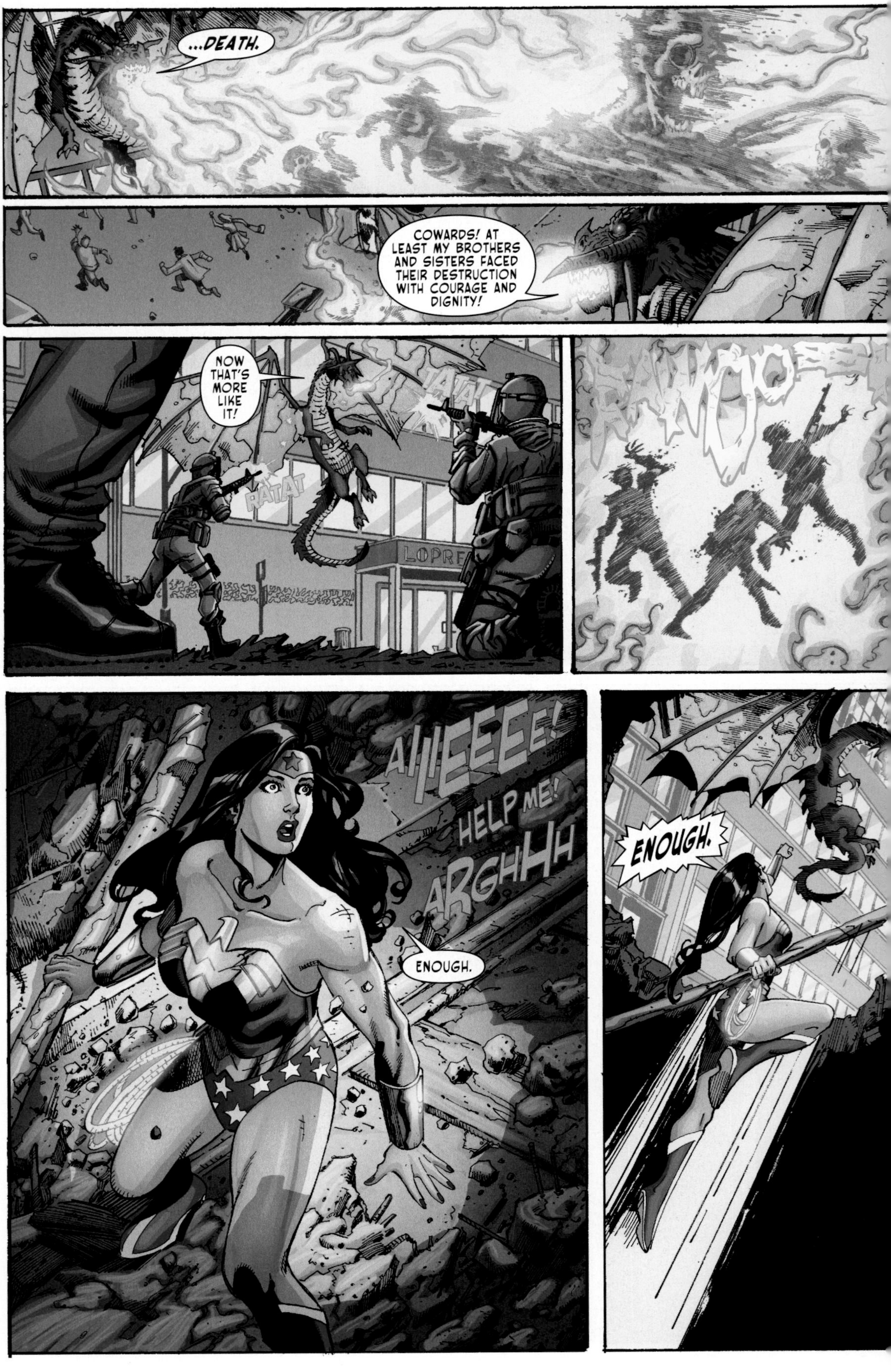
...DEATH.
COWARDS! AT LEAST MY BROTHERS AND SISTERS FACED THEIR DESTRUCTION WITH COURAGE AND DIGNITY!
NOW THAT'S MORE LIKE IT!
RATAT
RATAT
LOPRE
AIIEEEE!
HELP ME!
ARGHHH
ENOUGH.
ENOUGH.

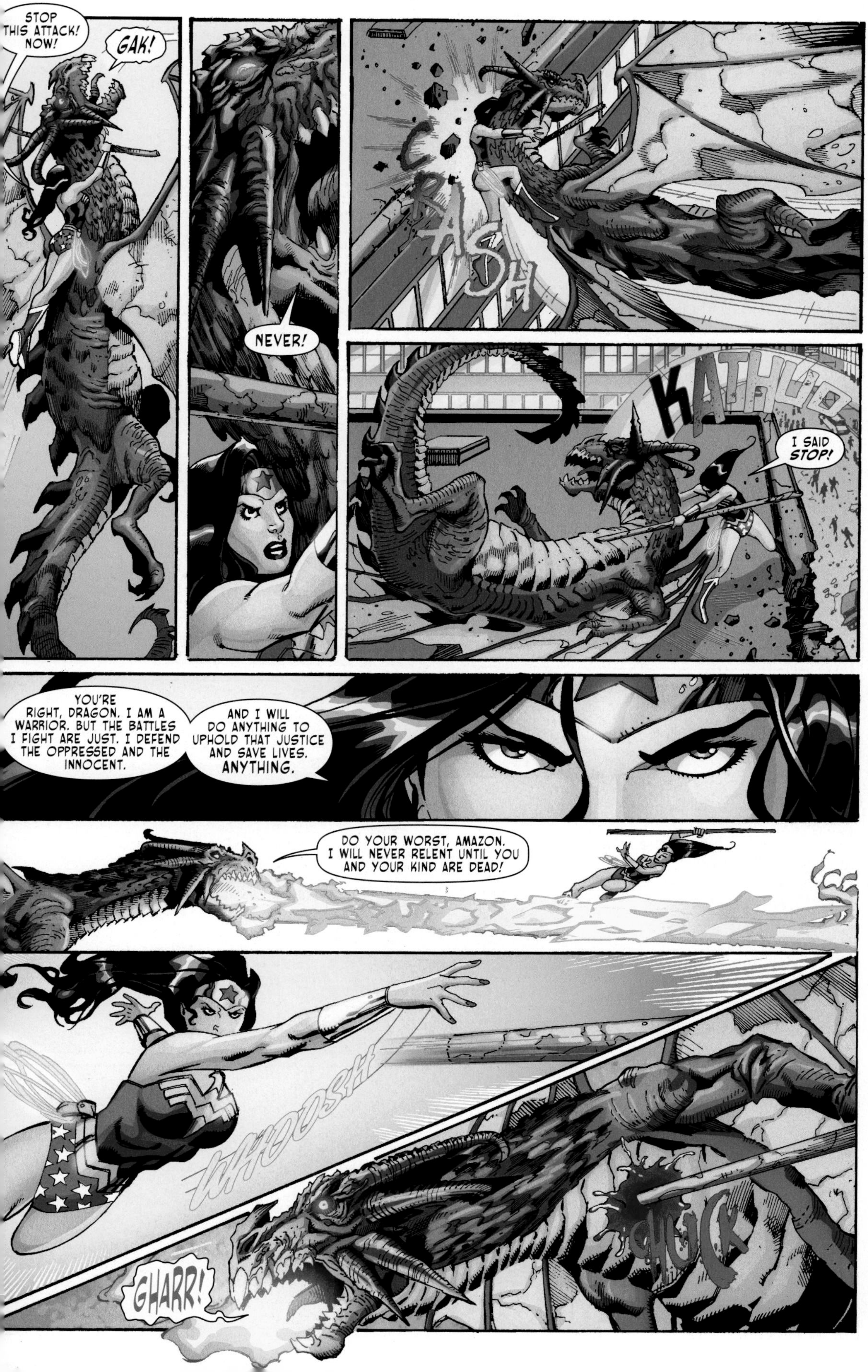
STOP THIS ATTACK! NOW!
GAK!
NEVER!
CRASH
KATHUD
I SAID STOP!
YOU'RE RIGHT, DRAGON. I AM A WARRIOR. BUT THE BATTLES I FIGHT ARE JUST. I DEFEND THE OPPRESSED AND THE INNOCENT.
AND I WILL DO ANYTHING TO UPHOLD THAT JUSTICE AND SAVE LIVES. ANYTHING.
DO YOUR WORST, AMAZON. I WILL NEVER RELENT UNTIL YOU AND YOUR KIND ARE DEAD!
WHOOSH
GHARR!
GUCK

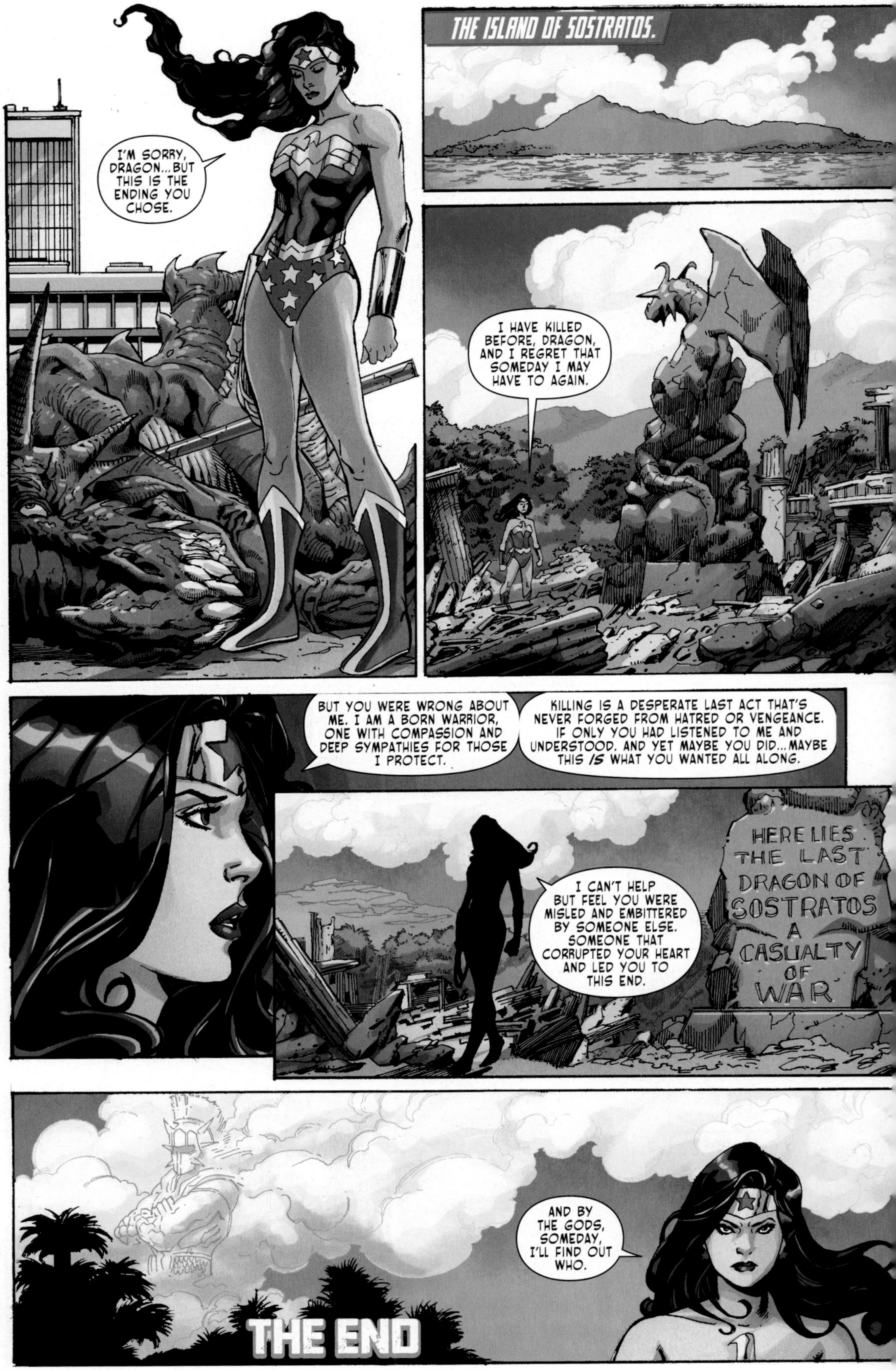
I'M SORRY, DRAGON...BUT THIS IS THE ENDING YOU CHOSE.
THE ISLAND OF SOSTRATOS.
I HAVE KILLED BEFORE, DRAGON, AND I REGRET THAT SOMEDAY I MAY HAVE TO AGAIN.
BUT YOU WERE WRONG ABOUT ME. I AM A BORN WARRIOR, ONE WITH COMPASSION AND DEEP SYMPATHIES FOR THOSE I PROTECT.
KILLING IS A DESPERATE LAST ACT THAT'S NEVER FORGED FROM HATRED OR VENGEANCE. IF ONLY YOU HAD LISTENED TO ME AND UNDERSTOOD. AND YET MAYBE YOU DID...MAYBE THIS *IS* WHAT YOU WANTED ALL ALONG.
HERE LIES THE LAST DRAGON OF SOSTRATOS A CASUALTY OF WAR
I CAN'T HELP BUT FEEL YOU WERE MISLED AND EMBITTERED BY SOMEONE ELSE. SOMEONE THAT CORRUPTED YOUR HEART AND LED YOU TO THIS END.
AND BY THE GODS, SOMEDAY, I'LL FIND OUT WHO.
THE END

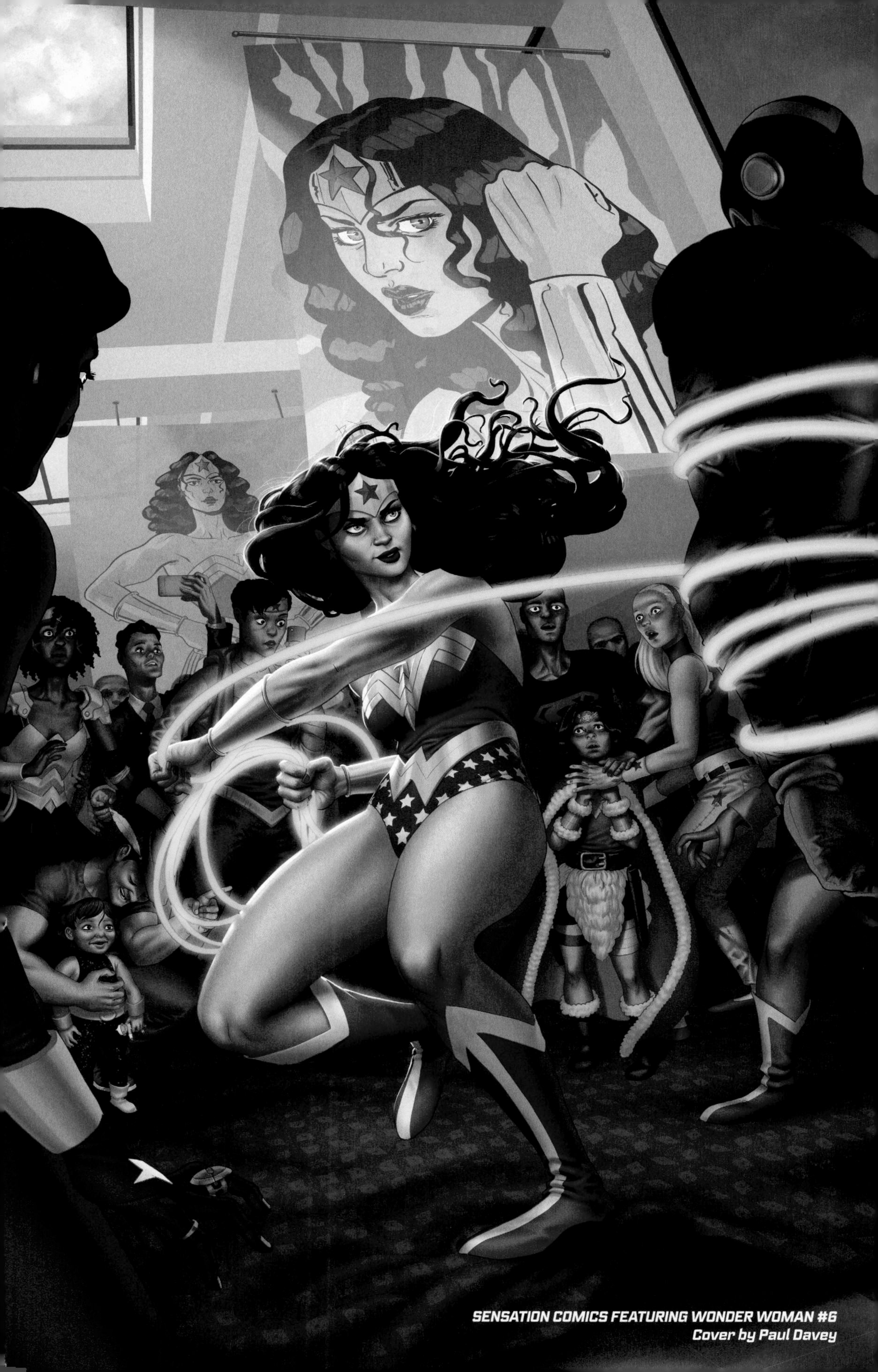

SENSATION COMICS FEATURING WONDER WOMAN #6
Cover by Paul Davey

SENSATION COMICS FEATURING WONDER WOMAN #7
Cover by Shane Davis, Michelle Delecki and Alex Sinclair

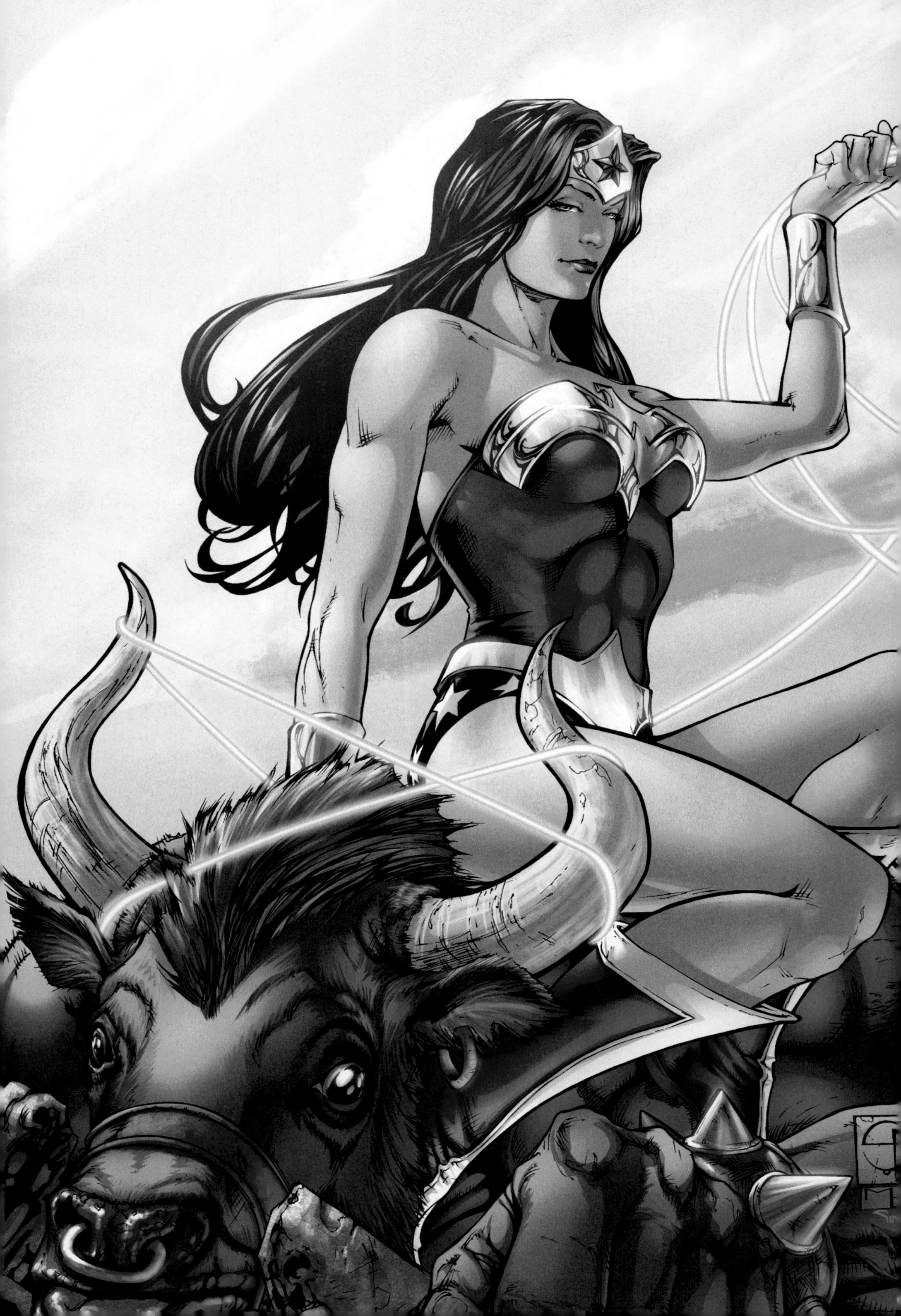

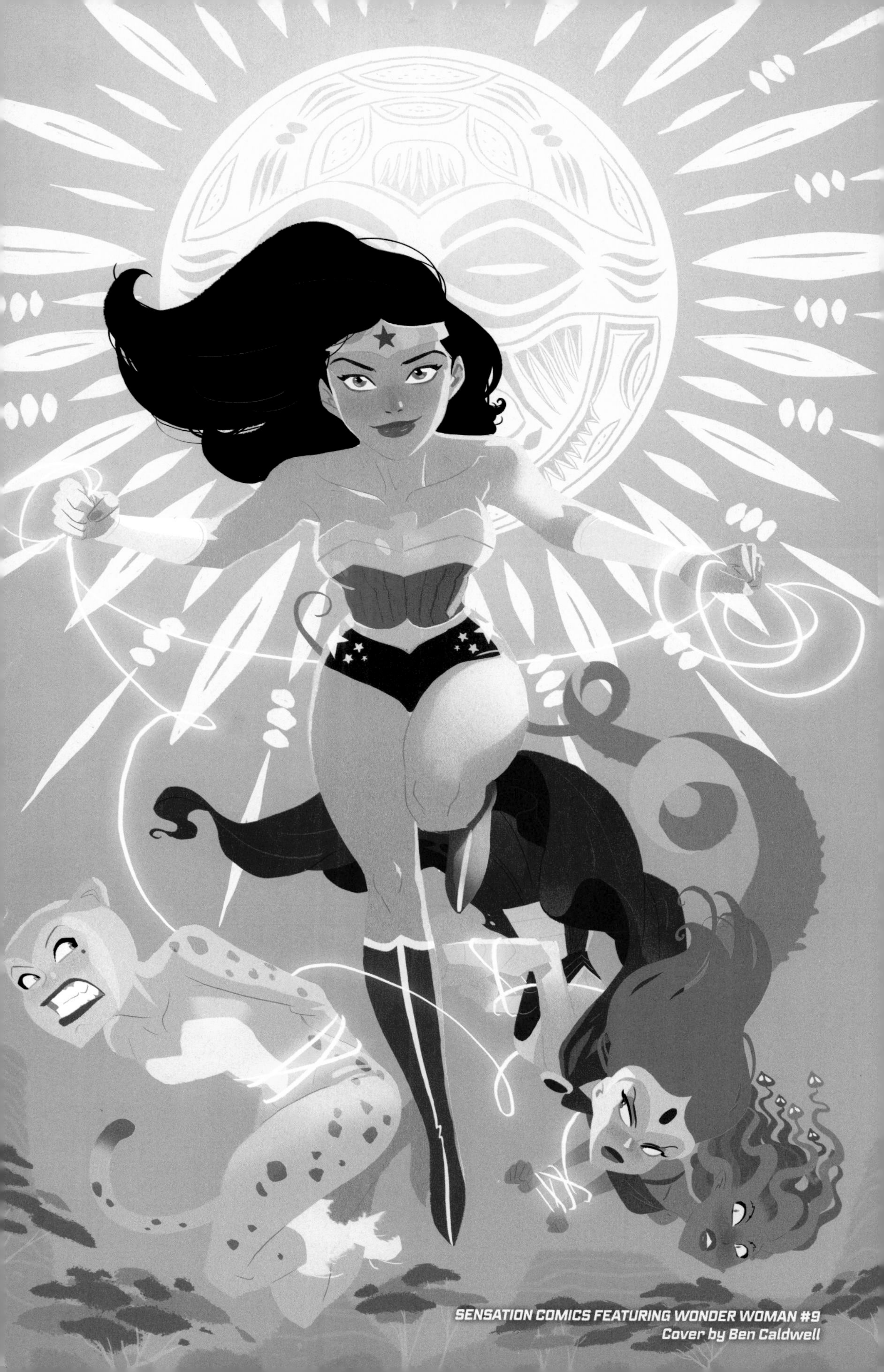

SENSATION COMICS FEATURING WONDER WOMAN #9
Cover by Ben Caldwell

SENSATION COMICS FEATURING WONDER WOMAN #10
Cover by Francesco Francavilla

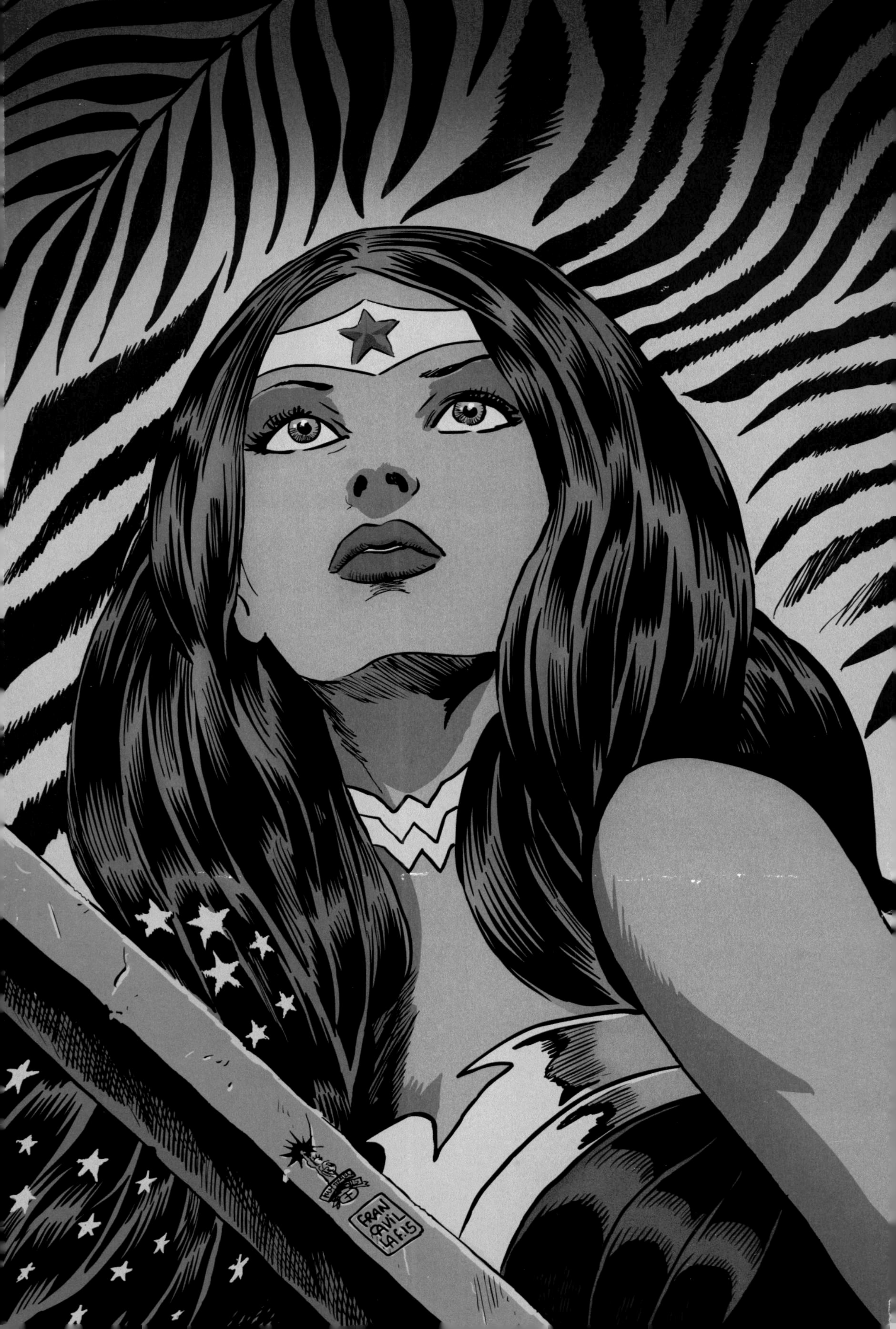